ENGLISH RADICALISM, 15

An exploration of the place of radical ideas and activity in English political and social history over three centuries. Its core concern is whether a long-term history of radicalism can be written. Are the things that historians label 'radical' linked into a single complex radical tradition, or are they separate phenomena linked only by the minds and language of historians? Does the historiography of radicalism uncover a repressed dimension of English history, or is it a construct that serves the needs of the present more than the understanding of the past? The book contains a variety of answers to these questions. As well as an introduction and eleven substantive chapters, it also includes two 'afterwords' which reflect on the implications of the book as a whole for the study of radicalism. The distinguished list of contributors is drawn from a variety of disciplines, including history, political science and literary studies.

GLENN BURGESS is Professor of History at the University of Hull. His publications include *The politics of the Ancient Constitution: an Introduction to English Political Thought 1603–1642* (1992), and *Absolute Monarchy and the Stuart Constitution* (1996).

MATTHEW FESTENSTEIN is Professor of Political Philosophy at the University of York. His recent publications include *Political Ideologies* (with Michael Kenny, 2005), and *Negotiating Diversity* (2005).

ENGLISH RADICALISM, 1550–1850

EDITED BY

GLENN BURGESS

University of Hull

and

MATTHEW FESTENSTEIN

University of York

CAMBRIDGE UNIVERSITY PRESS
Cambridge, New York, Melbourne, Madrid, Cape Town, Singapore,
São Paulo, Delhi, Dubai, Tokyo, Mexico City

Cambridge University Press
The Edinburgh Building, Cambridge CB2 8RU, UK

Published in the United States of America by Cambridge University Press, New York

www.cambridge.org
Information on this title: www.cambridge.org/9780521180818

First published 2007
Reprinted 2008
First paperback edition 2010

A catalogue record for this publication is available from the British Library

Library of Congress Cataloguing in Publication data

English radicalism, 1550-1850 / edited by Glenn Burgess and Matthew Festenstein.
p. cm.
Includes bibliographical references and index.
ISBN-13: 978-0-521-80017-4 (hardback)
ISBN-10: 0-521-80017-x (hardback)
1. Radicalism–England–History. I. Burgess, Glenn, 1961- II. Festenstein, Matthew. III. Title.

HN400.R3E64 2007
303.48′4–dc22

2006035547

ISBN 978-0-521-80017-4 Hardback
ISBN 978-0-521-18081-8 Paperback

Contents

List of Contributors vii

Introduction 1
Glenn Burgess

1 A politics of emergency in the reign of Elizabeth I 17
Stephen Alford

2 Richard Overton and radicalism: the new intertext of the civic ethos in mid seventeenth-century England 37
Luc Borot

3 Radicalism and the English Revolution 62
Glenn Burgess

4 'That kind of people': late Stuart radicals and their manifestoes: a functional approach 87
Richard L. Greaves

5 The divine creature and the female citizen: manners, religion, and the two rights strategies in Mary Wollstonecraft's *Vindications* 115
Gregory Claeys

6 On not inventing the English Revolution: the radical failure of the 1790s as linguistic non-performance 135
Iain Hampsher-Monk

7 Disconcerting ideas: explaining popular radicalism and popular loyalism in the 1790s 157
Mark Philp

8 Henry Hunt's *Peep into a Prison*: the radical discontinuities of imprisonment for debt 190
Margot C. Finn

9 Jeremy Bentham's radicalism 217
F. Rosen

10 Religion and the origins of radicalism in nineteenth-century Britain 241
J. C. D. Clark

11 Joseph Hume and the reformation of India, 1819–1833 285
Miles Taylor

AFTERWORDS 309

Radicalism revisited 311
Conal Condren

Reassessing radicalism in a traditional society: two questions 338
J. C. Davis

Index 373

Contributors

STEPHEN ALFORD, Fellow in History, King's College, Cambridge.

LUC BOROT, Professeur de Civilisation Britannique, Université Paul-Valéry Montpellier III.

GLENN BURGESS, Professor of History, University of Hull.

GREGORY CLAEYS, Professor of the History of Political Thought, Royal Holloway, University of London.

J.C.D. CLARK, Hall Distinguished Professor of British History, University of Kansas.

CONAL CONDREN, Professor of Politics, University of New South Wales, Sydney.

J.C. DAVIS, Emeritus Professor of English History, University of East Anglia.

MATTHEW FESTENSTEIN, Professor of Political Philosophy, University of York.

MARGOT FINN, Professor of History, University of Warwick.

RICHARD L. GREAVES, was Robert O. Lawton Distinguished Professor of History, Florida State University, until his death in June 2004.

IAIN HAMPSHER-MONK, Professor of Politics, University of Exeter.

MARK PHILP, CUF Lecturer in Politics and Tutorial Fellow, Oriel College, Oxford.

FRED ROSEN, Honorary Senior Research Fellow in the Bentham Project, and Emeritus Professor of the History of Political Thought, Department of History, University College London.

MILES TAYLOR, Professor of Modern History, University of York.

Introduction

Glenn Burgess

I

Radicalism is a term well-entrenched in the historian's lexicon. A search on the Royal Historical Society's on-line bibliography for British and Irish history retrieves nearly 300 books, essays and articles that use the word in their title.[1] The total rises to nearly 850 if the search term used is 'radical' rather than 'radicalism'. Radicals and radicalism are everywhere, at least from the sixteenth century onwards. They come in all sorts of varieties, popular and elite, of the left and of the right, Tory and Whig; British, English, Irish, Scottish and Welsh. But the word is, in many of its uses, curiously weak. We are likely to have a rough idea of the sorts of things that might be meant by calling someone a socialist, a conservative or a liberal, and a corresponding sense of what the equivalent 'isms' might look like, even if that sense quickly becomes complex and sub-divided. But what sense do we get from hearing someone described as a radical? We would assume that the 'socialisms' of different periods might show some resemblances (however forced or artificial), and there is a recognisable core meaning in describing Thomas More, Gerrard Winstanley and Karl Marx as communists. All of them envisaged an ideal society in which private property was abolished. They have all been described as radicals too, but it seems less clear what this label tells us about them.

The present collection of essays is a collaborative attempt to address three questions that are central to any understanding of the function of the terms 'radical' and 'radicalism' in the historian's conceptual toolkit. First, does it make sense to talk of the existence of 'radicalism' before that particular label was invented? (1820 is the first use of the term recorded in the *Oxford English Dictionary.*) Second, do the various people, ideas and groups to which the label 'radical' has been given by historians have anything in common with one another? And, third, is there in any sense a 'radical' tradition in English political culture, constituted by the transmission of 'radical' ideas through time? The book does not claim to have answered any of these questions. They are the sort of questions unlikely to receive agreed answers. Indeed, it may not be desirable that there are agreed answers, for the heuristic value of the radical/radicalism vocabulary may well be great in some circumstances and little in others, depending on the precise questions being asked and the way in which definitions are being constructed. The purpose of the book, instead, is to explore the sorts of problems raised by 'radicalism', and to try out a variety of solutions to them, some broad, some narrower and more local. Historians should be as conscious of the implications of the language they use, and as self-aware and self-critical, as they can be, and the present book is intended to contribute to the achievement of these notions. Its authors would varyingly like to restrict, refine or qualify discussions of radicals and radicalism, but they do not by any means speak with a single voice, and one would not wish them to do so.

This introduction will chart the terrain, identifying the sorts of assumptions that underline historians' discussions of radicalism, and the sorts of problems that arise from the use of the term as a label for political ideas and activity.

II

Much of the historical interest in 'radical' political thought (and activity) has developed since the 1950s and 1960s, and much of this interest has taken the form of *recovery*. The effort at recovery certainly goes back much further, at least to the late Victorian period; but was greatly aided by the interest that historians have developed more recently in 'history from below'. In the 1930s and 1940s, when A. L. Morton and his fellow Marxist historians embarked on the search for 'a people's history of England', the discovery of popular radicalism was itself a radical activity with political purposes. That has remained true of later developments, like labour history and the history of working-class movements. Certainly, they have not been the province of Marxists alone; but they have remained areas of scholarship attractive to those with some sympathy for radical politics. As Bryan Palmer has said of E. P. Thompson, he 'staked a historical claim for his own allegiance to an antinomian tradition that reached through the ranting impulse of sixteenth-century dissent into sects such as the Muggletonians'.[2]

It would be pointless to bemoan this fact. New areas of history are generally opened up by scholars whose motivations lie in the present rather than the past. Were it not so, historical scholarship really would be the province of Scott's and Carlyle's 'dry-as-dusts'. But, of course, these motivations do not provide a justification for the field. History develops as scholars refract the past through the changing concerns of the present; but it is always necessary to judge and assess the results by proper scholarly means. Frequently the enthusiasms that create new areas of interest also distort them; and then a second phase gives way to the first. It is arguable that the history of radicalism has had that second phase artificially truncated. Shifting concerns have led to the decline of labour history, Marxist history, and so on, before the assessment and absorption of their results had been completed.

The Marxist recovery of English radicalism

Though the radical dimensions of the English past, and especially of the English Revolution of the 1640s and 1650s, never altogether disappeared from view, it was in the twentieth century, and largely by Marxist and socialist historians, that the history of radical groups was recovered and constructed.[3] Central to this process (chronologically as well as in achievement) was the work of the Communist Party Historians' Group (CPHG), which flourished for a brief decade (1946–56), but had a remarkable impact on English historiography.[4]

Perhaps the most important thing to appreciate about the work of the British Marxist historians is that it is inspired by a good deal more than Marxist theory. In one of the bitter arguments that have from time to time fractured the British Left, Perry Anderson defended the claim that E. P. Thompson's work had 'cultural nationalist' elements.[5] Thompson did not take the charge well; but it nonetheless identified a feature of his work, and that of other early Marxist historians, from which much richness, depth and resonance have been derived. One of the central achievements of the British Marxist historians, in Harvey Kaye's assessment, 'has been the recovery and assemblage of a "radical-democratic tradition" in which have been asserted what might be called "counter-hegemonic" conceptions of liberty, equality, and community'. This is 'a history of popular ideology standing in dialogical relationship to the history of politics and ideas', running from the peasants' rising of 1381, through

Levellers, Diggers and Ranters, through Wilkes and the London crowds of the eighteenth century, to Chartism and beyond.[6] Appreciation of this point has been best addressed in the literature about E. P. Thompson, in whose work it is unmistakable, and, whose final posthumous work on William Blake seems to have addressed at the end some of his own deepest inspiration. While his chief interest was in an antinomian 'tradition' originating in the seventeenth century, and in the radicalisms of romanticism, Thompson could also appeal to 'the long and tenacious revolutionary tradition of the British commoner', 'a dogged, good-humoured, responsible tradition: yet a revolutionary tradition all the same'. From Levellers to Chartists, this tradition was chiefly one of 'moral revolt'. Careless of theory but resilient and humane, it sounds a lot like Thompson himself.[7]

But the impulse to recover a radical tradition in the English past was by no means unique to Thompson. It lay behind much of the historical thinking that surrounded the formation of the Communist Party Historians' Group. The group began as a collective endeavour to update A. L. Morton's pioneering work *The People's History of England* (1938), and at the heart of this endeavour was the further recovery of a native English radical tradition.[8] Dona Torr, reviewing an early edition of the writings of Gerrard Winstanley, proclaimed that 'the political history of the English working people began 300 years ago'. It was a slightly odd tradition that began in the mid-seventeenth century: 'The stream went underground. But many generations later the democratic demands of the Levellers arose again to powerful in Chartism, while Owen (through Bellers) recreated Winstanley's communism. This is our heritage.'[9] One might wonder where, exactly, underground was, but the important sentence here is the last. The core historical project lay in the relationship of present to past embedded in the recovering of a radical or revolutionary heritage that could make communism not an alien, foreign and unpatriotic implant into the green and pleasant lands of the sceptred isle but a suppressed, native tradition. Daphne May made the point emphatically:

> The Levellers were defeated. Two hundred years later, however, the working class, the Chartists, put forward similar demands which, as the result of hard prolonged struggle, have been substantially realised. In face of the workers, the capitalists have had to retreat. Bourgeois historians have tried to gloss over the revolutionary struggles of our people, and to present the growth of democracy as the story of 'freedom broadening slowly down, from precedent to precedent', thanks to our enlightened rulers. That leads to the conclusion, so convenient for

the ruling class, that the Communists with their nasty talk about class struggle are 'alien' to English politics. The fight of the Levellers (and many similar battles) demonstrate the opposite: that it is precisely the Communist Party which is the true heir and successor of the most heroic champions of liberty in the past.[10]

Christopher Hill pushed back further. 'The people of England', he maintained, 'have a past of which they may be proud – a history of working-class struggle . . . and of struggles for democracy earlier'. They should celebrate in remembering 1649 'the creative vision and capacity of the common people of England'. But the Levellers did not invent English radicalism *ex nihilo*, for they 'inherited . . . the medieval peasant tradition of revolt against landlords'. It was important to Hill, too, to be able to deny the claim that 'when twentieth century democrats or Communists claim kinship with Lilburne or Winstanley . . . we are like *nouveaux riches* trying to establish "a spurious pedigree"'.[11] His early essay on 'The Norman Yoke', first published in 1954, identified a distinctively native tradition of opposition and subversion, rooted in the continuity of the Norman Yoke motif and its account of a lost age of freedom and well-being. Hill traced this tradition from the late middle ages, through its heyday in the seventeenth century, and then into the nineteenth century, when it was to be replaced by modern socialist ideas.[12] The people's history that Hill and others in the CPHG were building, one recent and largely sympathetic commentator has noted, was one 'in which the class character of earlier rebels, revolutionaries and popular leaders was obscured by regarding them all as representatives of a national revolutionary tradition'.[13]

These views and this aspiration to a revolutionary heritage are embedded in some of the most widely read Marxist historical writings. The source of the spring that nourished the recovery of England's revolutionary past was A. L. Morton's *People's History*, but it must be admitted that this book itself did relatively little to identify a radical tradition in the English past. It was more concerned to tell the history of England as a history of class struggle, and to assess the changing character of social classes over time.[14] Some of Morton's later work, though, sounds a note that echoes in the writings of Thompson, Hill and others. His study of English utopian writing linked ideas across time in a variety of ways, indicating, for example, the persistence of ideas about Cockaygne (the land of plenty) through time, and finding that its late medieval form 'anticipate[s] some of the most fundamental features of modern socialism' as well as 'foreshadowing . . . Humanism, the philosophy of the bourgeois revolution'.[15] Links could be drawn between the 'simple men' who had written of Cockaygne, and future utopian writers, including Thomas More and William Morris.[16] Morton was not insensitive to intellectual change, generated by changing class structures and alliances, but there were important lines of continuity running through the dialectical history that he wrote. Thus, in one formulation, Thomas More is said to bring together Plato's 'aristocratic communism' and the 'primitive communism' of the medieval peasant, and is the link that binds both to modern 'scientific socialism'. More and the utopian socialism that he represented formed only one of the sources of modern socialism; but the other, a popular socialism, also had a long tradition from Munzer, through the Levellers, the French Revolution and the Chartists. One of the key differences between modern socialism and earlier socialism was that the latter could exist only in dream; but for modern socialism, the dream had become realizable. Fantasies were now being translated into facts.[17] In his study of William Blake, Morton delineated a broadly similar pattern. Blake himself was firmly located in an 'antinomian' and Ranter tradition, and the essential ideas in his writings could be found in the pamphlets of the English Revolution. But there was a much broader tradition than this, European as much as English, and 'with a continuous existence of several centuries':

> It was a revolutionary tradition, tenaciously held by the descendants of the small tradesmen and artisans who had formed the extreme left of the Commonwealthsmen: few things are held more tenaciously than such a tradition with the vestiges of a past glory about it, and if it was dying in Blake's time, this was only because it was being replaced by the more positive, powerful and apposite radicalism of Wilkes, Paine and Place. Blake's life and work, among other things, illustrate the conflict between these old and new trends in English radicalism – he himself attempted but never quite managed to reconcile them.[18]

Christopher Hill's major study of the radicalism of the English Revolution, *The World Turned Upside Down* (1972), though it continued the search for a radical pedigree, beginning with the proud boast that 'popular revolt was for many centuries an essential feature of the English tradition',[19] was largely unconcerned with issues of continuity and transmission. Assessing the impact of earlier ideas on the eighteenth century, he remarked, 'We need not bother too much about being able to trace a continuous pedigree for these ideas. They are the ideas of the underground, surviving, if at all, verbally: they leave little trace.'[20] This was a dangerous position, for Hill had little doubt that there was a continuous pedigree, and his remark might be read as an attempt to insulate that belief against the demand for evidence. He returned to the theme, although a few years later, in an essay 'From Lollards to Levellers', published appropriately in a collection honouring A. L. Morton.[21] This was, as Hill acknowledged, an inconclusive sort of essay – evidence again proved more elusive than he would have liked – but it was nonetheless alive with the possibility that an underground heretical and seditious tradition stretching from the later middle ages to the end of the eighteenth century might have existed.

Three approaches to radicalism: critique of the Marxist recovery

Historians should always be on the lookout for 'how' questions: take care of the 'hows', and the 'whys' will look after themselves. The people's (radical) history that emerged from the work of the CPHG and the historians associated with it raises a number of important 'how' questions.

It is possible to define at least three different approaches to radicalism, all of them with very different implications for our understanding of the subject.

The approach that has dominated the field, especially amongst the British Marxist historians, has constructed radicalism as an ideological tradition that has existed since (perhaps) the late middle ages. It rests upon a *substantive* definition of the term, in which radicalism is defined by identifying its core content. This remains relatively unchanged over time, and is transmitted from generation to generation. Witness, for example, E. P. Thompson's claim that 'it is above all in Bunyan that we find the slumbering Radicalism which was preserved through the eighteenth century and which breaks out again in the nineteenth'.[22] There is an assumption that radicalism is a consistent ideology with an underground existence over many centuries. Earlier and later radicals, who believe and do recognizably the same things, are part of the same tradition. So committed was Thompson to this view that he was able to suggest that, because antinomianism is found in the age of William Blake, then it must have existed amongst the radicals of the English Revolution. On that basis one could dismiss Colin Davis's arguments for the non-existence of an antinomian Ranter sect.[23] The argument is extraordinarily revealing of the depth of Thompson's commitment to the existence of a radical tradition, which here becomes an article of faith, in proud defiance of the historian's usual sense that you need contemporary evidence to prove that something happened.

This approach to radicalism usually gives it a class location. The continuous history of the radical tradition could, for those who adopted this approach, be rooted in the life-experience of peasants, proletarians and other subaltern classes, and so in class analysis could be found the natural explanation for it. Thus Christopher Hill could write, as we have seen, of a popular underground tradition of protest in ways that assumed hidden links and continuities between particular outbreaks of radical protest from the Lollards to the Levellers, and (no doubt) beyond. This is so in spite of two things (a) that Lollards and Levellers are as dissimilar as they are similar; and (b) that there is at best very limited evidence to support the idea of an historical continuity between the two.[24]

A second approach has been developed out of dissatisfaction with the first. It rests on a *functional* definition of radicalism, and has perhaps been most explicitly formulated by Colin Davis.[25] This approach defends the application of the term radicalism to diverse phenomena, even before the term itself became current in the early nineteenth century; but it need not assume any real historical connection between different examples of radicalism. It need not link them into a single continuous tradition of popular protest. Rather, it lays down basic functional criteria for recognizing radicalism, and suggests that any political ideas or activity that matches them can be understood as an instance of radicalism.

In Davis's early formulation a radical ideology needs to do three things. (1) It must delegitimate an old socio-political order; (2) it must re-legitimate an alternative or new socio-political order; and (3) it must provide a transfer mechanism that will change things from the old to the new. Many of the papers that follow are written with explicit or implicit acceptance of an approach like this, though not necessarily with any debt to Davis's work, and it has arguably become the most common of all outside Marxist circles.

However, functional approaches are not beyond criticism. Conal Condren is, perhaps, the leading theorist of a third approach, and he roots it in a critique of both substantive and functional understandings of radicalism.[26] We might term this third approach *linguistic*, for it rests heavily on a close study of word usage. Ultimately, it suggests that we should not use the term radicalism to describe any phenomena before the term was invented. To do so obscures the historical significance of the emergence of the word. But, beyond that, it misdescribes earlier ideas. Condren has especially emphasized the fact that, while the term radical suggests the willing and enthusiastic acceptance of innovation, premodern societies were more or less universally hostile to innovation, and thus to 'radicalism'. Those whom we call radical are the ones who have failed to make themselves look acceptable to their contemporaries, though invariably they have tried hard to do so. They have, in other words, tried hard not to be radicals. The key point in this is that any description of sixteenth- or seventeenth-century people as radical must misdescribe their language – and possibly as a result (though Condren is more cautious) their *intentions* too. They cannot and did not intend to be what we mean by the term radical. They thought of conserving and renovating, not of innovating. On the whole, they did not believe that change – fate or providence – was something amenable to human control. Thus, there is a dramatic difference between pre-modern ideas and modern ones, and applying the term radical to them (still more, linking them into a common tradition) obscures this fact altogether. In the essays that follow, Jonathan Clark, in particular, has given an historical exemplification of this approach.

III

Four particular problems

The three approaches outlined carry with them different attitudes to four topics that have been central to the history of radicalism, and it is worth identifying and commenting on each of these topics because they run in various ways, through many of the essays that follow. The key purpose is to identify the questions with which to interrogate the histories of radicalism that have been produced through the twentieth century.

Historical transmission

There has been a marked tendency, especially with the substantive approach, to understand the transmission of radicalism through time as a relay race, in which the baton of radicalism is passed on, hand to hand, down the generations. The baton, of course, stays the same, while those who carry it change. Certainly, some continuities can be found in 'radical' protest (the demand for universal manhood suffrage or for frequent parliamentary elections); but a number of points can be made. First, to concentrate on similarities can be to ignore even greater differences. Second, it is possible that 'radicals' at various times actually picked up ideas not from those before them in the radical tradition, but from the political culture that surrounded them. One of the effects that comes from postulating a radical tradition is that it divorces those in it from their contemporaries; yet, from the Levellers onwards, there is evidence to suppose that most 'radicals' relied on the exploitation of a common stock of ideas that they shared with 'non-radicals'.

A third point might be to consider an alternative mode of transmission altogether. This might draw upon the recent historical interest in reading habits and memory. It might stress the iconic significance of radical figures and a radical tradition. The key point is that, simply because later radical writers looked back on their predecessors and constructed a tradition in which to place themselves, there is nonetheless no reason to accept this as a real historical tradition. People remember the past inaccurately; they read creatively. What is particularly needed is a history of the way nineteenth-century radicals looked at the past. In so far as we have this, in Timothy Lang's book, we discover that when early Victorian radicals looked at the English Revolution, they tended to admire Hampden and Pym, not Lilburne and Winstanley.[27] The radicals, in their eyes, were Cromwell and the Independents, not Christopher Hill's plebeians. This changed over time, and we need to understand the changing status of iconic figures in this process. Very likely, in the end, we shall discover that the radical tradition identified by the British Marxist historians is but the last of a long series of attempts by radicals to identify a self-justifying tradition for themselves. Each of the attempts is of historical importance; but none of the traditions constructed actually existed until remembered and invented by politician or historian. Tradition has become mythology. A canon of radical writers is created, and the works in it read, reread, and misread.

This leaves us with the possibility that there was no significant continuity or transmission in the past – no radical tradition – and that such a thing has been created only in retrospect by radical historians writing their own pedigree. The result is history written with passion – but is it history that is reliable? Alternatively, is all historical writing prone to the same problem?

Radical ideas and social history

The history of radical thought and activity has been closely associated with social history, in the belief that radicalism was a class ideology. A number of difficulties immediately arise. In particular, when did class societies emerge? When is it appropriate to discuss politics in class terms? Whatever answer we give to that question, a good many historians (other than Marxists) might be prepared to believe that at least at the beginning of our period, the sixteenth and seventeenth centuries, class analysis is at best misleading.

This is important because of the problem of class-consciousness, and the links between that and the problems of radical intention suggested by Condren. It may make sense to talk of classes unaware of themselves; but for the historian of ideas and politics there will be something unsatisfactory in this. If class is to play an explanatory role in their work, then it needs to be linked to class-consciousness. Men and women need to be aware of and able to articulate their class identity and grievances. There is much evidence to show that they were not so able in early modern England, and that class has only limited explanatory value for the period.

If there is any truth in this, then a further point can be added to Condren's analysis. For many who adopt the substantive approach, radicalism is class-based protest. But, in fact, it is doubtful whether many early modern people constructed their social world in class terms, and therefore doubtful whether they could have intended to articulate a class protest. This does not, of course, mean that they could not make any social protest. But it does mean that they did not do so in the interests of a social class, but in some other way. This has important implications for our understanding of both the content and purpose of their thought and activity. The most recent work may, to a degree, be reversing some of this, but the problematic relationship of intellectual and ideological identity to social identity remains.[28] One approach – pregnant with possibilities for the history of radicalism (as indicated in Colin Davis's contribution to this book) – is *via* the idea of the 'unacknowledged republic', which captures the sense that a high proportion of English adult males, down to the level of the village and parish, were involved in their own self-government. If this were so, then the history of radicalism as a battle between the included and the excluded might need to be rethought.[29]

Religion

In his 1940 review of Christopher Hill's early work, George Orwell remarked that 'the main weakness of Marxism [is] its failure to interpret human motives. Religion, morality, patriotism and so forth are invariably written off as "superstructure" '.[30] It was religion that he had most in mind on this occasion, and it was to be religion that unsettled many Marxist approaches to England's radical past. There was always a tendency – perhaps not inevitable and certainly not uniform – to ignore the religious motivations of supposed radicals, and to attribute to them instead more modern-seeming concerns with social equality and political democracy. Or, perhaps more accurately, the modern (and secular) elements in these thinkers were accorded greater attention and weight than the early modern (and religious) ones. In the *ancien régime* world, did political and social conflict occur between social classes, or fractions of them, or between confessional groups? If the latter, then religion rather than class could be considered the key explanatory context for politics and political thought. This problematic idea, briefly sketched, provides one possible alternative to class-based analysis. It is arguable that all significant political conflict in the early modern period occurred between groups whose difference was primarily confessional. In this world, what we take to be radicalism was most often the dramatic political impact of extreme religious beliefs, beliefs that were followed sometimes without regard for political and social order. What distances this from modern radicalism is the fact that it was often unpolitical or even antipolitical, relying not on human agency but on God to transform the world. It was animated not by a vision of human freedom and equality, but by a vision of community with God. Glenn Burgess's chapter below applies this understanding to the English Revolution.

Indeed, if this is so, we might expect radicalism when it does emerge to be irreligious. Aware of the point, perhaps, Christopher Hill has tried hard but unsuccessfully to find irreligion in the English Revolution. This is a sign of the danger of prematurely identifying radicals: they find themselves forced to live up to a label of someone else's choosing. Modern radicalism has, indeed, often been irreligious; and in an earlier phase associated with heresy. Religion must be central to it, for you cannot have a radicalism resting upon human agency unless an antidote is found for the opium of the people. This need not lead to atheism or irreligion proper, but it most probably will lead to a critique of what are perceived to be the stupefying effects of religion, and a defence of the capacity of human beings to control and perfect their own affairs. We need to ask, then, when such a critique became available; and to understand the differences between modern political radicalism and the religious challenges to authority of the post-Reformation period.

Language and anachronism

The most fundamental of the problems raised by the differing ways in which radicalism can be approached concerns the historian's use of language. To what extent is the historian obliged to understand the past using concepts and/or language that were available to people in the past? To what extent is conceptual anachronism an enriching imaginative device that can help the historian to understand people in the past differently (better? more deeply?) from the ways in which they understood themselves?

Peter Munz, using Popper to transform Max Weber's distinction between *verstehen* (understanding) and *erklären* (explaining), has suggested that:

> If one is using the laws the people one is writing about would have used, one is understanding them because one is explaining them the way they themselves would have explained themselves. If, on the other hand, one is using general laws which are accepted and current in one's own modern world, one is interpreting the people of the past, because by explaining them to ourselves rather than explaining them in the way they would have explained themselves to themselves, one is foisting something on them they themselves had not thought of; and hence, one is literally interpreting them.[31]

Though Munz is here concerned with the historian's use of causal explanatory laws, the distinction he makes is applicable to the use of concepts and words. A moment's thought makes it clear that the historian has both to understand and to explain, though not necessarily at the same time. It follows that it cannot be the case that conceptual and linguistic anachronism is in itself evidence of poor historical practice. Historians have, for example, advanced a great many explanations for why a considerable number of early modern women were executed for the crime of witchcraft. Historians may seek to understand the contemporary belief that they were executed because they were witches, perhaps as a result of entering into a pact with Satan; but none would consider that understanding to provide an explanation of what happened.[32] The historian's knowledge is primarily the knowledge of the outsider and not the insider, and as such it must explain as well as understand. In seeking to explain, the historian cannot be bound by the language and concepts of the past.

To clarify this matter further it is worth distinguishing the explanation of human action from the explanation of other historical phenomena. The demographic historian, concerned with measurable and long-term patterns, extracted using various techniques from recalcitrant data, need not worry about the explanation of human action – at least not in the first instance. In explaining how human beings act – and we can consider for these purposes writing and speaking to be forms of action – it does seem important to ensure that the historian's conceptual vocabulary does not clash with the conceptual vocabulary of the past in such a way that historical explanations necessarily imply a false understanding of the ways in which people in the past saw their own worlds. This, it seems to me, is at the heart of the debates in this book. Does using the concept of 'radicalism' to group, link and explain thoughts and actions that took place before the early nineteenth century necessarily falsify the past? To what extent are we entitled (or obliged) to translate the actions and thoughts of people in the past into a vocabulary located in the present? Clearly, the answer must be – to quite a considerable extent. Historians can do nothing else if they are to represent the past to the present. Where then are the limits to be drawn – when does anachronistic language become a problem?

IV

There are many questions here, and none of them is intended to belittle the pioneering work of the historians of the Communist Party Historians' Group, and others whose passion for the radicals of the past was inspired by their commitment to a radicalism of the present. It is time, though, to take stock of this historiography, and to argue over its legacy. Let the debate commence.

NOTES

1 http://www.rhs.ac.uk/bibl/

2 Bryan D. Palmer, *E. P. Thompson: Objections and Oppositions* (London, 1994), pp. xii–xiii.

3 See for example Blair Worden's account of the historical fortunes of the Levellers in his *Roundhead Reputations: The English Civil Wars and the Passions of Posterity* (London, 2001), ch. 12.

4 Important accounts of the CPHG are Eric Hobsbawm, 'The Historians' Group of the Communist Party', in Maurice Cornforth (ed.), *Rebels and their Causes: Essays in Honour of A. L. Morton* (London, 1978), pp. 21–47; Bill Schwarz, '"the People" in History: The Communist Party Historians' Group, 1946–56', in R. Johnson, et al. (eds.), *Making Histories: Studies in History-Writing and Politics* (London, 1982), ch. 2; and Alistair MacLachlan, *The Rise and Fall of Revolutionary England: An Essay on the Fabrication of Seventeenth-Century History* (Basingstoke, 1996), ch. 3.

5 Perry Anderson, *Arguments within English Marxism* (London, 1980), ch. 5, pp. 146–7.

6 Harvey Kaye, 'E. P. Thompson, the British Marxist Historical Tradition and the Contemporary Crisis', in Kaye, *The Education of Desire: Marxists and the Writing of History* (New York, 1992), p. 101.

7 Thompson quoted in Bryan D. Palmer, *E. P. Thompson: Objections and Oppositions* (London, 1994), p. 79.

8 The other core text, which led to a famous debate on the transition from feudalism to capitalism, was Maurice Dobb's *Studies in the Development of Capitalism* (1946). The issues raised by it can be seen making an earlier appearance in the debate on Hill's *English Revolution* (1940) in the pages of *Labour Monthly*, 22 (1940), pp. 558–9, 651–5; and 23 (1941), pp. 90–3; while the collective statement of debates in the CPHG, 'State and Revolution in Tudor and Stuart England', *Communist Review*, July 1948, pp. 207–14, indicates the importance of the matters raised in Dobb's book to the Group. The transition debate is collected in Rodney Hilton (ed.), *The Transition from Feudalism to Capitalism* (London, 1978).

9 Dona Torr, 'Book Review', *Labour Monthly*, 26 December 1944, pp. 383–4.

10 Daphne May, 'The Putney Debates', *Communist Review*, January 1948, p. 27.

11 Christopher Hill, 'History and the Class Struggle', *Communist Review*, March 1949, pp. 476–8.

12 Christopher Hill, 'The Norman Yoke', in Hill, *Puritanism and Revolution: Studies in the Interpretation of the English Revolution of the Seventeenth Century*, (Harmondsworth, 1986), ch. 3; earlier version in J. Saville (ed.), *Democracy and the Labour Movement: Essays in Honour of Dona Torr* (London, 1954), pp. 11–66.

13 Ann Talbot, '"These the Times . . . This the Man": An Appraisal of Historian Christopher Hill', from the World Socialist Website (www.wsws.org), at <http://www.sws.org/articles/2003/mar2003/hill-m25_prn.shtml> accessed 05/01/2005.

14 Harvey J. Kaye, 'Our Island Story Retold: A. L. Morton and "The People" in History', in Kaye, *Education of Desire*, ch. 5.

15 A. L. Morton, *The English Utopia*, (London, 1952, reprinted 1978), pp. 32–45, esp. 43, 45.

16 *Ibid.*, p. 61.

17 *Ibid.*, pp. 76–7, 179, 275.

18 A. L. Morton, *The Everlasting Gospel: A Study in the Sources of William Blake*, (New York, 1966), pp. 11–12.

19 Christopher Hill, *The World Turned Upside Down*, (Harmondsworth, 1974), p. 13.

20 *Ibid.*, p. 381.

21 Christopher Hill, 'From Lollards to Levellers', in Maurice Cornforth (ed.), *Rebels and their Causes: Essays in Honour of A. L. Morton* (London, 1978), pp. 49–67.

22 E. P. Thompson, *The Making of the English Working Class* (Harmondsworth, 1968; original ed. 1963), p. 34.

23 E. P. Thompson, 'On the Rant', in Geoff Eley and William Hunt (eds.), *Reviving the English Revolution: Reflections and Elaborations on the Work of Christopher Hill*, (London, 1988), pp. 153–60; J. C. Davis, 'Fear, Myth and Furore: Reappraising the "Ranters"', *Past & Present*, 129 (1990), pp. 79–103.

24 An interesting reflection on relevant issues is now Andy Wood, *Riot, Rebellion and Popular Politics in Early Modern England* (Basingstoke, 2002).

25 J. C. Davis, 'Radicalism in a Traditional Society: The Evaluation of Radical Thought in the English Commonwealth 1649–1660', *History of Political Thought*, 3 (1982), pp. 193–213.

26 Conal Condren, 'Radicals, Conservatives and Moderates in Early Modern Political Thought: A Case of the Sandwich Islands Syndrome?', *History of Political Thought*, 10 (1989), pp. 525–42; Condren, *The Language of Politics in Seventeenth Century England* (Basingstoke, 1994), ch. 5.

27 Timothy Lang, *The Victorians and the Stuart Heritage* (Cambridge, 1995).

28 This is a rapidly developing and changing field. Perhaps the most important work has been that of Keith Wrightson on the language of social description. His recent work is pulled together in Wrightson, *Earthly Necessities: Economic Lives in Early Modern Britain 1470–1750* (New Haven, 2000).

29 Michael Braddick, *State Formation in Early Modern England c.1550–1700* (Cambridge, 2000); Steve Hindle, *The State and Social Change in Early Modern England, 1550–1640* (Basingstoke, 2000); Mark Goldie, 'The Unacknowledged Republic: Officeholding in Early Modern England', in Tim Harris (ed.), *The Politics of the Excluded c.1500–1850* (Basingstoke, 2001), pp. 153–94.

30 *New Statesman and Nation*, 24 August 1940.

31 Peter Munz, *Beyond Wittgenstein's Poker: New Light on Popper and Wittgenstein*, (Aldershot, 2004), p. 45.

32 For some provocative reflections, though, see Diane Purkiss, *The Witch in History: Early Modern and Twentieth Century Representations*, (London, 1996).

CHAPTER I

A Politics of Emergency in the Reign of Elizabeth I

Stephen Alford

In the third volume of his *Political Disquisitions* the Scottish philosopher James Burgh explored the historical dimensions of his call for the reformation of parliament. 'Before all other things', he wrote, 'there must be established a GRAND NATIONAL ASSOCIATION FOR RESTORING THE CONSTITUTION' as a statement of the established right of the English people to act in an extra-parliamentary way.[1] Working primarily from the British histories of David Hume, Burgh rehearsed some of the radically defining moments in the historical relationship between monarch and subject, from the barons' opposition to King John – 'the first attempt toward an association for a plan of liberty, according to Mr *Hume*' – to the proposal for a 'grand national association against popery' in 1680. For Burgh a purpose of these associations was the protection of protestantism; another was the safety of the crown. He recorded two other examples: a 'general association all over *England* for the defence of *Elizabeth*' in 1586, and 'afterwards for that of *William* and *Mary*'.[2]

James Burgh's account of these bonds between subject and monarch (or subject and subject) was naively simplistic, driven by a notion of historical progress and development which was deeply anachronistic.[3] Popular action in the sixteenth century, in the sense that Burgh understood it, did not exist, because the social and political structures of the Tudor polity were radically different from those of the late eighteenth-century state. The Elizabethan Bond of Association of 1584 (Burgh miscalculated the year) was not, in its origin, a popular or spontaneous response to crisis; nor was it a conscious alternative to parliamentary action. The text of this 'Instrument of an association' committed its signatories 'to thuttermoost of their power at all tymes to withstand, pursue, and suppres all maner of persons that shall by any meanes intend and attempt any thing dangerous or hurtfull to the honours, Estates, or persons of their Souveraynes'.[4] It was an orchestrated political statement of intent. 'Master secretory', William Cecil Lord Burghley, wrote to Sir Francis Walsingham 'late at night' on the day they had affixed their seals and added their signatures to the document, 'consideryng that this Association accorded uppon as yow know, is to be made publycque, by reason manny sortes of persons by degrees of offices and callynges, ar lyke to be partyes in the societe.'[5]

But the thrust, if not the detail, of James Burgh's interpretation of the Elizabethan Bond was perceptive and, in its own way, quite accurate. 'The Instrument of an association' was written and circulated to bind subjects into a common 'society' or 'fellowship' designed to protect the crown. It was also, by implication, strongly Protestant; a reaction to – and a protection against – the ideological divisions of continental Europe, the Catholic challenge to the legitimacy of Elizabeth I's queenship and the claim of Mary Queen of Scots; or, as the Bond put it, 'for the furtherance and advancement of som pretended titles to the Crown of this Realm, it hath ben manifest that the Life of our gracious Souverayn Lady Quene Elizabeth hath ben moost traiterously and devilishly sowght'.[6] This sense of danger had been with the regime since its inception in 1558, and it developed a definite intellectual and political form during the first Elizabethan decade.[7]

In fact, Elizabethan politics, and the political thinking that underpinned it, was a remarkably subtle mechanism. I would like in this chapter to explore the relationship between the mental world of Elizabethan councillors, the complexity of their inherited political thought, the broader implications of documents like the Bond of Association and 'A necessary consideration of the perillous state of this tyme' of 1569, the blueprint for 1584. There was a quite radical dimension to the politics of Elizabeth's reign. The basic proposition was that divinely ordained royal authority had a purpose. That purpose was the destruction of idolatry and its agents. A defined purpose became a mark against which to measure the exercise of kingly power; and royal authority measured was, fundamentally, royal power critiqued. This was a position shared by some of the most subversive writers and preachers of the 1550s and members of the Elizabethan regime's political establishment. There was also, by the 1560s, a clear notion of the principal duty of the members of (to borrow a phrase from the Instrument of Association) 'any Christian Realm or civile Societie'.[8] This was the defence of the kingdom's Protestant settlement: with or without the active participation of the queen, by subjects who were defining themselves as the citizens of a polity developing into a state in its modern sense.

I

The sixteenth century can look remarkably unradical. Strongly bound by hierarchy and an emphasis on order and social degree, successive regimes seem to have had an unlimited capacity to preach the virtues of obedience to established authority. John Cheke, for example, wrote his *The Hurt of Sedicion* against the rebels of 1549, but it was reissued in 1569, 1576 and 1641, 'Whereunto is newly added by way of Preface a briefe discourse of those times, as they may relate to the present'.[9] Raphael Holinshed printed Cheke's text in the editions of his *Chronicles* in 1577 and 1587.[10] Both Thomas Cranmer and Heinrich Bullinger published and preached on obedience during the reign of Edward VI.[11] But popular rebellion was only one form of radical action – and Tudor rebellions generally failed.

More effective and significant were critical readings of the nature of the polity which came from within the kingdom's 'political society'. Here, Tudor political culture can be deceptive. English thinking in the sixteenth century was active and responsive: it developed in a complex way, rested on a number of theses and counter-theses of the nature and exercise of political power, and depended heavily on political context.[12] In 1550, for example, Bishop John Ponet of Rochester preached on the authority of the king as supreme head of the church on earth next under God.[13] John Ponet the Marian exile, on the other hand, constructed a devastating critique of monarchy, clearly driven by the English political scene. These ideas must have been accessible to him during the Edwardian years, even if their implications were not immediately clear or obvious. *A Shorte Treatise of Politike Power* (1556) deployed scriptural text, natural law and English constitutional precedent to argue, ultimately, that royal power could be constrained.[14] For Ponet, human authority divinely ordained and the consent of a people to their governors could coexist. He took one of the most conventional platitudes of innumerable sermons and books on obedience to the powers that be ordained of God – that governors were ordained for the wealth and benefit of the people and for the preservation of the commonwealth – and transformed it into a basic test of the legitimacy of authority.[15] The crucial point was that this test could be applied by God in the afterlife and by subjects on earth.

John Ponet presents an interesting case study. Chaplain to Thomas Cranmer and Edward VI, he symbolized the Edwardian and Elizabethan political elite at its most connected. The Edwardian and Elizabethan MP Sir Peter Carew may have been involved indirectly in the composition of *A Shorte Treatise of Politike Power*.[16] John Jewel, later an Elizabethan bishop of London, was in Strasburg with Ponet.[17] Anthony Cooke – the father-in-law of William Cecil and of Elizabeth I's lord keeper of the great seal, Nicholas Bacon; and of the Elizabethan diplomat Henry Killigrew – bought Ponet's library after his death in 1557 and seems to have edited some of his work for publication.[18] Even in his thought, there is some serious common ground between Ponet and his apparently more conservative contemporaries. On a broad level of political analysis (even, arguably, at his most radical) Ponet strikes some familiar chords. His critique of the absolute power of monarchs, for example, rested on a number of assumptions. He argued that God's law, 'by which name also the lawes of nature be comprehended', was made solely by God, and so kings and princes 'are not joyned makers herof with God'.[19] So 'this absolute autoritie which they use' had to be either maintained by the reason of man or a usurpation of God's will.[20] Absolute power meant, for Ponet, the freedom to dispense with laws, 'and frely and without correction or offence doo contrary to the lawe of nature, and other Goddes lawes, and the positive lawes and customes of their countreyes, or breake them'.[21] 'Absolute' may not have been a word other writers would have chosen to deploy in this context, but, like Ponet, they would have found the notion of unlimited political power objectionable.

The nature of a monarch's power was a complex issue, and one which had long exercised the minds and pens of common lawyers. For John Ponet, the absolute power of princes and governors was morally unacceptable. Similarly, a common lawyer like James Morice acknowledged the fundamental and extensive prerogative powers of the crown but, using the work of Bracton and Fortescue and a corpus of statute law, defined the *exercise* of those powers very carefully.[22] In a lecture on the prerogative delivered in the Middle Temple in 1579, Morice explained that sovereign rule and absolute authority had often 'burst forth into hatefull Tirannye and Insolent Oppression' because, quite simply, princes were neither immortal nor immutable. So a better kind of monarchy had been established by common assent, whereby kings were guided by the law. The English monarch was not limited like a Venetian duke or a king of Sparta, but the exercise of sovereign authority was influenced in ways that reflected the needs and concerns of his subjects. On laws affecting the life, lands and goods of subjects, or the money they paid in taxation, the members of the body politic offered their counsel and consent. Parliament was 'the greate counsell of the Prynce and of the Realme': an expression of royal power and a point of contact between subjects and monarch.[23]

Although the worlds of Fortescue and James Morice and John Ponet appear, on the surface, to have been unimaginably distant, Ponet was nevertheless sensitive to these distinctions. He argued that there were two kinds of monarch: those who independently made the laws of their countries 'bicause the hole state and body of their countrey have geven, and resigned to them their authoritie so to doo'; and governors 'unto whom the people have not geven suche autoritie, but kepe it them selves'. Ponet denounced the first sort of kings as tyrants. But the authority of his second category derived from what he called 'the mixte state'.[24] This notion of 'mixed' government reflects the complexity of sixteenth-century notions of the location of political power, and it became, in many ways, a rallying cry of early Elizabethan writers and politicians. For Ponet, the 'mixte state' of the three distinct polities of monarchy, aristocracy and democracy had been by experience 'judged to be the best sort of all', because mixed commonwealths survived.[25] Sir Thomas Smith endorsed the mixed polity in his *De Republica Anglorum* (1565).[26] So did John Aylmer who, in 1559, described England not as 'a mere Monarchie, as some for lacke of consideracion thinke, nor a meere Oligarchie, nor Democratie, but a rule mixte of all these, wherein ech one of these have or shoulde have like authoritie'. The concept found its physical form in parliament, 'wherin you shal find these 3 estats'.[27]

In his essay on 'The Monarchical Republic of Queen Elizabeth I', Patrick Collinson explored Aylmer's defence of Elizabeth's fitness to rule (essentially that the kingdom was governed on her behalf) and pointed to the 'republican' implications of Aylmer's emphasis on mixed polity.[28] And these implications have deep resonances. Commentators like Aylmer must have understood the implications of this political model of the kingdom – in essence Sir John Fortescue's *dominium politicum et regale* at its most extreme. In 1573 the puritan Thomas Cartwright used the model of the mixed polity of the commonwealth to construct an equivalent constitution for the English church.[29] In doing so, he effectively challenged the notion of the absolute sovereignty of Elizabeth in matters ecclesiastical and temporal. It was a critique of royal power that Archbishop John Whitgift of Canterbury understood only too clearly.[30] In a published reply to Cartwright, Whitgift admitted that parliament represented the estates of the realm but maintained that because 'the judgements, confirmation, and determination resteth in the Prince, therefore the state is neyther Aristocratie, nor Democratie, but a Monarchie'.[31] But it was Cartwright's model, rather than Whitgift's, which underpinned the Elizabethan political creed of William Cecil and the analyses of authors as diverse as Thomas Smith, John Aylmer, John Ponet and Richard Hooker. For John Guy, this shared assumption represented 'the most powerful and subversive critique of the monarchy of Elizabeth I', a critique which 'emanated from the very heart of the regime'.[32]

John Ponet demonstrated how it was possible to construct a stunning analysis of the aims and limits of political authority. Working from conventional assumptions – that human authority was instituted by God for the wealth and benefit of all, and that it was the duty of governors to maintain justice, defend the innocent and punish the evil – Ponet demonstrated that 'Common wealthes and realmes may live, when the head is cut of, and may put on a newe head, that is, make them a newe governour, whan they see their olde head seke to muche his owne will and not the wealthe of the hole body'.[33] This conclusion rested on a reading of principles of political action which were subtle and highly ambiguous. But probably the most important point to grasp is that by the reign of Elizabeth the impact of political writing in the 1550s had done two things: first, it had encouraged authors like Ponet, John Knox, Christopher Goodman and (from a different perspective) John Aylmer to explore the nature of monarchical regimes; and second, it had encouraged these writers to take as their test of legitimacy a commitment to God. The 'true' religion became the prescriptive and authoritative guide to the actions of human governors.

II

This ideological reading of the nature of monarchy had complex origins. During the reign of Edward VI, writers and preachers emphasized the relationship between their own godly Protestant monarch and Old Testament models of reforming kings. Like eight-year-old king Josiah (2 Kings 22–23), Edward presided over the destruction of idolatrous images and the rediscovery of the book of the law. In court and public preaching, biblical translations and Edwardian printing, Josiah became a key element in the regime's presentation of itself, a providential mark of the authority of God in the reformation of the kingdom, and a counter to the insecurities of royal minority.[34] The implications of this ideological model of monarchy revealed themselves during the Marian half decade. Although historians have recognized that commentators like Ponet and Christopher Goodman wrote explicitly on subjects' obedience, it is easy to miss the implicit theme of Goodman's *How Superior Powers O[u]ght to be*

Obeyd of Their Subjects (1558) or John Knox's *The First Blast of the Trumpet* (1558). The Marian exiles had inherited from the Edwardian years strong notions of what regimes should and should not do. Although the nature of an individual's obedience to authority appears as a key theme in the writing of the period, so too does the template for a regime acceptable to the godly. When Christopher Goodman noted that 'To obey is good, but whome, wherin, and howe farre, ought to be considered', he encouraged his readers to ask searching questions about the essential nature of the polity in which they lived.[35]

The legacy of writers like Anthony Gilby, Christopher Goodman and John Knox was Elizabethan rather than Marian. In 1567 the Catholic Thomas Stapleton used passages from the works of Gilby, Knox, Goodman and Goodman's editor William Whittingham to demonstrate that the Protestants of Geneva wanted 'not only to deprive the Quene of her title of the Supremacy in causes Ecclesiasticall, but even in temporal too, and from al government'.[36] This was a conscious misunderstanding of the relationship of these men to Elizabeth – she was, after all, a monarch they found confessionally acceptable – but it was a point made by Stapleton with some justification. Patrick Collinson believes that 'the polemical critique of monarchy' is a more appropriate term than 'resistance theory' for the quite radical readings of political power presented by Protestant writers and politicians.[37] Elizabeth's subjects did not resist their queen but 'it does not follow that there was no ideological capacity for resistance'. Monarchy as 'a ministry exercised under God and on his behalf – in effect, the monarch as an accountable public officer – was a notion widely and commonly shared.[38]

For Protestants the destruction of idolatry became the defining mark of acceptable kingship. Christopher Goodman turned the conventional model of counsel on its head when he wrote that the office of royal counsellors was 'to brydle the affections of their Princes and Gouvernours, in geving such counsele as might promote the glorie of God; and the welthe of their contrie'. The antithesis of this was Mary Tudor, 'their ungodlie and unlawful Governesse, wicked Jesabel.[39] Like Jezebel and 'ungodly Athalia' (2 Kings 8, 11; 2 Chronicles 21, 22), 'instrumentes of Satan, and whipps to his people of Israel', Mary was a hypocrite and an idolatress.[40] For Goodman, the 'end of all offices' – of councillors, noblemen, rulers, justices, mayors, sheriffs, bailiffs, constables and gaolers – was humbly to promote God's glory 'and to defende all those whom he committed to your charge'. The kingdom's officers had betrayed their trust by banishing God's truth and changing religion into superstition and the true honouring of God into blasphemous idolatry.[41] These godly duties were taken equally seriously by the MPs and bishops of the parliamentary session of 1572. They condemned Mary Queen of Scots for the crime of idolatry in terms which were identical to Christopher Goodman's 1558 reading of one of their major texts, Deuteronomy 13.[42]

These models and assumptions were deeply embedded in the Tudor consciousness. When the Edwardian regime deployed the biblical examples of Corah and Dathan (Numbers 16) against its internal enemies – the rebels of 1549, who resisted godly reformation – it did so with a consciously ideological purpose. Corah and Dathan were punished because they challenged the authority of Moses and offended God with idolatrous sacrifices.[43] Equally, Saul's failure to obey God in his campaign against King Agag and his presentation of 'burnt sacryfyces & offerynges' (1 Samuel 15) meant that he was stripped of his kingly power. The example of Saul was used to condemn rebellion in 1549. It was also deployed in the parliament of 1572 during its debate on the punishment of Mary Stewart. Saul had been deceived by the 'shaddowe of honor', but honour was not an excuse to avoid the execution of justice, 'for in deed execution of justyce upon any person whatsoever is and ever hath bene accompted honorable'.[44] Magistrates in commonwealths were ordained, 'accordinge to the greatnes of the offences, [to] represse the wickednes of mankinde whereunto by coruption of nature they are inclined'.[45]

The English translation of the Bible printed in Geneva in 1560 became a key Elizabethan text. There were strong ideological implications in its marginal notes on the cruelty of Jezebel, the refusal of David to kill Saul in a private cause (something which would have been acceptable as a public act), and the failure of Asa to execute his wicked mother.[46] The Geneva Bible's introduction to the book of Deuteronomy (an important Tudor text on the duties of kingship) discussed God's promise 'to raise up Kings and gouvernours for the setting forthe of this worde and preservacion of his Churche'.[47] Just as important was the letter of dedication to Elizabeth I, in which the translators considered 'how muche greater charge God hath laid upon you in making you a builder of his spiritual Temple'. Josiah's destruction of idolatry was an instructive model. So was King Asa, who demonstrated that 'the quietnes and peace of kingdomes standeth in the utter abolishing of idolatrie, and in advancing of true religion'. Asa was a cautionary example. He began 'to be colde in the zeale of the Lord', feared the power of man, imprisoned the messenger of God and died after a period of war and oppression (2 Chronicles 14, 15).[48] This was not a fringe text. The letter to Elizabeth was printed in the editions of the Geneva Bible produced in the 1570s and 1580s by Christopher Barker, printer to the queen and a man closely associated with her principal secretary Francis Walsingham.

The translators of the Geneva Bible addressed Elizabeth as the natural agent of reformation in the tradition of Jehosophat, Josiah and Hezekiah. Equally, the queen was the defender of the godly and the principal agent in the prosecution of idolatry. The author of one text from the parliamentary session of 1572 assumed that the person 'bound in conscience to proceed with severitie' against Mary Stewart was Elizabeth.[49] When the queen's almoner, Bishop Edmund Gest of Rochester, constructed a defence of English military action against Scotland in 1565, he began with the assertion that 'Every prince ought to defende Christis religion . . . not onelye to defende it in his owne contree but also in the countrye next by him'.[50] This argument 'pro defensione relligionis' rested on the assumption that if 'inferiour magistrates' could act to defend God's religion 'much more maye an other prince'. Gest openly maintained that 'inferiore magistrates maye fight against there prince for the defence of goddes religion'.[51] So the duty to protect true religion could be shared, potentially, by the monarch, the governors of her realm; even, perhaps, on the model of Christopher Goodman, local officers of the parish.

III

The notion of a collective responsibility for the protection of the kingdom and its religion was one of the themes of a major document prepared by Elizabeth I's principal secretary, William Cecil, in June 1569. Cecil divided the text of 'A necessary consideration of the perillous state of this tyme' into two parts. The second section offered a solution to what, in the first part of the document, was a disturbing assessment of the weaknesses of Elizabeth's kingdom in a hostile and conspiratorial Europe. The solution was a prototype for 1584: an association of the queen's subjects for the defence of the person of Elizabeth, the preservation of the common peace of the realm, and the conservation of its religion.[52] The 'first and principall meane' to prevent crisis was the queen 'as the naturall head of all the Realme', who would, on the model proposed by Edmund Gest in 1565, help to protect the victims of religious violence and Catholic persecution on the continent.[53] The second line of defence – and the principal theme of the proposal – was the mobilization of the subjects of the crown for the defence of the realm.

'A necessary consideration' explored the strengthening of the relationship between monarch and subject, pushing it beyond the 'commen band which every subject by nature oweth to hir Majesty'.[54] This depended on a written statement of loyalty to the physical person of the queen, and, connected to that aim but distinguishable from it, the protection of the realm and its religion. In Cecil's summary of the bond's intentions, religion came first: 'mayntenance of Relligion, suerty of the Quenes person, Mayntenance and Contynuance of the Monarchy, conservation of the subjectes in peace'.[55] The oath was, by implication, an oath to the queen; but it was also a promise which bound initiates 'to associat them selves with all estates of their degrees', so the relationships it encouraged were horizontal as well as vertical.[56] Like the Instrument of Association of 1584, which deployed the vocabulary of 'society' and 'fellowship', 'A necessary consideration' was a declaration of a mutual commitment to a common cause.

The paradox is that the Bond of 1584 and the proposal of 1569 enhanced the role of the individual in a 'Christian Realm or civile Societie' and helped to demarcate the nature of the Tudor state. 'State' has to be used carefully for the sixteenth century, but in the context of 1569 and 1584 it is an appropriate substitute for 'polity' or 'commonwealth'. This was perhaps not the state of Thomas Hobbes and Quentin Skinner, in which the 'artificial person of the state', rather than the person of the monarch or any corporate body of natural persons, bore sovereignty.[57] But it was something different from the traditional and inherited notion of the political body or realm residing within the physical person of the monarch. In plans prepared in 1563 and 1585 for periods of emergency interregnum, Elizabethan privy councillors tested some of the fundamental assumptions of their political world. Public office became, in effect, separable from service to a living monarch. Institutions of government which were in theory little more than extensions of royal power and authority declared themselves capable of outliving the queen. The exercise of royal power was detached from the person of the monarch. In the transition from the governance of the kingdom as the royal *estate* to the commonwealth as *state*, the ability of Elizabethan councillors to isolate sovereignty, their sense of what this meant in terms of the governance of the realm, and their willingness to become representatives of that power are undoubtedly significant.

Both the plan for association of 1569 and the Bond of 1584 helped implicitly to define the relationship between the subject and the political community of which he was a member. Subscription to the Bond was, in theory, a matter of free and personal choice. Entry into 'this fellowshippe and societie' was a voluntary mark of an individual's loyalty to the regime.[58] 'A necessary consideration' was more prescriptive. In its model for the recruitment of local communities for the defence of the realm, it linked a subject's oath to his willingness to contribute money to the regime in a time of crisis. An individual who refused 'to associat him self in comen cause by oth and subscription' would be 'certified as a recusant'. But even a man who swore but failed to pay his contribution was liable to the same fate.[59] 'Recusant' is the key word here. In subscribing to the oath proposed for 1569, Cecil failed to distinguish between a commitment to the defence of the realm and the protection of Protestant religion in the kingdom – because, quite simply, the two were bound so closely together. The Elizabethan regime was extremely conscious of the religious loyalty of its political elite of senior clerics, noblemen and gentlemen at court and in the counties. 'A necessary consideration' established an important link between the regime's sense of ideological self identity and William Cecil's perception of subjects' capacity for political involvement: from privy councillors, bishops, noblemen, 'head gentlemen' and 'inferior gentlemen' to 'ecclesiasticall persons, merchantes, clothyers, farmors, howsholdors and such lyke'.[60]

In his exploration of the later Elizabethan plan for interregnum, Patrick Collinson pointed to the concealment of citizens within subjects.[61] The distinction is an important and real one. If the basic definition of a citizen is a member of a political community who has a defined role and an important part to play in the life and preservation of that community, then texts like the proposals for interregnum by council or oaths of association had some profound things to say about participation in the affairs of the realm.[62] 'A necessary consideration' was a draft; but the Bond of Association was widely circulated and signed, *en masse*, both by local gentlemen of substance and by men who could make only marks on the returns.[63] This was certainly not citizenship classically conceived in the form reconstructed by Markku Peltonen, a citizenship of 'public virtue and true nobility based essentially on the classical humanist and republican traditions';[64] or a reflection of the mental world of Elizabethan governors like William Cecil or Nicholas Bacon, driven by classical notions of public duty.[65] Equally, Elizabethan writers examined the governance of towns as municipal communities.[66] But these explorations and traditions coexisted with less historically driven or classically conceived notions of the role of individuals within communities. When the 'chieffe inabitants' of Swallowfield in Wiltshire gathered in 1596 to establish articles for effective self-governance, they produced a fascinating statement of the public responsibility of the 'company' in the creation of a disciplined Christian community and an efficient execution of the duties delegated to them by the crown.[67]

IV

This desire to preserve an ordered Christian and civil society was an acknowledged aim of the Elizabethan associations. The analysis of England's situation presented by William Cecil in 'A necessary consideration' clearly acknowledged the broad implications of the Marian works of men like Christopher Goodman and the translators of the Geneva Bible – that a godly realm must protect itself against the threat of Roman idolatry and promote the true religion – and sets them in the international political context of the 1560s. According to Cecil, the Catholic powers wanted to force dissenting 'states' to reconvert to Rome. For Cecil, there was an intimate relationship between the Catholic church and those in authority, because, in enjoying the material benefits of the church, the temporal powers wanted 'the authority of this pompe of the Chirch of Roome to be still kept in hir worldly state, without regard of the forme of the primative Chirch'. Persecution had become the principal method of reimposing papal authority. It was clear that the attempts by the Catholic powers to reduce 'their owne subjectes to this romish obedience' would be extended to other countries.[68]

The central argument of Cecil's paper was that England was the Catholic powers' principal target, the 'monarchy of Christendome of whose departure from Roome the Chirch of Roome hath ben most greved'. Foreign powers resented England's support for the persecuted godly of continental Europe. The fact was that the realm was 'so established by Lawes in good pollicy to remayne in freedome from the tyranny of Roome, and in constancy and conformity of true doctrine'. England was 'The best satled pollycy against Roome'.[69] It was, at its heart, a Protestant polity, and it is this clear confessional identity – this '*Protestant* state of the realm', as John Guy has put it – which became the defining factor in the call for its preservation.[70] This principle underpinned Cecil's claim in 1570 that the English polity was ecclesiastically distinctive.[71] And even *The Execution of Justice in England* (1583), in which Cecil argued that Catholics were not persecuted for their faith, established a strong relationship between claims of papal authority over England and the importance to a 'civil and Christian policy and government' of a protection against foreign Catholic aggression and the destruction of rebellion.[72]

The Elizabethan associations undoubtedly reflected the insecurities of continental politics and religion. One possible model for Cecil's draft of 1569 was produced in English translation in 1562 by one of the members of his household, the printer William Seres. The text of *The Treaty of Thassociation*, circulated by Louis de Bourbon, prince de Condé, explained why he and members of all estates had entered into 'Association' for the maintenance of the honour of God, the 'quiet' of the realm and the defence of the king.[73] The document justified the actions of the participants and bound them by oath into 'a felowship from hencefoorth of a holy companye one towardes another'.[74] As accessible to the Elizabethan regime were Scottish bonds of loyalty and revenge. In early modern Scotland, maintenance and protection were offered to men in return for service, counsel and a promise to keep their lord from harm. The bond could also represent an expression of purpose between men of equal social status, and there was an increasingly complex relationship between political alliance and public religious statements during the period of French occupation in the 1550s and Mary Stewart's personal rule in Scotland a decade later. The bond of Henry Lord Darnley in March 1566, with its promise to kill a number of 'privey persons' around the queen (principally David Rizzio) was a blunt but significant political statement. Equally, the 'band' of June 1567, sworn to revenge the murder of Darnley, bore some similarities to the English Instrument of Association.[75]

The impact of the Elizabethan Bond of 1584 was profound, both culturally and practically. Just over a century after its promotion, the text was used in 1696 as a model for an association to defend William III against the Jacobite threat.[76] The text of 1584 was printed as a pamphlet and circulated with a title which reflected the regime's heavy emphasis on the defence of Protestantism. 'The Instrument of an association for the preservation of her Majesties Royall person' became, in its Williamite incarnation, *A True Copy of the Instrument of Association . . . against a Popish Conspiracy*.[77] The Association of 1696 was given statutory backing with an act for the security of King William's person and of his government. This statute offers two insights into the importance of the politics of association and the political implications of a public declaration of loyalty to the crown. The first is that the security of the regime is conceived in explicitly Protestant terms. The 'Welfare and Safety of this Kingdom and the Reformed Religion' were seen to depend directly 'upon the

Preservation of Your Majesties Royal Person and Government'.[78] Reinforced by the oaths of supremacy and allegiance of 1689, the oath of association became a qualification for office. A refusal to swear the oath exposed an individual to 'the Forfeitures and Penalties of *Popish* Recusants Convict'.[79] The message of 1696 was clear: the security of the state rested on a Protestant kingdom with a Protestant king.

James Burgh explored this relationship between the association and the challenge to popery, but one example he did not use – and one which would have supported his notion of the association as a mechanism for independent action – was the declaration of the inhabitants of Maryland against their governor, Lord Baltimore, in 1689. The hundred years between the Elizabethan Instrument and the Glorious Revolution seem almost to disappear in the declaration's complaint that places of worship notionally dedicated to 'the Ecclesiastical lawes of the Kingdom of England' were instead 'converted to the use of popish Idolatry and superstition'. The link between tyrannical government and Catholicism is often implicit rather than explicit in Elizabethan writing, but by 1689 there was a clear relationship between arbitrary government and the popish subversion of the community.[80] Cecil's draft association of 1569 and the Instrument of 1585, using a shared vocabulary of fellowship and society, presented opportunities for political involvement and, importantly, linked that involvement to the protection of authority and true religion. The Maryland association, as a document subscribed by the persecuted, worked in reverse. The popish and arbitrary actions of their governor removed from the signatories their obligation to obey. They considered themselves 'discharged, dissolved and free from all manner of duty, obligation or fidelity to the Deputy Governor or Chief Magistrate here', because those in authority had 'departed from their Allegiance (*upon which alone our said duty and fidelity to them depends*) and by their Complices and Agents aforesaid endeavoured the destruction of our religion, lives, libertys, and propertys all which they are bound to protect'.[81] In the Maryland declaration, the protection of the Protestant state of the realm met a critique of authority made unacceptable by its ideology.

V

Radicalism or loyalism? The defence of personal monarchy or the protection of the state? The subordination of subject to monarch or the definition of the individual as citizen? It is predictably difficult to impose on the politics and political thought of the second half of the sixteenth century order and coherence. 'Radical' and 'conservative' lose their powers to define the politics of a century in which chaplains to the king became devastating critics of the exercise of human authority and privy councillors shared some of their core assumptions. The Elizabethan regime's instinct was to survive and to protect the continuity of governance. But this loyalism, in its public expressions of the need to defend secular and spiritual authority, assumed a complex form when the polity it sought to protect defined itself in explicitly ideological terms. Some of the strongest statements of this polity as a 'state' were written by men who wanted to conserve the essential features of personal monarchy and preserve the kingdom's ecclesiastical and ideological distinctiveness. The sixteenth century was responsible for the powerful association of stable governance and the 'true religion'. Notions of 'arbitrary' government perhaps came later, but the danger of 'popery' was a key element of the Elizabethan political consciousness.

The implications of political action were sometimes not immediately obvious to writers, preachers and politicians. 'Political thinking' perhaps offers a better sense of this than 'political thought': working documents for the privy council or debates in parliament could push conceptual boundaries just as effectively as text in print. But even Christopher Goodman's *Superior Powers* or John Ponet's *Shorte Treatise*, widely recognized as two major texts of political theory, were explicitly polemical; proof that established classics have to be read in terms of the environment which informed and produced them. Understanding the nature of political debate in the sixteenth century depends on an archaeological investigation of the vocabulary of politics: recovering fragments and decoding their meaning by positioning them in their own layer – the work of one author or a single decade or a contained political debate – but, at the same time, using them to map the broader dimensions of the whole site. A word like 'idolatry', for example, would have triggered different responses in the late 1540s, the middle 1550s and early 1570s. Contemporaries would have been attuned to these responses but they would have recognized too that there were profound similarities of meaning, and been able to point to a common resource of biblical reference and commentary. There were, in the political writings and speeches of the sixteenth century, subtle distinctions; there were also strong continuities.

It should not shock historians to discover that Elizabethans shared the language, assumptions and responses of the 1550s. One of the great achievements of the reign of Edward VI was the construction of a coherent culture of kingship. The regime promoted Edward as a godly king counselled by godly men, personally involved in an evangelical reformation of the realm; a reformation which was an expression of kingly authority and not a consequence of political manipulation. In woodcuts and printed text, representations of Edward served to underpin the claim that he was a young monarch doing what kings had a duty to do, with an ideological twist: caring for his subjects by administering the 'wholesome medecine' of the evangelical gospel.[82] Edwardians could write of the providential fashioning and preservation of Edward in his mother's womb, and explain how, during the king's infancy, idols were being beaten down by the clear light of the gospel. Providence was an ideal counter to the conventional pitfalls of royal minority. Edwardians inherited the key notion of Henry VIII's break with Rome and turned it into a force for ideological change. Cranmer explicitly linked the king's office of supreme head of the church on earth next under God to the second Josiah's reformation of the church.[83]

Elizabethans inherited a model of kingship which was, in its potential, massively powerful. They had to cope too with a serious debate on the limitations of female monarchy and the impact of the Marian exile. It was a complex political, religious and cultural heritage. The preservation of the realm was accepted as a profound political and moral duty. It was principally the responsibility of the prince to preserve God's people and their religion. But monarchs could, and sometimes did, refuse to accept the implications of their responsibilities to subjects. In 1572 Elizabeth I's bishops used the account of King David's refusal to order the death of his treacherous son Absalom (2 Samuel 19: 5–7) to argue that 'the infirmetye of too much pittie and indulgence towardes offenderes' was a dereliction of kingly duty.

> It is daungerouse for any Christyan prince and contrary to the worde of God with coullor of mercy and pittie to doe that whereby he shall discourage and kill the hartes not only of his owne good subjectes and faithfull councellores but also of all other naciones faithfully protestynge Godes religeon and his true worshippe. . . .

The bishops recounted how, moved by the words of 'his counseilore' Joab, David was 'contented to take another course which turned both to the comforte of his subjectes and his owne benefyte'.[84] Like Joab, Elizabeth's good subjects and faithful councillors recognized the need to challenge those who threatened the security of the queen's person, the stability of the kingdom and the promotion of God's truth, even if this meant, as it did in 1569 and 1584, associating themselves against the power of Antichrist.

NOTES

1 James Burgh, *Political Disquisitions*, 3 vols (London, 1774–75), III, pp. 428–9.
2 Burgh, *Political Disquisitions*, III, p. 430, 431.
3 For an account of this reading of English history, see T.M. Parssinen, 'Association, Convention and Anti-Parliament in British Radical Politics, 1771–1848', *English Historical Review*, 88 (1973), pp. 505–7.
4 The Instrument of an association for the preservation of her Majesties Royall person', 19 Oct. 1584: P[ublic] R[ecord] O[ffice, London], S[tate] P[apers] 12/174, fo. 10r.
5 PRO, SP 12/173, fo.134r.
6 PRO, SP 12/174, fo.10r.
7 Stephen Alford, *The Early Elizabethan Polity: William Cecil and the British Succession Crisis, 1558–1569* (Cambridge, 1998), pp. 43–70.
8 PRO, SP 12/174, fo.10r.
9 John Cheke, *The Hurt of Sedicion Howe Greveous it is to a Commune Welth* (London, 1549); and *The True Subject to the Rebell. Or the Hurt of Sedition, How Greivous it is to a Common-wealth* (Oxford, 1641).
10 Raphael Holinshed, *The Laste Volume of the Chronicles of England, Scotland, and Irelande* (London, l577), pp. 1677–96; Holinshed, *Chronicles* (London, 1587), pp. 1042–55.
11 Henry Jenkyns, ed., *The Remains of Thomas Cranmer*, 4 vols. (Oxford, 1833), II, pp. 248–73; Heinrich Bullinger, *A Treatise or Sermon of Henry Bullynger, Much Fruitfull and Necessarve for this Tyme Concernynge Magistrates and Obedience of Subjectes* (London, 1549).
12 For a recent essay, see John Guy, 'Tudor Monarchy and its Critiques', in John Guy, ed., *The Tudor Monarchy* (London, 1997), pp. 78–109.
13 John Ponet, *A Notable Sermon Concerninge the Ryght Use of the Lordes Supper and Other Thynges Very Profitable for All Men to Knowe Preached Before the Kynges Most Excellent Mayestye and Hys Most Honorable Counsel* (London, 1550), sig. {F6r–v}.
14 For an account of Ponet's political thought, see Winthrop S. Hudson, *John Ponet (?1516–1556): Advocate of Limited Monarchy* (Chicago, 1942), pp. 109–216; and Robert M. Kingdon, 'Calvinism and Resistance Theory, 1550–1580', in J. H. Burns and Mark Goldie, eds., *The Cambridge History of Political Thought 1450–1700* (Cambridge, 1991), pp. 194–6.
15 John Ponet, *A Shorte Treatise of Politike Power* (Strasburg, 1556), sig. {E7v}.
16 Hudson, *John Ponet*, pp. 84, 206–7; Christina Hallowell Garrett, *The Marian Exiles: A Study in the Origins of Elizabethan Puritanism* (Cambridge, 1938), pp. 256–7.
17 Hudson, *John Ponet*, p. 206.

18 Hudson, *John Ponet*, pp. 80, 87.
19 Ponet, *Shorte Treatise*, sig. B4r.
20 Ponet, *Shorte Treatise*, sig. B4r–v.
21 Ponet, *Shorte Treatise*, sig. B3r.
22 For a discussion of Morice in the context of the debate on prerogative power, see John Guy, 'The Elizabethan Establishment and the Ecclesiastical Polity', in John Guy, ed., *The Reign of Elizabeth I: Court and Culture in the Last Decade* (Cambridge, 1995), pp. 132–6; and James E. Hampson, 'Richard Cosin and the Rehabilitation of the Clerical Estate in Late Elizabethan England', unpublished University of St Andrews PhD dissertation (1997), pp. 37–9.
23 British Library, Additional MS 36081, fo. 239r.
24 Ponet, *Shorte Treatise*, sig. B5r–v.
25 Ponet, *Shorte Treatise*, sig. {A5r}.
26 Thomas Smith, *De Republica Anglorum*, ed. Mary Dewar (Cambridge, 1982), p. 52 (Book I, Ch. 6).
27 John Aylmer, *An Harborowe for Faithfull and Trewe Subjectes* (London, 1559), sig. H3r.
28 Patrick Collinson, 'The Monarchical Republic of Queen Elizabeth I', in Collinson, *Elizabethan Essays* (London and Rio Grande, 1994), pp. 35, 38.
29 Guy, 'Ecclesiastical Polity', pp. 126–9; Thomas Cartwright, *A Replye to an Answere Made of M. Doctor Whitgifte. Agaynste the Admonition to the Parliament* (Hemel Hempstead, 1573), p. 35.
30 Guy, 'Ecclesiastical Polity', p. 127.
31 John Whitgift, *The Defense of the Aunswere to the Admonition, Against the Replie of T.C.* (London, 1574), p. 182.
32 Guy, 'Tudor Monarchy and its Critiques', pp. 99–100; also Guy, 'Ecclesiastical Polity', pp. 126–49.
33 Ponet, *Shorte Treatise*, sig. {D7r}.
34 Margaret Aston, *The King's Bedpost: Reformation and Iconography in a Tudor Group Portrait* (Cambridge, 1993), pp. 26–53; Diarmaid MacCulloch, *Tudor Church Militant: Edward VI and the Protestant Reformation* (London, 1999), pp. 57–104.
35 Christopher Goodman, *How Superior Powers O[u]ght to be Obeyd of their Subjects* (Geneva, 1558), p. 35.
36 Thomas Stapleton, *A Counterblast to M. Hornes Vayne Blaste against M. Fekenham* (Louvain, 1567), pp. 23r–26r; quotation at p. 26r.
37 Collinson, 'Monarchical Republic', p. 119.
38 Collinson, 'Monarchical Republic', p. 120.
39 Goodman, *Superior Powers*, p. 34.
40 Goodman, *Superior Powers*, p. 96.
41 Goodman, *Superior Powers*, p. 95.
42 Gerald Bowler, '"An Axe or an Acte": The Parliament of 1572', *Canadian Journal of History*, 19 (1984), pp. 351–2; T.E. Hartley, ed., *Proceedings in the*

Parliaments of Elizabeth I, 3 vols (London, l981–95), I, p. 276; Goodman, *Superior Powers*, pp. 181–2.

43 John Foxe, *Actes and Monuments of these Latter and Perillous Dayes* (London, 1563), p. 696.

44 Hartley, ed., *Parliaments*, I, p. 279.

45 Hartley, ed., *Parliaments*, I, p. 275.

46 Collinson, 'Monarchical Republic', pp. 120–1.

47 *The Bible and Holy Scriptures Conteyned in the Olde and Newe Testament* (Geneva, 1560), p. 80.

48 *The Bible and Holy Scriptures Conteyned in the Olde and Newe Testament* (Geneva, 1560), sig. 2r–v.

49 Hartley, ed., *Parliaments*, I, p. 275.

50 British Library, Lansdowne MS 8, fo. 84r.

51 British Library, Lansdowne MS 8, fo.85v. For a discussion of the development of the notion of 'inferior magistrates', see Quentin Skinner, *The Foundations of Modern Political Thought*, 2 vols (Cambridge, 1978), II, pp. 127–8, 195–6.

52 PRO, SP 12/51, fo. 11v.

53 PRO, SP 12/51, fo. 11r.

54 PRO, SP 12/51, fo. 12r.

55 PRO, SP 12/51, fo. 11v.

56 PRO, SP 12/51, fo. 12r.

57 Quentin Skinner, *Liberty before Liberalism* (Cambridge, 1998), p. 3; also Quentin Skinner, 'The State', in Terence Ball, James Farr and Russell L. Hanson, eds., *Political Innovation and Conceptual Change* (Cambridge, 1989), pp. 91–112.

58 PRO, SP 12/173, fo. 136r; David Cressy, 'Binding the Nation: The Bonds of Association, 1584 and 1696', in DeLloyd J. Guth and John W. McKenna, eds, *Tudor Rule and Revolution* (Cambridge, 1982), p. 221.

59 PRO, SP 12/51, fo. 12v.

60 PRO, SP 12/51, fo. 12v.

61 Patrick Collinson, '*De Republica Anglorum*: or, History with the Politics Put Back', in Collinson, *Elizabethan Essays*, p. 19.

62 For an important discussion of the nature of citizenship, see Collinson, '*De Republica Anglorum*', pp. 17–19.

63 Cressy, 'Binding the Nation', pp. 223–5.

64 Markku Peltonen, *Classical Humanism and Republicanism in English Political Thought 1570–1640* (Cambridge, 1995), p. 12; cf. Michael Walzer, 'Citizenship', in Ball, Farr and Hanson, eds, *Political Innovation*, pp. 258–61.

65 Patrick Collinson, 'Sir Nicholas Bacon and the Elizabethan *Via Media*', *Historical Journal*, 23 (1980), p. 260; Alford, *Early Elizabethan Polity*, pp. 21–2.

66 Peltonen, *Classical Humanism and Republicanism*, pp. 69–73.

67 The implications of the Swallowfield articles are discussed in Collinson, 'Monarchical Republic', pp. 111–12; for an important contextual essay and a transcript of the articles, see Steve Hindle, 'Hierarchy and Community in

the Elizabethan Parish: The Swallowfield Articles of 1596', *Historical Journal*, 42 (1999), pp. 835–51.

68 PRO, SP 12/51, fo. 9v.

69 PRO, SP 12/51, fo. 10r.

70 Guy, 'Tudor Monarchy and its Critiques', p. 97.

71 Alford, Early Elizabethan Polity, p. 208.

72 William Cecil, *The Execution of Justice in England*, ed. Robert M. Kingdon (New York, 1965), pp. 31–5; quotation at p. 35.

73 Louis de Bourbon, prince de Condé, *The Treaty of Thassociation Made by the Prince of Condee, Together wyth the Princes, Knyghtes of Thorder, Lordes, Captaines, Gentlemen. & Others of Al Estates which He Entred or Hereafter Shall Entre into the Said Association, for to Mainteine the Honour of God, the Quiet of the Realme of Fraunce, and the State and Lybertie of the Kyng under the Governance of the Quene His Mother who is Authorized Thenunto and Establyshed by the Estates* ([London,] 1562).

74 Condé, *Thassociation*, sigs. A3v–A4r.

75 Jenny Wormald, *Lords and Men in Scotland: Bonds of Manrent* 1442–1603 (Edinburgh, 1985), pp. 143–5, 149–51.

76 Cressy, 'Binding the Nation', pp. 227–33.

77 Thomas Park, ed., *The Harleian Miscellany*, 10 vols (London, 1808–13), VII, pp. 132–5.

78 7 & 8 William III c. 27, printed in *Statutes of the Realm*, 11 vols (London, 1810–28), VII, pp. 114–17.

79 R[ichard] K[ingston], *A True History Of the Several Designs and Conspiracies against his Majesties Sacred Person and Government* (London, 1698), p. 197.

80 Michael G. Hall, Lawrence H. Leder, and Michael G. Kammen, eds., *The Glorious Revolution in America: Documents on the Colonial Crisis of 1689* (New York, 1972), p. 172.

81 Hall, Leder, and Kammen, eds., *Glorious Revolution*, p. 174; my italics.

82 Bernardino Ochino, *A Tragoedie or Dialoge of the Unjust Usurped Primacie of the Bishop of Rome*, trans. John Ponet (London, 1549), sig. Cc4r; Stephen Alford, *Kingship and Politics in the Reign of Edward VI* (Cambridge, 2002), pp. 32–56, 100–15.

83 Jenkyns, ed., *Remains of Thomas Cranmer*, II, p. 119.

84 Hartley, ed., *Parliaments*, I, pp. 278–9.

CHAPTER 2

Richard Overton and Radicalism: the New Intertext of the Civic Ethos in Mid Seventeenth-Century England[1]

Luc Borot

When he was reacting to the ideological debates of the Paris Commune in the Spring of 1871, Karl Marx complained that the French revolutionaries wasted their time rehearsing the issues of the previous revolutions instead of facing the revolutionary tasks of the present.[2] Marx's insights are confirmed by a glance backward at the 1848 revolutions, and forward from him to 1968. French historiography has long wondered whether the Paris Commune was like the dawn of something new, or like the dusk of the *ancien régime* of working-class movements. In August 1944, when the Paris Resistance took control of the Hôtel de Ville, they were repeating what their forebears had done in all the previous Paris revolutions. In May 1968, Daniel Cohn-Bendit prevented the most radical part of the student movement from marching on the presidency at the Palais de l'Élysée. This choice reveals that the mental patterns which structured the political imagination of the student movement were moments like the storming of the Winter Palace in the Soviet revolution, not the French revolutionary traditions. It also betrayed the shift in political realities undergone by France in a century: the symbolical seat of power directly addressed by the protesters was national, not local. Radicalism and revolutions are traditionalist phenomena in many ways, and their symbolic choices reflect the values and representations that are widespread in the societies from which they emerge. It should not be surprising to observe the same process in the traditionalist and deferential societies of early modern Europe within which people like the Levellers were acting.

Two terms in this title beg for definition: 'radicalism' and 'intertext'. Is it indeed legitimate to use the terms 'radical' or 'radicalism' before they were claimed by a specific school of political thought? Two criteria will be ascribed to 'radicalism':

1. A current of thought will be called 'radical' when it advocates more thorough policies than those advocated by the opposition movement it associates with, or by the new authorities in the revolutionary situation of mid seventeenth-century England.
2. As historians of the eighteenth century remind us, radicalism defined itself by an appeal to constitutional reformation, an issue with which the Levellers were definitely concerned.

Is it completely legitimate to import into historical scholarship a literary methodological notion like 'intertext'? 'Intertext' means more than 'quotations' or 'parody,' or even 'plagiarism,' though these devices are intertextual phenomena. All writers construct a world of words that weaves other authors' words into theirs. Whether they do it consciously or not depends on their conceptions and practices of composition. They also weave common places, proverbs, beliefs and historical allusions into their writing, and all this constitutes an 'intertext.' Bunyan has a different 'intertext' from Milton's or Sir Thomas Browne's, and Overton's is different from Lilburne's. Their respective positions within English society, their education, their positions within English Protestantism, produced different intellects that are reflected in individualized referential corpora. This chapter's argument is that Overton's 'intertext' is more radically subversive than Lilburne's because the former borrows from a wider referential corpus which extends far beyond the 'godly' tradition and the common law to include popular traditions and proverbs, and because he develops a very subtle way of interweaving biblical references with colloquial language when he decides to challenge his Leveller fellows in the summer of 1649. Though the two men share much of the godly party's collective background of hagiography and martyrology, Overton's work with biblical quotations sharply contrasts with Lilburne's extremely deferential use of the idiom and behavioural patterns of 'Puritanism'.

Were the Levellers the dawn of English radicalism? Did the Levellers embody the sunset of pre-modern popular grievances? Both questions can receive positive answers, and would also raise new questions from other corners.[3] The Levellers, if the term can be safely used, although there never really was a unified and uniform movement, were certainly looking backward to old and obsolete myths of Englishness, referring to an obsolete legal system of oppression based on wise saws and old instances, and marketed to them, as it were, as the doctrine of their liberty. Yet, they also initiated some of the most characteristic grievances of English radicalism: yearly parliaments, manhood suffrage (more or less comprehensive), parliamentary salaries, to name but a few demands of various Leveller petitions or pamphlets, were also on John Wilkes's platform in the 1770s and were high on the list of grievances of the Chartists in the 1830s and 1840s. Not unlike the French revolutionaries of the nineteenth century, the English radicals of the seventeenth thought of themselves as belonging to a tradition, or rather, to converging streams of tradition, or, to get closer to the point, to streams of tradition revealed by the idioms (religious, legal, political or otherwise) that these people were speaking. This essay's main concern is to show how such a pithy author as Richard Overton managed to reinsert the vocabulary of popular festive traditions within an ideological context that was so deeply pervaded by the values of godliness.

The presence of a Marprelatist intertext in Overton's early Marpriest tracts has already been tackled by, among other critics, Joseph Frank, Margot Heinemann and Nigel Smith.[4] Our attention will bear on the *Appeale from the Degenerate Representative Body*, of July 1647, Overton's narrative in the *Picture of the Council of State* of April 1649 and *The Baiting of the Great Bull of Bashan*, published in July 1649, after the burial of Rainsborough, the execution of the king, the institution of the Commonwealth, the May Day Agreement of 1649 and the repression of the Burford mutiny by Oliver Cromwell. In *The Baiting of the Great Bull of Bashan*, Overton blends evangelical references with allusions to the prohibition of popular festivals. He deplores the lack of punch, as it were, of his Leveller comrades, his 'brethren of the sea-green order' as he calls them, and he seems to blame them for accepting the new moral order imposed by the men in office, as if their contention against king and Church had only been that there were Whitsun ales in churches, lewd dancing around the Maypoles, and that these abuses were to be repressed.

Overton's catchwords are freedom, mirth and reason: 'all [God's] communications are reasonable and just, and what is so, is of God,'[5] or: 'Mirth sure is of divine instinct'.[6] The very title of the pamphlet, with its allusion to bull baiting (one of the traditional bugbears of the 'godly sort') and to tyranny (one of the accusations they had levelled against the king), is a humorous provocation to the several shades of Army Puritans (to use a loose term) represented in the Council of State and in the Rump. The sources for the association of the bulls of Bashan with tyranny and oppression are Amos 4.1 and Psalm 22.2. Patrick Collinson has painted a portrait of Puritanism as a form of popular culture,[7] but he did not include a description of this very original popular form of radical Protestantism, which has some of its roots in the satirical vein of the Marprelate and anti-Marprelate tracts, and resulted in the Leveller practice of exposing tyranny and mock-sanctity.

The first element of my argument that needs defining is the mode of civic intervention within which Overton's writings must be studied: those who had no right to civic participation, viz. to the choice of the legislators, had to resort to spectacular modes of political intervention. This remains a dominant feature of radical action. The second element, which is going to be analyzed at the end, is the intertextual creativity of Overton's later writings as a radical alternative to Lilburne's classical godly stance.

One important dimension of radicalism in the first sense, is its modes of action. English radicalism in the seventeenth century already belonged to a nexus of traditions, among which were some spectacular modes of resistance and action. Others have already pointed out that Foxe's *Acts and Monuments of English Martyrs* were a constant source of role models. Lilburne was already perceived in his day as a master of self-staging, and the examples of apprentices, gentlemen and artisans resisting the arbitrary power of Bishop Bonner and his crew represent an obvious stock of role models. The common points between the Leveller militants and the Marian martyrs was the stubborn character of the judges they were confronted with, and the extra-legal forms of the procedures that were used against them. When Overton complained that he, his brother and his wife were being detained 'without due process of law', in *An Appeale from the Degenerate Representative* in 1647, he was describing a situation that the Protestants tried under Mary Tudor had previously experienced. Yet, he did not share their language and stance as much as his associate Lilburne did. Overton was a better master of language, but Lilburne was a better master of public appearance. Like the Marian martyrs and the Leveller rank and file, the Leveller leaders had to use the spectacular form of action or testimony that shall here be called intervention, when they were illegally deprived of their right to civic participation (or when they were socially barred from it).

The civic ethos and habitus manifested during the English Revolution can be characterized as the result of a process that started under Henry VIII with such educational treatises as Sir Thomas Elyot's *Book named the Governor*. The development of courtier handbooks, treatises for lords of manors, copyholders, Justices of Peace, the introductions to rhetorical treatises and classical translations continued this process, and shaped the figure of the local gentleman as magistrate, or as councillor, either in the spheres of Parliament or in the ethereal circles of the court.[8] The struggles of an MP like Sir Peter Wentworth in the 1576 Parliament illustrate the shift from a conception of the councillor as courtier to the self-image of the knight of the shire or burgess as councillor of the monarch, grounded on the belief that the MP is a representative of the dynamic vested interests of the kingdom.[9] The syntheses of the common law produced in the same decades by Coke, Bacon and others accompanied this process. This is a native trend of the English gentry's tradition of citizenship. According to Pocock and Fink, it has an Italian, Greek and Roman parallel which they call 'classical republicanism', or 'civic humanism'.[10] To them, it results in the development of the Harringtonian-Sidneian model of aristocratic republican citizenship. It is also possible to argue that the two traditions influence each other so much that the distinction can often seem artificial.[11]

Less artificial is the distinction between these streams of tradition and the English Protestant mode. Its elaboration began with the desire of the Elizabethan Church to generate an identity to strengthen the unity and uniformity of the Church. Foxe's 'Book of Martyrs' is an essential component of this new civic education, that reached out to people that classical and legal culture would only reach with difficulty. The speeches of the Marian martyrs as they stood in Foxe's book were read in public, since most reading in early modern England was public and was an integral part of the sociability of an oral culture. Their theatricality, the pathos of their rhetoric certainly acted as a set of models. The development of separatist, Brownist, Presbyterian activism, the novelty of the anti-prelatical opposition, fashioned another habitus and ethos. The way such streams of tradition got mingled in varying ways in the evolution of the Leveller movement is one of this essay's focuses.

Deprived of the franchise by their relative lack of fortune, most of the people who had an interest in the victory of the Levellers' ideas could find that petitioning, demonstrating, 'being there' at the public punishment of their leaders, was a means to express their views. The same had been true when some Puritan leaders had been repressed by the Stuarts. It can sometimes be difficult to draw the line between these demonstrations and the mob behaviours of the London crowds,[12] but they became increasingly strong from the beginning of the Long Parliament. The development of newsbooks and newsheets after 1641, the multiplication of political rumours while the Houses were in session, put the Parliament under the pressure of crowd movements in the City, to which petitions from the provinces added a new dimension, very much resembling what we now call public opinion.[13] Even the disenfranchised could express their views through the medium of intervention, though they were excluded from the more dignified mode of civic participation.[14] The Leveller petition of 11 September, 1648 was one of the highlights of Leveller action.[15] It was printed separately, and was entirely reprinted by the newsbook that was closest to the Levellers' positions, *The Moderate*.[16] In later pamphlets, Overton and Lilburne refer to it as one of the strongest manifestations of support from the mass of the people for the positions they were upholding in front of the growing power of the Army grandees.[17]

With the Civil War in the summer of 1642, men who had no voting rights ventured their lives in the Parliament's cause, and with the creation of the New Model Army in 1645 the inner conflicts among the officers and between the soldiers and officers led to a development of political debate that has been extensively documented.[18] As appears in the army debates of November 1647, some soldiers effectively demanded universal franchise, although the Agreements of the People and the proposals of the Leveller leaders never went so far. Yet, as some of these soldiers then complained, and as Cromwell confirms, they were fools to have committed their lives and goods in the cause of the Parliamentary gentry in the hope that they would obtain a political reward for their sacrifice, in the guise of an extension of franchise. As one of them put it, a man who was enfranchised before he ventured his life and goods in the Parliamentary army may lose his money and goods and therefore lose his freehold and his franchise in the adventure.[19] Debating, petitioning, were rights claimed by the soldiers with their Solemn Engagement of 1645, but they were regularly losing some of them as the social élites confirmed their control of the war machine and of the political machinery of power conquest.

Petitioning the king and commons directly and through bills was regarded as an ancient mode of political action in English constitutional history; it became a daily mode of intervention in the 1640s. The State Papers and the newsbooks of the time are full of lists of private or community petitions, or of regimental petitions. When the right of the soldiers to petition was curtailed in 1647 and 1649, they used pamphlets to justify their petitions and to inform the nation that the army leaders wanted to impose silence on those men that had become mere instruments of war to them. When Overton helped some of them, he advocated himself and them, and staged the soldiers as witnesses (that is, as martyrs) of the cause of England's freedom, in *The Hunting of the Foxes*.[20] After the repression of the Burford rebellion in the spring, and the extinction of public liberties in the autumn of 1649, the last mode of intervention that was left to those who intended to resist the new rulers now perceived as traitors to the cause was conspiracy. Yet, as the Protectorate and Restoration have shown since, conspiracy has a considerable drawback for the people in power: it has a strong tendency to provide the opposition with martyrs, a detail that the Protectorate and Restoration leaders had completely overlooked. Changing an enemy into a martyr was a form of mismanagement that Cromwell had avoided as long as possible, when he tried, with variable results, to win Lilburne over to his side in the early years of the civil war, but which he totally failed to do after the king's execution.[21] The figures of Lilburne, Overton and Charles I as martyrs do deserve some consideration in the light of the Foxean inheritance of Leveller action. These shared references and behaviours may be one of the explanations for the complicity that appeared between Levellers and royalists under the Protectorate, and in which Overton and Lilburne were personally involved.

The Elizabethan Church had required every parish church in the land to own a copy of Foxe's martyrology, popularly known as 'Foxe's Book of Martyrs'. The figures portrayed by Foxe could provide role models to several age-groups and social types, such as wives, maids, apprentices, ministers, artisans, merchants, gentle folk. The national mythography of the Protestant elect nation built itself on this encomium of a wide panel of witnesses of the faith. When the Presbyterian scholar and propagandist William Prynne had his ears cut off for his religious dissent under Charles I, he was able to stage his martyrdom to his benefit. When other victims of arbitrary power like Burton and Bastwick were released from jail with him on another occasion, their enthusiastic welcome by the London population resembled the worship of living saints.

Foxe's book clearly covered the whole spectrum of rank, age and gender. The dialogues between the judges and the martyrs were almost certainly made up: considering the average education level in the 1550s, it is difficult to imagine a weaver or an apprentice in his late teens discussing points of scholastic philosophy with a bishop.[22] Foxe obviously oriented his character construction towards the defence of Protestant doctrine, and the portraiture of his martyrs as exceptionally gifted and orthodox theologians contributed in the construction of heroic figures.

A relevant instance of radical pre-history in the English Reformation can be found in the comparison of the weaver Thomas Tomkins with Mucius Scaevola: it fulfils several functions in Foxe's work, and it must have had deep echoes in the minds of early seventeenth-century Puritan readers and listeners. Tomkins was arrested, tried, tortured and burned by Bishop Bonner in 1555. When Bonner wanted to try his faith by torture, he held Tomkins's hand over a candle, and then, Foxe writes:

> Tomkins afterwards reported to one James Hinse, that his spirit was so rapt up, that he felt no pain. In the which burning he never shrank, till the veins shrank and the sinews brast, and the water did spurt into Master Harpsfield's face.[23]

The parallel between Tomkins and Scaevola that follows, enables Foxe to draw another parallel, between Bonner and the Etruscan king Porsenna. Tomkins is greater than Scaevola, because he was fighting for the Christian truth that he knew, whereas Bonner was worse than the pagan Porsenna, since Porsenna spared his enemy and sent him back to his country, whereas the would-be Christian Bonner had the true Christian burned at the stake. In the apologetical tradition, the Christian must be better than the pagan who only had the seeds of true virtue in him, so the Christian persecutor can but be worse than the pagan persecutor, since the latter did not have the advantage of Gospel revelation. As Porsenna was a civil tyrant, so is the bishop's power a tyranny, though spiritual: such analogies run through the whole body of antiprelatical polemic.

To the readers, these parallels would take on a new meaning in the late sixteenth century and in the seventeenth century, when Roman history, partly through the discovery of Machiavelli and other Italian thinkers, got integrated within a new political idiom, which was in part to inspire such different people as constitutional monarchists, republican Puritans, the republicans of the Vane-Harrington-Sidney line and some Levellers too, if Sexby's late *Killing no Murder* is a relevant example.

Some sociological patterns applied by the Levellers in their self-fashioning as martyrs and/or heroes can also be tracked back to Foxe. In her article 'Gender and Politics in Leveller Literature', Ann Hughes gives a very insightful analysis of the Levellers' narratives of their families' trials, and her analyses of the Leveller leaders' wives' petitions throw much light on the construction of their reputations as archetypal 'godly households'.[24] What she identifies with such accuracy is something like a sociological pattern with which other godly families could identify, and through which the Levellers could appear as fully-fledged Protestants unfairly persecuted.

When Foxe reports on John Rogers's persecution, he insists on a dialogue between Bonner and the translator of the Matthew Bible, concerning his wife. The bishop denies him the right to have visits from his wife because she is not so. To the persecutor, although they had been married eighteen years and had ten children, as Rogers had been a priest, his marriage was *ipso facto* invalid since Mary's repeal of Henry VIII's laws.[25] The martyr can then ridicule the bishop for the hypocrisy of the priests who keep 'whores' to satisfy their lusts. The apologetical narration of martyrdom is all the more complete since the martyr can extol the new family values against the abuses of the Roman Church. The existence of his ten children overbalances the claims of the old religion's clergy to chastity and virtue. Likewise, in the story of young William Hunter, a sixteen-year old apprentice, Browne, a priest who prosecutes Protestants, asks the boy's father to deliver his son to be tried. The father rejects the money offered him, returns home, meets his son and offers to pretend that he never found him at home. The virtuous young man will return to the persecutors to be tried, and to keep his father out of harm's way.[26] Even his brother was ready to die like him.

Another godly household out of Foxe is the Warne family, in which the husband, wife and her daughter from her first marriage, were in that order sent to the stake. The three had been caught when attending a secret communion service in London, and the three died for it. The young woman, at the age of twenty, was ministering to her imprisoned parents when her employer told the bishop's men that he suspected her of sharing her family's faith. She was at the same time a model of filial piety and of Protestant piety.[27]

These particular examples illustrate the origin of some of the radical features which can be identified in the Levellers' modes of action if we admit the first definition of radicalism outlined above. The spectacular dimension of Leveller behaviour and interventions, the self-assertion of righteousness, the emphasis on household unity in action and martyrdom, build up a picture of extreme commitment to the cause. The activists are antitypes of the Foxean martyrs, and they embody the truth of the cause against its corrupters. In republican terms, they are an incarnation of *virtù* against corruption. Their experience provides a touchstone to test the honesty and righteousness of any other person who stands up to uphold the cause. Happy are they if they are persecuted for the cause, since their persecutors' fathers did the same to the prophets of old, to paraphrase Matthew 5.11–12: to a Bible-nurtured mentality like the godly sort, such patterns of thought gave means to discern the goodness of the tree by its fruits. To take up Christopher Haigh's phrase about the evangelical current in early Tudor England, this culture contributed in 'the making of a minority',[28] well into the post-1660 dissenting *milieu*.

In terms of intellectual archaeology, this moment of English Protestant culture can be read as a first instance of the link that will become explicit in the eighteenth century between radicalism and religious dissent.

The Leveller master of martyrdom, who was often martyr-Prynne's own martyr, was John Lilburne. Clarendon writes that: '... by reading the Book of Martyrs, he raised in himself a marvellous inclination and appetite to suffer in the defence, or for the vindication, of any oppressed truth, and found himself very much confirmed in that spirit'.[29] His skill in the art of self-promotion won him thousands of admirers and quite a few enemies. His best victories were won by appealing from the arbitrary jurisdiction that was trying him, to the law of God, the law of nature, or the liberties of freeborn Englishmen. He was always able to find an authority above his judges, or more fundamental than theirs. His self-advertising as Freeborn John, the champion of the liberties of the common Englishman made his name very popular. His line of defence, by appealing to fundamental laws and to the right of the people by inheritance, was also used by King Charles in his trial. When Overton was sued by the Council of State with Lilburne, Walwyn and Prince, a few months after the execution, he was able to find words that echoed the king's.[30]

During his trial, Charles I cast himself as the champion of the liberties of the people, a posture that he had only assumed once before, in his answer to the parliament's Nineteen Propositions in June 1642, probably under the influence of his advisers Culpeper and Hyde. For several days he used devices that Lilburne was wont to use, and in particular the illegitimacy of the Court, and the absence of grounds to judge him according to the fundamental laws of the kingdom. Once denied the right to make this point good, the king more regularly returned to the more 'liberal' accents of Freeborn John. This quote is from one of the news pamphlets that were printed almost every day during the trial, *A Perfect Narrative of the whole Proceedings of the High Court of Justice in the Trial of the King.*[31] On January 20, 1648/9, the king responded to Bradshaw's accusations in these words: 'Let me know by what lawful authority I am seated here, and I will answer it, otherwise I will not answer it',[32] and further:

> I will stand as much for the Priviledge of the House of Commons, rightly understood, as any man here whatsoever. I see no House of Lords here that may constitute a Parliament, and the King, too, should have been. Is this the bringing of the King to his Parliament? Is this the bringing an end to the treaty in the public faith of the world?[33]

Two days later, in the next session reported in the same number of the *Perfect Narrative*, he claimed:

> It is not my case alone, it is the freedom and the liberty of the People of England, and do you pretend what you will, I stand more for their liberties. For if power without law may make laws, may alter the fundamental laws of the kingdom, I do not know what subject he is in England, that can be sure of his life or any thing that he calls his own.[34]

When Overton had to speak in his own defence in front of the Council of State, he also used the argument of illegitimacy, as he explained in his narrative of *The Picture of the Council of State*, when he, in his turn, addressed Bradshaw:

> Sir, what title to give you, or distinguish you by, I know not; indeed, I confess I have heard by common report that you go under the name of a Councel of State; but for my part, what you are I cannot well tell; but this I know, that had you (as you pretend) a just authority from the Parliament, yet were not your authority valuable or binding, till solemnly proclaimed to the people [. . .].[35]

And further:

> [. . .] For my part, Gentlemen, I do utterly refuse to make answer unto any thing in relation to my own person, or any man or men under heaven; but do humbly desire, that if you intend by way of charge to proceed to any trial of me, that it may be [. . .] by the known established Law of England, in some ordinary Court of Justice appointed for such cases (extraordinary ways being never to be used, but abominated, where ordinary ways may be had) and I shall freely submit to what can be legally made good against me.[36]

In front of exceptional jurisdictions, Lilburne, Overton and the king had resorted to vocabularies that sounded like that of the martyrs facing Bonner and his crew. Overton never tried to stage himself as a martyr, though in 1646, when he was describing the insults that his wife had received when she was arrested, with himself and his brother, or when he described the plight of his three children left in the streets on their parents arrest, he did echo the 'godly household' archetype identified above in Foxe's *Acts and Monuments*, an allusion which the readers could not miss.[37] On the other hand, the iconography of Lilburne's trials (in two senses of the word) and tribulations,[38] and the *Eikon Basilikè* that established Charles I as a Christian martyr raised these two figures to the same eminence as the *Golden Legend* saints of the Catholic world, or as the Marian martyrs. As Nigel Smith rightly says in his paper on the Marpriest tracts, Overton, like Marprelate, was to influence people who were 'the farthest away from him in terms of the political and religious stances of 1645'.[39] But should we not also consider that, in his later writings, he was more or less consciously plagiarizing the king's behaviour? After all, the king's words to the High Court had been officially published, and many pamphlets and newsbooks had reported the king's speeches, so that it was not unlikely that Overton had read them and that he could expect his readers to have recollections of the trial, which was not very distant.

One of the legacies that the Levellers shared with other English people of other political persuasions was therefore the awareness that public behaviour, when in conformity with established English Protestant role models, was a political language in its own right, that petitioning was a mode of political intervention for the unenfranchised and disenfranchised, and that *visible* action could make up for constitutional participation. The two major political actors (in the theatrical sense of the word) of the period, Lilburne and the king, could be presented as two antitypes of the Foxean martyrs, on each side of the English Revolution's struggles.

On the other hand, what a man like Overton proved in his literary production, was that a political idiom is a mode of action. If Margot Heinemann (quoting Marie Gimmelfarb-Brack) is right, in his youth Overton was involved in theatrical practice at Cambridge. Following Don Wolfe, Heinemann also argues that Overton is likely to have been the author of anonymous pamphlet-plays in the early 1640s (e.g. *Canterbury his Change of Diet* of 1641);[40] if this is true, he was more aware than the other Leveller authors (John Harris excepted) of the evocative power of dialogue, and of the directness of theatre's appeal to both the intellect and the senses. Like the colloquies and dialogues of the Renaissance, Overton's playlets and the apostrophes in his non-dramatic pamphlets dramatize and actualize the opposition of ideas and ideals at very specific moments in the Revolution.

Beyond the intertext of drama and martyrology that so deeply influenced Leveller intervention, Overton invented a new intertext. Against the pious prohibition of May Games and revels, of Christmas and Easter, of the theatres, against the attacks on freedom of the press and freedom of petitioning, he found a way to blend the language of popular pastimes and pastoral festivals with the biblical idiom of the godly party. More humane than the terrible beauty of martyrdom, the ideal that Overton tried to promote was the godly mirth of the liberated people, the remedy against the godly melancholy and tyranny of Hollis, Prynne, Cromwell and Ireton. He seems to have elaborated this ideal in a gradual way: his last pamphlet was the most pathetic, and the most luminous appeal to his fellow Levellers and to the free people of England.

Three pamphlets more particularly testify of Overton's evolution in the second half of the 1640s: *The Appeale from the Degenerate Representative* (April 1647), *The Picture of the Council of State* (April 1649), and *The Baiting of the Great Bull of Bashan* (July 1649).

In spite of the two years between the first pamphlet and the other two, some circumstances of their production are similar on several points: the arbitrary arrest, examination and imprisonment, but the political context is very different.

In April 1647, the Leveller movement was coming together, and the Presbyterians still apparently control the House of Commons, whereas in the spring and summer of 1649, the Independents were in power, the Levellers and royalists were on the front-line of repression, the party was dissolving as its members react differently to the new regime; another difference was that the 1647 pamphlet was a defence of Overton himself and of his wife, brother and children, whereas in 1649, the four Leveller leaders were writing from their jail in their own defence.

Another major difference between the *Appeal* and the other texts, is that the political doctrine of the Levellers was more consistently established, after dozens of pamphlets, months of debating and the elaboration of the Agreements of the People. The *Appeal* contained Overton's first mature version of his political thought, and was concluded by a series of articles towards constitutional and social reform.[41] Some of these grievances were to appear in the three Agreements of the People.

The concision of the style and the efficiency of the technical legal argument demonstrate that Overton was becoming a more style-conscious writer and was able to adapt his rhetoric to the audience and to the circumstances. It will soon be shown that he was also elaborating a new style of allegorical biblical quotation, but it is important to describe first the way he developed what Nigel Smith has called his 'writing of inversion', remaining faithful to some of the original features of this style as they had appeared in *The Araignment of Mr Persecution*, like apostrophe, proverbs, metonymy and calumniation.[42] These devices remain, but others appear, of a more momentous nature.

Despair – or wisdom – drove Overton to address the people through a genre that reaches beyond the satire of his early playlets. The biblical intertext had always been very strong in his writings, but he now turns it into a form of art. The festive, even carnivalesque, dimension of popular culture was always an important stock of metaphors and similes, but they were becoming central, and all this was merging into a new intertext.

The technique of biblical word-association begins to change in the *Appeale* of 1647. It is possible to compare Overton's treatment of parables in the *Appeale* and in the *Baiting*. In the *Appeale*, the treatment of the parable of the compassionate Samaritan (the title of a pamphlet by Walwyn) weaves biblical reference and political meditation together:

> It is not the part of the just and merciful freemen of England to behold the politic body of this commonwealth fallen amongst a crew of thieves, as Hollis, Stapleton, etc. stripped of its precious raiment of freedom and safety, wounded and grovelling in its blood, even half dead, and pass by on the other side like the merciless priest and the levite: no, now is the time for the compassionate Samaritan, to appear to bind up its wounds, to pour in wine and oil to engage in the defence and preservation of a distressed miserable people [. . .].[43]

The pattern of priestly tyranny that is so characteristic of radical Protestantism and of Overton (and already observed in Foxe) is present, but the metaphor of the commonwealth as the wounded man of the parable equates the people as a whole with the compassionate Samaritan. Their responsibility and their Christian duty is to help the commonwealth, therefore to help themselves, since they are both matter and makers of the Commonwealth, as Hobbes would write (in a different philosophical context) in *Leviathan* in 1651. The parable begins with an appeal to the 'just and merciful freemen of England' and ends in the deploration of the plight of the 'distressed miserable people'; the former are a part of the latter, and must help the people to become a commonwealth.

This is also the sort of appeal that is recurrently voiced in the *Baiting*, to criticize popular passivity in front of the May Day Agreement:

> When tis put upon the personal test for execution, O then one hath bought a piece of ground, and must be excused; another a yoke of oxen, and he must go see them; and a third hath married a wife and therefore must please her. Friends, be not offended, this is a crime deserves your repentance; I condemn you not all, it is but some few; a little leaven you know leaveneth the whole lump; therefore do ye beware of the leaven of the Pharisees; it much retardeth your motions and blasteth their fruits; the public is a loser thereby, and your cause receiveth damage.[44]

The apologies out of Luke 14.19 must remind the reader of the tale of the parable: a man has made a great supper, but the guests will not come, so the master invites the poor and the cripple to the feast. The English people are wasting the occasion to settle the Commonwealth on new grounds, and the Levellers are to them as the master to the guests, and like God to his unfaithful people. The word-association technique in the leaven metaphor combines the Gospels (the intimation 'Beware the leaven of the Pharisees' is in Mat. 16.6, Mark 8.15 and Luke 12.1) and the Pauline epistles ('a little leaven leaveneth the whole lump': 1 Cor. 5.6, Gal. 5.9). It is one more attack on the hypocrisy of the Independents, a central theme of the *Baiting*: the supporters of the petition of 11 September, 1648 are lulled into passivity or fear by the Independents' claim that the fight is over. The Levellers' function must now be to arouse their brethren into speedy action. Overton thought that a more elaborate form of intertext appealing to a broader spectrum of cultural references would enable them to do so, and this is what he resorted to, as if he wanted to take his last bow in grand style. This must be the greatest literary and ideological innovation of Overton's career.

The popular and festive references that pervade Overton's writings have already been studied by Smith and Heinemann concerning the Marpriest tracts.[45] Both have overlooked the power of his later methods of composition. In 1649, Overton still resorted to proverbs, but he either used them at face value or he altered them to create a new idea.[46] Among the classical proverbs he uses in the *Baiting* are 'like a shoulder of mutton to a sick horse' (Tilley S399),[47] 'to strain at a gnat and swallow a camel' (Tilley G150; Mat. 23.24, in which Christ curses the hypocrisy of the Pharisees),[48] 'touch pitch and you shall be defiled' (Tilley P358; perhaps also an echo of a speech by Falstaff in *1 Henry IV*).[49] All these proverbs are uttered within a couple of pages, with a great density of word play. Overton also turns proverbs upside-down in utterances like: 'My brethren of the sea-green order, take a little wine with your water, and I'll take a little water with my wine, and it will temper us to the best constitution'.[50] The second formula is the attested proverb (Tilley W112), whereas the first one is an inversion. Overton's 'writing of inversion' revives the lexicalized metaphor of the proverb, and associates his energy and clear-sightedness with the strength of wine. Some proverbial utterances are not attested by Tilley or Brewer, but they echo biblical references, for instance: 'like music to the house of mourning',[51] which echoes Eccl. 7.

Festive metaphors and similes were already present in the *Appeal*, but they become a structuring device in the *Baiting*. In a previous pamphlet, Overton had likened himself to a dog baiting the bull of tyranny,[52] and used obscene words to denote the Independents. He reacts to the hostile responses this language had prompted, and reminds his critics that worse incivility is daily committed by the present rulers of England under the cloak of sanctity:

And so of my metaphor of the Bull, the use of the word Genitals, Pox, etc. you may say is uncivil in the Letter, but how uncivil I pray in the Moral? Know ye not that whosoever shall but fasten on the genitors or parents of the peoples ruin, so as to pinch the grand impostors and deluders of the times, he burns his fingers, is smit with *the Morbus Gallicus* of the enslaving sword.[53]

The spirit of mirth does not rule the spirits of the Levellers in the Summer of 1649:

Love envieth not, it judgeth the best; I had thought with two or three merry jigs to attempt an uproar in all the laughers in England, but I see you are a company of dull souls, mirth with you is like a shoulder of mutton to a sick horse, or worse, you straight convert into melancholy, trample it under your feet, turn again, and are (some of you) ready to rent me.[54]

The first sentence is an elaboration on 1 Cor. 13.4, but the rest combines proverbs and references to dance and laughter. Yet, this is not the most elaborate combination.

Concerning his obscene wit, replying to his critics, he writes:

What if I had turned fidler in that paper, Christ himself useth the simile of a piper, saying, we have piped unto you and ye have not danced (Mat. 11.17). And truly I think we (the four poor sea-green fidlers in the Tower) may take up the same saying, We have piped unto you ever since the first of May, the most pleasant tune of the Agreement of the People, but ye have not danced up so roundly as so sprightly a tune deserves.[55]

The parable in Matthew 11.17 authorizes a transgression of the new moral order, in which, as he writes further:

Religion is turned into melancholy; [. . .] he, that cannot whine, pipe, weep and hang down his head like a bulrush and seem sad unto men, is prophane, light, hath not any thing of God in him, is a reprobate, is condemned and censured of all, as neither fit for Church or Commonwealth; and thus it cometh to pass; my mirth is heightened to such a transgression, even to cast me under the present Anathema of the now godly party.[56]

The tune of constitutional reform is like the tune of the word of God, the Levellers, here again, are in a prophetical position, humorously assimilated to the role of the May Day musicians, whose profane tunes had been the bugbears of the godly sort since the reign of Elizabeth.

Overton confirms what Hobbes was to explain in the mid-1660s in his *Behemoth, or the Long Parliament*: the Independents and Presbyterians were overtaken by more radical critics, which the thinker of Malmesbury calls 'a brood of [the Puritans'] own hatching'.[57] The people who had supported the Leveller movement for the past two or three years had occasion to see that the struggle for the liberties of the people was not one and the same thing as the fight for the continuation of the Reformation in the Church. Yet, they were removing or silencing their support for their own cause, now the Independents were holding the reins of power. It looks as though Overton, with his usual clear-sightedness, had understood that the rhetoric of the Army Puritans had convinced the people who had supported the revolutionary movement, that the process had now come to an end, that enough blood had been spilt (and this was understandably a reason to end the fight), and that there was no need to embark on a new campaign for a freedom that was gained, since the most obvious agencies of tyranny, *viz.* the king, Lords and bishops were no more.

He was certainly echoing the feelings of many ordinary country-folk, who were being deprived of their traditional festive cycles both in their religious life and in the rituals of their immemorial pastoral experience. As Ronald Hutton has shown in *The Rise and Fall of Merry England*, there was much resistance to the abolition of agrarian festivals in many rural areas.[58] Likewise, it must have been extremely difficult to understand the abolition of religious festivals like Christmas and Easter. The cultural revolution of the two decades of 'godly rule' was a complete failure, as Christopher Durston and John Morrill have shown.[59] Yet, some were weary of the revolution, as Overton regrets:

> I have known, when things as unserious as my last sheet, dressed out in the youthful attire of mirth, hath found a very large acceptance not only with you, but even with this generation of men, that are now the enemies of the people; and I think if I have not forgot the Araingment of Persecution [. . .] that I myself have been one of those who have had the honour of such acceptances: But O tempora! O mores! how few are the same yesterday and today? success changeth men's minds as the wind doth the weathercock.[60]

Overton's rhetoric strayed very far indeed from the spirit of the 'godly' movement, for even godly militants from the artisan class like Nehemiah Wallington delighted in the narrative of God's visitations upon the Sabbath breakers and May-Day dancers, as his collection of judgement stories, preserved in the British Library, shows. Wallington reports that:

> In 1639 in Salisbury, a jolly fellow brewed strong ale to maintain sport on the Lords day, and in the month of May would have a Maypole set up on the Lords

> day; and on the night before, he and his jovial crew went in despight of the Puritants to cut the tree, and in the Lords day in the morning, he driving his three horses down the hill, [. . .] the tree not being tied fast in the cart turned round by reason of one wheel going higher than the other, and so fell over, beat out the fellows brain abroad upon the ground, and there ended their sport; and instead of a mad merry-making of the May game, had the sad burying of a profane fellow and the horse and cart for it.[61]

The mentality of popular Puritanism was built on the memory and practice of collective resistance to enforced conformity, it was a culture of shared trials, with its metrical psalms sung while the saints 'gadded to sermons' in procession to the churches of their favourite preachers, away from their own parishes, communities bonded together by private meetings to 'seek the Lord' together, but a culture that was also marked by a constant struggle against the profanity of their fellow workers, farmers, merchants, apprentices, etc. Now, Overton was opening another perspective for the humbler godly: there existed a merry godliness, truly English in its roots, in its descent from the Marian martyrs, from the resistance to Laudian abuses, a godly citizenship that could be called more truly English than the dreary one because it could endorse the harmless rural merriments of the pastoral tradition. This merry godliness was the state of mind required to further the aims of the *Agreement of the Free People of England*. The date of 1 May cannot have been chosen by the authors of the Agreement without this set of allusions in mind. The festival of the rebirth of nature inaugurates the new constitutional era of the political freedom of the English people. A Wallington was trapped in the mental framework shaped by the representations of the Puritan élites. By adhering to such patterns of belief and judgement, an artisan could hope to share the conversation and worship of his social betters, to become their equal in saint-hood. Yet, this could estrange him from the bulk of his colleagues and neighbours. Bunyan's autobiography and Wallington's diary provide much evidence for this: the seeker for saint-hood is not popular in the work-place.

Overton was opening new perspectives in religion, politics and society, with such tenets as: reason is the mark of God, godliness cannot be melancholy and Christ is mirth. All this should be interpreted as a radical redefinition of the relationship between the people, religion and politics. As thinkers like Marcel Gauchet have shown, the passage of Western civilization into modernity is best described as an exit from religion, and in political thought, as a transition from heteronomy (the State derives its modes of legitimization and its laws from an outside source) to autonomy (the State is its own law-giver).[62] To me, Richard Overton embodied a very original moment of this intellectual transition.

In the *Appeal*, Overton (like Winstanley who was to call God 'the Creator Reason') suggested that nothing irrational could come from God. The laws of England must be 'englished', the legal system must be made rational, penal procedures must be made to conform to the laws and reason must preside over the religious debates of the people. This was an important contribution of the *Appeal* to Overton's philosophical development. These demands were shared by many other Levellers, but men who came from very different ideological backgrounds, like Hobbes and Harrington, would definitely have agreed that these were major items on the agenda of political reform. The philosophical systems of these authors were incompatible with Overton's theories (and even more with Winstanley's idea of 'the Creator Reason'), and the function played by these items in their theories gave them a rather different value, but on these points, Overton was travelling by a different route to the same harbour.

Overton's insistence on the Agreement of the People in the *Baiting* links him forward to our second definition of 'radicalism': political improvement through constitutional reformation. Political reform would only occur if the people took upon them the task of initiating a new social and political covenant. This idea had been constantly behind the Agreement projects since the autumn of 1647, but as Overton presents it, for the first time the people have not negotiated it with apparent allies like Cromwell or Ireton, but they were stepping forward to offer it to the people. If our argument has been right so far, *i.e.* that Overton's *Baiting* marked a turning point in his long-acquired awareness of the Independents' betrayal of a heretofore common cause, then the May Day Agreement was the instrument of political reformation that the people were to turn against their new leaders. Since the proclamation of the Commonwealth, and especially after Burford, the Grandees' deception was too manifest, so the declaration of the people's autonomy by the voluntary ratification of the Agreement would be the best solution. In English history, this would be looking back to something like the Elizabethan Bond of Association at a time when the Engagement controversy was about to start, following ideological assumptions and with a style of casuistry that left the Levellers' designs far behind.[63] The *Baiting* is Overton's last 'intervention' to support a project that would have made 'participation' the birthright of many more, though not of all, Englishmen.

The notion that mirth is 'of divine instinct', a formulation that appears in the *Baiting* amongst other criticism of Puritan hypocrisy, is Overton's most daring jibe at the godly. The physiological language centred on melancholy and the balance of humours harks back to Jonsonian comedies of humours, late Elizabethan satires and to the Marprelate stock of metaphors.

> But (my friends) your gravity (which I am afraid hath too much of melancholy in it) cannot more move me to a more serious dialect, than my own affections incline me, I prize both in their places; as I affect the one, I respect the other: for sure, modest mirth tempered with due gravity makes the best composition, most natural and harmonious: God in the temper of our natures as he hath made us earth, so hath he enlivened that dull lump with the element of fire, which is the forma formans, the giver and preserver of being and motion, and the original of that habit of laughter: Therefore mirth sure is of divine instinct, and I think I may boldly say, more natural than melancholy, and less savours of the curse.[64]

The melancholic has the wrong sort of temper for the *Agreement of the People*: '[melancholy] is the root of the root of all wickedness, covetousness; for where have you seen a melancholy man that's not covetous? and a covetous man seldom proves a good commonwealthsman'.[65] Liberation from the political consequences of the curse implies the purgation of religious and political melancholy, of those peccant humours that poison the people's spirits ... but not the body politic, since the old organicist allegory is far from the Leveller stock of similes and metaphors.

The new civic ethos that emerges from these witty and lucid complaints of Richard Overton is made of honesty, homely godliness, tolerance, a desire for peace and justice, and a definite courage in the face of danger and oppression. From the streams of civic tradition that had contributed elements to the English revolutionary fighters of various tendencies, Overton rejected the gloomiest and bloodiest. He adapted the common-law element to open a perspective of constitutional reformation, whereas Lilburne uncritically and contradictorily applied the old patterns of Cokean argument. Overton altered the old Roman motto into *dulce est pro patria pati*, changing the last word to 'suffering' instead of 'dying'.[66] Suffering for the good old cause does not imply dying for it. Overton's revolutionary spirit, like his religion, was not morbid. He had begun his literary career in the Marprelatist tradition, he was ending it in an act of spiritual, political and literary utopianism. To return to our initial mythological meditation and to the historiographical debates about the Levellers' modernity, one argument should contribute to establish Overton among the first thinkers who elaborated a doctrine of political autonomy, as opposed to the traditional conception of heteronomy: for James I, Filmer, or even Lilburne, the law of God was above all other laws. For absolutists, human beings were on Earth under a political power as a part of their expiation for the sin of their first parents, in accordance with Augustine's teachings. The norm (*nomos*) of political order was outside this very order, in God, and the king was under him and answerable to him only. With authors like Hobbes, heteronomy became philosophically un-arguable, and power found an autonomous justification. Overton's originality is that his God is not an avenging God: His law and His humour are close to those of plain-dealing Englishmen, and His wrath will strike the melancholics. The people have found a way to define the foundation of their autonomy by writing the Agreement, and the means to achieve such autonomy by subscribing their names to it. Men are making laws for themselves, and God thinks that it is good. In many ways, Overton's 'people' were mature for autonomy, and therefore they were stepping into political modernity. Though such a sweeping simile is usually found illegitimate in 'revisionist' historiography, I hope to be forgiven if I write that the 'merry godliness' of Overton's new civic outlook could be seen as foreshadowing Orwell's 'common decency,' this hidden trait of the common man's character that would forever prevent the British ever to yield to fascism. Yet, in spite of the jollity and jocularity of Overton's tone in the *Baiting*, his humour very often sounds like the definition that Kierkegaard gave of it: the politeness of despair.

NOTES

1 I thank Professor Colin Davis of the University of East Anglia, and Prof. Jonathan Scott of the University of Pittsburgh, for their helpful remarks on this paper.

2 Karl Marx, *The Civil War in France*, address to the council of the first International, May 30, 1871, in *Marx and Engels, Basic Writings on Politics and Philosophy*, ed. Lewis S. Feuer (London: Fontana, 1984), 415. He also voiced the same complaints in his letter to the Internationalist Communeux Léo Frankel and Eugène Varlin on 13 May 1871, Karl Marx, *La guerre civile en France 1871*, Classiques du marxisme (Paris: Éditions sociales, 1975) 113.

3 Joseph Frank, *The Levellers. A History of the Writings of Three Seventeenth-Century Social Democrats: John Lilburne, Richard Overton, William Walwyn* (Cambridge, MA: Harvard UP, 1955; New York: Russell and Russell, 1969) 129–30 and 248–52 for the first thesis, 255–56 for the second.

4 Frank 48–52, Margot Heinemann, *Puritanism and Theatre. Thomas Middleton and Opposition Drama under the Early Stuarts* (Cambridge: CUP, 1980) 251–52, Nigel Smith, 'Richard Overton's Marpriest Tracts: Towards

a History of Leveller Style,' *The Literature of Controversy: Polemical Strategy from Milton to Junius*, ed. T. N. Corns (London: Cass, 1987) 39–66, esp. 54, and *Literature and Revolution in England, 1640–1660* (New Haven Yale UP, 1994) 297–304.

5 *An Appeale from the Degenerate Representative Body of the Commons of England [...] to the Body Represented, The Free People in General ...*, in *Leveller Manifestoes of the Puritan Revolution*, ed. D. M. Wolfe (London: Cass, 1967) 158, and see Frank 51–52.

6 *The Baiting of the Great Bull of Bashan*, in *Revolutionary Prose of the English Civil War*, eds. Howard Erskine-Hill and Graham Storey (Cambridge: CUP, 1983) 149.

7 Patrick Collinson, 'Elizabethan and Jacobean Puritanism as Forms of Popular Culture,' *The Culture of English Puritanism, 1560–1700*, eds. Christopher Durston and Jacqueline Eales (Basingstoke: Macmillan, 1996) 32–57.

8 Luc Borot, 'Conseiller, courtisan, citoyen: trois figures de la participation politique du sujet dans l'Angleterre moderne,' *Civisme et citoyenneté: une longue histoire*, ed. Luc Borot (Montpellier: Université Paul-Valéry, 1999) 93–141. Felicity Heal and Clive Holmes, *The Gentry in England and Wales 1500–1700* (London: Macmillan, 1994) 166–275.

9 Sir Peter Wentworth's speech, 8 February 1576, *Proceedings in the Parliaments of Elizabeth I*, ed. T. E. Hartley, vol. 1: 1558–1581 (Leicester: Leicester UP, 1981) 425–434.

10 J. G. A. Pocock, *The Machiavellian Moment* (Princeton: Princeton UP, 1975) 323–422; Zera Fink, *The Classical Republicans* (Evanston: Northwestern UP, 1945).

11 Borot 113–122.

12 For an example of mob behaviours, see the narrative of an apprentice riot against the Spanish ambassador Gondomar in April 1621, in Joseph Mead's letters of news to Sir Richard Stuteville, BL Harleian ms 389, fol. 48v–49v.

13 David Zaret, 'Petitions and the Invention of Public Opinion in the English Revolution,' *American Journal of Sociology* 101.6 (1996): 1497–1555. The MPs' participation in the process of publicization is analyzed by Sheila Lambert in 'The Beginning of Printing for the House of Commons, 1640–42,' *The Library* 6th series 3.1 (March 1981): 43–61.

14 Frank 257.

15 In *Leveller Manifestoes*, 279–290.

16 *The Moderate* (9), 12 september 1648, sig. I2v–I4v, Thomason E.462 (32), N&S 413.2009.

17 *Baiting* 148. On the literary techniques that reveal the Levellers' popular target, see Frank 255–62, esp. 257; I cannot agree with Frank (e.g. 259) when he writes that the literary impact of the Levellers was negligible, or that Overton's literary contribution was small, but Frank's presentation of the rhetorical approach of the group is interesting. For a better appreciation see Heinemann, *Puritanism and Theatre* 239–252, esp. 251–52 for a criticism of Frank's judgement.

18 Mark Kishlansky, *The Rise of the New Model Army* (Cambridge: CUP, 1979); Austin Woolrych, *Soldiers and Statesmen: the General Council of the Army and its Debates 1647–1648* (Oxford: OUP, 1987).
19 William Clarke, *The Clarke Papers, vol.* I–II, ed. C. H. Firth (1891–1894; London: Royal Historical Society, 1992) 305, 320, 325, 333.
20 *The Hunting of the Foxes [. . .] by five Small Beagles (late of the Army). Or The Grandie-Deceivers Unmasked [. . .]* (21 March 1649), *Leveller Manifestoes* 355–383.
21 François Guizot, *Études biographiques sur la révolution d'Angleterre* (Paris: Didier, 1851) 159–160; Ann Hughes, 'Gender and Politics in Leveller Literature,' eds. Susan D. Amussen and Mark A. Kishlansky, *Political Culture and Cultural Politics in Early Modern Europe* (Manchester: Manchester UP, 1995) 164–165.
22 John Foxe, *The Acts and Monuments of these latter and Perilous Dayes, touching Matters of the Church* (1563; London: J. Daye, 1570, STC 11223) 1714–15: dialogue between the young apprentice William Hunter and bishop Bonner.
23 Foxe 1710.
24 Hughes 162–188.
25 Foxe 1662.
26 Foxe 1713.
27 Foxe 1751, 1878, 2030.
28 Christopher Haigh, *The English Reformations* (Oxford: OUP, 1993) 187.
29 Edward Hyde, Earl of Clarendon, *History of the Great Rebellion*, ed. W. D. Macray (Oxford: Clarendon P, 1888) XIV:50. Smith considers Lilburne's case in *Literature and Revolution* 132, and n.12, referring to Joan Bennett, *The Eloquent I: Style and Self in Seventeenth-Century Prose* (Madison, 1968) 68–79, and John R. Knott, *Discourses of Martyrdom in English Literature, 1564–1694* (Cambridge: CUP, 1993) 144–150.
30 Smith also noticed this Foxean connection in 'Marpriest Tracts,' 56–57.
31 *A Perfect Narrative of the whole Proceedings of the High Court of Justice in the Tryal of the King in Westminster Hall, on Saturday the* 20. *and Monday the* 22. *of this instant January. With the several Speeches of the King, Lord President, and Solicitor General. Published by Authority to prevent false and impertinent Relations* (London: John Playford, 23 January 1648/9). In '"Vive le roi!" ou "Mort au tyran!"? Le procès et l'exécution de Charles Ier dans la presse d'information de novembre 1648 à février 1649,' *Figures de la royauté en Angleterre de Shakespeare à la Glorieuse Révolution*, eds. François Laroque, and Franck Lessay (Paris: Presses de la Sorbonne Nouvelle, 1999), 143–164, I argue that this official narrative must have been supervised by its own licenser, Gilbert Mabbot, the editor of the Leveller newsbook, *The Moderate*.
32 *Perfect Narrative* 6.
33 *Perfect Narrative* 6.
34 *Perfect Narrative* 11.

35 *The Picture of the Council of State* (April 1649), Richard Overton's narrative, in *The Leveller Tracts: 1647–1653*, eds. William Haller and Godfrey Davies (1944; Gloucester, MA: Peter Smith, 1964) 220.
36 *Picture of the Council of State*, Overton's narrative, *Leveller Tracts* 222.
37 For another interpretation of Mary Overton's trials, Hughes 170–172.
38 Two of these prints are in *The Levellers in the English Revolution*, ed. G. E. Aylmer (London: Thames and Hudson, 1975) 8, 17. On the difference between Lilburne and Overton as martyrs, see Smith, 'Marpriest Tracts,' 54–55.
39 Smith, 'Marpriest Tracts,' 62.
40 Heinemann, *Puritanism and Theatre* 245 and n23, 24, refers to D. M. Wolfe, 'Unsigned Pamphlets of Richard Overton,' *Huntington Library Quarterly* xxi (Feb. 1958): 167–201; Smith, 'Marpriest Tracts,' 49–50, and *Literature and Revolution* 298.
41 *Appeale, Leveller Manifestoes* 189–95.
42 Smith, 'Overton's Marpriest Tracts,' 55–56.
43 *Appeale, Leveller Manifestoes* 179.
44 *Baiting* 150–51.
45 Smith, 'Overton's Marpriest Tracts,' 60; Heinemann *Puritanism and Theatre* 245–249.
46 The reference work for proverbs is Morris Palmer Tilley, *A Dictionary of the Proverbs in England in the Sixteenth and Seventeenth Centuries* (Ann Arbor: U of Michigan P, 1950).
47 *Baiting* 148.
48 *Baiting* 148.
49 *Baiting* 152; *1 Henry IV*, ed. David Bevington, The Oxford Shakespeare, Oxford Classics (Oxford: OUP, 1994) 2.4.396–400.
50 *Baiting* 150; Smith, 'Marpriest Tracts,' 48–49.
51 *Baiting* 148.
52 Richard Overton, *A Sacred Decretall* (London, 1645), sig.*2r is reprinted in Smith, *Literature and Revolution* 301 (Figure 13). It represents a bull writing at a table, tossing up a soldier's figure with his horns.
53 *Baiting* 147
54 *Baiting* 148.
55 *Baiting* 147.
56 *Baiting* 149–50.
57 Thomas Hobbes, *Behemoth, or the Long Parliament*, ed. F. Tönnies (1889; Chicago: U of Chicago P, 1990) dialogue III, 136.
58 Ronald Hutton, *The Rise and Fall of Merry England* (1994; Oxford: OUP, 1996) 111–199.
59 Christopher Durston, 'Puritan Rule and the Failure of Cultural Revolution, 1645–1660,' Durston & Eales 210–233; John Morrill *The Nature of the English Revolution* (London: Longman, 1993) ch. 1:7: 'The Church in England 1642–1649,' 148–175.
60 *Baiting* 149.

61 Nehemiah Wallington, A Memorial of God's Judgments, British Library, Sloan MS 1457, fol. 15v. Spelling and punctuation modernized for clarity's sake.

62 Marcel Gauchet, *Le désenchantement du monde. Une histoire politique de la religion* (Paris: Gallimard, 1985); *La religion dans la démocratie. Parcours de la laïcité* (Paris: Gallimard, 1998); 'Essais de psychologie contemporaine', *Le débat* 99 (March-April 1998): 164–181; 100 (May-August 1999): 189–206.

63 The debates concerning this Bond and the 1576 Act for the Queen's Safety can be followed in the diary of Sir William Fitzwilliam for 28 November 1584, Hartley *Proceedings*, vol. 2 (London and New York: Leicester UP, 1995) 141–152.

64 *Baiting* 149.

65 *Baiting* 149.

66 *Baiting* 150.

CHAPTER 3

Radicalism and the English Revolution

Glenn Burgess

Since the publication of Christopher Hill's *The World Turned Upside Down* in 1972, the radical groups of the English Revolution have continued to attract attention. Some of that attention has reinforced Hill's account, but much of it challenges the terms with which Hill approached the subject. The present chapter attempts to take stock of the results, and to provide the broad outlines of an account that takes seriously the criticisms of the Hill paradigm that have been advanced.

HISTORIOGRAPHY AND THE ENGLISH NEO-REFORMATION

It is often said that historians are much more concerned with origins and causes than they are with consequences, effects or 'aftermath'. It may therefore be worthy of note that we probably have a clearer understanding of the afterlife than of the origins of mid-seventeenth-century English radicalism. Although the full legacy of the English Revolution still awaits its historian, it is possible to piece together a reasonably clear idea about the ways in which subsequent generations remembered (or forgot) Levellers and radicals, and an even fuller knowledge of the subsequent fortune of commonwealth and republican ideas.[1] But historians have never developed even the agreed outlines of an account of the origins of Civil War radicalism, or an agreed way of placing its occurrence in an early modern historical context. Indeed, they have generally avoided asking too many questions about its origins.

In 1982, Colin Davis identified many of the problems.[2] How can historians make sense of the sudden outburst of radicalism in a 'traditional' society, that is to say, in a society that valued custom and order highly, and devalued innovation? In part, as Davis made clear, that question can resolve itself into a search for the source of ideas of sufficient force to overthrow the strong in-built preference for renovation and preservation over innovation. Radical theories have, in the first instance, to delegitimate an old order; they have then to provide the means for legitimating a new one. For Davis, those who produced such theories in seventeenth-century England were unique in European history before the French Revolution. Hill's approach to these radicals, with its emphasis on their forward-looking character, failed to explain them historically precisely because it took them out of their time in this way. Instead, Davis encouraged us to understand them in terms of their use of available resources for legitimation and delegitimation.

More recently, Conal Condren has developed rather further the view that 'radicalism' is difficult to envisage in an early modern or 'traditional' society.[3] He suggests that historians of the pre-modern world should abandon the concept of radicalism altogether. Condren's case is at its strongest when he argues that labelling someone 'radical' inevitably misdescribes the language actually used in the seventeenth century. In effect, although Condren avoids putting the matter in this way, such misdescription ascribes a false intentionality to its subjects. In most cases, they were not seeking to be 'radical' – indeed *could* not possibly have understood their own motives or intentions in relation to such a term. 'Radicalism' is thus an intolerable anachronism, which must distort the phenomena that it purports to describe. Many of those whom historians wish to praise as radical are people who have failed in their efforts to claim the protective mantle of tradition. The languages of the early modern 'radical' were diverse, and are seldom well described as indicative of 'radicalism'. The label is primarily dispositional and, therefore, its use will impute disposition, and by extension intention, contrary to the nature of the surviving linguistic evidence. Most of those whom we call 'radicals' spoke the language of conservation, restoration, reformation or purification. Understanding is thus prevented by application of a label. Historians can only abandon the term, and uncover the discrete and particular phenomena that it has mysteriously cloaked. This might amount to the demand that historians concentrate on understanding the patterning of the evidence – the political vocabularies of the English Revolution – and become much more parsimonious in the application of dispositional labels, which by their nature amount to invariably dubious imputations of intentionality.

Condren's arguments attack the very root of the radical paradigm that underlay Hill's great book of 1972. That paradigm had its roots in the late nineteenth-century rediscovery of radical pamphleteering. Its pedigree runs from the German Marxist 'revisionist' Eduard Bernstein,[4] through the Left Book Club, the Communist Party Historians' Group, and on to Hill.[5] In *The World Turned Upside Down* an entire tradition of inquiry was summed up with great erudition and humanity, and given paradigmatic status. Since 1972 it has not been without its critics – Davis (especially his book on the Ranters[6]) and Condren themselves; but others including Kenyon, Kishlansky, Morrill and Clark have let their dissent be known.[7] Nonetheless, it is perhaps true to say that 'revisionist' historiography has, in general sought a victory altogether too easy. Too frequently, it has attempted to marginalize radicalism rather than to understand it.[8] We still lack a post-revisionist view that is as comprehensive as Hill's. One function of this essay is to raise questions about what such a view ought to look like. Should it retain the concept of radicalism and seek a new understanding of it, or should it abandon the concept and replace it with a more nuanced and varied understanding of the terrain that it once occupied?

Hill's critics have, nonetheless, successfully identified several assumptions of his approach that are both characteristic and debatable. Any new synthesis must itself consider the validity of these assumptions, and, if necessary, construct an account that avoids them. First, there is the initial belief that radicalism – however diverse – is at some level a single phenomenon, that a diverse array of groups and individuals have enough in common to share a collective label. Second, there is a common interpretative mood, which praises radicalism for its anticipation of modern progressive ideas (democracy, socialism, communism, toleration, liberalism, constitutionalism and materialism can all be involved in this). In part, this mood is built into the term radicalism. Its nineteenth-century origins tend to give it inescapably modern resonances. Third, there is a belief that the best way of understanding the origins of radicalism, and of locating it in the early modern world, is through class analysis. Radical ideas were a class ideology, arising from the social experience of particular social groups, and were part of a long (largely underground) tradition of radical social protest that could be traced back to the middle ages.

Each of these assumptions requires careful unpacking. This will be undertaken in reverse order.

The third assumption that can be found underlying Hill's work is the least relevant to my later argument; nonetheless, it deserves brief discussion here. Class analysis of radicalism has not, so far, proved productive.[9] There are some obvious general reasons for this, not least the serious methodological doubts that must attach to any attempts to link social class and ideas. Gerald Aylmer, in a provocative essay that tried to look empirically at the social origins of Leveller leaders, rightly remarked: 'Nor, even if it could be shown that they came predominantly from one kind of social background rather than another, should this be taken as the cause of their holding the ideas which they did, still less as explaining the worth or significance of those ideas'.[10] Much research, in good part inspired by Hill's approach and generalizations, has revealed the extent to which the radical option was a minority choice for every social group. David Underdown's work has uncovered the existence of popular Royalism and popular traditionalism.[11] This has made it impossible to sustain any assumption that an easy link can be drawn between plebeian social experience and radical politics or religion.

Furthermore, an increasing number of microhistorical studies – models might by Christopher Marsh on the family of love, and Andy Wood on Derbyshire miners[12] – have revealed connections between the social experience of individuals and communities, religion and politics that are incredibly diverse. Some, notably Andy Wood, remain sympathetic to class analysis, but nonetheless show a sensitivity and subtlety in its use that moves us far from the over-simplifications of the past. The same intricacy of connection and awareness of the need for an understanding of class that allows for multi-causality and avoids determinism is apparent, too, in John Walter's recent account of the Colchester plunderers of 1642.[13] Walter makes it very clear that class hostility, though it may have had a role in stimulating the riots of 1642, falls well short of providing an adequate explanation of the patterns those riots followed.[14] Jim Alsop's patient investigation of the life and business career of Gerrard Winstanley has revealed all sorts of fascinating detail, none of which provides by itself an adequate social explanation for his brief radical phase, still less for anyone else's.[15]

It is perhaps still too early to tell exactly where recent work is tending. Some of the most innovative work on early modern society and economy has recently achieved synthesis at the hands of Keith Wrightson;[16] but we are still searching for a framework that can bring together society and economy, politics and culture. The evidence of recent work might suggest that it will be quite unlike the Marxist one that Hill endorsed.[17] It is likely to be *pointillist*, extensively multi-causal, explicitly anti-deterministic and non-hierarchical. Social experience and culture interact, but neither determines the other. It might yet turn out to be possible to identify long-term continuities in the history of religious nonconformity. There is some evidence, gathered by Margaret Spufford and her students, to suggest that families that were once supporters of Lollardy, became centuries later adherents of Quakerism and dissent, but we are a long way from understanding fully the implications of this, even if the pattern can be sustained on a broader front.[18] This essay, however, without denying the possibility of linking social experience to political and religious beliefs, will take a different approach to the subject.

The second of Hill's assumptions raises the question of how radicalism should be *evaluated*. Unfortunately, it exacerbates rather than reduces the problem of locating radicalism historically. To view radicals as thinkers before their time, as anticipators of one's own reading of modernity, is explicitly to alienate them from their own historical worlds.[19] The approach has served as a neat way of combining a reason for the failure of radicalism – historical circumstances were not yet ready for it – with a positive evaluation of the objectives that radical groups had. It rescues them from their own failure, blame for which is instead attached to circumstance. This begs too many questions to be of value. Just how modern were the ideas of radical groups? Is it really true that their failure is not a product of their own ideological weaknesses? Anachronism of one sort or another is never easy to avoid, and we might best take the anachronism that has existed in the evaluation of seventeenth-century radicalism as a challenge. Can we generate an account of radicalism that is not constructed in such terms; one, indeed, that explicitly rejects modernizing interpretations of the objectives of radical writers? In facing such a challenge it is necessary directly to confront Condren's objection that the use of political languages prevalent in mid seventeenth-century England has generated evidence that it is difficult to redescribe using the dispositional label 'radical'. That, in turn, demands an answer to the question of whether the terms 'radical' or 'radicalism' should be applied to the period at all. There is always an underlying constraint: our use of the term 'radicalism' can only be justified as a way of mediating between past and present, them and us, if it retains *both* meaningful, non-anachronistic application to the past, *and* sufficient connection with our own sense of what a radical is or should be. If it can be argued that a seventeenth-century 'radical' can always be more precisely described by some other term, then why not use that other term? This is *not* a matter of using only words that existed in the past, of describing the past in its own terms: it is a matter of ensuring that our vocabulary does not falsely impute ideas and attitudes to people in the past, and (equally) that it does not construct false traditions and continuities.[20] 'Radicalism' risks doing both.

Hill's first assumption – that there is an identifiable phenomenon of sufficient coherence to be given the label 'radicalism' – directs us to this core matter of defining and identifying. This is the assumption most vulnerable to Condren's suggestion that no one in the English Revolution wrote or spoke in ways that might justify our efforts to impute to them without distortion an intention to be radical. For him, the creation of a radical phenomenon and a radical tradition is entirely a retrospective enterprise, in which historians pick out things that seem to them radical in modern terms and lump them together. The case that he makes is a strong one, and there can be little doubt (as we shall see) that the way in which the terms 'radical' and 'conservative' have been applied to seventeenth-century thinkers have been damaging to our understanding of them. Should we abandon these labels and find another identity for our erstwhile radicals? It is tempting to answer in the affirmative. But efforts to purge historians' vocabularies are seldom effective, and it might be as well to ask instead whether the things that are often grouped together as examples of radicalism really belong together, what they have in common, and in what ways the term 'radicalism' is appropriately applied to these common features.

What follows is a preliminary attempt to answer these questions. Three distinctive features of this attempt can be identified.

1. In the first instance it uses a relatively simple *functional* definition of radicalism: radicalism involves the capacity to envisage and justify the structural transformation of social, economic, religious or political institutions. 'Radicalism' here labels an attitude to the *status quo*, and it must remain a mater for historical inquiry to decide whether those who do demand the structural transformation of an existing order actually have anything more substantial in common with one another. Nonetheless, it is this definition that determines who shall be included in the category. But this cannot be the end of the matter for two reasons. First, should it turn out that nothing more than a disposition of antagonism to the existing order links these people, then it would be necessary to reconsider whether a common label for them is appropriate. And, second, a functional definition does not by itself deal with the problems of intentionality, implicitly raised by Condren and others. We might decide that Levellers and Diggers, Quakers and Harringtonians made demands that required the structural transformation of an old order: but did they see things in this way? Did seventeenth-century 'radicals' have a language or languages in which to speak of structural transformation? And, even if they did, does this

place them in a field in which they can be distinguished from 'conservative' or 'moderate' thinkers who lacked or refused to employ such language?

2. These last questions serve to identify my approach as primarily linguistic.[21] Radicalism, if that is the right word, need not be seen as a phenomenon with a continuous existence. Rather it was forged, and forged repeatedly, from the discursive and cultural materials – e.g. from the languages – that lay to hand. The task of explaining it lies first in identifying what languages existed, and the range of their possible exploitation and subversion. Radicalism is a matter of context rather than of intellectual substance. To explain it, we should be interested less in the transmission through time of any radical 'essence', and more in the occasional radical *uses* of ideas drawn from a broader political culture not itself radical.[22] In the longer term, the continuity of languages of legitimation can itself provide a spurious continuity for radicalism. This is so because, to take a single example, the language of the 'ancient constitution' will itself structure the ways in which the idea of the ancient constitution can be either subverted or redeployed by radicals. So long as the ancient constitution remains an important ideological defence of the *status quo*, then critics of that *status quo* will find occasion to counter it. And they are likely to do so in similar ways.
3. Much, if not all, of what has been identified as 'radicalism' in mid-seventeenth-century England shares a common linguistic context and character. It is only by exploring this that we can hope to decide whether it remains useful to apply the label 'radical' to it. There is no doubt that the languages of custom and tradition played a pervasive legitimating role in the period, but there were limits to their purchase. Civil and worldly traditions and customs ruled only so long as they were not seen to conflict with the will of God. Those languages capable of visualizing an active interventionist God, whether providential[23] or apocalyptic, were inherently capable of being turned against worldly customs. This is most obviously true of the language of millenarianism, and we know (thanks to Lamont, Capp, Christianson and others[24]) that millenarianism was a rapidly-evolving and well-entrenched element in Elizabethan and early Stuart religious culture. For many, the English Revolution unleashed an active God against the laws, institutions and customs of the world. That Revolution, which we would do better to think of as a second Reformation – the English Neo-Reformation – was pervaded from the beginning

with the sense of an active God who would judge and punish, direct and control. It is this language, developed at length in the Fast Sermons to parliament,[25] that was exploited by many of those who have been labelled radical. So, by this concept of a neo-Reformation I mean to indicate, as one recent historian put it, that in the 1640s 'England experienced its own Radical Reformation'.[26]

PROBLEMS OF DEFINITION AND IDENTIFICATION: LOCATING THE LEVELLERS

Before we can develop in more detail the themes just identified, it will be useful to consider an example of the problems engendered by the use of the label 'radicalism'. Doing that will also help us to gain a clearer sense of the divisions within the ideological space that was occupied by the king's opponents in the late 1640s.

Politically, the most significant of all the groups usually labelled radical were the Levellers, but they are not an easy group to locate on the ideological terrain of the English Revolution. Consider, for example, their relationship with the army. It is no exaggeration to say that the way in which historians have understood the Leveller relationship with the army has always focused on the extraordinary debates that took place in Putney church in the autumn of 1647. Colin Davis has summarized the usual view: 'These debates have often been depicted as the more or less unsuccessful attempt of the conservatives, Cromwell and his son-in-law, Henry Ireton, to defeat the radical, proto-democratic Levellers'.[27] Such an interpretation provides a classic example of Conal Condren's point that 'radical' functions as one of a field of dispositional labels, and gains much of its force from the ways in which it relates to other terms in the field, especially 'conservative' and 'moderate'. But does this labelling help us to understand the Levellers and their relationship to their contemporaries?

Arguably not, I would suggest. A case can be made for the claim that it is precisely this sort of labelling that has produced a dramatic mislocation of the Levellers amongst their contemporaries. At the very least, the labelling prematurely forecloses on our interpretative options. When Henry Ireton's Army *Remonstrance* of November 1648 adopted the Leveller language of agreement of the people, was Ireton becoming more radical, or was the idea of agreement becoming more conservative? When the Levellers condemned the regicide and the new Commonwealth on grounds of constitutional propriety and the rule of law, were they more or less radical than the republic they opposed? What the questions suggest is that the application to the Levellers of the label 'radical' has served to render as normal their clash with the army grandees in 1647, and as marginal their rapprochement with them late in 1648. It renders the latter episode more difficult to understand than it would be if it were accepted that, far from being divided as conservative and radical, army and Leveller ideologies were always very similar. Why, indeed, should things not be the other way around? Why was not 1647 the anomaly, in which Cromwell and others took a harder line against Leveller ideas than they might otherwise have done in order to preserve army unity? Have we been misled by the (atypical) Putney debates? Were not the debates at Putney in 1647 as much as those at Whitehall in 1648–9, debates within a grouping of like-minded people? What is normal and what is marginal – who was 'radical' and who was 'conservative' – and when?[28]

Even at Putney there was more agreement than the heated debates might at first suggest.[29] Ireton was not, in the end, at least, opposed to extending the franchise, being troubled chiefly by the fear that any appeal to *natural* rights would be fatal to property rights. He seems to have consented to a compromise formula on the franchise, which allowed 'That all soldiers and others, if they be not servants or beggars, ought to have voices in electing those which shall represent them in Parliament, although they have not forty shillings per annum in freehold land'.[30] And he definitely sat on a committee that recommended that the Commons should decide on the franchise 'soe as to give as much inlargement to Common freedome as may bee, with a due regard had to the equality [=equity?] and end of the present Constitution in that point'. The recommendation also made it clear that all who had fought for Parliament ought to have the vote.[31] The debates resulted in broad agreement about extension of the franchise, and the Levellers themselves were subsequently careful to preserve their credentials as defenders of *limited* franchise extension and preservers of property rights.[32] Equally interesting is the fact that on 30 October, and again in the poorly-recorded days of debate at Putney in early November, committees of which Ireton was a member, produced a series of recommendations that very clearly embraced a political programme broadly similar to that of the Levellers' Agreement of the People, though in ways that brought it into alignment with the proposals earlier accepted by the army leadership, the Heads of the Proposals.[33] Describing one side as 'conservative' and the other 'radical' gives the positions of political groups a rigidity and inflexibility that they did not possess.[34]

Part of the problem is that the terminology seems incapable of capturing the shifting alliances and ideologies of the period. But, more fundamentally, application of the 'conservative'/'radical' dichotomy reduces our capacity to understand the relationship between army and Levellers because it arbitrarily fixes a particular episode – indeed virtually a single day – in that relationship (29 October 1647) as the benchmark. It is worth looking at a little of the evidence from 1649, after the breach between army and Levellers. John Lilburne began the work that marked his divorce from the Independents and the army, *Englands New Chains Discovered* (February 1649), by noting how the Levellers 'have bin the first movers in concerning an Agreement of the People'. He was acknowledging that 'the Officers of the Army' had now adopted the same strategy, and had presented to the Rump their own Agreement of the People (on 20 January 1649). Lilburne proceeded to offer a critique of this document, but it is clear enough that this critique was offered – with whatever degree of bitterness – by someone who was working with the same terms as those whom he attacked. Even Lilburne had the grace to acknowledge the ground shared between himself and 'this honorable House, his Excellency, and the Officers of the Army'. He differed from them on 'particulars', though he also suspected that the officers were insincere, and that their show of principle masked an ambition 'to attain to an absolute domination over the Common-wealth'.[35] But, of course, part of the force of that perception came from the charge that grandees were betraying principles that they appeared to share with Lilburne and his friends.

Turning to examine the 'particularities' on which Lilburne differed from the officers, we find no clear guidance for deciding which is the more 'radical'. For example, the Officer's Agreement proposed that among the powers of the Representative would be the 'erecting and abolishing of Courts of Justice'.[36] Lilburne rejected this in what was effectively the language of the traditional and ancient constitution. It would give the Representative power to abolish 'the usual way of Tryals by twelve sworn men of the Neighborhood... [which] ought to remain unalterable'. Furthermore, he objected to the erection of the High Court of Justice, which tried the king. This too undermined 'that great and strong hold of our preservation', trial by jury.[37] Elsewhere, it was made clear that the king had been destroyed by arbitrary authority, and his trial could only have been constitutionally valid if it had rested on the authority of a new Representative based upon a proper Agreement of the People.[38]

Is it more radical to kill a king or to protest that his killing infringes the right to trial by jury? Is it more radical to use the sword to make a revolution, or to protest at the lack of constitutionality involved? The questions seem to me largely pointless. The relationship between Levellers and army was not fixed into any particular pattern, and it is not at all apparent how the application of the conservative/radical dichotomy to the relationship ever does anything but obscure what was really happening. It is clear that by late 1648 the army generals, in the person of Henry Ireton, continued the willingness evident even in 1647 to accept much of the Leveller programme. This is only a puzzle if we assume, as we should not, that 'conservative' officers had no interest in the ideas of 'radical' thinkers; it is as plausible to assume that Leveller ideas were merely one articulation of principles that had broad appeal to what we might call the 'Independent' grouping (of which the Levellers were a part). What is interesting is the thing that still divided Levellers and army even at the height of their rapprochement (November–December 1648).

Ireton's *Remonstrance* is a revealing document. There are many points at which it embraces – or is designed to suggest that it embraces – a Leveller programme.[39] Yet it is not a Leveller document, and that is primarily because of its darker sense of the political realities. Ireton appreciated that, for all the talk of an Agreement of the People, the people themselves were most likely to agree to a settlement in which the king had a central role. The people had now won 'a full conquest' over their king, and by right of conquest – one of the king's own principles – they could do with him as they saw proper.[40] There was, however, a catch. Ireton was frank in his assessment of the fact that, amongst that very people in whose name the king had been conquered, he had acquired the reputation of being a lover of peace and freedom who would restore 'trade and plenty'. If Charles were given the chance again to foment civil war, then it is likely that the people would support him, blaming parliament for the excessive exactions they had already borne.[41] In such circumstances, it would be dangerous to enter into any settlement that gave the king a continuing constitutional presence in England. He would have the means to win back all that he had lost, supported by the people.[42] Ireton did not shirk from telling parliament that it must force freedom on the people:

> . . . what you contend for is their general, fundamental, and perpetual Liberties; for the preservation whereof you will be forced to press upon them in particular matters, against their present ease and freedoms; and the people being ordinarily more affected with the latter, as more immediate and sensible, and less with the former, which are more remote and to them less intelligible, the king closing with

them under pretence of the latter, which they can feel, may easily engage them to the prejudice of the former, which they hardly discern.[43]

Not surprisingly, therefore, Ireton was tougher minded than the Levellers usually were about the need in this context for arbitrary power.[44] Furthermore, an Agreement of the People would be sought only *after* the new Representative was in place.[45] The difference between Ireton and the Levellers in November 1648 was scarcely the difference between conservative and radical ideologies: it was the difference between two contrasting estimates of how to implement a shared political programme.

This gives some indication of the ways in which labelling groups radical and conservatives serves to close down our interpretative options, and to get in the way of looking clearly at things in the past. But the example might also encourage us to find other ways of dividing up the ideological space occupied by the king's opponents in the 1640s and later.

A preliminary attempt might begin by identifying two markers, both of them concerned with the relationship between God and man, and both of them raising fundamental questions about the ideological and linguistic construction of the political sphere in the mid-seventeenth century. These markers can best be understood as two questions.

1. *First, did God deal with the consciences of men mediately through a church, or immediately with individuals?* The answers given to this question helped to determine whether people would separate a realm of conscientious freedom from a realm of coercive politics (whether civil or ecclesiastical). Presbyterians, willing as they were to countenance a persecuting and coercive church answered this question in one way, while many Independents came to answer it in another, and to embrace a limited liberty of conscience.[46] There was always, perhaps, an ambiguity in the Independent position (evident from the *Apologetical Narration* of 1644 onwards) – should they embrace a tolerationist position, or reject separatism and toleration, and rest their case for Independent church government on an appeal to the model presented in the scriptures as the word of God? – and this ambiguity was to be the subject of discussion in the Whitehall debates late in 1648 (see below). Independents were not at all agreed that the magistrate had no role in the policing of religious matters. But there is no doubt that some of the Independents (including the Levellers) developed a powerful case for the view that the secular magistrate, even when his authority rested as it properly should on the consent of the people, could not interfere with men's consciences. Such a view tended to

define the political sphere as one that God himself insisted was to be kept apart from the sphere of conscience (though we should not suppose that this meant either the secularisation of politics, or the exclusion from political control of all that we might think of as religious).[47] As John Goodwin put it, we 'stand diametrally bent against the dictatoring, and law-giving by men, in the things of God', but this posed no challenge to civil authority in its own sphere.[48] A good many Independents and sectarians stood together in their commitment to a religious sphere largely beyond the reach of civil politics, a commitment that grounded claims for liberty of conscience.

2. *Second, did God interfere directly in the civil politics of human communities?* In the work just cited, Goodwin reassured his readers that 'the kingdomes and powers of this world, need not fear either the numbers or power of the Saints, for taking away their crowns . . . untill the world that now is be translated into that which is to come'.[49] Just how reassuring that was would depend on exactly when and how the world which is to come would appear. The important distinction was not between those who were and were not millenarians. Goodwin clearly was a millenarian, but (here at least) his understanding of civil politics was insulated from his millenarian beliefs. The same is true of the Levellers. Individually, many of the Leveller leaders held millenarian beliefs, but there can be little doubt that they nonetheless accepted the provisional legitimacy of a political sphere that was shaped by human consent and decision. God so created the world that he left to human beings the freedom to control and shape their political worlds. He did not intervene directly.[50] Nor was it true that millenarianism was the only language in which an active God could be envisaged. A providential God might be just as interfering. But the essential contrast that I wish to draw is between those Independents and sectaries who accepted that civil politics existed as a separate realm of human choice, and those sectaries who thought that God was in the present actively involved in political matters, and destroying the crowns and sceptres of civil authority. The Levellers in this view take furthest and develop in the most sophisticated fashion what is an Independent view of the relationship between religion and politics.

These, then, are essential markers in what we might call the religious construction of the political sphere. What I shall argue in the remainder of this paper is that the phenomenon often referred to as radicalism is best understood as a product of precisely this, the religious construction of politics.

MAPPING RADICALISM?

The clearest approach to this argument can be made through a consideration of the Whitehall debates, fully and adequately recorded only for one day (14 December 1648). These reveal the Leveller Wildman and the Independent Ireton as alternative faces of the same coin. Each was troubled by the arguments of men whose approach to religion and politics was very markedly different from that of Levellers and Independents. Ireton was troubled because he thought that these men licensed anarchy; Wildman because, for very similar reasons, he feared that they licensed tyranny. It boiled down to a matter of judgement: are we more threatened by our fellow citizens or by our rulers? The two men agreed on liberty of conscience and on the immunity of consciences from human control. The question was whether the civil sovereign should, for the sake of peace, have the right to punish the outward man for such unsocial sins as atheism and blasphemy. Ireton was troubled by the fact that peace and order were impossible if the sovereign had no authority to repress 'anything which men will *call* religion'.[51] He was worried that, under cover of religion, anything could claim immunity. Wildman on the other hand looked at matters from the opposite end: 'God hath not given a command to all magistrates to destroy idolatry, for in consequence it would destroy the world'. Every magistrate was a fallible human being, therefore 'the probability is greater that he will destroy what is good than prevent what is evil'.[52]

Ireton and Wildman, Independent and Leveller, were debating within an agreed framework,[53] sharing a preference for agreement and consent, liberty of conscience and the view that God's political activity was all mediate and not immediate. Wildman might concede that 'authority hath been broken in pieces' by God's judgement, but it was for men to find for themselves 'a new way of serttling this nation, which is a new constitution'.[54] But whereas Ireton was perturbed by the fallibility of the people, above all by the dangers of popular Royalism, Wildman and the Levellers were fatally untroubled by such matters, behaving as if the people were possessed of sound political values and only rulers needed to be distrusted. The difference was (again) as much pragmatic as principled.

We might want to talk still of Leveller 'radicalism'; but nonetheless Independents and Levellers had more in common than either shared with those whose 'radicalism' Levellers are often thought to have shared but who, in fact, constructed a very different radical politics. Their voices were certainly heard at Whitehall. Colonel Thomas Harrison declared that the time had come when:

> the powers of this world shall be given unto the hands of the Lord and his Saints, that this is the day, God's own day, wherein he is coming forth in glory in the world, and he doth put forth himself very much by his people, and he says, in that day wherein he will thresh the mountains, he will make use of Jacob as that threshing instrument.

That perspective led Harrison to give only very hesitant support to the Agreement of the People that Ireton and the Levellers could for a time both accept:

> I judge . . . that this Agreement will fall short. I think that God doth purposely design it shall fall short of that end we look for, because he would have us know our peace, our agreement shall be from God, and not from men. And yet I think the hand of God doth call us to hold forth to this nation, and to all the world, to vindicate the profession that we have all along made to God, that we let them know that we seek not for ourselves but for [all] men.[55]

The Agreement was not, as for Ireton and the Levellers, the path to settlement, to what Cromwell would later call healing and settling; it was a temporary step, allowing the people of God to show their good faith, but inevitably doomed to failure.

Witness, too, remarks made by Joshua Sprigge at Whitehall. Whereas for Ireton, the main problem with the draft *Agreement of the People* was its blanket protection of liberty of conscience, Sprigge found this the only acceptable feature of the document. But his commitment to it was provisional and temporary; its value to him negative. In a fallen world, the Godly had to be protected from persecution, of course, but one could also look forward to a time in which such protection might become redundant. 'It is God's design, I say, to bring forth the civil government, and all things here below, in the image and resemblance of things above'. It was a mistake, into which the English had fallen, to 'have measured religion and the appearances of God according to the rules and ends of policy'. As a result, God has 'taken us to pieces' and 'brought forth the government of the sword'. No human Agreement could now settle things; 'God will bring forth a New Heaven and a New Earth'. In the meantime, one could only 'restrain the magistrate' so that he could not persecute God's people.[56]

From this perspective, the value of liberty of conscience was negative. It was necessary as part of the task of destroying the forms of worldly religion, and preparing the stage for God's triumphant performance. It was necessary to protect the Godly in a fallen world, but important only until God made possible the rule of the Saints. There is little sense of a *politics* of religious toleration, of toleration as a pre-requisite for any satisfactory human social and political existence, as there was for the Levellers.

Many of the groups and individuals who are often included in the category of 'radicals' adopt an approach to the interaction of politics and religion that is markedly different from that of Levellers and Independents. The first Fifth Monarchist petition of 19 February 1649 is a good place to start:

> 1. There is a kingdom and dominion, which the church is to exercise on the earth, 2. that extends to all persons and things universally, which is to be externally and visibly administered, 3. by such laws and officers, as Jesus Christ our mediator hath appointed in his kingdom. 4. It shall put down all worldly rule and authority (so far as relates to the worldly constitution thereof) though in the hands of Christians: 5. and is to be expected about this time we live in. 6. This kingdom shall not be erected by human power and authority, but Christ by his spirit shall call and gather a people, and form them into several less families, churches and corporations; and when they are multiplied, 7. they shall rule the world by general assemblies; or church-parliaments, of such officers of Christ, and representatives of the churches, as they shall choose and delegate, which they shall do, till Christ come in person.[57]

There are two particular features in this that serve to define this particular sort of 'radicalism', should we wish to continue using that term. First, there is the problematic nature of political agency. Because so much of the work is to be done by an active God, there are doubts about what human beings are actually contributing to the process of change. Second, and following neatly from this, there is the precarious existence of a political realm. It is not just that the commonwealth has become folded into the church (for churches can be political communities too). More significantly, the existence of politics is temporary, a holding pattern awaiting God's final intervention in human affairs; and, as such, its value is entirely negative. Men or women can achieve nothing positive; they can destroy corrupt worldly institutions, recognize their homelessness in the world, perhaps build temporary shelter for themselves, and wait for something better. There was no sense, as there was for Levellers and Independents, that political activity was worthwhile in itself.

These features can, of course, be found in many others whom we label 'radical'. They lie, for example, behind many of the interpretative disputes that have arisen over the Digger, Gerrard Winstanley. Historians have veered between materialist economic readings of his motives and millenarian-religious ones; they have argued over whether the Digging experiments of 1649–50 were actions intended to transform the social world, or forms of symbolic activity with a religious meaning. More recently, some have suggested that the very distinctions upon which the dispute rests are inapplicable to Winstanley.[58] I'm not sure that Winstanley thought so. He conveyed very clearly a sense that destroying worldly inequalities was itself an act of spiritual significance, and a sign of our contempt for worldly things. Private property had to be eradicated because those who possessed it could never be free of sin, and because its very existence destroyed the aboriginal equality of God's creation. The Fall had occurred when 'selfish imagination . . . working with covetousness, did set up one man to teach and rule over another; and thereby the spirit was killed'. He condemned 'teachers and rulers' because both over-valued the external material world (that was the meaning of covetousness). Teachers did so because they looked for the principles of morality in the material husk of a fallen world.[59] The problem came when men abandoned the indwelling spirit and 'sought content from creatures and outward objects'.[60] There is a terrible irony in materialist readings of Winstanley: they locate the heart of his message in a world upon which he turned his back. They made his message little more than another example of what he condemned as covetousness, seeking content in outward objects.

Coupled with this was an *apolitical* stress on divine rather than human agency. When he explained his Digging activities, Winstanley emphasized his own passivity, 'I was made obedient to the word'.[61] Indeed Winstanley's *political* radicalism scarcely exists. Built into the argument of his works (most explicitly the *New-Year's Gift*) was a three-part hierarchy of agency. God would in time utterly transform the world; in the meantime the civil authorities could do much to facilitate the process without infringing individual property rights; individual men might act only within the established laws and structures until such time as God altered the conditions of their action. Winstanley was as keen to distance himself from sword-levelling as the Levellers were from any sort of levelling. God not man was the only radical activist. When Winstanley turned his back on the fallen world, he turned his back on politics, radical or otherwise. It has not been sufficiently noted that when Winstanley spoke of *human* action, he spoke of it within traditional boundaries of passivity and legal restraint. Radical or revolutionary change might be envisaged, but only as the work of God.[62]

Similar things are true of Abiezer Coppe, the 'Ranter'. Winstanley called Christ 'the great Leveller';[63] Coppe spoke for him as the 'mighty Leveller . . . coming . . . to Levell in good earnest'.[64] Coppe, however, was more like the Fifth Monarchists than Winstanley in allowing men considerable capacity for negative action. He encouraged them to live a life of Christian charity and to show contempt for all worldly forms. But it was the Leveller Christ who would deal with those who refused to do so, and Coppe's thought lacked altogether a politically constructive dimension. Other Interregnum groups, often lumped into the radical category, followed a path that led them to a denial of the value of politics altogether. The Quakers certainly possessed a sense of the radical transformation of the world, but they lacked altogether a sense that this would be the work of man. Their political thought – if such a term can be considered applicable – rested in the belief that those reconciled to God had no use for human ordinances, but would nonetheless live in respect of the magistrate, at least so long as he provided them with protection. They expected little more from him than that. As Barry Reay has put it, 'Quakerism is devoid of any coherent and identifiable political philosophy'.[65] Muggletonians were more obviously politically quiet, but not because they valued political obedience. Rather, they thought civil politics to be so insignificant as to be not worth bothering about. Reeve tellingly asked 'if Magistrates act any unjust things in their places, is any man sure that another Power should act better?'[66] All men acted unjustly; only from God could anything better be expected. Far from revolutionary, Reeve actually suggested that civil rulers had a divine and providential warrant for their authority that made all resistance sinful.[67] That still did not mean that much good could be expected of them, or of what we would call politics.

Much effort from historians has gone into awarding points for degrees of radicalism, distinguishing between the more passive groups (Muggletonians, Quakers), and the activists (Diggers, Ranters). But compared to the Levellers, whose understanding of God's relationship to the human world allowed room for political action, all of these groups were 'passive'. This surely is the main case to be made against applying to them the word 'radical'. The problem is not that they could not envisage dramatic change, or did not believe that the world would and should be turned upside down. The problem is that if radical is a political category it is difficult to apply it to groups whose understanding of the nature of the world devalued the political. Human choice and human action counted for little. The world in which they lived would be made better – but not by men, whose sinfulness meant that little could be hoped from them. These groups had an *anti-politics* rather than a politics. They saw human action as feeble, as perhaps able to destroy, but as unable to construct. The best men could do was wait on God. Thus they all wrestled with the problem confronted by the Fifth Monarchist, John Tillinghast: what did it mean, he asked, to wait on God?

> [W]e are not to waite as Idlers doe for helpe in a ditch, and cry God helpe us, but we are to wait as if we would have it by our very strifing & strugling, yet notwithstanding there must be a quiet waiting on God for his time, so it should be with us, for this new Covenant mercy; waite for it patiently, be content with it in Gods own time, when he shall bring it forth . . . .[68]

As if: this was not a ringing endorsement of the hope to be expected from human action. Indeed it seemed to render such action pointless, something to be undertaken *as if* it might achieve a result that God, in fact, would produce in his own good time.

This analysis is tending towards a paradox: when extreme groups were most political (as was the case with the Levellers), then calling them 'radical' serves to understate or marginalize their political involvement in the world of Civil War Independency; on the other hand those 'religious radicals' who can imagine a world fundamentally change do so without articulating any politics, let alone a radical politics. If this was radicalism, then it amounted to the imagination of God's transformation of the world, and this fact made it next to impossible for radical writers to generate an account of human agency of the sort we find in modern radical political theories.

Underlying this point is the central argument and conclusion of this essay: what has come to be called radicalism in the English Revolution is a product of the religious construction of the political sphere. Looked at in this way, there is a marked difference between Levellers and many others, the difference between a politics of consent and a world in which the political is denied all independent existence. Can we really justify our effort to find radicals in a world in which radical political activity is rejected, either because it frowns upon innovation, or because it allows innovation to God and not to man? To call these people radical is very often to attribute to them implicitly a theory of human action that they explicitly repudiated. There seems to be no single thing that we can call 'radicalism' in the English Revolution. At least two quite different configurations of the relationship between politics and religion in the period have been put together as examples of radicalism (and the picture would get even more complicated if it took into account that 'radical' republicanism of the 1650s).[69] What remains important is that 'political' thinking in the 1640s was conducted within the context of the 'Neo-Reformation'. From that perspective Ireton and the Levellers were together in believing that the religious and political oppression of the English people would only be solved by institutions that they (all or some) would build for themselves; while the 'religious radicals' believed instead that nothing people built was likely to serve well the purposes of God. The centrality of this divide to the debates of the period is such that it cannot be useful to talk of a radicalism that spans it.

NOTES

1 Most recently, for example, there are the contributions of Tim Harris and Blair Worden to Michael Mendle (ed.), *The Putney Debates of 1647: The Army, the Levellers and the English State* (Cambridge, 2001), chs 11 & 12. Information can also be found in works as diverse as Timothy Lang, *The Victorians and the Stuart Heritage* (Cambridge, 1995); and Margot Finn, *After Chartism: Class and Nation in English Radical Politics, 1848–1874* (Cambridge, 1993), ch. 1. On the immediate aftermath see especially Richard L. Greaves' trilogy *Deliver Us from Evil: The Radical Underground in Britain, 1660–1663* (Oxford, 1986); *Enemies under His Feet: Radicals and Nonconformists in Britain, 1664–1677* (Stanford CA, 1990); and *Secrets of the Kingdom: British Radicals from the Popish Plot to the Revolution of 1688–89* (Stanford CA, 1992). Classic accounts of the republican legacy include Caroline Robbins, *The Eighteenth-Century Commonwealthman* (Cambridge MA, 1959); J. G. A. Pocock, *The Machiavellian Moment: Florentine Political Thought and the Atlantic Republican Tradition* (Princeton, 1975); and Edmund Ludlow, *The A Voyce from the Watch Tower, Part Five: 1660–1662*, ed. Blair Worden (London, 1978).

2 J. C. Davis, 'Radicalism in a Traditional Society: The Evaluation of Radical Thought in the English Commonwealth 1649–1660', *History of Political Thought*, 3 (1982), pp. 193–213.

3 Conal Condren, *The Language of Politics in Seventeenth Century England* (Basingstoke, 1994), ch. 5; and his earlier article, Condren, 'Radicals, Conservatives and Moderates in Early Modern Political Thought: A Case of the Sandwich Islands Syndrome?', *History of Political Thought*, 10 (1989),

pp. 525–42. Cf. also Lotte Mulligan & Judith Richards, 'A 'Radical' Problem: The Poor and the English Reformers in the Mid-Seventeenth Century', *Journal of British Studies*, 29 (1990), pp. 118–46.

4 For a brief account of Bernstein see Leszek Kolakowski, *Main Currents of Marxism: Volume 2: The Golden Age* (Oxford, 1978), ch. 4. Bernstein's book, translated into English in 1930 as *Cromwell and Communism*, was part of an attempt initiated by Karl Kautsky to write a history of socialism, to which enterprise Kautsky himself contributed *Thomas More and His Utopia* (1888).

5 Accounts (differing in their degree of sympathy) can be found in R. C. Richardson, *The Debate on the English Revolution Revisited* (London, 1988); and Alastair MacLachlan, *The Rise and Fall of Revolutionary England: An Essay in the Fabrication of Seventeenth-Century History* (Basingstoke, 1996).

6 J. C. Davis, *Fear, Myth and History: The Ranters and the Historians* (Cambridge, 1986).

7 For example, J. C. D. Clark, *Revolution and Rebellion: State and Society in England in the Seventeenth and Eighteenth Centuries* (Cambridge, 1986), esp. pp. 97–103; also Clark, *English Society 1688–1832: Ideology, Social Structure and Political Practice during the Ancien Regime* (Cambridge, 1985), ch. 5; Mark Kishlansky, 'What Must Be', in Gordon Schochet (ed.), *Religion, Resistance and Civil War* (Folger Shakespeare Library: Proceedings of the Folger Institute Center for the History of British Political Thought, Volume 3, 1990), pp. 83–90; John Morill, *The Nature of the English Revolution* (London, 1993), esp. ch. 14.

8 The best example is J. P. Kenyon's review of *The World Turned Upside Down*, in *The Spectator*, 8 July 1972. For more sympathetic assessments of Hill's legacy see Barry Reay, 'The World Turned Upside Down: A Retrospect', and David Underdown, 'Puritanism, Revolution and Christopher Hill', both in Geoff Eley and William Hunt (eds.), *Reviving the English Revolution: Reflections and Elaborations on the Work of Christopher Hill* (London, 1988), pp. 53–71, 333–41.

9 The clearest assertions in Hill's work of an underground tradition of popular or plebeian radicalism are in 'Plebeian Irreligion in 17th Century England', in Hill, *England's Turning Point: Essays on 17th Century English History* (London, 1998), ch. 8; and 'From Lollards to Levellers', in Hill, *Religion and Politics in 17th Century England (The Collected Essays of Christopher Hill, Volume Two)* (Brighton, 1986), ch. 7.

10 Gerald Aylmer, 'Gentlemen Levellers?', in Charles Webster (ed.), *The Intellectual Revolution of the Seventeenth-Century* (London, 1974), ch. 8, p. 103.

11 Especially David Underdown, *Revel, Riot and Rebellion: Popular Politics and Culture in England 1603–1660* (Oxford, 1985).

12 Christopher Marsh, *The Family of Love in English Society, 1550–1630* (Cambridge, 1994); Andy Wood, *The Politics of Social Conflict* (Cambridge, 1999); also Wood, 'Beyond Post-Revisionism? The Civil War Allegiances of

the Miners of the Derbyshire "Peak Country"', *Historical Journal*, 40 (1997), pp. 23–40.

13 John Walter, *Understanding Popular Violence in the English Revolution: The Colchester Plunderers* (Cambridge, 1999).

14 E.g. *ibid.*, pp, 281–4, 341–7.

15 For a summary of the results of this work see James D. Alsop, 'Gerrard Winstanley: What Do We Know of his Life?', in Andrew Bradstock (ed.), *Winstanley and the Diggers 1649–1999* (London, 2000), pp. 19–36. A particularly pointed attack on the use of Winstanley's social background to explain his later radicalism is Alsop, 'A High Road to Radicalism? Gerrard Winstanley's Youth', *The Seventeenth Century*, 9 (1994), pp. 11–24.

16 Keith Wrightson, *Earthly Necessities: Economic Lives in Early Modern Britain* (New Haven, 2000).

17 A Marxist approach still has its powerful defenders, notably James Holstun, *Ehud's Dagger: Class Struggle in the English Revolution* (London, 2000).

18 Margaret Spufford (ed.), *The World of Rural Dissenters, 1520–1725* (Cambridge, 1995); also Adrian Davies, *The Quakers in English Society 1655–1725* (Oxford, 2000), pp. 129–33.

19 Davis, 'Radicalism in a Traditional Society' is valuable on this theme.

20 Cf. J. C. D. Clark, 'Religion and the Origins of Radicalism in Nineteenth Century Britain', ch. 10 below. See also Clark, *English Society 1660–1832* (Cambridge, 2000), ch. 4.

21 Cf Iain Hampsher-Monk, 'The Languages of Radicalism: The "Failed" English Revolution of the 1790s as Linguistic Non-Performance', ch. 6 below.

22 On the concept of *usage* see Conal Condren, *The Statue and Appraisal of Classic Texts: An Essay on Political Theory, Its Inheritance, and the History of Idea* (Princeton, 1985), ch. 5. Condren sees the term as a more precise substitute for *influence*; I'm using it here as a more precise alternative to *tradition.*

23 See especially Alexandra Walsham, *Providence in Early Modern England* (Oxford, 1999); and Blair Worden, 'Providence and Politics in Cromwellian England', *Past & Present*, 109 (1985), pp. 55–99.

24 On millenarian languages see William M. Lamont, *Godly Rule: Politics and Religion 1603–60* (London, 1969); Paul Christianson, *Reformers and Babylon: English Apocalyptic Visions from the Reformation to the Eve of the Civil War* (Toronto, 1978); and Bernard Capp, The Political Dimension of Apocalyptic Thought', in C. A. Patrides & Joseph Wittreich (eds.), *The Apocalypse in English Renaissance Thought and Literature* (Manchester, 1984) ch. 4.

25 An excellent summary of this theme in J. C. Davis, *Oliver Cromwell* (London, 2001), pp. 118–24. For the Fast Sermons see John F. Wilson, *Pulpit in Parliament: Puritanism during the English Civil Wars, 1640–1648* (Princeton, 1969); and Stephen Baskerville, *Not Peace but a Sword: The Political Theology of the English Revolution* ((London, 1993). See also my discussion in Glenn Burgess, 'Was the English Civil War a War of Religion? The Evidence of Political Propaganda', *Huntington Library Quarterly*, 61 (1999), pp. 173–201.

26 John Coffey, *Persecution and Toleration in Protestant England 1558–1689* (Harlow, 2000), p. 212.

27 Davis, *Oliver Cromwell*, p. 26.

28 The fullest accounts of the relationship are Austin Woolrych, *Soldiers and Statesmen: The General Council of the Army and its Debates 1647–1648* (Oxford, 1987); and Ian Gentles, *The New Model Army in England, Scotland and Scotland, 1645–1653* (Oxford, 1992), chs 6–10.

29 Cf. Mark Kishlansky, 'Consensus Politics and the Structure of Debate at Putney', *Journal of British Studies*, 20 (1980–1), pp. 50–69.

30 A. S. P. Woodhouse, *Puritanism and Liberty* (London, 1951), p. 452; Woolrych, *Soldiers and Statesmen*, pp. 243–4.

31 C. H. Firth (ed.) *The Clarke Papers* (London, 4 vols 1891–1901), I, pp. 365–6.

32 For example, Wolfe, *Leveller Manifestoes*, pp. 269, 288.

33 Firth (ed.), *Clarke Papers*, I, pp. 363–7, 407–10. For the 'Heads of the Proposals' see S. R. Gardiner (ed.), *Constiutional Documents of the Puritan Revolution* (Oxford, 3rd ed., 1906), pp. 316–26.

34 Gentles notes the convergence (*New Model Army*, p. 217), but in what frame of reference is he right to call it 'surprising'?

35 W. Haller & G. Davies (eds.), *The Leveller Tracts* 1647–1653 (Gloucester MA, 1963), pp. 157. 161.

36 D. Wolfe (ed.), *Leveller Manifestoes of the Puritan Revolution* (New York, 1967), p. 347.

37 Haller & Davies, *Leveller Tracts*, pp. 158, 161–2.

38 *Ibid.*, p. 422.

39 It is true that the most pro-Leveller portions of the *Remonstrance* were added at Leveller request late in the drafting process, but it is nonetheless clear that Ireton was himself willing to make changes that would render the document more acceptable to the Levellers. See Haller & Davies, *Leveller Tracts*, pp. 415–9; and discussion in Joseph Frank, *The Levellers* (New York, 1969), pp. 171–3; and Gentles, *New Model Army*, pp. 273–4.

40 Citations are from the text of the *Remonstrance* in William Cobbett, (ed.), *The Parliamentary History of England*, 36 vols (London, 1806–20), iii, cols 1078–1127, at col. 1096.

41 *Ibid.*, cols 1102–4.

42 *Ibid.*, cols, 1104–6.

43 *Ibid.*, cols 1105–6.

44 *Ibid.*, cols 1087–8.

45 *Ibid.*, cols 1124–5.

46 Useful accounts of the debates of the 1640s are Robert S. Paul, *The Assembly of the Lord: Politics and Religion in the Westminster Assembly and the 'Grand Debate'* (Edinburgh, 1985); Ernest Sirluck (ed.), *The Complete Prose Works of John Milton: Volume Two* (New Haven, 1959), pp. 53–136; and George Yule, *Puritans in Power: The Religious Legislation of the Long Parliament 1640–1647* (Abingdon, 1981).

47 For an important (and valid) re-emphasis on the wide degree of religious pluralism that was defended by some in the 1640s, and their corresponding conception of the civil state developed see John Coffey, 'Puritanism and Liberty Revisited: The Case for Toleration in the English Revolution', *Historical Journal*, 41 (1998), pp. 961–85.

48 John Goodwin, *Theomachia; or The Grand Imprudence of Men Running Hazard of Fighting Against God* (London, 1644), pp. 47–8.

49 *Ibid.*, p. 48.

50 One of the best statements of this view is the opening of Overton's *An Arrow against all Tyrants*, in Andrew Sharp (ed.), *The English Levellers* (Cambridge, 1998), pp. 55–8.

51 Woodhouse (ed.), *Puritanism and Liberty*, p. 146.

52 *Ibid.*, p. 161.

53 Cf. Carolyn Polizzotto, 'Liberty of Conscience and the Whitehall Debates of 1648–9', *Journal of Ecclesiastical History*, 26 (1975), pp. 69–82.

54 Woodhouse (ed.), *Puritanism and Liberty*, pp. 127–8.

55 *Ibid.*, p. 178.

56 *Ibid.*, pp. 134–6.

57 Quoted from Keith Lindley, *The English Civil War and Revolution: A Sourcebook* (London, 1998), p.p. 175–6.

58 A good survey of the debates, with references to other contributors to them, can be found in Andrew Bradstock, 'Sowing in Hope: The Relevance of Theology to Gerrard Winstanley's Political Programme', *The Seventeenth Century*, 6 (1991), pp. 189–204.

59 Winstanley, *The True Levellers Standard Advanced*, in George Sabine (ed.), *The Works of Gerrard Winstanley* (New York, 1965), p. 252.

60 Winstanley, *New Law of Righteousnes*, in Sabine (ed.), *Works of Gerrard Winstanley*, p. 156.

61 Winstanley, *A Watch-word to the City of London and the Army*, in Sabine (ed.), *Works of Gerrard Winstanley*, p. 315.

62 See especially Winstanley, *A New-Years Gift for the Parliament and Army*, in Sabine (ed.), *Works of Gerrard Winstanley*, pp. 353–403, esp. 389–91.

63 *Ibid.*, p. 391.

64 Abiezer Coppe, *A Fiery Flying Roll*, in Nigel Smith (ed.), *A Collection of Ranter Writings from the 17th Century* (London, 1983), p. 97.

65 Barry Reay, *The Quakers in the English Revolution* (New York, 1985), p. 40.

66 John Reeve, *A Divine Looking-Glass: or, The Third and Last Testament of Our Lord Jesus Christ* (London, 2nd ed. 1661), p. 57.

67 *Ibid.*, p. 59.

68 John Tillighast, *Mr. Tillinghast's Eight Last Sermons* (London, 1655), pp. 38–9.

69 The danger of sticking to the label is illustrated in Jonathan Scott, *England's Troubles: Seventeenth-Century English Political Instability in European Context* (Cambridge, 2000), e.g. pp. 245–6. In assuming that 'radicalism' is an entity with some coherence to it, Scott is compelled to tell what is essentially

a single story embracing Levellers, 'religious radicals', and a bit later republicans. But it is not always clear that the episodes from which Scott builds his account are all part of the same story. There is, for example, some truth in the claim that 'the origins of English radicalism lay . . . in the deepening of the reformation process' (236). That is true – of Coppe or Winstanley – but it is not so obviously true of Lilburne or Harrington.

CHAPTER 4

'That Kind of People': Late Stuart Radicals and their Manifestoes, a Functional Approach

Richard L. Greaves

On Christmas eve, 1683, the Scot James Stewart, having been arrested for smuggling letters from the exile community in the Netherlands to London, professed not to know the conspirator Robert Ferguson 'nor any of that kind of people'.[1] Both Stewart and his interrogator(s) understood what sort of people he meant. Indeed, contemporaries used a variety of terms, mostly pejorative, in referring to them. Typically the critics of 'that kind of people' spoke of them as fanatics or the disaffected, often linking the terms together. At the burial of the Particular Baptist Henry Jessey in September 1663, the *Newes* reported that 'a strange Medly of *Phanatiques*' accompanied the corpse.[2] The term was used indiscriminately for such people as Protestant nonconformists, the northern rebels in 1663, Sidney Bethel, the Whigs, the militant Covenanters organized as the United Societies, and the 'many enthusiastique fanaticall men' who comprised the main body of Covenanters.[3] Not surprisingly, the imprecision could cause problems, as in the summer of 1683, when local magistrates received orders to confiscate weapons from the disaffected; one official asked the lieutenant of Dover Castle if there were 'any notice or direction what principle or profession I ought [to] take for a distinction of disaffection'.[4] The Earl of Lindsey thought the order extended to all people justly suspected of being potential supporters of an insurrection.[5] Whatever their shortcomings, terms such as fanatic, disaffected and ill-affected were normally clear enough to convey the user's meaning. Such words indisputably referred to those who had serious disagreements with the government or the established church, often to the point of being considered a security threat.[6]

The disaffected were also commonly described as factious and seditious, terms that underscored their perceived threat to the commonwealth. At the Northamptonshire quarter sessions in the autumn of 1681, the grand jury used these locutions to depict those who had petitioned for

James' exclusion in the elections for the Oxford Parliament, and the English ambassador Thomas Chudleigh applying the same words to dissident exiles in the Netherlands.[7] Opponents of the Whigs sometimes referred to them as factious, as when the mayor of Chichester complained in February 1685 that 'factious spiritts' were hoping to elect previously seditious members to the next House of Commons, or when a Tory poet damned 'the *Factious Crew*' in 1682.[8] When the government investigated the Rye House plotting, 'factious' became a handy adjective with which to tar its opponents, even those not implicated in the conspiracies.[9] Seeking to distance himself from the plotting as the government's investigation unfolded, the Whig newswriter Giles Hancocke pledged to do what he could to disclose the schemes of factious dissenters, effectively linking Protestant nonconformists to treasonous activity.[10] The Privy Council had already ordered magistrates to disarm those who attended 'seditious Conventicles'.[11] No one surpassed Roger L'Estrange in tarring sectaries with the brush of sedition, for he was intent on demonstrating 'the Unanimous Agreement of All the Several Sectaries for the Common Destruction of the Government'.[12] The blanket indictment was spurious, but even James, Duke of York, thought all 'Phanatical discenters' favoured a commonwealth.[13] In the minds of some people, sectaries were disloyal or fanatical; to a Tory poet the Whig martyr Stephen College, for instance, was an 'Incorrigible *Zealot*'.[14] The Devon grand jury referred in August 1683 to the horrid designs of sectaries and fanatics, going so far as to adjudge all conventicles 'Seditious and treasonable consults, where the Subversion of our Religion and Goverment is designed', and all nonconformist ministers to be participants in a conspiracy against the king and government.[15] Clearly, such locutions as sectary, nonconformist and dissenter[16] were often employed in partisan and defamatory ways.

Opponents of the disaffected liked to depict themselves as loyalists, especially in the 1680s, yet those of a different persuasion would not have seen themselves as 'the disloyall party',[17] at least with respect to the country's welfare and a commitment to Protestantism. On the contrary, an anonymous Whig author thought that when the truth about plotting was known, 'those persons, who now go under the Name of Loyallists, will be as obscure as their Knavery is now publick'.[18] In their own minds the dissidents were 'the godly party' and the 'Sober people',[19] although it is hardly likely that Catholics and many conformists would have characterized the religiously and politically disaffected as godly. An interesting exception occurs in a letter to Secretary of State Leoline

Jenkins describing a small trader named Alexander Wallis, whom the residents of Barnstaple deemed:

> a man fanatically inclin'd, and disaffected to the government . . .: But as to his behaviour, and comon conversation, hee is not given to any debauchery, but a sober man, very reserv'd, and of few words. And as to his Credibilitie, and what beliefe morally may bee given to him, hee hath as to that particular, a fair, and unblemish'd reputation.[20]

For the most part, however, loyalists portrayed their foes with such locutions as 'the ill people', 'the restlesse party', 'the Caballisticall men', rebellious subjects, dangerous and restless men, schismatics, 'persons of unquiet Spirits' and the '*Damn'd Rebellious Crew*'.[21] In July 1662, Charles II himself, fearing an insurrection, blamed 'Persons of desperate Principles'.[22]

Thus the contemporary lexicon was not lacking in words and phrases to limn those substantively at odds with the late Stuart regimes, the established church, or both. But with the usual exception of such religious terms as nonconformist and dissenter, the contemporary words and phrases had pejorative or partisan connotations that masked the complexities which were part of late seventeenth-century society. Some Protestant laity patronized dissenters while conforming themselves, and some were more interested in good preaching than differences over liturgy and polity. The Bristol merchant James Holloway 'professed himself neither a *Dissenter* from the *Church of England*, nor joyn'd with them altogether', and Arthur Annesley, Earl of Anglesey, did not let fundamental ecclesiastical differences keep him from worshipping in the Church of England on Sunday mornings while periodically listening to nonconformist ministers preach in his chapel on Sunday afternoons.[23] This is neither to deny nor to underestimate the reality of substantive differences between groups, but it is a warning that any terminology which focuses on delineating such groups tends to mask the existence of individuals – perhaps in significant numbers – who, by minimizing the differences, manifested a fluidity that mocks the historian's efforts to categorize. The boldest assertion of this fluidity may be Jonathan Scott's claim that 'with the important exception of some hardliners on both sides, 1678's "whigs" *were* 1681's "tories"'.[24] The historian's challenge is to recognize fluidity without losing sight of the basic differences that internally sundered each of the three kingdoms during the late Stuart period. Although some of the fissures, particularly those of a political nature, underwent periodic flux, they were nevertheless real and were recognized as such by contemporaries. The most stable divisions were in the religious sphere, but even here the differences between Presbyterians and many adherents of the Church of England were less pronounced than those that separated the former from Baptists and Quakers.[25] Yet visions of limited Protestant ecumenicity remained alive in the late seventeenth century,[26] and in most respects the greatest divide remained that which separated Protestants and Catholics. As Lord William Russell was about to be executed in 1683, he hoped that 'all our unhappy Differences [might be] removed, and that all sincere Protestants would so far consider the Danger of Popery, as to lay aside their Heats, and agree against the Common Enemy; and that the Church-men would be less severe, and the Dissenters less scrupulous'.[27] But Protestantism was riven by 'Heats', and so too was the political realm.

Contemporary terms have unquestionable value in depicting these differences, though nearly all are subject to legitimate criticism. Fanatic, schismatic and factious have an unmistakably pejorative connotation, and seditious has clear legal overtones. Disaffected is perhaps less objectionable, though it was regularly used in a negative, partisan sense. Positive terms such as loyalist, godly and the sober sort imply that those of a different persuasion were less loyal, spiritual and upright, or even disloyal, ungodly, or dissolute, but this was often untrue. A strictly linguistic approach – confining historical analysis, as Conal Condren has proposed, to 'the vocabulary around which argument was organised' – is subject to limitations at least as serious as those levelled against a functional approach. The latter has the advantage of employing a general term to refer to the disaffected that is not freighted with contemporary value judgements, whether positive or negative. Of course, any term, including radical, can be given associations by users, and Condren rightly notes that modern analysts have associated radical with 'democratic, laudable, edifying, progressive and worthy'.[28] My point is that historians of the seventeenth and eighteenth centuries can and should explicitly define the term radical to exclude such affiliations. Employed without such value associations, radical is useful in discussing groups of an otherwise disparate nature – for instance, Quakers and republicans, rebels and Baptists, Fifth Monarchists and Covenanters – for analytical purposes. Those who use an anachronistic term such as radical have an obligation, as Condren argues, to provide 'criteria to justify its explanatory or its descriptive use'.[29]

Etymologically, seventeenth-century Englishmen understood radical to mean, *inter alia*, fundamental, root, primary, or thorough.[30] It is, then, in the spirit of the contemporary meaning to use radical to denote a proponent of fundamental change that strikes at the root of existing institutions and assumptions. Although anachronistic, this usage builds on the contemporary understanding of the adjective radical, and it does so in a way that privileges no contemporary group because the term, defined in this manner, is neutral. It also captures the full range of those deemed by loyalists to be disaffected, fanatical, schismatic or factious. The term radical thus has considerable utilitarian value as long as its anachronistic nature is remembered and no assumption is made of a continuous radical tradition that spans the centuries. If such a tradition exists, it must be demonstrated through historical evidence. It is also worth remembering that the notion of a tradition is itself an invention of one age as it appropriates the past for its own purposes, and is thus anachronistic. This essay will discuss only the linkage between the 1640s and 1650s on one hand and the period 1660–1689 on the other.

Restoration radicals are characterized in large measure by their attempt to implement the unfinished agendas of the 1640s and 1650s. Because of the varied nature of those earlier agendas, it is more accurate to speak of radical traditions than of a single tradition. Contemporaries themselves recognized differences, as in the Baptist-Quaker feuding, or the disparate political views of Lord Russell and Algernon Sidney, or the dissimilar tenets of the Cameronians (a group of militant extremists among the Covenanters) and Robert West's Rye House cabal. Yet all of them shared a fundamental hostility to one or more aspects of the Stuart regime and a desire to implement sweeping changes, however differently those may have been formulated, or however disparate the means proposed to attain those ends. When used in the context of the seventeenth century, 'radicalism' refers in a general sense to this fundamental hostility and a belief in the necessity for comprehensive reforms, not a common set of specific tenets or proposed changes. In referring to radicalism, it is crucial not to ignore the substantial differences between radical groups. In this sense the question of transmitting radicalism is inaccurately posed, given the absence of a common core of specific principles. In discussing the seventeenth century, the term 'radicalism' – or, more accurately, if unconventionally, 'radicalisms' – is a convenient way to describe the commitment or disposition to effect fundamental changes in the body politic, religion, society, or the economy, or some combination thereof.

Defining a radical as an advocate of sweeping, substantive change raises the problem of determining what constitutes such fundamental transformation. There is no simple answer because the historian is assessing matters of degree in the context of a range of possibilities that alter over time. An accurate contextual understanding is consequently a *sine qua non* for any assessment of what constitutes radical commitment or behaviour. Generally, radicals espouse disobedience to an existing regime, socioeconomic structure, or religious establishment, typically by such means as physical resistance, ranging from assaults on magistrates to open rebellion; assassination or kidnapping; illegal publishing and the dissemination of banned works; participation in unlawful assemblies or conventicles; violent, destructive acts against institutions or the propertied; and attempts to overthrow a government. Radicals can also confine themselves to legal actions intended to bring about fundamental changes in church or state; for the most part, many Protestant nonconformists in the period 1660–1689 were radicals because they contested the legitimacy of the established church and simultaneously asserted a right to freedom of conscience that challenged the state's historic claim to compel people to worship according to its dictates, although without resorting to violence. The nature and form of the challenge to existing authority vary in accord with the range of options, again emphasizing the importance of context in assessing whether someone can be appropriately deemed a radical. The situational dimension recognizes that altering contexts can prompt people to become radicals or cease being such. Following his arrest for stealing the crown jewels, Thomas Blood left his radical ways to become a royalist informer, whereas Arthur Capel, Earl of Essex, who served the crown as lord lieutenant of Ireland and then as one of Charles' key advisors, ultimately participated in a conspiracy for a general insurrection. Moreover, it was possible to be radical in one aspect of life but not in others; Quakers such as Anthony Sharp and Samuel Clarridge denounced the established church, refused to pay tithes and church rates and would not take oaths, yet both served as aldermen in Dublin, and Sharp was master of the weavers' guild.[31] Total opposition to the established order is not a necessary criterion to be a radical.[32]

In assessing whether a person, group, or movement is radical, we can profitably adapt Colin Davis' functional methodology, which defines a radical as one who delegitimates the old order, justifies a new one and proposes means to implement the latter.[33] By striking at the roots of contemporary institutions and assumptions, seventeenth-century radicals delegitimated the old order, nowhere more obviously than in religion, though proponents of republicanism no less effectively struck at the heart of monarchy. The radicals' visions of a new order were neither uniform nor sometimes even compatible, but they shared a deep-seated enmity to the existing order. For many, the goal was a voluntary system of religion, with no place for compulsion, legally enforced theological tenets and polities, or mandatory tithing, whereas in politics some sought a commonwealth, others a reformed monarchy and some a theocracy. Those manifestoes which deal with social issues, such as immigration, tax reform, free trade and the abolition of primogeniture, not only reflect the socioeconomic concerns of various dissident groups but also indicate the audiences to which they hoped to appeal. Proposed social and economic reforms were not, however, common to all the declarations. The radicals differed as well in their proposed means to introduce a new order, some embracing rebellion or assassination, others less militant political action, and yet others, such as the Quakers and many dissenters, nonviolent but illegal resistance.

Nor did seventeenth-century radicals concur with respect to the authorities to which they appealed as justification for their actions and beliefs. Scripture, historical precedent, natural law, reason, the divine will (as manifested, for example, through the Quakers' understanding of the inner light) and freedom of conscience were all cited by radicals at one time or another. In fact, the various radical strands are distinguished in part by the authorities to which their adherents appealed. Many radicals subscribed to a belief in the working of divine providence in human affairs, and this gave force to their commitment to fundamental change as a manifestation of divine intentions. For those dissidents, belief in providence did not inhibit change; rather, it cloaked the demand for change in religious garb that reinforced their convictions.[34] Some of the manifestoes, particularly those of the Vennerites and the Covenanters, evince a belief, similar to that espoused by various opponents of Charles I in the 1640s, in providence as divine judgement against not only individuals but also an entire political and religious establishment. Stephen Marshall might well have remarked, as did the Vennerites, on 'the great and good designe God hath in this strange Providence, whereat most are confounded; to punish and spue out of his mouth a Lukewarm People, who had not a thorough spirit for the Work' of reformation.[35] This is not to imply that the Vennerites were the heirs of Marshall and his colleagues, but to recognize that the demands of many post-1660 radicals continued to be deeply rooted in religious convictions, including a sense of providence as the outreach of a deity exercising an activist role in human affairs and exhorting the godly to function as his agents.[36]

Whether radicals couched their proposals in providential or secular language, they did so by appealing to one or more authorities. The core of any radical programme is not innovation for the sake of change, but *transformation* based on a commitment to fundamental tenets grounded in authority. Those authorities might change (though not in all cases, especially in religion), but pre-modern radicals shared a belief in the need to transform core institutions because of authorities they found compelling. Looking to the past did not preclude someone from being a radical; the key question was how one used the past in relationship to the present and as a potential shaper of the future. Late Stuart radicals and their opponents often appealed to the same authorities in making their cases against each other, clearly finding different meaning in such authorities as history, Scripture and natural law.

Elsewhere I have documented the existence of various radical strands in the three decades following the Restoration, arguing that the radical threat to the Stuart regime should not be underestimated even though some of the conspiracies were never implemented.[37] Seven insurrections occurred during a twenty-eight-year span, and an eighth, planned for Dublin and Ulster in early 1663, was quashed on the eve of the revolt. Six of the other seven were exclusively radical affairs: the Fifth Monarchist uprising in London in January 1661, the northern rebellion in the autumn of 1663, the Galloway insurrection in 1666, the Bothwell Bridge uprising in 1679 and the Argyll and Monmouth rebellions in 1685. Radicals helped shape and participated in the revolution of 1688–89, though many others were involved as well. Moreover, radicals assassinated the archbishop of St Andrews in May 1679, kidnapped the Duke of Ormond in December 1670, stole the crown jewels in May 1671 and plotted to murder Charles and James in the early 1680s. Elements of the Good Old Cause survived the Restoration, helping to make the ensuing three decades a period of protracted struggle. In a speech to the House of Lords in March 1664, Charles observed that the recent trials of the northern rebels demonstrated that the crown's old enemies were still active.[38] As Colonel Edward Warren faced execution for his role in the Dublin plot, he spoke of 'the Just and honest Cause which now lyeth in dust and some days would have terefyd the greatest monarks'.[39] 'Busie Fellows of the old Leaven' attracted attention at Nottingham in May 1665.[40] In fact, the Good Old Cause lived on, and commentators during the Restoration crisis of 1677–83 would draw parallels between the 1640s and the events unfolding before them.

> If *Murders, Treasons,* and such Crimes go free,
> As they have done of Late, with great Applause;
> What need they care, how wicked then they be,
> So they can carry on the *Good Old Cause*?[41]

The popular hostility to the traditional political and religious order that continued throughout the post-1660 decades provided a reservoir of potential manpower on which radical schemers could draw, and though they ultimately failed to utilize this resource to accomplish their ends, the threat could not be ignored by the government. Such people and the causes they espoused were not imaginary, though they never comprised a homogeneous movement characterized by uniform objectives.

The full spectrum of radical opinion in this period, including sectarian groups such as Quakers and Baptists, political theorists such as Sidney and John Locke, and radical Whigs in London and Bristol, is too large to analyze in this essay, but an overview of twenty radical manifestoes offers an opportunity to explore common as well as disparate themes, the role of religion, the degree of historical continuity with earlier radicals and the common thread of opposition to the Stuart regime as the first step in implementing transformative change. These manifestoes did not share a uniform vision of what those reforms should be, thereby underscoring the existence of various radical strands. The divergences are in part situational, for they reflect the disparate conditions in England, Scotland and Ireland, and the altered circumstances between the 1660s and very early 1670s on the one hand and the late 1670s and 1680s on the other.

The revolutionary declarations can be loosely grouped into four clusters, though differences existed within those clusters. The first group comprises three English declarations, beginning with *A door of hope: Or, a call and declaration for the gathering together of the first ripe fruits unto the standard of our Lord King Jesus* drafted for Thomas Venner's Fifth Monarchist uprising in January 1661. The following year, the government apprehended the London distiller and tobacco merchant Thomas Tong and his confederates, who were allegedly part of a conspiracy to restore the commonwealth and possessed a declaration setting forth their aims. The third manifesto, written by the Independent minister Edward Richardson, *A door of hope opened in the valley of Achor for the mourners in Sion out of the north*, was for the use of the northern rebels in the autumn of 1663. Two Irish declarations comprise the second cluster: an undated remonstrance, probably composed in late 1661 or 1662 and reportedly signed by hundreds, and the 1663 manifesto of Lieutenant Thomas Blood, the Presbyterian minister William Lecky, Colonel Thomas Scott (son of the regicide) and their fellow Dublin plotters. Seven Covenanter declarations make up the third cluster: the statement of the Galloway rebels (November 1666), the documents issued by the insurgent Covenanters at Rutherglen (May 1679), Glasgow (June 1679) and Hamilton (June 1679), and the declarations of the Cameronians at Queensferry (June 1680), Sanquhar (June 1680) and Lanark (January 1682). The final cluster comprises four draft declarations of the Rye House plotters,[42] the general manifesto of the Argyll rebels (May 1685), the Earl's personal declaration, Monmouth's manifesto and Hugh Speke's *Third declaration*, ostensibly drafted for William of Orange (December 1688).

A comprehensive analysis of radical strands would require the examination of more than the manifestoes, for in varying degrees these are propaganda documents tailored for the intended audiences. The extent to which the declarations seek to do this varies, with arguably the most conscious attempt to reach as many people as possible being the documents produced by the Monmouth and Argyll rebels. The Irish proclamations of the early 1660s, the Rye House manifesto and Speke's declaration likewise were unmistakably composed with a view to attracting adherents. The Vennerites openly appealed to those who at least shared the same common enemies and hostility to the same perceived political, social and religious ills – 'the negative part of our Cause'.[43]

Although each of these manifestoes may appropriately be termed radical, the various groups responsible for them manifest striking diversity. Even among the Covenanters, the Cameronians (later known as the United Societies), as militant extremists, are an offshoot of the more broadly based Covenanting movement that had taken up arms in the Galloway and Bothwell Bridge insurrections. Like the Cameronians, Thomas Venner and his followers were an extremist group, but the latter were Independents, the former, Presbyterians. The Tong schemers and northern rebels espoused the Good Old Cause, whereas the Dublin plotters, an alliance of Presbyterians and Independents, were especially concerned with the Irish land settlement and fidelity to the Solemn League and Covenant. The draft declarations of the Rye House conspirators were the work of men with disparate religious views and backgrounds – lawyers, ex-military men, the brewer Zachary Bourne and Robert Ferguson, a Scottish minister who had served as an assistant to the famed Independent minister John Owen. Some of the same men subsequently rallied around Argyll and Monmouth, and Ferguson and John Wildman went on to support William of Orange, for whom Speke served as a double agent.

With the possible exception of the Rye House draft declaration noted in Lord Grey's account, each declaration includes material dealing with religion, thus ruling out any suggestion, at least for this period, that radicals were irreligious. This is not to say that all were pious, though Francis North, Baron Guilford, probably went to the opposite extreme in describing the 1660s as a time when 'there was at work underground, other partys of Republican Atheists, who were for overturning all, & restoring their fancyed Commonwealth, & their titles to Crowne– & church–lands'.[44] The Rye House plotter Robert West was reportedly an atheist, and an anonymous Tory author, writing in 1681, thought those who inveighed against arbitrary power were conventiclers and atheists who read '*Hobs*'s Divinity'.[45] These are, of course, defamatory characterizations, and they are evidence only of the extent to which some opponents of the radicals attempted to paint them as irreligious.

Reflecting popular feeling, manifesto drafters believed anti-popery was a useful, potent cry. The Vennerites cast *A door of hope* in internationalist terms, resolving never to sheath their swords until Babylon has been destroyed: 'We shall in a holy Triumph... go on to *France, Spain, Germany*, and *Rome*, to destroy the Beast and Whore'.[46] The northern insurgents did the same, pledging to eradicate '*Gog* and *Magog*, Pope and Turk, with all their adherents'.[47] In Ireland the Dublin cabal warned that Protestants were being ruined because the government countenanced Catholicism.[48] The draft of a declaration probably prepared by this group stirred anew the fears of another uprising like that of 1641: The 'bloodie papists that were the leaders of the people [responsible for] that barbarous Massacre, were now the first that tasted of [Charles'] Royall clemency'.[49] Although the focus of the Covenanters' religious animus was prelacy – the immediate threat – more than Catholicism, the manifesto of the Argyll rebels damned both as suppressive.[50] Among the Rye House plotters, Captain Thomas Walcott's proposed declaration apparently intended to do little more than echo the familiar war cry against popery and arbitrary government, the same approach used in the Monmouth declaration.[51] In sharp contrast, Speke's *Third declaration* made the rescue of the three kingdoms from slavery and popery its principal theme, threatening dire punishment to Catholics in open arms, with weapons in their houses, or holding any civil or military office contrary to law, and to any who assisted or submitted to them. Fanning the fear, Speke warned that large numbers of Catholics were in the area of London and Westminster, presumably preparing to burn the cities, massacre the inhabitants, or join forces with an invading French army to extirpate Protestantism. All Catholics were therefore to be disarmed and secured. Thus Speke, whose brother had been hanged as a Monmouth rebel, brought to the

Williamite revolution a strong dose of the anticatholicism that was now ingrained in society.[52]

Although the manifestoes were in general agreement on their opposition to Catholicism, only the Vennerites and northern rebels called for an international crusade to expurgate it, and there was no unanimity on what the correct religious policy should be. The Vennerites and the Cameronians responsible for the Lanark declaration explicitly looked for the rule of King Jesus, an emphasis shared by the Baptists but not the Presbyterians (who stressed a preaching ministry) among the northern revolters.[53] The Covenanters, of course, professed their allegiance to the National Covenant and the Solemn League and Covenant, and the Dublin plotters and northern rebels also affirmed the Solemn League and Covenant; by expressing approval of the Covenanters, the Argyll rebels did the same.[54] The Dublin conspirators and northern insurgents somewhat incongruously professed adherence to both the Solemn League and Covenant, which prescribed adherence to the example of the best Reformed churches, and liberty of conscience, but the Dublin cabal clearly intended to confine religious freedom within the bounds of the Solemn League and Covenant.[55] In contrast, the Tong plotters, the Rye House conspirators, and the Monmouth rebels, appealing to a broader constituency, favoured toleration for all Protestants, and the Tong cabal also wanted to make it treason to disturb the meetings of religious groups.[56] The Covenanters sought a presbyterian polity for the church, and their antipathy to prelacy was shared by the Tong and Dublin plotters and the Argyll rebels.[57] Among the Rye House conspirators, Ferguson demanded the termination of bishops, deans and chapters because they 'eat the fat of the land without makeing any return for it', but his compatriots in West's cabal opposed him, fearing such a demand would alienate the present tenants or those who hoped to profit by acquiring episcopal lands, a telling example of how materialistic concerns could temper ideology.[58] The Tong colluders and northern insurgents condemned the Book of Common Prayer, the Galloway rebels defended the Directory of Worship and the Argyll forces opposed any attempt to enforce human inventions in the church, but otherwise the declarations generally ignore forms of worship.[59] Although millenarianism is often linked to radical religious groups, the manifestoes reflect little of it, the principal exceptions being the general tone of the Vennerites' declaration and the northern rebels' interest in the conversion of the Jews and the coming of Christ's earthly reign.[60] The manifestoes make it clear that their authors were neither irreligious nor heretical; Reformed Protestantism undergirds most of them, though the Tong schemers (who wanted to unite all sectaries[61]), the Rye House cabal, and the Monmouth insurrectionists (who refer positively to Reformed Protestantism) were willing to embrace Baptists and Quakers as well as the mainstream Protestant groups.

For the Vennerites and the Covenanters, political considerations were subordinate to religious issues, but this was not the case with the Rye House conspirators and the Monmouth rebels, for whom religion was only one among many important concerns. The latter groups were not primarily animated by a vision of community with God, nor can most of their radical principles be explained in terms of the impact of their religious convictions. Although Jonathan Clark's dictum 'that the conceptual framework of disaffection continued for many decades [beyond the seventeenth century] to be provided by theology'[62] is generally true, the proposed Rye House manifestoes and the Monmouth declaration are early examples of radical documents that are not primarily framed in religious terms. In part this reflects the disparate interests of these radicals and in part their desire to reach the largest possible audience. The Tory and Dublin plotters and the northern rebels gave substantive attention to religion, but without making other subjects subordinate; even in their case it would be misleading to argue that religion was the key explanatory issue, as it clearly was for the Vennerites and the Covenanters.[63]

The manifestoes differ sharply in the attention they accord to political matters and to their views on such subjects. This is apparent with respect to the various positions on monarchy. The Dublin plotters, the Galloway rebels and the Hamilton declaration explicitly avowed monarchy, whereas Monmouth asserted his title to the throne but opted to let a 'free' parliament decide whether to make him king, his hesitation stemming primarily from divisions among his key supporters over kingship *versus* a republic.[64] The draft manifesto which Ferguson read to Monmouth and his supporters professed support for Charles and pledged no 'considerable alteration in the government'.[65] The Tong conspirators insisted on a commonwealth, whereas the northern insurgents were willing to embrace a reformed monarchy or a commonwealth.[66] The West cabal was also flexible, preferring a weak executive in any case, but the Vennerites and the Cameronians who issued the Queensferry and Lanark manifestoes favoured theocracy.[67] The Vennerite, Queensferry, Sanquhar, Lanark, Argyll and Monmouth declarations explicitly denounced one or both of the Restoration-era monarchs. In the words of the Cameronians who issued the Sanquhar testimony, "[we] disowne Charles Stewart (who has been reigning, or rather we may say tyranizing on the throne of

Brittain . . .) as having any right or title to, or interest in the croun of Scotland or goverment, as forfaulted yeares since by his perjuring and breach of Covenant with God and his church, other breaches in matters ecclesiasticle, and by his tyranny'.[68]

Differences are apparent as well with respect to views concerning parliament. The Tong cabal wanted to recall the Rump but then hold annual elections for parliament, whereas Edward Richardson, whose views helped to influence the northern rebels, proposed the return of the Long Parliament.[69] In contrast, the Galloway insurgents endorsed the traditional privileges of parliament, indicating no desire to alter the form of government.[70] The Hamilton declaration called for a free parliament, a demand Monmouth and Speke would subsequently make in 1685 and 1688 respectively, indicating a free parliament's appeal to a diverse range of dissidents.[71] The draft declaration which Ferguson presented to the Monmouth cabal indicated a willingness for parliament to settle all matters in dispute.[72] Among the other Rye House conspirators, Walcott, who had ties to Shaftesbury and was probably acquainted with Locke's political views, showed West the draft of a declaration that rehearsed the Stuarts' support of popery and arbitrary government, concluding 'that the Government was dissolv'd, and the people at Liberty to settle another'.[73] Reflecting issues important to radical London Whigs, West and his cohorts advocated a bicameral parliament, annual elections, a ban on proroguing or adjourning parliament without its consent, a weak executive veto and parliamentary election of a council of state. The House of Lords would be retained, but only nobles who supported the 'design' would retain their hereditary status; all others would be life peers, with replacements selected from the House of Commons when they died. According to this plan, parliament would control the militia and nominate justices of the peace, judges, sheriffs and other officials.[74] No declaration was finalized, and in the spring of 1683 the cabal reportedly agreed on five points that would be conveyed to Monmouth on the eve of the planned uprising: annual parliaments, to sit as long as they had business to transact; the people's right to control the militia; the right of counties to elect their sheriffs; liberty of conscience; and the degrading of all nobles who had acted against the people's interest.[75] By degrading they presumably meant stripping titles and perhaps estates from the miscreants. Argyll's declarations were much less specific, condemning James for ruling contrary to law, insisting the current House of Commons had been fraudulently elected and rejecting James' claim to the throne because the English House of Commons had voted to exclude him.[76]

The most sophisticated of the declarations, that of Monmouth incorporated some of the points that had been made in the Rye House discussions. This almost certainly reflects the fact that contact between his group and West's was maintained by Walcott and Ferguson; in fact, the latter drafted the Duke's manifesto. Evincing the likely influence of Walcott and Locke, the declaration averred that 'all the boundaries of the Government have of late been broken, & nothing left unattempted, for turning our *limited Monarchy* into an *absolute Tyranny*'. In addition to indicting James as a murderer, Catholic usurper, traitor and tyrant, the manifesto offered a political programme designed to save the country from popery and arbitrary government. As the Rye House schemers had proposed, parliaments would be elected annually and sit without prorogation or dissolution until all grievances had been redressed and petitions answered. Monmouth's statement called for new laws to provide for the election of sheriffs by freeholders, place the militia under the sheriffs' control, repeal the Corporation and Militia Acts, institute life tenure for judges subject to their good behaviour, bar ignorant and scandalous men from the judicial bench, restore traditional charters, and ban a standing army without parliamentary consent (a point also made in the Argyll declaration).[77] Clearly, the reforms envisaged by the Rye House plotters and the Monmouth rebels were far more extreme than those proposed in other declarations, underscoring the diversity of political aims and degrees of sophistication (or lack of it) among various radical groups.

The revolutionary manifestoes evince a range of views on taxes as well. The Vennerites naively called for the repeal of all taxes, and the northern rebels went nearly as far with their proposal for an end to subsidies, benevolences, customs, the excise and hearth and gift taxes.[78] Other radicals were more discriminating: the Tong cabal opposed the levying of customs on seamen (whom it hoped to enlist for its insurrection) and the hearth tax, calling as well for a prohibition on the payment of government officials out of the public treasury.[79] With the exception of the Queensferry declaration, which deemed taxation unlawful if the money were used to suppress conventicles, and the Lanark manifesto, which condemned Charles' exorbitant taxes,[80] the Covenanter statements were silent on taxation, as were both Argyll declarations. In contrast, the Rye House conspirators, a largely urban group, were willing to accept a land tax and a moderate excise on luxury items, but not a hearth tax. Reflecting the interests of traders, they opposed the customs, calling for England to become 'a free port'. They also wanted taxes designated for 'particular uses', which signalled their interest in fiscal responsibility.[81] Perhaps not wanting to diminish tax revenue should he gain the throne, Monmouth was content merely to complain that James had invaded people's estates with his proclamations concerning customs and excise taxes; the crux of his objection had more to do with parliamentary rights than the level of taxation.[82] The various positions – or lack of them – on taxes are further evidence of the disparity of political aims and sophistication among late Stuart radicals.

The declarations also varied sharply with respect to their interest in and views on economic matters other than taxes. The most ambitious economic programme was that of the Vennerites, who proposed to abolish primogeniture, copyhold and customary tenure. The export of raw materials, including fuller's earth (for cloth manufacturing) and unwrought leather, would be prohibited, and forests would be preserved and expanded. In addition to terminating lordship as well as monarchy, the Vennerites called for reform of the debt law, employment for the indigent and the cessation of begging.[83] Among the Covenanters, who were likewise religious zealots, virtually no interest was expressed in economic reforms, though the Lanark declaration protested against Charles' grinding of the poor.[84] The Tong plotters, who joined in the demand to abolish the nobility, espoused two unusual concerns, one insisting on a programme of social welfare for seamen (whom they hoped to recruit, as we have seen), and the other clamouring for the confirmation of all public land sales.[85] In addition to confirming the estates of those who held them in May 1659, the Dublin conspirators protested against the restoration of estates to Catholics, but they manifested no interest in economic reform, apparently because their concern focused on landowners.[86] In contrast, the northern rebels were broadly interested in the welfare of the poor, unemployment and the decay of trade, but they offered no proposals to deal with these problems.[87] Generally, then, economic considerations, other than a dislike of taxes, were not at the core of the radical manifestoes, with the exception of those issued by the Vennerites and the Dublin schemers (whose interest in preserving estates was pivotal). Even in the case of Venner's movement, the economic proposals were but one facet of militant millenarianism, though a 'class' element is clearly evident in their denunciation of 'the old bloody, Popish, wicked Gentry of the Nation' and their call for the abolition of nobility.[88] As a group, the manifestoes do not indicate any simple correlation between radical beliefs and class identity, which is not surprising given the fact that the groups responsible for the declarations reflected a broad social spectrum.

This diversity is further reflected in some of the idiosyncratic proposals in the manifestoes. Venner's group wanted to introduce democratic government in towns and guilds, and it proposed to use the spoils of war to establish a treasury to fund its crusading army. Reflecting their socioeconomic concerns, the Vennerites also urged the abolition of capital punishment for theft.[89] For their part, the Tong cabal was interested in using treason laws against their foes, punishing any who, once the commonwealth had been re-established, attempted to restore the monarchy, the House of Lords, or government by a single person and any who refused to obey parliament as long as it remained loyal to these principles.[90] The Dublin plotters spoke of defending the English interest in the three kingdoms, restoring the traditional privileges of corporations in the three realms, paying the arrears of Protestant troops in Ireland and assuring the English of their right to retain the Irish estates they possessed on 7 May 1659.[91] One of the aims of the northern rebels was revenge on those responsible for punishing alleged plotting in the early 1660s. Moreover, these insurgents, like the Vennerites before them, denounced the prevalence of immorality in society, explicitly singling out blasphemy, the theatre, inebriety, adultery and theft.[92]

The Covenanters generally protested against fines, imprisonment, quartering, torture and exile, or what the Queensferry manifesto summarized as violations of their 'civill rights & liberties'. The authors of this declaration anticipated governing by the laws of Israel, especially in matters of life and death, with three exceptions: the laws regarding slavery, which do not accord with Christian liberty; the laws governing divorce, which they deemed a temporary concession to the Israelites' hardened hearts; and polygamy, which they adjudged a sinful custom that was discordant with marriage as originally instituted. For their adherence to the Hebrew laws the Cameronians expected to be associated in the minds of others with the Fifth Monarchists, 'but if this be ther fyfthe monarchie wee both are and ought to be such and that according to [God's] word'.[93] In the Lanark declaration the Cameronians proposed to return church and state to what they had been in Scotland in 1648–49, thereby extricating the Scots from tyranny.[94]

Enunciating very different concerns, the Rye House conspirators sought the naturalization of all aliens, a ban on future immigration and security measures to protect Anne so she could marry 'some honest Country Gentleman, and raise a breed for keeping out all Forraign pretences to the Crown'. Ferguson added that Charles' illegitimate sons should be allowed to live, though compelled to labour as common porters and watermen. Reiterating concerns that had been prominently voiced in the 1640s and 1650s, West's cabal proposed to orient some Oxford and Cambridge colleges toward 'Mechanicall Arts' and agriculture rather than training 'a supernumerary clergy'.[95] The general Argyll manifesto was also something of a potpourri, opposing the Dutch wars (because of the Protestant bond), condemning torture, insisting on the restoration of those who had suffered under the Stuarts and pledging to establish a new government, while the Earl's personal statement demanded the return of all property belonging to him and his father which had been expropriated by the state.[96] No less varied, the Monmouth declaration demanded the reversal of all treason convictions in the alleged Presbyterian plot and of all penalties imposed on Protestant dissenters by the penal statutes. It also promised to try James for the reputed murder of Charles and to restore the traditional charters.[97]

Some of the declarations made a conscious effort to underscore continuity with the past, the most obvious example being the frequent references to the Solemn League and Covenant, and, to a lesser extent, the National Covenant in the Dublin and Scottish manifestoes. Another is the identification with what the Sanquhar declaration called 'our free reformed mother the church'.[98] Even the Monmouth declaration appealed, as we have seen, to the Protestant Reformed religion, clearly implying that the Duke's enemies were of a different persuasion.[99] In the same spirit, the Argyll manifesto pledged to restore Protestantism and explicitly praised the Covenanters.[100] The Reformed Protestant tradition was further reflected in the northern rebels' resolve to model ecclesiastical polity on that of the best Reformed churches (as well as the Bible) and the reference to John Calvin in the Queensferry declaration.[101] Continuity with the more recent past was underscored by the Tong cabal's and northern insurgents' open appeal to the Good Old Cause the former's plan to recall the Rump and the Glasgow declaration's avowal of the 1648 Engagement.[102] Perhaps the most striking expression of continuity was the Vennerites' determination 'to take down their Masters, those Regicides quarters' on the gates of London and the heads on Westminster Hall and London Bridge, though they explicitly denounced Oliver Cromwell's alleged apostacy.[103] The indebtedness to Reformed Protestantism and some of the radical acts of the 1640s and 1650s was deliberate, though hardly uniform. Within the Restoration era itself, the Cameronians consciously fostered this sense of continuity by referring not only to the Solemn League and Covenant but also to preceding Covenanter manifestoes: the Sanquhar declaration cited the Rutherglen statement with approval but denounced the Hamilton manifesto because the latter accepted monarchy, and the Lanark declaration in turn endorsed the statements proclaimed at Rutherglen and Sanquhar.[104] The importance of Reformed Protestantism to these radical groups should warn against any simplistic correlation of the radical with the heterodox in the seventeenth century.[105]

Continuity enhanced a sense of authority, helping to vindicate new manifestoes by linking them to historic events, people, or documents considered praiseworthy. In this sense, tradition – albeit selectively chosen – was important to radicals. In a negative fashion they also invoked tradition by depicting their archenemies as innovators. In the minds of the Galloway revolters, Charles was the principal culprit, having forsaken his pledge to rule Scotland according to biblical precepts, the National Covenant and the Solemn League and Covenant. Instead he had ordered the Covenants burned and established episcopacy 'in its height of tyranny'.[106] Similarly, the remonstrance of hundreds chastised Charles for refusing to honour the Declaration of Breda, and the Hamilton manifesto recounted how God's people had been 'groaninge under, the overturninge of the worke of reformation, the Coruptions of doctrine, the slightinge of worshipe–despyseing of ordinances, the Changeing of Ancient church disciplnge & Governement'.[107] The usurper – the innovator – was Charles II, insisted the Cameronians, and in his personal statement Argyll similarly denounced James II for having 'abandoned and invaded' the people's religion and liberties.[108] The most effective attempt to indicate continuity by attacking the enemy's break with traditional government and religion is found in Monmouth's declaration, which begins by linking the Duke's cause to government as 'originally Instituted by *God*, and *this* or *that* forme of it chosen and submitted to by *Men*, for the peace[,] happiness & security of the *Governed*, & not for the private Interest, & personall greatness of those that Rule'. In recent years England's limited monarchy had been transformed into an absolute tyranny and its Protestantism undermined by popery; the real plotter is the usurper James, whose actions 'hath been but one continued conspiracy against the *Reformed Religion* & rights of the *Nation*'. A lengthy indictment of his alleged crimes follows, including the burning of London, a confederacy with France, the third Dutch war, the popish plot and Essex's assassination.[109] The intent was to ward off the imputation of doing something radical, especially the recourse to arms against the king, by presenting the Duke's cause in the guise of conserving traditional liberties and religion. This is not to suggest that Monmouth and his lieutenants were deliberately being deceptive; on the contrary, they probably believed what they were saying, yet a number of their proposals – annually elected parliaments, life tenure for judges subject to good behaviour and religious freedom for all Protestants – amounted to fundamental changes that struck at the roots of contemporary institutions, and thus were radical. This, too, they must have understood. To ask whether late seventeenth-century radicals were conservers or innovators is to pose a false dichotomy.

Although the proposals of late seventeenth-century British radicals were varied, they reflect a common sense of shared persecution. Nowhere is this feeling more obvious than in the title of the Sanquhar proclamation: 'The Declairation and Testimonie of the Trew Presbeterian Anti-prelatick Anteristain [i.e. Anti-erastian] Persecuted Partie in Scotland'.[110] The remonstrance of hundreds cited the impending ruin of those excommunicated by bishops, and the Dublin plotters recounted how they and their families had been delivered like prey to the 'barbarous and bloodie' murderers whose cruelty had reputedly led to the deaths of 150,000 Protestants in Ireland in 1641. Their manifesto was issued on behalf of Ireland's 'poor suffering protestants'; 'we may undoubtedlie as David did conclude that evill is determined against us'.[111] The northern rebels intended their declaration 'to revive the prisoners of hope and awaken the dead witnesses of the lambe', whereas the Covenanters who promulgated the Hamilton manifesto contended that God's people had endured cruelty, injustice and oppression at the hands of prelates and 'malignants'.[112] The Argyll insurgents promised redress to those who had suffered under the Stuarts, protested against illegal executions and torture and expressed support for ejected clergy.[113] Monmouth's declaration embodies the fullest account of suffering in any of the manifestoes, claiming that 'all that is *Sacred*, and *Civil*, or of regard amongst men of Piety, or Vertue [has been] Violated'. It went on to promise a longer remonstrance recounting the persecution, tyranny and grievances to which the people had been subject.[114] Sustained persecution provided the justification for all of these groups to plan or engage in rebellion, which in their minds was self-defense.[115] Better to 'dye like men, than live worse then slaves,' the northern insurgents proclaimed.[116]

The radical manifestoes also share several common themes, each of which is framed in the language of protest. Dislike of Stuart rule is one such theme, though expressions of it varied in intensity. In the time-honoured manner, the Dublin conspirators concentrated their attack on the king's evil advisors, specifically citing the Duke of Ormond.

The authors of the Hamilton manifesto took a similar position, averring that they fought to defend Charles 'in the preservation & defense of the true religion & liberties of the kingdome,' even while resisting his government.[117] The draft manifesto Ferguson read to Monmouth, Essex, Sidney and their cohorts likewise insisted that they meant no harm to Charles, seeking only to liberate him from his evil counsellors.[118] The Vennerites, denouncing 'the bloody Family of the *Stuarts*' and boasting that they would bind all monarchs in chains, and the Tong cabal, which called for the commonwealth's return, were obviously no supporters of the Stuarts, yet their focus was not those kings' shortcomings. In contrast, the Sanquhar, Lanark, Argyll and Monmouth declarations included intensely personal attacks on Charles and James, castigating both men as brutal tyrants. Accusing Charles of having committed thousands of misdemeanours against church and state, the Lanark testimony cited him for 'exceeding al measure devine or human, tyrannically obtruding his will as a law'.[119] Another theme common to the declarations was a protest against Catholicism, typically coupled with charges of arbitrary rule. This theme featured dramatically in the Vennerites' and the northern rebels' proclamations of an international crusade to extirpate popery, in the expression of concern among dissidents in Ireland over the return of estates to Catholics, in the Covenanters' heated attacks on popery and prelacy (echoed in Argyll's declaration), in the Monmouth manifesto's accusation that James was conspiring against Protestantism, and in Speke's blatant attempt to rally support for William by fanning anti-Catholic hatred. The radicals' language of protest encompassed both political and religious concerns.

The revolutionary manifestoes discussed in this chapter reflect the often disparate strands that can usefully, if anachronistically, be described as radical. This is not to suggest that these declarations represent the totality of radical expression in the late Stuart period. The Quakers, for example, are virtually excluded from the groups responsible for these declarations, notwithstanding the Tong cabal's claim that 'severall forces in the Countrey were already listed of *Fifth-monarchy-men*, *Anabaptists*, and fighting *Quakers*'.[120] Although a handful of Friends participated in the Monmouth rebellion,[121] none of them seems to have had any part in drafting the Duke's declaration. Many Baptists and Independents had no role in any of the groups that discussed or produced the revolutionary manifestoes, but their hostility to the established church and the penal laws mark them as radical because they challenged the regime's claim to possess the right to impose religious uniformity and its reliance on the established church as a fundamental bulwark of monarchy. Likewise, the republican tenets espoused by Algernon Sidney and his allies in the early 1680s, Essex and John Hampden, are radical because their implementation would have led to the overthrow of monarchy. Although I have not explored the full range of radical individuals and groups in the late Stuart period, I have suggested the usefulness of the term 'radical', demonstrated the variety of political, religious and socioeconomic views expressed in the manifestoes, and noted a deliberate sense of continuity between this period and preceding ones.[122]

NOTES

1 *Calendar of state papers, domestic, 1683–84*, 164–65. I would like to thank Glenn Burgess and Robert Zaller for their critiques of an earlier version of this chapter.

2 *Newes* 2 (10 September 1663), 16.

3 Public Record Office, London, State Papers (henceforth PRO SP) 29/81/53, 93; 29/277/179; 29/294/15; *Newes* 11 (12 November 1663), 83; PRO SP 29/408/171; 29/417/38; 29/421/131; 63/340, p. 38; *A collection of letters addressed by prelates and individuals of high rank in Scotland and by two bishops of Sodor and Man to Sancroft archbishop of Canterbury*, ed. William Nelson Clarke (Edinburgh, 1848), 83 (quoted).

4 PRO SP 29/427/20.

5 PRO SP 29/425/129.

6 British Library, Additional Manuscripts (henceforth BL, Add. MSS) 41,810, fol. 30r; PRO SP 29/84/103; 29/425/68, 111; 29/275/162; 29/417/38; 29/430/67.

7 PRO SP 29/92/77; 29/417/71; BL Add. MSS 41,810, fol. 56v.

8 PRO SP 31/1/19; *A poem to the Right Honourable Sir J[ames] B[utler] Knight* (London, 1682), [2]. Cf. PRO SP 29/417/176.

9 PRO SP 29/430/64; 29/431/21.

10 PRO SP 29/427/89.

11 Cumbria Record Office, Kendal, MS WD/Ry, Box 35, Privy Council to Sir Daniel Fleming, 4 July 1683.

12 PRO SP 29/432/17.

13 *Archives ou correspondance inédite de la Maison D'Orange-Nassau*, ed. G. Groen Van Prinsterer, 2nd ser., book 5, 1650–88 (Utrecht, 1861), 422.

14 PRO SP 29/421/196; *Collections of the Massachusetts Historical Society*, 8:214; *A poem (by way of elegie upon Mr Stephen Colledge* (1681), 2 (quoted).

15 PRO SP 29/430/67. Cf. Thomas Pomfret, *Subjection for conscience-sake asserted* (London, 1682), 2, 21.

16 Cf. PRO SP 29/430/35; SP 31/1/7.

17 PRO SP 29/424/149; 29/429/175 (quoted); 29/431/21; 29/436/134.
18 *The Tory-poets: A satyr* (London, 1682), sigs. A2v–A3r.
19 PRO SP 29/103/60 (quoted); John Pinney, *Letters of John Pinney 1679–1699*, ed. Geoffrey F. Nuttall (London, 1939), 36.
20 PRO SP 29/437/64.
21 *Calendar of state papers, domestic, 1678*, 168 (quoted); *Archives*, ed. Prinsterer, 489 (quoted); PRO SP 29/417/60 (quoted); 29/432/48; 29/433/137; SP 31/1/68 (quoted); SP 44/68, p. 309; BL, Add. MSS 41,812, fol. 20r; *A poem to the Right Honourable Sir J. B. Knight*, [1].
22 BL, Egerton MSS 2543, fol. 92r.
23 *The history of the Whiggish-plot* (London, 1684), 68; BL, Add. MSS 40,860, fols. 13r–14v, 20v, 21v, 34r. Anglesey's chaplain was the dissenter Benjamin Agas, and the earl was also close to Dr John Owen, the noted Independent.
24 Jonathan Scott, *Algernon Sidney and the Restoration crisis, 1677–1683* (Cambridge, 1991), 47.
25 For the intense disputes between Baptists and Quakers see T. L. Underwood, *Primitivism, radicalism, and the Lamb's War: The Baptist-Quaker conflict in seventeenth-century England* (New York, 1997).
26 Richard L. Greaves, *John Bunyan and English nonconformity* (London, 1992), 6–8.
27 *The last speech & behaviour of William late Lord Russel* (London, 1683), 2.
28 Conal Condren, *The language of politics in seventeenth-century England* (New York, 1994), 149, 168.
29 *Ibid.*, 151.
30 Cf. the title of a Tory tract: *A letter to a friend. shewing from Scripture, fathers and reason, how false that state-maxim is, royal authority is originally and radically in the people* (London, 1679).
31 For both men see Richard L. Greaves, *Dublin's merchant-Quaker: Anthony Sharp and the community of Friends, 1643–1707* (Stanford, 1998).
32 Cf. Condren, *The language of politics*, 153.
33 J. C. Davis, 'Radicalism in a traditional society: The evaluation of radical thought in the English Commonwealth, 1649–1660,' *History of political thought* 3 (1982): 202–3.
34 One of the more interesting examples of the belief in providence occurred when the Bothwell Bridge rebels thought Monmouth's arrival in Scotland was 'a most favorable providence'; in fact, the Duke used his army to quash the insurrection. BL, Add. MSS 23,244, fols. 14v–15r.
35 *A door of hope: Or, a call and declaration for the gathering together of the first ripe fruits unto the standard of our Lord King Jesus* [1661], 2.
36 Cf. Alexandra Walsham, *Providence in early modern England* (Oxford, 1999), 290–99.
37 Richard L. Greaves, *Deliver us from evil: The radical underground in Britain, 1660–1663* (New York, 1986); *Enemies under his feet: Radicals and nonconformists in Britain, 1664–1667* (Stanford, 1990); *Secrets of the kingdom: British radicals from the Popish plot to the revolution of 1688–1689* (Stanford, 1992).

38 *Journals of the House of Lords*, 11: 582. Cf. PRO SP 29/75/54.1.
39 PRO SP 63/314/24.
40 *Intelligencer* 35 (8 May 1665), 297.
41 *A poem to the Right Honourable Sir J. B. Knight*, [2]. Cf. Robert Hearne, *Loyalties severe summons to the bar of conscience* (London, 1681). A Whig poet turned the charge around, satirizing 'the *Good Old Tory Cause*,' linking it to 'the infantry of old Rebellious *Rome*.' *The Tory-poets*, sig. A2v, p. 1.
42 This essay refers to proposed declarations by Thomas Walcott (BL, Add. MSS 38,847, fol. 91r), two by Robert West's cabal (BL, Add. 38,847, fols. 96r-v, 102r, 104v; *Copies of the informations and original papers relating to the proof of the horrid conspiracy against the late king, his present Majesty, and the government*, 3rd ed. [London, 1685], 77), and one, probably by Robert Ferguson, that was read to Monmouth, Essex, Sidney, Russell, and their allies (Ford Lord Grey, *The secret history of the Rye-House plot: and of Monmouth's rebellion* [London, 1754], 39–40).
43 *A door of hope*, 4.
44 BL, Add. MSS 32,520, fol. 181r-v.
45 Greaves, *Secrets of the kingdom*, 335; anon., *The complaint of liberty & property against arbitrary government* (London, 1681), 2.
46 *A door of hope*, 3.
47 *Mercurius publicus* 1 (3–10 January 1661), 13; Evan Price, *Eye-salve for England* (London, 1667), 6.
48 Trinity College, Dublin (henceforth TCD), MSS 844, fols. 223r–224r.
49 National Library of Scotland (henceforth NLS), Wodrow MSS, Folio XXVI, fol. 141r.
50 Edinburgh University Library (henceforth EUL), MSS La.III.344, vol. 2, fol. 63r; Bodleian (henceforth Bodl.), Carte MSS 45, fols. 514r–515r; BL, Add. MSS 23,246, fol. 63v; London *Gazette* 2036 (21–25 May 1665).
51 BL, Add. MSS 38,847, fol. 91r; *The declaration of James Duke of Monmouth* (1685), bound in BL, Lansdowne MSS 1152), 2.
52 [Hugh Speke], *By His Highness William Henry, prince of Orange. A third declaration* (1688), 3–8.
53 *A door of hope*, 3, 5, 9–10; *Mercurius publicus* 1 (3–10) January 1661, 12; EUL, MSS La.II.89, fols. 137r–138r; BL, Add. MSS 33,770, fol. 38r.
54 TCD, MSS 844, fols. 223r–224r; NLS, Wodrow MSS, Folio XXVI, fol. 141r; BL, Add. MSS 38,656, fol. 80r; Add. MSS 23,125, fol. 198r; Bodl., Carte MSS 45, fols. 484v–485r, 514r–515r; EUL, MSS La.III..344, vol. 2, fol. 63r; EUL, MSS Dc.1.16, no. 22; Add. MSS 23,246, fol. 63r; EUL, MSS La.II.89, fols. 137r–138r; London *Gazette* 2036 (21–25 May 1685).
55 BL, Add. MSS 37,206, fol. 117r; Add. MSS 33,770, fol. 37v; NLS, Wodrow MSS, Folio XXVII, fol. 141r.
56 *A true and exact relation of the araignment, tryal, and condemnation of Tho. Tongue, George Philips, James Hind, Francis Stubbs, John Sallows, Nathaniel Gibbs* (London, 1662), 15; BL, Add. MSS 38,847, fol. 96v; *Copies of the informations*, 77; *Declaration of Monmouth*, 5.

57 PRO SP 29/66/41; *True and exact relation*, 6; Patrick Adair, *A true narrative of the rise and progress of the Presbyterian church in Ireland (1623–1670)*, ed. W. D. Killen (Belfast, 1866), 273; NLS, Wodrow MSS, Folio XXVII, fol. 141r; London *Gazette* 2036 (21–25 May 1685).

58 BL, Add. MSS 38,847, fol. 104v.

59 [William Hill], *A brief narrative of that stupendious tragedie* (London, 1662), 39; BL, Add. MSS 38,856, fol. 79v; Add. MSS 23,125, fol. 198r; London *Gazette* 2036 (21–25 May 1685).

60 BL, Add. MSS 38,856, fols. 79v–80r.

61 *True and exact relation*, 15; [Hill], *A brief narrative*, 34.

62 J. C. D. Clark, *Revolution and rebellion: State and society in England in the seventeenth and eighteenth centuries* (Cambridge, 1986), 110–11.

63 Mark Knights reaches a similar conclusion in his study of the London livery companies, noting that political, social, and economic considerations sometimes overrode religion without rendering the latter inconsequential. 'A city revolution: The remodelling of the London livery companies in the 1680s,' *English Historical Review* 112 (November 1997): 1177.

64 TCD, MSS 844, fols. 223r–224r; BL, Add. MSS 23,125, fol. 198r; Bodl., Carte 45, fols. 514r–515r; EUL, MSS La.II.89, fol. 136r-v; *Declaration of Monmouth*, 7.

65 Grey, *Secret history*, 39–40.

66 [Hill], *A brief narrative*, 14, 34; BL, Add. MSS 38,856, fol. 80r.

67 BL, Add. MSS 38,847, fol. 96r-v; *A door of hope*, 9; *Mercurius publicus* 1 (3–10 January 1661), 13; EUL, MSS Dc.1.16, no. 22; EUL, MSS La.II.89, fols. 137r–138r. Melissa Zook's denial of republican sentiment among all 'radical Whigs' is contradicted by the evidence. In early 1683 Essex, Sidney, and John Hampden favoured a commonwealth, and the West cabal wanted an executive so weak that the limitations on his power 'reduc'd the prince to a meer Duke of Venice'. Melinda S. Zook, *Radical Whigs and conspiratorial politics in late Stuart England* (University Park, PA, 1999), xix; Grey, *Secret history*, 42; BL, Add MSS 38,847, fol. 96v (quoted). For Sidney's republicanism see Scott, *Sidney and the Restoration crisis*, 111–12, 220–64.

68 *A door of hope*, 1; EUL, MSS Dc.1.16, no. 22; BL, Add. MSS 23,246, fol. 63r (quoted); EUL, MSS La.II.89, fols. 137r–138r; London *Gazette* 2036 (21–25 May 1685); *Declaration of Monmouth*, 2–7.

69 Samuel Parker, *History of his own time*, trans. Thomas Newlin (London, 1727), 62–63; BL, Add. MSS 33,770, fol. 5v.

70 BL, Add. MSS 23,125, fol. 198r.

71 EUL, MSS La.II.89, fol. 136r-v; *Declaration of Monmouth*, 7; [Speke], *Third declaration*, [3]-4.

72 Grey, *Secret history*, 39–40.

73 BL, Add. MSS 38,847, fol. 91r. The Cameronians advocated a similar view, insisting that 'the people that have all power radically in themselves may assume the fiduciall Trust', with the authority to vest it 'in the fountain till

the Lord choise such as he will establish'. EUL, MSS La.III.350, fol. 54r. On this point see also [Ferguson], *An impartial enquiry into the administration of affair's in England* (1683), 3–4, 28, 79–80.

74 BL, Add. MSS 38,847, fol. 96r-v. Cf. Gary S. De Krey, 'London radicals and revolutionary politics, 1675–1683', in *The politics of religion in Restoration England*, ed. Tim Harris, Paul Seaward, and Mark Goldie (Oxford, 1990), 154–55.

75 *Copies of the informations*, 76–77.

76 London *Gazette* 2036 (21–25 May 1685).

77 *Declaration of Monmouth*, 2 (quoted), 4–6; London *Gazette* 2036 (21–25 May 1685).

78 *A door of hope*, 10; BL, Add. MSS 38,856, fol. 79r; Add. MSS 33,770, fol. 5v.

79 PRO SP 29/66/41; *True and exact relation*, 10; Parker, *History*, 62.

80 EUL, MSS Dc.1.16, no. 22; EUL, MSS La.II.89, fols. 137r–138r.

81 BL, Add. MSS 38,847, fol. 102r.

82 *Declaration of Monmouth*, 3.

83 *A Door of Hope*, 5, 10; *Mercurius publicus* 1 (3–10 January 1661), 13.

84 EUL, MSS La.II.89, fols. 137r–138r.

85 *True and exact relation*, 10; PRO SP 29/66/41.

86 NLS, Wodrow MSS, Folio XXVII, fol. 141r.

87 BL, Add. MSS 38,856, fol. 79r.

88 *A door of hope*, 8, 10.

89 *Ibid.*, 5, 10.

90 Parker, *History*, 62–63; [Hill], *A brief narrative*, 34.

91 TCD, MSS 844, fols. 223r–224r; Thomas Carte, *An history of the life of James Duke of Ormonde*, 2 vols (London, 1736), 2:268; NLS, Wodrow MSS, Folio XXVII, fol. 141r.

92 *A door of hope*, 5; BL, Add. MSS 38,856, fol. 79r.

93 BL, Add. MSS 23,125, fol. 198r; Bodl., Carte MSS 45, fols. 514r–515r; EUL, MSS Dc.1.16, no. 22 (quoted).

94 EUL, MSS La.II.89, fols. 137r–138r.

95 BL, Add. MSS 38,847, fol. 104rv.

96 London *Gazette* 2036 (21–25 May 1685).

97 *Declaration of Monmouth*, 6–7.

98 BL, Add. MSS 23,246, fol. 63v.

99 *Declaration of Monmouth*, 2–3.

100 London *Gazette* 2036 (21–25 May 1685).

101 BL, Add. MSS 38,856, fol. 80r; EUL, MSS Dc.1.16, no. 22.

102 Parker, *History*, 62–63; BL, Add. MSS 38,856, fol. 79v; *True and exact relation*, 15; [Hill], *A brief narrative*, 34; EUL, MSS La.III.344, vol. 2, fol. 63r.

103 [James Heath], *A brief chronicle of all the chief actions so fatally falling out in these three kingdoms* (London, 1662), 66 [mspr. 56]; *A door of hope*, 3.

104 EUL, MSS Dc.1.16, no. 19; BL, Add. MSS 23,246, fol. 63v; EUL, MSS La.II.89, fols. 137r–138r.

105 Jonathan Clark has made the strongest case for the link between heterodoxy – Arianism, deism, and Socinianism – and political resistance. I am suggesting only that much of the radical activity and thought in late seventeenth-century Britain was grounded in Reformed Protestant principles rather than the heterodox 'isms'. J. C. D. Clark, *The language of liberty 1660–1832: Political discourse and social dynamics in the Anglo-American world* (Cambridge, 1994). I have sketched the importance of the Reformed Protestant tradition in 'Radicals, rights and revolution: British nonconformity and roots of the American experience', *Church history* 61 (June 1992): 151–68. For a contemporary recognition of the radical potential in Reformed thought, see the Tory Thomas Venn's contention that Calvinist principles were wholly inconsistent with monarchy. PRO SP 29/29/417/38. The Calvinist John Owen espoused a doctrine of active resistance in 1682; *A brief and impartial account of the nature of the Protestant religion* (London, 1682), 12. An early example (*c.* 1665) of the alleged link between deists and 'dangerous' people can be found in PRO SP 29/143/140.

106 BL, Add. MSS 23,125, fol. 198r.

107 Bodl., Carte MSS 32, fol. 294r; Carte MSS 45, fols. 514r–515r.

108 EUL, MSS Dc.1.16, no. 19; London *Gazette* 2036 (21–25 May 1685).

109 *Declaration of Monmouth*, 1–2.

110 EUL, MSS Dc.1.16, no. 19.

111 Bodl., Carte MSS 32, fol. 294r; NLS, Wodrow MSS, Folio XXVII, fol. 141r.

112 BL, Add. MSS 38,856, fol. 79r; Bodl., Carte MSS 45, fol. 514r.

113 London *Gazette* 2036 (21–25 May 1685).

114 *Declaration of Monmouth*, 3, 8.

115 NLS, Wodrow MSS, Folio XXVII, fol. 141r; BL, Add. MSS 38,856, fol. 79v; Add. MSS 23,125, fol. 198r; EUL, MSS La.III.344, vol. 2, fol. 63r; Bodl., Carte MSS 45, fols. 514r–515r; *Declaration of Monmouth*, 8. I am not suggesting that a disposition to embrace suffering, which was a fundamental part of the ethic of dissenters, especially the Quakers, was common to all radicals; most of those in Monmouth's circle were not so disposed. Richard L. Greaves, 'The "Great Persecution" reconsidered: The Irish Quakers and the ethic of suffering,' in *Protestant identities: Religion, society, and self-fashioning in Post-Reformation England*, ed. Muriel C. McClendon, Joseph P. Ward, and Michael MacDonald (Stanford, 1999), 212–13; Greaves, *John Bunyan and English nonconformity*, 169–83.

116 BL, Add. MSS 38,856, fol. 80r.

117 NLS, Wodrow MSS, Folio XXVII, fol. 141r; Bodl., Carte MSS 45, fols. 514r–515r (quoted).

118 Grey, *Secret history*, 39–40.

119 *A door of hope*, 8 (quoted); EUL, MSS Dc.1.16, no. 19; EUL, MSS La.II.89, fols. 137r–138r (quoted); London *Gazette* 2036 (21–25 May 1685); *Declaration of Monmouth, passim.*

120 *Kingdomes intelligencer* 50 (8–15 December 1662), 804–6.

121 Richard L. Greaves, 'Shattered expectations? George Fox, the Quakers, and the Restoration state, 1660–1685,' *Albion* 24 (Summer 1992): 256–57.

122 For radicals in the decades following the revolution of 1688–1689, see Gary Stuart De Krey, *A fractured society: The politics of London in the first age of party 1688–1715* (Oxford, 1985), 7–8, 49–58, 63–66, 177–91.

CHAPTER 5

The Divine Creature and the Female Citizen: Manners, Religion, and the Two Rights Strategies in Mary Wollstonecraft's Vindications

Gregory Claeys

This paper challenges the common view that Wollstonecraft extends her conception of rights from men to women in her evolution from the *Vindication of the Rights of Men* (1790) to the *Vindication of the Rights of Woman* (1792). Instead, it argues, Wollstonecraft is primarily concerned in both texts not with rights but with manners, and it is this concern which permits her most compelling accomplishment: the effective demolition of any fixed boundary between a male 'public' and a female 'private' or domestic sphere. Wollstonecraft's concept of rights, in fact, takes two forms in the second 'Vindication', and her most radical rights argument is not elaborated in relation to her account of manners, but in the context of her much-neglected religious beliefs.

Few any longer read Mary Wollstonecraft's so-called first 'Vindication', the *Vindication of the Rights of Men*. Produced hastily in a few short weeks at the end of 1790, it glimpsed fleeting fame as the first response to Burke's *Reflections on the Revolution in France*, and sufficient critical acclaim to offer a useful fillip to its author's literary career. With few internal divisions or pauses, the tract was sent to the printers sheet by sheet with the ink barely dry, but its forceful, occasionally beautiful style succeeded in scoring a few points off Burke. But it was soon eclipsed by Thomas Paine's *Rights of Man* (1791–2), James Mackintosh's *Vindiciae Gallicae* (1792) and Godwin's *Enquiry Concerning Political Justice* (1793), which became and remain far better known radical responses to Burke and the revolution debate generally.

Yet the text, of course, remains of interest less in itself than in relation to the more famous second 'Vindication', the *Vindication of the Rights of Women* (1792), which over thirty years before William Thompson and Anna Wheeler's *Appeal of One-Half the Human Race* (1824) and nearly eighty before J. S. Mill and Harriet Taylor Mill's *The Subjection of*

Women (1869), first set forth the principles which became central to the modern women's movement, though its demands seem remarkably modest today. Nonetheless the development of Wollstonecraft's thought from the first to the second 'Vindication' has rarely been examined carefully; and I propose here to offer a re-reading of the relationship between the two texts as a means of explaining Wollstonecraft's central themes and assessing why, despite its title, most of the second 'Vindication' seems to have far more to do with 'manners' than with 'rights' per se.

Until fairly recently Wollstonecraft was rarely located within histories of the critique of manners in this period.[1] But the 'main argument' of the second 'Vindication', as Wollstonecraft herself expresses it, is that those who support the 'cause of virtue' must permit women to become educated to be the companion of man. Failure to do so will result in women halting 'the progress of knowledge and virtue'.[2] This was a striking argument in itself for its time. What is most radical in Wollstonecraft's text, however, particularly in light of the development of later feminist thought, is the assertion that private morality is the chief source of public virtue, and that male tyranny in the domestic sphere thus inhibits public morality, notably by imposing an education in tyrannical principles upon children who are destined to become citizens under what was widely trumpeted as the most free constitution in the world.

Nonetheless, it is paradoxical that it is precisely where Wollstonecraft seems to be at her most *radical*, in eroding a crucial distinction between public and private forms of virtue, that she also appears in some respects most *traditional*, in supporting the view that marriage and motherhood remain the chief occupation and fulfilment for most women. Moreover, it was Wollstonecraft's *second* argument about rights, derived from a notion of divine intention, which seems to be most traditional and alien to more secular modern readers, yet which was in fact far more radical in its implications. This concept of equality, which was, we will see, not gendered, pointed towards a much more all-encompassing egalitarianism by arguing that the Creator did not intend any difference in character to exist between men and women. Seen from this perspective, Wollstonecraft's much-neglected religious views – whose sources and development cannot be explored here – were not tangential to, but *central* to the main arguments of the *Vindication of the Rights of Woman*.[3] In order to see how the tension between these two rights claims develops, we must first briefly recall the arguments of the first 'Vindication'.

Wollstonecraft's starting point in the *Vindication of the Rights of Men* (1790) is the 'rights of humanity', or 'the rights of men and the liberty of reason'.[4] But while she early on introduces the theme of rights, Wollstonecraft in fact is more concerned to juxtapose two notions of manners, one, challenging the status quo, based on reason; the other, already widely accepted as the dominant role model for female behaviour, unduly fixated on sensibility. Burke's reaction to the French Revolution, and his effusive affection for the *ancien régime* and the trappings of aristocracy, chivalry and courtly life, Wollstonecraft claims, succumb to the sensibility and compassion which are the grand mania of the day. Burke's 'pampered sensibility', the fumes of his emotionalism rising to 'dispel the sober suggestions of reason', prevents him from recognizing the cause of justice as embodied in the French Revolution.[5] But justice, Wollstonecraft says, now entails the defence of 'such a degree of liberty, civil and religious, as is compatible with the liberty of every other individual with whom he is united in a social compact, and the continued existence of that compact'. This liberty, everywhere fenced in by 'the demon of property', must be recognized by all those who build their morality and religion on 'the attributes of God'.[6] Burke, by contrast, reverences not reason, but only 'the rust of antiquity . . . the unnatural customs, which ignorance and mistaken self-interest have consolidated'. Those who uphold similar principles, the few who tyrannize over the many, are not cultivated as a result of their education, but warped by its tendency, according to the dictates of European civilization, to refine 'the manners at the expence of morals, by making sentiments and opinions current in conversation that have no root in the heart, or weight in the cooler resolves of the mind'.[7] We see quite early on, thus, that Wollstonecraft's main strategy concerns a juxtaposition of one form of manners, or more properly morals, based on sincerity, to the 'courtly insincerity' and 'politeness' which, by merely making 'sport with truth', demand disguising our sentiments and perpetrating an ethos of falsehood throughout social relations.[8]

It is usually recognized that this is a common radical and 'dissenting' claim against the ruling classes and courtly culture; a plea for sincerity would play a crucial role, with a similar aim, in Godwin's *Enquiry Concerning Political Justice* (1793) as well.[9] The ideal of politeness under attack was a fairly recent invention. Since the end of the seventeenth century, writers like Shaftesbury, Addison, Steele and Hume had attempted to construct a new model of commercial and increasingly urban manners which once and for all time could dispel the myth of the supposed, much vaunted, superiority of ancient patriotism, and especially the civic devotion of the Greek and Roman republicans, by comparison with the more refined, self-indulgent, private but sociable manners of the moderns.[10] In the second half of the eighteenth century David Hume, most notably, had attempted to defend as intrinsic to the achievements of commercial society a notion of politeness which was partly modelled on courtly culture, while avoiding what Hume regarded as its extremes of 'affectation and foppery, disguise and insincerity'. Hume asserted that modern politeness, whose essence was a 'mutual deference or civility, which leads us to resign our own inclinations to those of our companion, and to curb and conceal that presumption and arrogance so natural to the human mind', owed its origins to gallantry. This form of civility arose in particular where a chain of dependency from prince to peasant existed, which provoked 'in every one an inclination to please his superiors, and to form himself upon those models which are most acceptable to people of condition and education'. Its great social advantage lay in the suppression of natural feelings and affectation of polite deference and respect 'which civility obliges us to express or counterfeit towards the persons with whom we converse'. Gallantry, Hume assumed, tended to correct the gross vices between the sexes, and by comparison with ancients, who left their women at home, and the barbarians, who simply enslaved them, men now compensated for their physical superiority over women by deference and generosity. Indeed Hume was even willing to concede that men would themselves find their manners softened, polished and refined by the company of virtuous women. It was for these reasons, among others, that Hume proclaimed the age of refinement to be both the happiest and most virtuous in history, with the increasing sociability and, even more, *humanity*, incident to urban life compensating sufficiently for the growing individualism of commercial societies. In Hume's account of manners, politeness in an urban context thus bears much of the weight which would otherwise fall on a theory of justice, morality and civic duty. For Hume is persuaded that greater humanity results from the social intercourse of commercial society than from that of any preceding social stage.[11]

Yet this account of the improved treatment of women by men, while it for Hume and others demonstrated the palpable superiority of modern civilization, was still reliant upon an ideal of gallantry to govern men's behaviour towards women, and thus fell far short of Wollstonecraft's demands. These echoed similar claims by John Brown, James Burgh (whose widow Wollstonecraft had befriended) and other republican writers in seeking a more austere, stoic and puritanical reformation of manners against the general trend towards libertinism which is now usually regarded as characterizing relations between the sexes from the Restoration until about 1800.[12] From the start of her career as a writer,

Wollstonecraft had developed the theme of moral reform through piety. It was central to her first published work, *Thoughts on the Education of Daughters* (1787), which warns of the refinement of female manners unchecked by religious sentiment.[13] It re-appears in some of the works she translated for Joseph Johnson, such as *Young Grandison. A Series of Letters from Young Persons to Their Friends* (2 vols, 1790). It looms large in her first novel, *Mary: A Fiction* (1788), with its injunctions to Christian virtue to 'govern the wayward feelings and impulses of the heart'.[14] It also plays a role in her occasional essays for Johnson's *Analytical Review.* One such piece reminded readers that God was 'the source of all perfection';[15] while another condemned that 'sickly feminine sensibility' which was too often the product of female education in the period, and derided female novelists for poisoning 'the minds of their sex, by strengthening a male prejudice that makes women systematically weak'.[16] A third insisted that education need treat men and women similarly, there being no 'characteristic difference' between them.[17]

Such demands were also echoed in more conservative, and especially evangelical quarters, by a major campaign against aristocratic profligacy led by Hannah More, whose *Thoughts on the Importance of the Manners of the Great to General Society* appeared in 1788, which attacked, amongst other things, 'The substitution of the word *gallantry* for that crime which stabs domestic happiness and conjugal virtue' [adultery], terming this 'one of the most dangerous of all the modern abuses of language'.[18] The efforts of William Wilberforce, too, were crucial in curbing excessive drinking, gambling and philandering amongst the upper classes over the course of the next century. Wilberforce's *A Practical View of the Prevailing Religious System of Professed Christians in the Higher and Middle Classes in This Country Contrasted With Real Christianity* (1797) appeared at the same time as the furore over Godwin's ruthlessly honest *Memoir* of Wollstonecraft, ensuring that her early ideals were forgotten amidst the censorious abuse heaped upon her conduct during much of the 1790s.[19] And even at the level of high theory, William Paley, whose *Moral and Political Philosophy* (1790) became a standard text for educated discussion of ethical issues over the next several generations, reminded readers of the perils of fornication, seduction and adultery, and condemned 'All behaviour which is designed, or which knowingly tends to captivate the affection of a married woman' as 'a barbarous intrusion upon the peace and virtue of a family'.[20]

There was thus some common ground between Wollstonecraft and the evangelicals early in the decade. For Wollstonecraft, who quotes

Hume in this context and clearly frames him as a target, gallantry was merely a 'cold unmeaning intercourse . . . this vestige of gothic manners'.[21] Polite culture masks an inequality of ranks which inhibits 'true happiness', for the latter derives solely 'from the friendship and intimacy which can only be enjoyed by equals'.[22] It is bonded to that arrogance of the propertied which prevents them from looking for natural rights 'which men inherit at their birth, as rational creatures', and which leads them to concede, with Burke, the value only of precedent, of the rights of the Englishman instead of those of the human being, of the virtues of the citizen rather than those inspired by the image of God.[23] Such prejudices are typical of 'the vulgar', by whom Wollstonecraft means both the rich and the poor, all of whom are mostly 'the creatures of habit and impulse', the rich from laziness and lack of mental exercise, the poor from necessity and inadequate education. Incapable of higher thought, the rich in particular achieve at the most Burke's 'Gothic affability', a form of politeness which is a mere substitute for true humanity and which is, other radical Whigs like James Mackintosh agreed, a reversion on Burke's part to an earlier, pre-commercial moral ideal.[24] Those beneath them, particularly the middle classes, in turn multiply their vices by 'apeing the manners of the great'.[25] Such arrogance, Wollstonecraft charges, prevents Burke from recognizing the inhumanity of the game laws and impressment, and leads him to turn a blind eye to the corruption of Crown and government. Reverence for property, in particular, limits benevolence within the family, and encourages the brutal treatment of children. Daughters suffer 'legal prostitution' in arranged marriages, after flirtatious coquetishness, in return for some share of the wealth, while younger sons are sacrificed to the elder heir. Most, prevented from early marriages by parental will, descend into immorality and weaken both mind and body thereby. Here is the well of morality first poisoned, although 'natural parental affection' was meant to be 'the first source of civilisation'.[26]

Inequality of property thus undermines family morality as well as producing 'an unmanly servility, most inimical to true dignity of character'.[27] Luxury, 'effeminacy' (which like most republican writers, Wollstonecraft equates with personal weakness and civic inadequacy), vice and idleness pervade the world of wealth. The ethos of romance and chivalry, the spiritual by-product of aristocracy, are now, however, on the wane, for the passions underlying them are slowly being dispelled by the progress of reason. Burke claimed that Britain could make no progress in morals, politics and the idea of liberty, and contended that morality originated in 'untaught feelings'. Wollstonecraft instead forces the point that virtue derives from the understanding, is based in justice and is 'concentrated by universal love'. This is in turn underpinned by a fear of as well as a reverence of God which aids self-reverence, and which indeed can alone promote it.[28] Wollstonecraft follows with what most modern readers may treat as a digression on the dangers of religious establishments, the immorality of tithes and of the corruption of the clergy by their association with the nobility. In fact these religious themes, which demonstrate how far Wollstonecraft had strayed from the Anglicanism of her upbringing towards the Dissent of her London radical friends, would remain vital to her perspective in the second 'Vindication'. Indeed, they would provide Wollstonecraft with her most powerful argument in favour of sexual equality.

So far we have seen that most of Wollstonecraft's concentration in the first half of the *Vindication of the Rights of Men* is upon the roots of morality rather than upon rights *per se*. Moral behaviour, in turn, rests upon the capacity for reason. Wollstonecraft's central contention in this respect is that since 'those men who are obliged to exercise their reason have the most reason', these are 'the persons pointed out by Nature to direct the society of which they make a part'. Talents are not hereditary, and this disqualifies from rule 'the profligates of rank, emasculated by hereditary effeminacy'. This is by no means an unqualified republican idea. Wollstonecraft concedes the point (in reference to the members of the French National Assembly) that the founders of the Roman state, for example, had only been partially civilized, and had sometimes refined the manners, but rarely the morals, of their people. (She otherwise commends 'that enthusiastic flame which in Greece and Rome consumed every sordid passion'.) What Wollstonecraft instead seeks is a moral meritocracy, 'everything respectable in talents', which is clearly not represented in the British House of Commons. Nor could it be, for few there have laboured for their knowledge, much less their bread, and hence they know not that 'every thing valuable must be the fruit of laborious exertions'.[29]

The improvement in morality Wollstonecraft seeks will, she claims, result only from an increase in liberty, 'the mother of all virtue', by which she means in part greater social equality of the type she often associated with the United States. This helps her to justify the seizure of church lands in France. But it must also result from increased humanity, though less from benevolence than from the recognition of just rights, particularly the right of the poor to 'more comfort than they at present enjoy', which she proposes might be aided by, for example, dividing great estates.[30] Yet by and large the practical politics of the first 'Vindication' are extraordinarily moderate. Despite her own friendship with Richard Price, the leading British target of the *Reflections*, Wollstonecraft surprisingly even concedes to Burke, 'for a moment . . . that Dr Price's political opinions are Utopian reveries'. Her sympathies here, despite the invocation of the rights of man, do not in all matters lie with the 'democratists'.[31] For here, among the majority, is not where morality and the sources of enlightenment should be sought. For while the rich have 'polished vices', insincerity, the debauchery of luxurious ease, the poor are 'scarcely above the brutes', debauched not by riches and power but the crushing burden of life at the subsistence level.[32]

Let us now turn to the arguments of the second 'Vindication'. Like the first, it is as much concerned with manners as rights, proclaiming, famously, that 'it is time to effect a revolution in female manners'.[33] Its chief target is those, like Rousseau, who have sought to foist, by educational dogma as well as force, what Wollstonecraft regards as an inferior character upon the female sex, in order to bolster the rule of a 'male aristocracy'. The barrier to the progress of morality which Wollstonecraft now is concerned to assail, however, is less the overly deferential respect paid to rank and custom which Burke had commended, than tyranny within the family. This inhibits, by coercion, the freedom of women and thus the wisdom and virtue of both sexes. This is particularly the case because women who are insufficiently educated cannot foster the love of mankind in their families which needs to be passed on to their children, both because they are not active citizens, and because of the overbearing authority of the husband and father. Wollstonecraft's crucial assumption here is that 'every family might . . . be called a state', whose morality, when 'polluted in the national reservoir, sends of streams of vice to corrupt the constituent parts of the body politic'. The principles of rule within the family are thus exactly analogous to those in society at large. But as a result, the pestiferous principles of divine right and patriarchalism, seemingly vanquished by the events of 1688, have in fact found their last great secure refuge hidden in the bastion of the family, where children are normally raised in despotic principles of unconditional obedience and blind respect whose suitability to *public* life was now widely dismissed by most. This theme had been hinted at in the *Vindication of the Rights of Men*, where Wollstonecraft had suggested that 'the character of a master of a family, a husband, and a father, forms the citizen imperceptibly, by producing a sober manliness of thought, and orderly behaviour'.[34] But this notion is now expanded into a full-scale theory of the relations between public and private morality. Wollstonecraft's starting point is well-known, but nonetheless worth quoting once again:

> Contending for the rights of woman, my main argument is built on this simple principle, that if she be not prepared by education to become the companion of man, she will stop the progress of knowledge and virtue; for truth must be common to all, or it will be inefficacious with respect to its influence on general practice. And how can woman be expected to co-operate unless she know why she ought to be virtuous? unless freedom strengthen her reason until she comprehend her duty, and see in what manner it is connected with her real good? If children are to be educated to understand the true principle of patriotism, their mother must be a patriot; and the love of mankind, from which an orderly train of virtues spring, can only be produced by considering the moral and civil interest of mankind, but the education and situation of woman, at present, shuts her out from such investigations.[35]

Private morality thus subverts the public, for children can themselves scarcely become good citizens in these circumstances. Moreover, the reverse was also true, for as Wollstonecraft would emphasize elsewhere, 'the private duty of any member of society must be very imperfectly performed when not connected with the general good'.[36]

Important as this conception is in foreshadowing later feminist discussions of the public/private dichotomy, the rights claimed for women here are nonetheless contingent and limited in two crucial ways. Firstly, they depend on a wider theory of the progress of reason and virtue and the repression of passion. That is, Wollstonecraft assumes that public virtue, and a claim for the extension of citizenship and greater social equality, are crucial elements in a necessary reform of public life and politics in order to halt the slide towards oligarchy and despotism, themes in this period which are now widely associated with a broadly 'republican' world-view.[37] But it is also quintessentially Christian, since here, for Wollstonecraft, as in the first 'Vindication', the character of God provides 'the only solid foundation for morality'.

Indeed, we can now appreciate that the importance of her religious mission to Wollstonecraft in the second 'Vindication' has been much underestimated. For Wollstonecraft even demands of her female readers that they recite a sort of (admittedly latitudinarian) catechism of belief in one God, powerful and wise, who has ordered all harmoniously.[38] Moreover, women's claims to equal rights are also contingent on the social role of education and the rearing of children, which Wollstonecraft concedes is 'the peculiar destiny of woman', and which gives them special claims vis-à-vis the advancement of citizenship. This view leads

Wollstonecraft to give stress to the improved performance of women's traditional roles which would result if they were freed from male tyranny. 'The conclusion I wish to draw, is obvious', writes Wollstonecraft: 'make women rational creatures, and free citizens, and they will quickly become good wives, and mothers'. Now, therefore, women languished as merely inferior mothers and housekeepers. 'Women cannot be confined to merely domestic pursuits', Wollstonecraft elsewhere notes, because 'they will not fulfill family duties, unless their minds take a wider range'.[39] Wollstonecraft here thus claims that women themselves have a right to be educated based on the wider social good which would result from their improved role as family members, rather than a right based in their inherent status as rational creatures. Though she argues that the aim of all education is 'to enable the individual to attain such habits of virtue as will render it independent', the basis for proclaiming this right is one of utility and function, namely women's contribution to education and to public virtue, rather than a claim based on the innate capabilities of women.[40] And this right in turn presumes that they can renounce the prevailing notion of the ideal character of womanhood, forced upon them by the lack of recognition of their rights, in order to practice greater modesty, chastity, virtue and rationality. In this sense marriage remains 'the foundation of almost every social virtue'. Earning one's own subsistence might still be 'the true definition of independence'. But it is not an ideal to which most women would be able to aspire.[41] Instead, women's domestic roles are reinforced, though these functions themselves, for Wollstonecraft, will clearly be considerably more pleasurable, and meaningful, to exercise.

The theme of female virtue and character thereafter becomes central to the second 'Vindication', which considers women in the middle and upper social ranks in particular (though sometimes Wollstonecraft's generalizations appear to apply to all women). The general question of woman's character had been touched on, though tangentially, in the first 'Vindication'. Here Wollstonecraft had challenged Burke's view of women, which seemingly insisted 'that *littleness* and *weakness* are the very essence of beauty; and that the Supreme Being, in giving women beauty in the most supereminent degree, seemed to command them, by the powerful voice of Nature, not to cultivate the moral virtues that might chance to excite respect'. Here, too, Wollstonecraft had condemned the resulting 'laxity of morals in the female world', which resulted when women were forced to coquet themselves in order to counterbalance male hostility to their just claims, and insisted that true virtue could flourish 'only among equals'.[42]

But among the shifts in argument we witness in the *Vindication of the Rights of Woman*, a religious argument now emerges as central to a new rights claim offered by Wollstonecraft. Whatever biological differences there are between men and women, both are 'human creatures' whose capacities are regulated by 'the governing passion implanted in us by the Author of all good, to call forth and strengthen the faculties of each individual'. For 'the grand end of existence' is 'the attainment of virtue', and 'the nature of reason must be the same in all, if it be an emanation of divinity'. If women lack souls, or are otherwise designated as inferior to men on theological grounds, this argument will be difficult to make, for Wollstonecraft's second rights claim is based not on function, but on nature. Wollstonecraft's God, the grand creator of nature, the instiller of the 'sublime and the amiable' (in Godwin's description), was 'not less amiable, generous, and kind, than great, wise and exalted',[43] far too wise, indeed, to have ever intended excluding half the human race from his bountiful legacy.

By contrast to this divinely-guided natural ideal, however, women's character now derives from circumstances, not innate propensity. Women are now educated to be sweet, docile, delicate, dependent and full of sensibility, their whole beings straining to be fulfilled in marriage. But for Wollstonecraft, 'elegance is inferior to virtue . . . the first object of laudable ambition is to obtain a character as a human being'.[44] Clearly the idea of virtue, and the antitheses of 'manners' and 'morality', often juxtaposed in the first 'Vindication', are also central here.[45]

Much of the second 'Vindication' in fact covers similar ground as the first. We find here the same general critique of Britain's 'preposterous distinctions of rank, which render civilization a curse, by dividing the world between voluptuous tyrants and cunning envious dependents'. Derided, again, is an overly-respectful attitude towards property: riches and honours prevent men from cultivating their understanding, and virtue, defined in terms of independence, 'the grand blessing of life, the basis of every virtue', is now extended to encompass women's virtue in turn, in a comprehensive widening of oppositional, and particularly republican, ideology.[46] Condemned, too, is the system of British political patronage, prone to multiplying 'dependents and contriving taxes which grind the poor to pamper the rich'.[47] An overly contrived sensibility which excites the emotions and subverts reason, virtue and 'austerity of behaviour' is again the target, and one solution again proferred is that liberty generally diffused produces virtue and wisdom, and that the cause of progress requires greater social equality; indeed any improvement in women's position is contingent upon increasing equality, which implies that women must become more independent of men just as the poor must of their masters.[48] As in the first 'Vindication', Wollstonecraft here also contrasts the character of the rich to that of the middling ranks, who are paid homage as possessing the 'most virtue and abilities', often because they place education ahead of marriage for money. Nonetheless, Wollstonecraft also concedes, rather unusually, given her readership, that most female virtue is to be found in 'low life', where greater heroism emerges in the face of true adversity and where the maxim she elsewhere invokes, that 'pleasure is the business of woman's life, according to the present modification of society', hardly applies.[49] Some of the standard radical themes of the era also crop up, such as an opposition to a standing army and the vices of an established clergy.

But Wollstonecraft's main assault here is clearly on the distinction between 'a supposed sexual character' and a 'human character', her chief emphasis being that women are educated to be weak and submissive, and have foisted upon them these manners, the insincere semblance of authentic being, a mere role, which is to be contrasted to true morality.[50] Crucial here is the parallel Wollstonecraft establishes between the character of women and that of the wealthy, who, like women, says Wollstonecraft, quoting Adam Smith, do little labour, engage in little abstract thought and are overly sentimental: 'women in general, as well as the rich of both sexes, have acquired all the follies and vices of civilization, and missed all the useful fruits'. Clearly this parallel, the most important analogy in the second 'Vindication', is not meant to apply to all women, but to Wollstonecraft's chief audience, the middle and upper classes, where 'morality is very insidiously undermined, in the female world, by the attention being turned to the shew instead of the substance'. Nonetheless, it is here, and in the character of the courtier, whose 'artificial mode of behaviour' is equally condemned by Wollstonecraft, that we see most clearly the extension of a wider eighteenth century radical critique of corruption in the 'Vindication' to the treatment of women in British society.[51] In this regard, the analogy Wollstonecraft draws between the character of a standing army and that of women is also important, however: in both, manners are learned before morals, and largely from the same source: the puffed-up ideal of gallantry. Instead, Wollstonecraft argues, both men and women should base their behaviour upon 'the character of the Supreme Being', the wise, the good and potentially perfect.[52] Both sexes should eschew the effects of luxury, which leads men to indulge their appetites more than women, and which engenders, through the debauched inclinations of men, the chief cause of female depravity and a means of subverting public morals. Both should recognize that one set of virtues, 'chastity, modesty, public spirit, and all the noble train of virtues, on which social virtue and happiness are built, should be understood and cultivated by all mankind'.[53]

Thus, Wollstonecraft insists, in a profound critique of radical as well as more traditional forms of political thought, there is no point in searching, with philosophers, for public virtue solely outside the relations of fathers, husbands, wives and mothers, in the citizen's willingness to place public duty before private interest and to sacrifice the particular to the general will. No distinctively public sphere of this sort exists, for the distinction between a female domestic sphere and a male political sphere has been burst asunder: 'public spirit must be nurtured by private virtue, or it will resemble the factitious sentiment which makes women careful to preserve their reputation, and men their honour'. This, then must be the task of the legislator, who should endeavour 'to make it the interest of each individual to be virtuous; and thus private virtue becoming the cement of public happiness, an orderly whole is consolidated by the tendency of all parts towards a common centre'. But this in turn requires, if women's private virtue is to become a 'public benefit', that they 'have a civil existence in the state, married or single'. There is thus a reciprocal relationship between public and private virtue. The second 'Vindication' concludes, with explosive implications for traditional concepts of political virtue and the public sphere, that

> To render women truly useful members of society, I argued that they should be led, by having their understandings cultivated on a large scale, to acquire a rational affection for their country, founded on knowledge, because it is obvious that we are little interested about what we do not understand. And to render this general knowledge of due importance, I have endeavoured to shew that private duties are never properly fulfilled unless the understanding enlarges the heart; and that public virtue is only an aggregate of private.[54]

Much of the plea of the second 'Vindication' is thus cast in the shape of a paean to the advantages of a 'revolution in female manners'. Better educated women would make better friends and wives, as well as lending dignity to single life. Men would be released from slavery to their appetites, and marriages would flow from affection alone. Children would be better educated, and less blindly obedient once an overly selfish respect for property had been removed. The effects of circumstances on character are thus the same for women as for men; in both, fashion, delicacy and sensibility corrupt, debase and foster dependence. But given equal opportunity, women can avoid false notions of beauty and delicacy, and instead, giving less stress to politeness, cultivate sincerity and humanity. Yet feminists have often been exasperated by the limits of this vision. To Wollstonecraft, marriage would become 'the foundation of almost every social virtue', with passion subsiding into friendship and greater modesty prevailing with both sexes.[55] But we must recall that Wollstonecraft regarded as her 'main argument' the value of domestic but truly virtuous and more independent women to the general cause of social virtue. As Ursula Vogel has stressed, Wollstonecraft's idea of domestic virtue thus forms an integral part of her moral critique of a civilized society corrupted by wealth and privilege'.[56] Family and public life are nearly analogous, and this is a substantial departure from the republican and oppositional tradition out of which Wollstonecraft largely emerges, which while it clearly also supported the cause of private morality, did so on a broadly patriarchalist foundation. Otherwise, while women are to become citizens, to emerge into the harsh light of the public from the shadows of the private sphere, they remain within a more or less traditional conception of the sexual division of labour, and are still assigned a specialized, distinctive sphere of competence, which some have associated with a romantic notion of a distinctive female nature.[57] Women have certainly gained greater autonomy here, but their liberation is far from complete. Instead, a stronger plea for independence is instead derived from a subordinate argument in the text itself, which is based on Wollstonecraft's idea of God's design in creating the human species.

Clearly there is thus some conflict between the two types of rights claims Wollstonecraft puts forward. Where the rights of women are subordinated to the cause of the progress of virtue, and it is the reformation of women's manners which is of crucial importance, women's pleas are set within a traditional context of the nuclear family, where their role as agents of education is paramount; and in a largely republican image of society, where the aim of creating virtuous citizens is fundamental. Women here are far from equal with men; for they are still separated by function, if at least eventually considerably nearer equal than they had been in the past. In Wollstonecraft's second rights claim, however, based on theological premises, the intent of the Deity in creating humanity implies that women become as independent as possible, 'the grand end of their exertions' being to unfold their own faculties and acquire the dignity of conscious virtue'.[58] Here no such subordination to male-dominated systems of power (or theories of politics) is evident.

Like the best-known republican of the era, Thomas Paine, – a man of 'strong sense' in Wollstonecraft's view [59] – who derived subsequent rights claims from the notion that God had created human beings in his image,[60] Wollstonecraft also rests her most radical argument on divine intention, indeed upon the same supposition about the Creation. As a mere citizen, woman remained tied to a specialized function dictated by the nature of citizenship, for her special contribution to the public good was the education of virtuous youth. Only as a divine creature, destined to reason exactly like the male of the species, is she truly equal and free, no longer shackled by function. But Paine, and the overwhelming majority of radical and republican writers in this period, had not extended such arguments to women as such, but, while condemning unchastity as a vicious aspect of aristocratic culture, often lent their weight to ideas of dual, unequal natures. Thus Thomas Christie, in his *Letters on the Revolution of France* (1791), commended the new French government for 'not raising [women] out of their natural sphere; in not involving them in the cares and anxieties of State affairs, to which neither their frame nor their minds are adapted' by allowing women to succeed to the throne.[61] Thus Capel Lofft, too, while dismissing a 'frivolous and insulting Gallantry', even upheld an idealized notion of chivalry, indeed insisting that a republican form of government would be most likely to restore 'not its Pomp indeed, but its true Value: its Simplicity, its Purity, and Elevation'.[62] Paine, while deriding Burke's famous claim that '*The age of chivalry is gone! [and] The glory of Europe is extinguished for ever!*' had said little about the implications of such changes for women.[63] The few reformers we know of this period who apparently adopted feminist ideas, such as the physician William Hodgson, active in the London Corresponding Society, who planned to publish a work entitled *Proposals, for Publishing by Subscription, A Treatise Called the Female Citizen: or, A Historical, Political, and Philosophical Enquiry into the Rights of Women*, (?1796), did not advance far in such endeavours. The reaction against the cause of the rights of man was alone sufficient to ensure this after 1793.

CONCLUSION

The primary context for understanding both 'Vindications' is a late eighteenth-century debate about improving manners in which Wollstonecraft builds upon three main premises: that manners in modern societies have become 'factitious and corrupt', and are usually an inferior and mere 'painted substitute for morals';[64] that true morals are derived from a combination of republican and Christian sources; and that women inhibit the cause of virtue generally by having a character forced upon them which is inimical to its practice. Another way of phrasing this is that this character is imposed by the failure to recognize women's rights, but I have emphasized here that in fact an emphasis on rights runs a distant second in Wollstonecraft's efforts to establish her case. In fact Wollstonecraft's conception of rights remains much the same in both 'Vindications', being based on the notion that all have a right to independence granted by God. In this sense the second 'Vindication' does not extend the theory of rights of the first 'Vindication', as is usually assumed, though Wollstonecraft's emphasis on the right of women to independence is clearly stronger, and comprises also a right to education based on the social and political consequences, especially increased patriotism, which would ensue. Instead, it is the critique of manners which is extended, and the analogy between public and private morality, which in this form goes well beyond republican writers, most of whom (even including the feminist historian Catherine Macaulay, a role model for Wollstonecraft) had not stressed women's rights in this way.

NOTES

1 An exception is Mitzi Meyers, 'Reform or Ruin: 'A Revolution in Female Manners'', in Harry Payne, ed., *Studies in Eighteenth Century Culture*, 11 (1982), pp. 199–216, which stresses (203) the proximity of some of Wollstonecraft's views and those of, for example, the evangelical reformer Hannah More. On the general context, see especially Maurice J. Quinlan. *Victorian Prelude. A History of English Manners 1700–1800* (New York, Columbia University Press, 1941), pp. 40–102, Muriel Jaeger. *Before Victoria. Changing Standards & Behaviour* (Chatto & Windus, 1956), pp. 118–38, Joanna Innes, 'Politics and Morals: The Reformation of Manners Movement in Late Eighteenth-Century England', in Eckhart Hellmuth, ed. *The Transformation of Political Culture. England and Germany in the Late Eighteenth Century* (Oxford University Press, 1990), pp. 57–118, and G. J. Barker-Benfield. *The Culture of Sensibility. Sex and Society in Eighteenth-Century Britain* (University of Chicago Press, 1992), especially pp. 359–68, which assumes Wollstonecraft to have been central to the 'gendering' of sensibility in this period, though it does not look closely at the relationship between the texts examined here.

2 *Vindication of the Rights of Woman* (1792) (*The Works of Mary Wollstonecraft*, William Pickering, 1989, vol. 5, pp. 65–266), p. 66. All subsequent references will be to this edition, which contains both texts under discussion. For commentary, see also Barbara Taylor's introduction to her edition of the second 'Vindication' (E. P. Dent, 1992).

3 Godwin later described her religious ideas as 'almost entirely of her own creation' (*Memoirs of the Author of a Vindication of the Rights of Woman*, Penguin Books, 1987, p. 215. Claire Tomalin, for example, stresses of Wollstonecraft's religious views that she, with many other radical Dissenters, was not much concerned with church attendance, but 'retained a tenuous but stubborn belief in God' (*The Life and Death of Mary Wollstonecraft*, Meridian Books, 1974, p. 76). Her brief account of the second 'Vindication' (pp. 103–7) similarly ignores the continuing significance of Wollstonecraft's religious views. Two recent full-scale studies of Wollstonecraft's thought do not go far to clarifying the central religious context of the second 'Vindication'. See Gary Kelly, *Revolutionary Feminism., The Mind and Career of Mary Wollstonecraft* (Macmillan, 1992), pp. 107–39, which focuses on the question of manners; and Virginia Sapiro. *A Vindication of Political Virtue. The Political Theory of Mary Wollstonecraft* (University of Chicago Press, 1992), which though it pays closer heed to the issue of Wollstonecraft's religious views (see esp. pp. 44–52), does not take up the view expounded here. Little attention is paid to religion, much less its implications for Wollstonecraft's view of rights, in any edition of the second 'Vindication', for example in Miriam Kramnick's Penguin edition (1978) or Barbara H. Solomon and Paula S. Berggren, eds., *A Mary Wollstonecraft Reader* (Mentor, 1983) or Ulrich H. Hardt, ed., *A Critical Edition of Mary Wollstonecraft's Vindication of the Rights of Woman* (Whitson Publishing Company, 1982). Moreover, the theme is virtually ignored even such well-known and wide-ranging accounts of Wollstonecraft's ideas as: Carolyn W. Korsmeyer's 'Reason and Morals in the Early Feminist Movement: Mary Wollstonecraft', reprinted in *A Vindication of the Rights of Woman*, ed. Carol H. Poston (Norton Books, 1988), pp. 285–97; Elissa S. Guralnick, 'Radical Politics in Mary Wollstonecraft's *A Vindication of the Rights of Woman*', *ibid.*, pp. 308–17; 'Mary Wollstonecraft Stoic Liberal-Democrat', *Canadian Journal of Political and Social Theory*, 1 (1977), 59–74; G. J. Barker-Benfield, 'Mary Wollstonecraft: Eighteenth Century Commonwealthwoman', *Journal of the History of Ideas*; 50: (1989), 95–115; and Anca Vlasopolos, 'Mary Wollstonecraft's Mask of Reason in *A Vindication of the Rights of Woman*', *Dalhousie Review*; 60: (1980), 462–71. Much more interesting in this regard, though it does not pursue these arguments in the direction which interests me here, is Mervyn Nicholson, 'The Eleventh Commandment: Sex and Spirit in Wollstonecraft and Malthus', *Journal of the History of Ideas*; 51: (1990), 401–21. See also Carol Kay, 'Canon, Ideology, and Gender: Mary Wollstonecraft's Critique of Adam Smith', *New Political Science*; 15: (1986), 63–76. The general religious context is explored in Ursula Henriques. *Religious Toleration in England 1787–1833* (Routledge and Kegan Paul, 1961), Roland Stromberg. *Religious Liberalism in Eighteenth-Century England* (Oxford University Press, 1954), Richard Barlow. *Citizenship and Conscience. A Study in the Theory and Practice of Religious Toleration in England During the Eighteenth Century* (University of

Pennsylvania Press, 1962), and Knut Haakonssen, ed. *Enlightenment and Religion. Rational Dissent in Eighteenth Century Britain* (Cambridge University Press, 1996).

4 Wollstonecraft, *Works*, vol. 5, p. 7. For commentary on the first 'Vindication' see especially Mitzi Meyers, 'Politics From the Outside: Mary Wollstonecraft's First *Vindication*', *Studies in Eighteenth Century Culture*; 6: (1977), 113–32, G. J. Barker-Benfield, 'Mary Wollstonecraft: Eighteenth Century Commonwealthwoman', *op. cit.*, and Gary Kelly, *Revolutionary Feminism., The Mind and Career of Mary Wollstonecraft* (Macmillan, 1992), pp. 84–106.

5 Wollstonecraft, *Works*, vol. 5, pp. 8–9. A good general treatment of Wollstonecraft's view of sensibility is Mary Poovey, 'Mary Wollstonecraft: The Gender of Genres in Late Eighteenth-Century England', *Novel: A Forum on Fiction*, 15 (1982), 111–26.

6 Wollstonecraft, *Works*, vol. 5, p. 9.

7 Wollstonecraft, *Works*, vol. 5, p. 10.

8 Wollstonecraft, *Works*, vol. 5, pp. 7, 201.

9 See William Godwin, *Enquiry Concerning Political Justice* (1793) (repr. Penguin Books, 1976), pp. 321–32.

10 On 'politeness' in the political thought of this period, see in particular J. G. A. Pocock, *Virtue, Commerce, and History* (Cambridge University Press, 1985), pp. 37–50.

11 David Hume, *Essays Moral, Political and Literary* (1903 edn.), pp. 127–8, 120, 278. Wollstonecraft quotes Hume on character (*Works*, vol. 5, p. 124).

12 For Burgh, e.g. see his *An Account of the First Settlement . . . of the Cessares* (1764), reprinted in my *Utopias of the British Enlightenment* (Cambridge University Press, 1994), e.g. pp. 111–120.

13 Wollstonecraft, *Works*, vol. 4, pp. 32–3.

14 Wollstonecraft, *Works*, vol. 1, p. 61.

15 Wollstonecraft, *Works*, vol. 7, p. 66.

16 Wollstonecraft, *Works*, vol. 7, pp. 109, 370.

17 Wollstonecraft, *Works*, vol. 7, p. 314.

18 Hannah More. *The Works of Hannah More* (11 vols, 1830), vol. **II**, pp. 36–7.

19 The standard survey of the origins of this movement is Ford K. Brown. *Fathers of the Victorians. The Age of Wilberforce* (Cambridge University Press, 1961).

20 William Paley. *The Works of William Paley* (5 vols, 1837), vol. **I**, p. 189.

21 Wollstonecraft, *Works*, vol. 5, pp. 166–7.

22 Wollstonecraft, *Works*, vol. 5, pp. 10–11.

23 Wollstonecraft, *Works*, vol. 5, p. 14.

24 Wollstonecraft, *Works*, vol. 5, p. 16. On this view of Burke, see my discussion of the radicals' treatment of the *Reflections* in my *Thomas Paine: Social and Political Thought* (Unwin Hyman, 1989), pp. 66–71.

25 Wollstonecraft, *Works*, vol. 5, p. 23.

26 Wollstonecraft, *Works*, vol. 5, p. 22.

27 Wollstonecraft, *Works*, vol. 5, p. 24.

28 Wollstonecraft, *Works*, vol. 5, pp. 34, 39. An account which treats this theme as central to the first 'Vindication' is Gary Kelly. *Revolutionary Feminism. The Mind and Career of Mary Wollstonecraft* (Macmillan, 1992), p. 96.
29 Wollstonecraft, *Works*, vol. 5, pp. 40–1.
30 Wollstonecraft, *Works*, vol. 5, pp. 105, 52, 55, 57.
31 Wollstonecraft, *Works*, vol. 5, pp. 18, 21. Wollstonecraft's brief review of Price's *A Discourse on the Love of Our Country* (Works, vol. 7, pp. 185–7) is however laudatory.
32 Wollstonecraft, *Works*, vol. 5, p. 58.
33 Wollstonecraft, *Works*, vol. 5, p. 114.
34 Wollstonecraft, *Works*, vol. 5, pp. 157, 23.
35 Wollstonecraft, *Works*, vol. 5, pp. 249, 221, 66–7.
36 Wollstonecraft, *Works*, vol. 5, p. 256.
37 See, e.g., J. G. A. Pocock, *The Machiavellian Moment. Florentine Political Thought and the Atlantic Republican Tradition* (Princeton University Press, 1975). On the spectrum of republican thought in this period, see my 'Republicanism, Commerce and the Origins of Modern Social Theory in Britain, 1796–1805', *Journal of Modern History*, vol. 66, (1994), 249–290.
38 Wollstonecraft, *Works*, vol. 5, pp. 114, 252–4.
39 Wollstonecraft, *Works*, vol. 5, p. 245.
40 Wollstonecraft, *Works*, vol. 5, pp. 261, 250, 68, 247, 66, 90.
41 Wollstonecraft, *Works*, vol. 5, pp. 140, 155.
42 Wollstonecraft, *Works*, vol. 5, pp. 45–6.
43 William Godwin. *Memoirs of the Author of a Vindication of the Rights of Woman* (Penguin Books, 1987), p. 215.
44 Wollstonecraft, *Works*, vol. 5, p. 172, 181, 122, 75.
45 E.g., Wollstonecraft, *Works*, vol. 5, pp. 51, 60.
46 Wollstonecraft, *Works*, vol. 5, pp. 215, 133, 211, 65–6.
47 Wollstonecraft, *Works*, vol. 5, p. 214.
48 Wollstonecraft, *Works*, vol. 5, pp. 82, 106, 129, 136, 211, 263, 211. This can be seen as demonstrating further how far republican ideals, like some forms of socialism later, provided a straightjacket for early feminism.
49 Wollstonecraft, *Works*, vol. 5, pp. 136, 145, 124.
50 Wollstonecraft, *Works*, vol. 5, p. 122.
51 Wollstonecraft, *Works*, vol. 5, p. 201, 205.
52 Wollstonecraft, *Works*, vol. 5, p. 114, 129, 127.
53 Wollstonecraft, *Works*, vol. 5, p. 209.
54 Wollstonecraft, *Works*, vol. 5, pp. 208, 210, 215, 219, 264.
55 Wollstonecraft, *Works*, vol. 5, pp. 114, 116, 119, 222–5, 113, 140.
56 Ursula Vogel, 'Rationalism and Romanticism: Two Strategies for Women's Emancipation', in Vogel et al., *Feminism and Political Theory* (Sage, 1986), p. 31.
57 Ursula Vogel, 'Rationalism and Romanticism: Two Strategies for Women's Emancipation', in Vogel et al., *Feminism and Political Theory* (Sage, 1986), pp. 17–46.

58 Wollstonecraft, *Works*, vol. 5, p. 95.
59 Wollstonecraft, *Works*, vol. 7, p. 396.
60 Thomas Paine, *Rights of Man*, ed. G. Claeys (Hackett Publishing Company, 1992), pp. 37–8.
61 *Political Writings of the 1790s* (8 vols, Pickering and Chatto, 1995), ed. G. Claeys, vol. 1, p. 245.
62 *Political Writings of the 1790s* (8 vols, Pickering and Chatto, 1995), ed. G. Claeys, vol. 2, pp. 294–5.
63 Thomas Paine. *The Writings of Thomas Paine*, ed. Moncure Conway (4 vols, New York, 1906), vol. 2, p. 287.
64 Wollstonecraft, *Works*, vol. 5, p. 66, 60.

CHAPTER 6

On Not Inventing the English Revolution: the Radical Failure of the 1790s as Linguistic Non-Performance

Iain Hampsher-Monk

This chapter considers whether, in the light of the recent focus on the linguistic character of political action, it makes sense to ask whether the failure of British radicalism in the 1790s can be explained by reference to features of the languages of politics available to and used by radicals of the time. There are two issues here, one substantive and one methodological. The substantive issue is to consider the range and character of the languages used by radicals.[1] The methodological is to consider what might be meant by asserting the primacy of language in our understanding of historical political events. Lurking below (and occasionally above) the surface of each of these is an issue which was hotly debated during the conference associated with these papers – the question of the identity of radicalism itself.

Anglophone historians of political thought have become used to the idea of identifying 'languages' of politics within which individual writers and thinkers can be located.[2] By 'language' is meant a particular pattern of vocabulary, conventions of discourse and set of associations which operate within a relatively distinct area of the wider, natural language. The languages of natural rights and utilitarianism are two such. Identifying the language used by an historical agent can have real explanatory and interpretative power. Knowing the linguistic conventions and associative valencies carried within particular patterns of speaking (and we suppose, thinking) enables us to make informed interpretative decisions at points of textual ambiguity, to ascribe plausible premises where arguments in the original have been abridged, and to link different thinkers and writers together in virtue of their common subscription to a certain linguistic world.[3] Pocock's seminal study, *The Ancient Constitution and the Feudal Law*, showed how the languages of ancient constitutionalism and feudal law were identified – largely through their being embedded in professional groups such as common lawyers, Parliamentarian and Royalist publicists. In this sense a particular political theory might be seen as part of the sociology of knowledge of a particular group – rather in the way that Kuhn depicted orthodox science within scientific communities.[4] There was an understandable tendency to regard such languages as more-or-less identifiable with particular political positions. But whilst it is true that particular languages may, over time, acquire historical connotations which render them more amenable to being deployed in certain ways rather than certain others, it seems clear that such valencies are ultimately a matter for historical investigation. However uncongenial the language of neo-Harringtonian republicanism was to the emergence of the commercial economy, Pocock and many of those working in his wake have been concerned not merely to show its opposition to the development of that society, but rather to chart the processes by which it came to accommodate it.[5] The link between a language and a particular political position is not exactly a contingent one – the hermeneutic character of the relationship between the two guarantees that – but it is one that requires historical demonstration, and this reveals that such limits are stronger at some times than at others.[6]

This contingency seems to be related to, and to bear on, another issue central to the linguistic character claimed for political action, namely the degree of agency capable of being exerted by individuals. To what extent are authors 'constructed', that is to say are their linguistic performances determined, by the linguistic world in which they live, and to what extent are they free to formulate innovatory or unorthodox speech acts? A strong linguistic determination thesis, such as that advocated by some French post-structuralists, virtually eliminates authorial agency in favour of linguistic determination. Abandoning any determinative link between the language and the particular linguistic performance, however, has the effect not only of freeing the author, but weakening the explanatory power of the language in relation to the particular deployment of it. If authors can say whatever they like it is not clear how knowledge of the particular language they use to say it in can help us to narrow down equivocal meanings in their speech.[7] Both Anglophone and French historians agree on the importance of identifying the linguistic component of historical understanding, but whereas the latter have tended to see the individual trapped within, the former present individuals as agents of, linguistic and hence social change.[8] At the extreme the political actor can be seen as a linguistic magus, not defined by, but standing behind and dextrously manipulating the conventions which define the political world (and other less prestigious beings).[9]

Those who sought significant change in the political institutions of late eighteenth-century Britain did not speak a single language. In this as in other senses radicalism was 'fragmented'.[10] Writers used a range of languages with which to engage the world confronting them. This very diversity suggests authors exercised some freedom if only in choosing which language to use. In this sense they were in thrall neither to a particular language of radicalism, nor to the orthodoxies latent in some of the languages they deployed for radical purposes. Having said that, it is clear that language, like any medium, imposes constraints and limitations on its users. One of the features of the approach which sees the degree of linguistic determination as a contingent and variable property of historically contextualised actors rather than a universal and necessary feature of human consciousness is that it can perform an explanatory role in helping us to understand, as Quentin Skinner has put it, what they were '"*doing in*" saying what they said'.[11] That is to say, to put it more colloquially, we can understand where speakers are *coming from*, but we can also understand where they were going, or rather, where they were trying to take their audience.

Amongst these languages deployed by radicals, and well discussed by commentators have been the languages of natural right used by Paine, Thelwall and a number of lesser figures, the civic language of political corruption used by Christopher Wyville, the ancient constitutionalism so doggedly and unchangingly propounded by Major Cartwright from 1774 to 1823 – a record which of itself must challenge the claim that theorists are necessarily influenced by their historical context – and the language of religious millenarianism found in such diverse characters as the deeply mystic William Blake and the no less deeply rationalistic Joseph Priestley. It is tempting, particularly in the case of some of these languages to see them as peculiarly radical, but this would be a mistake. Their origins were often of quite a different political complexion from the uses to which they were put. The language of natural right and contract had originally been – and as Burke and a significant group of high Anglicans would insist, still was – quite capable of supporting a relatively authoritarian interpretation of the Whig-Anglican settlement.[12] The language of civic corruption was as much Tory as Whig in origin.[13] The identity of the ancient constitution had been fought overduring the English Civil War by Whigs and Tories in the late seventeenth and early eighteenth centuries, and, as Janet Lee has shown, was to be fought over again at the start of the nineteenth.[14]

The language of religion, conventionally deployed in defence of the revolution settlement, could, when 'enthusiastic', be hugely subversive and yet even in this mode be a force for political conservatism.[15] The valencies and possibilities of languages were changed by changing circumstances. Within the context of the development of a polite and commercial society the assertion of natural rights was apt to be seen, even on a charitable interpretation, as a nostalgic call for a return to a simple and agrarian society – less indulgently as an invocation of the economic (and social) crudity of the state of savage nature.[16] Both Thelwall and Paine responded to this by elaborating ways – ways still with us – in which economic entitlement under natural right to as much land as one could work could be supplied in cash to the individual through redistributive taxation, and indeed could be increased to meet the demands of the more sensitive and cultivated inviduality made possible by the new society.[17] Whilst some radicals – Cartwright is an example – seemed only to use one language, they nevertheless had little difficulty in joining with others who articulated their demands in a different way; and many radicals were opportunists, exploiting evidently moderate or nostalgic positions for reformist or radically transformative looking ends which they were evidently capable of conceiving independently of the particular idiom in which they formulated their claim at any one time. This diversity amongst individuals who nevertheless often saw themselves as members of a group sharing common aims, suggests that radicals were not defined or determined by language but deployed it as agents for their own purposes.

An extreme example of this creative opportunism shows how even as unpromising a thinker as Hume could be recruited to mount an attack on a certain conception of property rights in order to clear the way for redistributive taxation.

Hume had argued that the institution of property could be explained from the coincidence of the utility that resulted from the stability of possession and the mental association formed in the mind through the intimate proximity between the person and their belongings. Repeated association of a person with a particular object has the effect – common in Hume's philosophical psychology – of leading the mind to ascribe another relation to the two besides the associative one, which, reinforced by our desire to keep what we owned, and the utility that followed from stability of possessions, could, with the aid of reflection, be formalized into a rule that people should enjoy security of their possessions – the first rule of justice.[18] Elaborations of the principles of property too, derive from aspects of the associative propensity of the human mind; succession or inheritance from the nearness of the relationship. On the death of the proprietor, the mind, which already associates the property indirectly with the offspring via the dead parent 'is apt to connect them still further by the relation of property'. This relationship is reinforced by what Hume claims is the utilitarian rule, derived from an observable fact, namely that 'men's possessions shou'd pass to those, who are dearest to them, in order to render them (the giver not the receiver) more industrious and frugal'.[19] Hume stressed that such rights are 'principally fixed by the imagination, or the more frivolous properties of our thought'.[20]

Although this derivation of property rights was viewed nervously by some for precisely the 'imaginative' feature of them that Hume singled out as their distinguishing character, the substantive import of his theory was nevertheless impeccably consistent with the status quo, the 'revolution settlement', with the inviolability of property and the maintenance of existing distributions.[21]

Even this, apparently recalcitrant, material, however, was appropriated by radical political economists looking for a theory which would justify redistributive taxation without threatening the stability of property rights. John Millar, writing as 'Sidney' to the *Scots Chronicle* in 1796[22] complained that the existing extremes of inequality were productive of great disutility since the idle rich had no incentive to develop or exercise their talents whilst the poor had no incentive to try. The effects of inequality thus invaded 'every connecting link, contaminating the morals of the whole nation'.[23] Inequality stifled economic growth – the poor must spend all they have on necessities, the rich engage in careless economic speculation threatening healthy competition, misdirecting investment and so retarding the 'general accumulation of riches'.[24] Millar accepted enough of the new political economy and its fragile basis in human psychology to be wary of simple redistributive taxation as disappointing reasonable expectations, discouraging the poor from labour and precipitating consumption in anticipation of the imposition of taxation.[25] Yet he identified one point in the Humean account where such utilitarian considerations fail to obtain, where the associative arguments supposedly give rise to reasonable expectations, and failed to obtain, and allowed the opposing claims of the utility which derived from more equal distribution to prevail – and that was at the point of inheritance.

Sidney acknowledged Hume's perception in identifying the associationist bases of the rule of heritability of property and even elaborated them: near relatives are often 'much connected with the deceased . . . are associated with him in the minds of neighbours ... present at the deathbed, and so can begin the possession immediately'. As a result of these features 'we are naturally led, by habit, to consider it a just rule'.[26] But primogeniture – a relic of the warlike clan society where a single chief was needed – is in fact, reflects Sidney – and whatever its associationist basis – a most unnatural practice, running counter to familial affection, and utility alike. It dispossesses the younger siblings and precludes the deployment of the beneficial principle of desert. Furthermore even testamentary right seems 'scarcely to have any foundation in the actual principle of justice. When a man is dead his dominion over external objects must be completely at an end'. Given that property right derives from the association in the mind between person and goods, once death intervenes and such a connection can no longer exist 'the rights attendant on this connection can no longer subsist. Sidney calls testamentary right a 'right of ruling beyond the grave' and he can hardly have used Paine's notorious phrase innocently.[27] Such a right has no root in natural feelings or association; it is 'merely a creature of the civil state and its abolition would provoke no disutility: no relaxation of industry would follow from the abolition of testaments: there would still be sufficient motives to prompt us to exertion'. Death or estate duty, consequently, would undermine none of the associative grounds of property in human psychology; nor is it affected by the economic arguments for property rights through diminishing the incentives to create or care for wealth.[28] Such a tax would diminish the absolute size of large holdings but the resulting wider dispersal of property would favour not only increased productivity but the incentives to moral and cultural improvement. Miller's argument thus succeeded in turning to radical purpose even the uncongenial language in which Hume – amongst others – had married associationist psychology with utilitarian speculation in seeking to ground political economy.

I have dwelt on Millar's argument at some length partly because it is less familiar than most and partly to demonstrate the ingenuity of radicals in forging arguments from unlikely sources. Although illustrative of the radicals' eclecticism and opportunism, it is also illustrative of the other feature of the languages of radicalism which I have tried to stress, namely that late eighteenth-century radicalism in Britain operated within patterns of discourse which were not the peculiar preserve of radicals. This had other implications to which I now want to turn. For whilst this 'connectedness' may have given their arguments a plausibility and a purchase on political reality denied to the more extremist political visionary, (although it didn't stop them being denounced as such) it may, by the same token, also have denied them the possibility of achieving any truly revolutionary distance from that reality. Indeed the existence of such a shared political language was emphasized by Cartwright and Cobbet in the post-revolutionary period as a distinguishing feature of English political culture. Cartwright, writing in 1812, drew attention to the supposed fact that there had been a revolution in France precisely *because* the people had no shared political language, no familiar landmarks such as Magna Carta and the Bill of Rights, to which they could appeal. 'The national mind of France was in utter darkness forming a complete contrast to the public mind of England.'[29]

Back in 1789, of course, British radicals, typically following Price, had seen the French Revolution as a model for a domestic effort to complete the work left undone in 1688. Although the government of the day took such threats seriously, historians – particularly those committed to explanations rooted in models of social causality, or even the balance of social forces – have had little problem in dismissing such aspirations as implausible.[30] However, from Furet's programmatic rejection of the social interpretation of revolutionary history through to the work of Lynn Hunt and Keith Baker, we have recently been encouraged to recognize the 'linguisticality of the revolution'.[31] This is entirely congruent with our earlier emphasis on speech act theory, and the further sense in which innovatory political action is irreducibly linguistic. Whilst we can assassinate kings through mere physical force, it is only through speech that monarchy can be abolished and replaced by something else. The Declaration(s) of the Rights of Man, the Declaration that the Third Estate was the nation, the establishment of the Constituent Assembly, the abolition of the monarchy, were all themselves speech acts. Cumulatively, they comprised a revolution and participants' recognition of that fact helped to constitute the Revolution as an act of aware conceptual and linguistic creativity.[32]

But if the revolution was essentially a linguistic, declaratory performance, was the British non-revolution a *failed* linguistic performance? Or to put it less tendentiously, were there features of the discourses deployed by British radicals which help to account for the 'failed British Revolution', or, at the very least, had implications for the possibilities of formulating revolutionary statements? The 'failure' of the British revolution is of course a question-begging notion,[33] yet radicals of the 1790s looking back certainly felt they had failed – even if some of them, notoriously, were glad they had done so. If making a revolution is a kind of speech act, might the British have failed through having the wrong kind of speech available, or through failing to deploy it adroitly enough, or through mere syntactical incompetence? If this sounds puckish, it is meant to be, and I am aware that such speculations provoke reflection as much on the 'revolution as speech act' theory as they do on the character of British radicalism.

POLITICAL IMPLICATIONS OF CONTINUITIES

Reading the tracts and treatises of the 1790s in the light of some familiarity with the literature of the 1640s and the 1650s, operating as they do within millenial, natural right, civic and ancient constitutionalist languages, one sees familiar but long-dormant arguments being unpacked from inherited premises, premises which had long seemed to some to seem less threatening through being only premises. Such premises were only partly unpacked in the debates surrounding Wilkes, the American War and the County Movement. To contextualize is an inherently conservative activity. To see, as we now do, the arguments of radicals in the 1790s in the context of patterns of discourse established in the previous century, or in the earlier 1700s, is to see them as part of an ongoing conversation, a set of moves and counter-moves within a linguistic game comprising, if not exactly stock responses, then at least offering scope for extemporization within a limited repertoire. Yet by the 1790s something appeared to have changed, something which charged words with meanings and valencies which they had not hitherto had, linking them to actions far more threatening and subversive than they could on their own have possessed.

To characterize that something as the French Revolution is, whilst true, only minimally illuminating. The construal of the French Revolution was crucial to the way it impacted on British politics. Yet as already emphasized, and as commentators have consistently pointed out, one dimension of the debate about France was the way in which what the French were understood to be doing was consistently mediated through the categories of what the English had already done. One test of the degree to which radicals were or were not able to make potentially revolutionary claims lay in the extent to which they were able to escape the past. The problem for English radicals was that, unlike the case in France, the content of 'revolution' did not have to be constructed out of present acts, it was already embedded in their past. For there was a revolution in English political language and it had been accomplished a century before. Any new declaratory act of revolutionary founding had therefore first to escape the caul of legitimating authority exercised over the English political imagination by 1688.

Even to deal with the issue of 1688 was tacitly to acknowledge its authority. Price's interpretation of that constitutional monstrosity, the Convention Parliament, as a convention (governed by natural rights) rather than as a parliament, sought to read back into the Glorious Revolution what only the Americans and barely yet the French had achieved, the declaratory performance of a revolutionary founding. Yet even in doing so he conceded that whatever it was that had been done then possessed political authority over his contemporaries. Thus formulated, his claim lay open to refutation through an historical demonstration that the protagonists had not in fact sought to declare what he attributed to them. That the act of foundation was a linguistic act, Burke, and most of his opponents seemed to agree, but, paradoxically to us, this meant that the present import of the events of 1688–9, was to be settled through establishing the identity of the linguistic acts performed at that time.

Price was wrong about 1688, and the way Burke sought to demonstrate this was to show what it was those who enacted and later defended the Glorious Revolution took themselves to be doing at the time. This he did through the increasing deployment of textual evidence, and those principles of interpretative plausibility and charity used by modern historians of ideas seeking to understand the past. As Burke reminded his readers, the Convention Parliament, in declaring itself to be, and subsequently validating its acts through, a parliament in law, strenuously sought to deny to itself extra-ordinary, and what was now coming to be called revolutionary, credentials. And those who defended 1688 against the ultra-legitimist Dr Sacheverall in 1710 did the same. A 'foundational' reading of 1688 by Price and others was seen by Burke to be a Trojan Horse for the introduction of the principles of 1789. Burke depicts the radicals inviting their audience into a hall of mirrors in which 1789 is claimed to be a reflection of 1688, but in which the image of 1688 is itself a reflection of 1789. The purpose as so often in radical discourse, claimed Burke, was to establish in the minds of the people, what appeared to be an innocent and benign – even familiar – principle from which, once rooted in their minds, revolutionary implications could be drawn.

Mackintosh's *Vindiciae Gallicae* almost escapes Price's pitfalls. For the most part he sticks closely to his brief – defending France – and by and large he separates out the issues of 1688, 1789 and the demands of the English present. However, he devotes the fifth section to a vindication of the English admirers of the revolution, and to Price's interpretation of

1688. This defence equivocates between claiming that Revolution's authority as the basis for the popular basis of government, and claiming that the revolution merely demonstrates the deployment of principles which could be established on purely other grounds. 'We, who conceive that we pay purest homage to the authors of that (1688) Revolution, not in contending for what they then did, but for what they now would do, can feel no inconsistency in looking on France, not to model our conduct, but to invigorate our spirit of freedom'.[34]

Paine was exceptional amongst radicals (he had after all had the experience of participating in one revolutionary founding already). He did not, like Price, claim the authority for his programme by showing it was the same as what the political actors of 1688 *thought themselves to have been doing*, or even, like Mackintosh, that it was congruent with, and in the spirit of 1688. Paine asserted the outright irrelevance of the protagonists by denying that whatever they thought they were doing could have any authority over the present generation.[35] Indeed he went out of his way to denigrate the heroes of 1688 by pointing out that, in claiming to establish institutions which were authoritative over their successors they were guilty of the same tyranny as that for which James himself had been expelled: the only difference was '... that one was an usurper over the living, and the other over the unborn'.[36] Such an argument is clearly radical, at the cost, as Burke had already pointed out in *Reflections*, of making impossible the establishment of continuing institutions with any intrinsic authority beyond the will of those operating them.[37]

This claim about Paine's success in avoiding embroilment in the interpretation of the meaning of 1688 for the present seems to rest on attributing to him some clear-sightedness about the issue which my other two exemplars lacked. As Keith Baker argued in the case of France – the Revolution needed to be created conceptually before it could be conducted actively, and that process of invention was necessarily a work of piecemeal self-discovery, fuelled, in the French case, by the absence of real possibilities for further extemporization within the existing languages of the ancient regime. Mark Philp has argued that for many British radicals too the deployment of political arguments, like the engagement in political action, was a process of self-definition. Such self-definition was not always controlled by the self being defined. The rapidly changing context often lent a meaning to words which the speaker may not have intended.[38] When challenged in print or in the law-courts they may have been forced for the first time to come to terms with the implications of their assertions – to avow or disown them, to travel further towards a destination which might yet turn out to be Hounslow or Windsor.[39] It seems that for some of them, it was only as the interaction between historical events and the logical implications of the positions they had adopted played themselves out that some of them realized what they had been saying. At this point the alternatives of dismounting with Tooke, or snapping their 'squeaking baby trumpet of sedition' appeared as options.[40]

This, what one might call ultra-contextualist, view of how radicals came to define themselves and the meanings of their statements in relation to surrounding events, reinforces the sense in which one might argue that they were not fully in control of their language – even that in some sense it was constructing them. It certainly demonstrates a failure to address the crucial issue on which the possibility of revolutionary change hinged – the act of taking the initiative away from pasts and institutions – which through language, defined the actor, and the making of claims and the performance of an act at once emancipating its assertors from what had gone before and a foundation of what might then follow. Whether such a speech act could be formulated in the available languages or, if formulated, publicly performed was the crucial issue. Such an act involved not merely cognitive possibilities but an existential commitment and our question relates to how these are connected. Yet to engage in an argument about whether it had already been performed (and thereby acknowledge that this made a difference) was certainly to be diverted from the business of performing it in the present.

Price and in his wake Macaulay, Mackintosh, Cartwright, Wyville and later Cobbett, all became embroiled in an argument about whether such an act had been performed in 1688. In doing so they predisposed themselves against the possibility that it might yet be performed and so acquiesced in what Burke called the 'powerful prepossession to antiquity'[41] which so characterized English political culture. The British radicals, instead of declaring a new constitution, typically became involved in an extended and distracting argument about the status of their existing one. It was the possibility – insisted on by Sieyes – of breaking completely free from inherited structures, linguistic as well as social and political (supposing these distinctions to be operable), which Burke surely rightly perceived to be the fearful nub of the issue; natural rights were only one way in which this might be advanced.

In contrast with France, there were few such revolutionary moments in Britain, and the disposition to argue within and about inherited patterns, a disposition so lauded by Burke, contributed to this.[42] Paine's claim that the world was as new to each generation as it was to the first expressed the conditions for such revolutionary action, but few, even of the radicals seemed to believe him.[43] Radicals in Britain pursued, sought, recovered, explained and vindicated their natural rights; most characteristically they sought a restoration of them. What they never succeeded in performing was that most political of speech acts, the collective declaration of them. Thus irrespective of whether such an act might have been politically successful, they never achieved that linguistic breakthrough that would have put it to the test.

There were three moments at which they might have done so and which can be litmus tests for revolutionary breakthrough. They were the two national conventions which met in Scotland in December 1793, and the British Convention which was called but never met in 1794. These were regarded with great suspicion by the government at the time and occasioned exemplary treason trials in Scotland. Historians seeking to stress the possibility of revolution in Britain have regarded them as positive evidence. Intuitively this seems plausible. The idea of a convention has associations with both the idea of a contract and a supra-constitutional collective action – particularly in light of the events in America in 1787 and in France. As another contributor to this collection shows, the concept of a convention had a history in British thought, yet, like revolution, once again this encumbered it with contextual ties which inhibited it from becoming truly universal and emancipatory. James Burgh and Obadiah Hulme had proposed conventions in the 1770s – not to replace, but to precipitate reform of the Commons. Burgh claimed such a convention could be called 'by all men of property, friends to liberty and able commanders' which nodded strongly to conventional conceptions of 'the people'. Jebb had called for one in 1780, elected by householders, but intriguingly, although he asserted its competence to replace the role of a corrupt Commons he still regarded it as co-ordinate with the King and Lords![44] In the immediate context of the execution of Louis and the proclamation of the Convention of the French People, 23rd January 1793, the word took on a much more explicitly revolutionary and foundational meaning than hitherto. Yet Joseph Gerrald's pamphlet 'A Convention the only means of Saving us from Ruin', later that same year nevertheless reassured his readers that under the Anglo-Saxon constitution a convention (the Folk-moot) had met annually to review the conduct of both King and Parliament (the *Witenagemote*).[45]

Despite the provocative language and revolutionary forms of address in the 1790s, radicals' understandings of the convention was quite consistent with these earlier models – it was an extra-parliamentary political body, but not one designed to substitute for existing insitutions. They were not constitutive of the act of reformation, but were a means of seeking it. The London Corresponding Society delegates to the Edinburgh Convention were instructed to pursue 'annual parliaments and universal suffrage by rational and lawful means'. They were pledged to 'adopt the firmest measures provided they are constitutional'.[46] Although both the convention and the LCS passed motions declaring that a convention would be recalled in the even of laws being passed to prevent freedom of assembly or to bring in foreign troops, the status and aim of such an assembly was left vague, but the London Corresponding Society's conception of their actions: 'to obtain a compleate Representation is our only aim . . . we are not engaged in Speculative and Theoretical schemes' – as well as their tactics, seeking to 'adopt a remonstrance to each of the three branches of the legislature against dangerous innovations . . . upon the valuable parts of our laws and constitutions' clearly suggest a body designed to exert pressure on rather than supplant the legislature.[47]

A LINGUISTIC REVOLUTION AS A PRECURSOR OF REVOLUTIONARY LANGUAGE?

The inherited linguistic modes within which ideas tended to be expressed seemed indeed, for many, if not most radicals, to preclude the possibility of revolutionary speech-action. Nevertheless there is perhaps a sense in which the revolutionary moment was both present and perceived to be so on the part of some radicals and by those in authority, and yet in a way which attention to the literal and surface text of the radicals' theories fails to capture.

The famous story of Pitt refusing to prosecute Godwin's *Political Justice* on the grounds that a book costing three guineas could not possibly pose a threat to the political order, however apocryphal, is symptomatic of an age in which the crucial issues were less what was being said but by who, where, and to whom.[48] William Ogilvie's 1781 *Essay on the Right of Property in Land*, anthologized ever since along with radical claims by Spence, Thelwall, Paine, Godwin, Proudhon and George,[49] argued that the Lockean natural right to an equal share in land persisted even in contemporary society and overrode conventional property rights. He did not stop at the principle but derived from it a programme in which states ought to guarantee to every citizen 'as much as would fall to his share in an equal partition of the territory of the state among the citizens'. He recommended this to the attention of 'the friends of all mankind', but Ogilvie was professor at the University of Aberdeen and his tract did not engage the attention of the authorities.[50]

Almost the mirror image of this is the case of Henry Redhead Yorke, whose 'seditious' speech to a crowd on Castle Hill in Sheffield in May 1794 led to his prosecution. In his defence Erskine pointed out that Yorke's 'speech' comprised lengthy readings from that Whig hero, John Locke's *Second Treatise of Government.*[51] Context is clearly doing a lot of work here in defining the nature of the radical. Nor was it only context that was seen as relevant: the range of forms in which political statements were promulgated continually threatened existing genres, and with them perhaps more than mere literary form. The periodical compilations of Spence, Eaton and Lee owe much to chap-books, the content often a mining of Whig heroes and classical sources for sound bites and *bons mots* bizarrely recruited to support plebeian political aspirations. Whilst their content confirms the inclusivity of the British political language: the form, the ridicule, the subversive dictionaries, the eager embracing of the swinish identity offered by Burke by contrast have overtones of a threatening charivari and the incipient instauration of a true counter-culture.[52] Moreover the ostentatious way in which newly politicized social and economic groups published their 'proceedings' (records, accounts and minutes of organizations and their meetings and correspendence)[53] becomes not only a new and significant genre but the enacted implication of a political theory about the range and agency, the public identity and interconnectedness of radical political society and societies. These are political actions less in virtue of any speech act contained within their texts than in the very act of their publication. The medium, not the content, in this case is the message, the very fact and facility of such 'electric' (a favoured neologism) communication evincing and comprising the political mobilization of hitherto unpoliticized people from different parts of the country. It was in these very acts of publicly communicating, debating and assembling over national political issues that the revolutionary moment was most nearly approached as they and certainly the government clearly sensed.

Yet there is a further point to be made about the meta-textual aspects of linguistic radicalism. At the outset I made the Skinnerian point that a focus on languages can help us to understand, not merely by identifying the language being deployed but by (and as a result) being able to identify the way and extent to which radicals were innovative. In a sense it enables us to gauge the degree of their radicalism. But there is a further dimension of this. Speakers and writers I have been saying, may be operating *with* language to perform innovatory speech acts. Foundational declarations, declarations of rights, redefinitions of 'the people', of what is to count as 'independence', of what counts as 'property' are classic examples of this kind of tactical speech act, in and through which political change is effected through verbal agency. But they might also take a more strategic view. They may seek to operate *on* language, to seek to change that language, either syntactically or in terms of the way it was socially embedded in order to make possible speech acts which were impossible or inhibited by language in its current state. The ascription of such strategic action presupposes our being able to show that agents were aware that political language itself, as opposed to particular propositions or theories formulated in it, needed revision. This strategic preoccupation is clearly an element of radical thinking in the period.

Many commentators have remarked on the political aspects of issues of style and tone in the literature of the period.[54] Nor is this sensitivity to the salience of language a construction of modern historical commentators; it was an issue consciously addressed and commented on by participants at a number of levels. Burke's language is a recurrent theme of Paine's: it is 'gay and flowery' (but without any ultimate point), 'a dramatic performance', 'a pathless wilderness of rhapsodies'. Most interesting of all, Burke is not in control of this language, but rather is himself constructed (and constricted) by it: 'He degenerates into a composition of art' and 'lives immured within the Bastille of a word, and surveys at a distance the envied life of man'.[55]

At the most obvious level radicals adopted and advertised their plain and direct style, often linking these qualities to claims of honesty and purity of motive: 'I speak', wrote Paine, 'an open and disinterested language, dictated by no passion but humanity'. By contrast, he claimed, the opponents of the revolution 'hold out a language which they do not themselves believe, for the fraudulent purpose of making others believe it . . . to keep up the common mystery'.[56] Mary Wollstonecraft ironically apologized to Burke for her failure to 'twist her periods' for not having learned the 'equivocal idiom of politeness; or how to 'disguise her sentiments' before telling him what 'liberty in its simple unsophisticated sense' was.[57] 'A single expression', claimed Paine, 'boldly conceived and uttered, will sometimes put a whole company into their proper feelings, and whole nations are acted upon in the same manner'.[58] The appeal to plain-speaking was clearly a potent one, turned by Burke against the radicals for their supposed espousal of 'French metaphysics' and picked up by Hannah More in 'Village Politics' which sought to show the confusion that resulted from ordinary working men being beguiled by abstractions such as 'liberty'.[59]

Plain speaking, for the more self-aware radicals, was a self-conscious attempt to undermine what many saw as the 'spell' cast over a people's political perceptions by esoteric or artificial language. This clarity was related to reason itself and clearly has undertones of the century-long deist critique of religious mystery, a critique which would leave only the plain truths of a more or less universal religion, or as others may secretly have hoped, the dissolution of religion altogether.[60] This clarity and appeal to intuitive truths – whilst they stuck to it – enabled the radicals to avoid becoming enmeshed in the existing languages of politics, in assessing, for example, by just how much the franchise could safely be enlarged to recover the independence of the Commons, without delivering it to the dependent poor, in deciding how natural rights could be reformulated within commercial society without undermining its undoubted benefits, in deciding what help the theory of associationism could be in formulating an inheritance tax whilst maintaining that security of expectation on which commercial society depended. All of them laudable reformist aims but none of them revolutionary, or, arguably even radical.

The radical's championship of 'plain speaking' was a recognition of the way in which the English language abounded (indeed still abounds) in numerous informal codes and linguistic distinctions used to exclude unqualified speakers from political discourse. Far from being a merely stylistic preference this became something of a longer-term radical preoccupation with overcoming the linguistic barriers to political agency.

One obvious tactic was education – to bring to the newly mobilized political actors awareness of the political resources of the culture they sought to influence. Legally constrained from talking about contemporary politics at public meetings, Thelwall lectured to artisan audiences on 'The Roman Republic' and 'Oratory', eventually establishing a school for the teaching of speech in London. The purpose, his prospectus announced, was 'the Preparation of Youth for the more liberal Departments of Active Life'.[61] When Cobbet, whose radicalism in the 1790s to be sure lay in the future, came to write his *Grammar* (the second edition ostentatiously dedicated to Queen Caroline as 'amongst all the Royal personages of the age the only one that appears justly to have estimated the value of The People') he did so as a conscious political act designed to enable every young man 'to assert with effect the rights and liberties of his country' and to create amongst those who read it 'numerous formidable assailants of our insolent high-blooded oppressors'.[62]

An alternative, ambitious and much more counter-hegemonic tactic was to seek to destroy the very distinction between cultivated and demotic speech through the creation of a new language. Thomas Spence seems to have hinted at this as early as 1782. His campaign for literacy and spelling reform based on a phonetic script named after his utopian community of Crusonia was not merely to make the acquisition of literacy easier, it was 'to free the poor and stranger, the industrious and innocent from vecsatious[sic], tedious and ridiculous absurdities . . .'.[63]

Horne-Tooke's *Diversions of Purely* took this programme to a higher plane. In seeking to break down the linguistic markers of class, Tooke's argument, buttressed by much scholarship, attacked the whole concept of linguistic vulgarity. This involved a detailed rebuttal of claims that only classical languages permitted the more sophisticated linguistic and philosophical tasks. He flatly denied the superiority of classical languages over Anglo-Saxon, deprecated as distorting the intrusion of classical grammar into 'common speech' and denied attendant claims that abstraction was only possible in an English – or by English speakers – enriched by classical terminology.[64] Linked to this was his attack on the whole obfuscating role of metaphysics in public life (which classical and romance-language-derived words supported) a role which he thought could only be dissipated by critical etymology. There are strong parallels here with Bentham's programme of exorcizing fictitious entities, and Bentham, although he took a different route, acknowledged a debt to Tooke.

A language purged of misleading abstraction, of class identifiers, and transparent in its referents would, thought Tooke, be incapable of supporting political imposture. Truth, Fraternity and Justice would emerge into clear conceptual focus and become a reality at one and the same time – it was perhaps a lot to ask of grammar.

NOTES

1 I have explored some of these in earlier articles cited below and in a survey article on which some of present discussion draws: 'Radicalism or Radicalisms? Radicals' ideas of property in eighteenth-century Britain', in *Der Eigentumsbegriff im englischen politischen Denken* ed. Günther Lottes (Bochum, 1995).

2 This aspect of the 'linguistic turn' is associated particularly with J. G. A. Pocock. For a programmatic statement and exemplifying articles see his 'The Concept of a Language and the *métier d'historien:* some

considerations on practice' in *The Languages of Political Theory in Early-Modern Europe*, ed. Anthony Pagden (Cambridge, 1987).

3 See Pocock's list in 'The Concept of a Language', pp. 26–7.

4 Pocock did for a time use the language of the Kuhnian paradigm, see some of the essays in *Politics, Language and Time* (London, 1972).

5 'If I had wanted to write a work called 'The Catonic Moment' I would have done so', Pocock, 'A Reconsideration impartially considered' *History of Political Thought* I, p. 541 (1981).

6 Pocock and Skinner have both insisted that it is in grasping how a language is deployed, not by its mere identification, that we come to historical understanding.

7 Quentin Skinner, 'Analysis of Political Thought and Action' in J. Tully (ed.) *Meaning and Context, Quentin Skinner and his Critics* (Cambridge and Oxford, 1988), p. 105 insists on the difference between 'the unexceptionable claim that any agent who is engaged in an intended act of communication must be limited by the prevailing conventions of discourse, and the further claim that he must be limited only to *following* these conventions'.

8 This agent-passivity seems even truer of the German genre Begriffsgeschichte, see my 'Speech Acts, Languages or Begriffsgeschichte' in *History of Concepts: Comparative Perspectives*, ed. Hampsher-Monk, Tilmans and Van Vree (Amsterdam, 1998).

9 For example, Quentin Skinner, 'The Principles and Practice of opposition: the case of Bolingbroke versus Walpole' in *Historical Perspectives: Essays in Honour of J. H. Plumb*, N. McKendrick (ed.) (London, 1974).

10 Mark Philp, 'The Fragmented Ideology of Reform' in *The French Revolution and British Popular Politics*, Mark Philp, ed. (Cambridge, 1991).

11 Skinner, '"Social Meaning" and Social Action' in Tully (ed.) p. 83ff; Skinner, 'Analysis of Political Thought and Action'.

12 *English Society 1688–1832*, J. C. D. Clark (Cambridge, 1985), Robert Hole, *Pulpits, Politics and Public Order in England 1760–1832* (Cambridge, 1989) Bishop Samuel Horsley championed a contractual view of the English Constitution – although in terms which notoriously led him, according to Cobbett's version, to claim that 'individuals had nothing to do with the laws except obey them'. See *High Church Prophet, Bishop Samuel Horsley (1733–1806) and the Caroline tradition in the later Georgian Church*, F. C. Mather (Oxford, 1992), p. 232.

13 The initial elaboration of it is associated with the later, opposition career of Viscount St John, Lord Bolingbroke. See *Bolingbroke and his Circle, the Politics of Nostalgia in the age of Walpole*, Isaac Kramnick, (Cambs. Mass., 1968) esp ch. 4, and J. G. A. Pocock, *The Machiavellian Moment* (Princeton, 1975) esp ch. xiii, 'The Neo-Machiavellian Political Economy'.

14 On 'ancient constitutionalism' in the seventeenth century the classical exposition is, *The Ancient Constitution and the Feudal Law . . . a Reissue with a Retrospect*, J. G. A. Pocock (Cambridge, 1987 [1957]), see the conceptual and

historical discussion *The Politics of the Ancient Constitution*, Glenn Burgess (Pennsylvania, 1992); on the revival of the contest for the identity of Ancient Constitutionalism in the aftermath of the French Revolution see Janice Lee 'Political Antiquarianism Unmasked: the Conservative Attack on the Myth of the Ancient Constitution' *Bulletin of the Institute of Historical Research;* 55: (1982) pp. 166ff.

15 Methodism was notoriously the *conservative* expression of religious enthusiasm.

16 Burke presses this to the radical's discomfiture: 'How can any man claim, under the conventions of civil society, rights which do not so much as presuppose its existence .... Men cannot enjoy the rights of an uncivil and of a civil state together' *Reflections on the Revolution in France*, (Harmondsworth, 1968), p. 150.

17 See John Thelwall, *Rights of Nature* (1795) in Greg Claeys, ed. *The Politics of English Jacobinism: Writings of John Thelwall* Pennsylvania, 1995, and Tom Paine, *Agrarian Justice* (1795) and see my 'John Thelwall and the Eighteenth-Century Radical response to Political Economy' *Historical Journal* 34; 1: (1991), and more widely Greg Claeys, 'Republicanism and Commerce in Britain 1796–1805' *Journal of Modern History*; 66 (1994).

18 *Treatise of Human Nature* ed. Selby-Bigge, 2nd Edn. (Oxford, 1978) III, Of Morals, part 2, sect.iii, p. 503–4 (& Fn.).

19 *Treatise*, pp. 510–13.

20 *Treatise*, p. 504.

21 Such, certainly was Hume's position, and he was seriously alarmed at the political consequences of increased taxation. See J. G. A. Pocock, 'Dying Thoughts of a North Briton', in J. G. A. Pocock, ed. *Virtue Commerce & History* (Cambridge, 1985).

22 Millar, or possibly by his pupil John Craig. Collectively published as *Letters of Sidney, on Inequality of Property* (Edinburgh, 1796). There is a modern edition *Letters of Crito e Letters of Sidney*, ed. Vincenzo Merolle (Rome, 1984). This cites the original pagination.

23 *Letters of Sidney*, Letter IV, p. 12.

24 Letter VI, pp. 24–6.

25 Letter IX, *passim*.

26 Letter XI, p. 56.

27 Paine had famously denounced Burke's claim that the acts of the Parliament of 1688 bound the present generation as 'the vanity and presumption of governing beyond the grave' *Rights of Man*, introduced Eric Foner (Harmondsworth, 1985), pp. 41–2.

28 *Letters of Sidney*, Letter XIII, pp. 62–66.

29 John Cartwright, *Six letters to the marquis of Tavistock, on a reform of the House of Commons of Parliament* (1812) p. 24. 'France, ... had no *appeal* to the *principles* of a Constitution by which the nation had *consented* to be governed [nor] reference to *precedents*, in which the wisdom of their ancestors, by *such appeals*, had at former periods successfully resisted arbitrary power,

renovated liberty, reinvigorated the law and given repose and prosperity to the community'. By contrast, in Britain and in America 'it is to be observed that in an appeal to known rights and to a *constitution*, here are plainly marked the *boundaries* of Reform; here are distinctly shown the *landmarks* at which Reform *if allowed to take its* course will naturally stop'. And see Cobbett: It was the misfortune of the French People, that they had no great and settled principles to refer to in their laws or history ... for want [of which] they fell into confusion; they massacred *each other* ... Let us therefore congratulate ourselves, that we have great constitutional principles and laws, to which we can refer, and to which we are attached' *Political Register* (1816) p. 568.

30 Ian R. Christie *Stress and Stability in Late Eighteenth-Century Britain: Reflections on the British Avoidance of Revolution* (Oxford, 1984), but see Roger Wells 'English Society and revolutionary politics in the 1790s: the case for insurrection' in M. Philp, ed. *The French Revolution and British Popular Politics* (Cambridge, 1991), for the counter case, made on the basis of the same kind of evidence.

31 Keith Baker, *Inventing the French Revolution* (Cambridge, 1990), p. 8.

32 'The revolution as historical fact was irrevocably translated (as Mably had hoped) into the revolution as political act' *Ibid.*, p. 223.

33 This has not inhibited historians from addressing it as an issue. See fn 30.

34 *A Defence of the French Revolution* in *Miscellaneous Works of the Right Honourable Sir James Mackintosh* (London, 1851), p. 618.

35 'what rule or principle can be laid down that of two non-entities, the one out of existence, and the other not in, and who can never meet in this world, the one should control the other..?' *Rights of Man*, esp. pp. 42–3.

36 *Rights of Man*, pp. 43–4.

37 'By this unprincipled facility of changing the state as often and as much, and in as many ways as there are floating fancies or fashions the whole chain and continuity of the commonwealth would be broken. No one generation could link with the other. Men would become little better than flies of a summer.' Edmund Burke, *Reflections on the Revolution in France ...* (Harmondsworth, 1969) pp. 192–3.

38 D. O. Thomas gives the striking example of Dr Price, who, the year after the famous anniversary dinner, in proposing a toast to 'the Parliament of Britain – may it become a NATIONAL Assembly' almost certainly did not mean what that now seems to imply. *The Response to Revolution*, D. O. Thomas (Cardiff, 1989), cited in Philp 'The fragmented ideology...', p. 55.

39 At Tooke's defence at his trial for treason in 1794 he had distanced himself from the more extremist elements of the movement by pointing out that if one is on a coach bound for Windsor one can always chose to dismount at Hounslow. (*State Trials* 25, 330) For an account of the trials *The Friends of Liberty*, Albert Goodwin, (London, 1979), chapter 9, p. 356.

40 Coleridge to (his brother) George Coleridge, ca. 10 March 1798, in *Collected Letters of Samuel Taylor Coleridge*, ed. Earl Leslie Griggs, VI volumes (Oxford, 1956–71), vol. I, p. 238.
41 *Reflections*, p. 118.
42 Günther Lottes stresses the importance of a parallel institutional difference between English and French Radicals – whereas the former 'could and had to refer to an existing representative system, the French could breathe the purer air of theoretical discourse.' 'Radicalism, revolution and political culture' in Philp, *The French Revolution...* p. 81.
43 Tom Paine, *Rights of Man* (Harmondsworth, 1985) p. 67.
44 T. H. Parssinen, 'Association, convention and anti-parliament in British radical politics', 1771–1848. *English Historical Review* 88, 1973.
45 Joseph Gerrald, *A Convention the only means of preserving us from ruin* (London 1793), p. 88. Gerald even cites Burke's *Present Discontents* to the effect that ultimately the defence of the constitution might require 'the interposition of the general body of the people', p. 85.
46 'Articles of Instruction' LCS Journal of the General Committee 10–24 October 1793 (Add MSS 27812, 73–7v) Printed in *Selections from the Papers of the London Corresponding Society* ed. Mary Thrale (Cambridge, 1983), p. 86; *State Trials*, vol. 24, col. 36.
47 London Corresponding Society, *Address to the Nation* (1793), in M. T. Davies ed. *London Corresponding Society 1792–1799* (London, 2002) vol. 1, p. 113; London Corresponding Society, *Address to the Nation* (1794) p. 219; and in Iain Hampsher-Monk, ed. *The Reaction to the French Revolution, texts from Britain in the 1790s* (Cambridge, 2005), p. 266ff. On the convention see Goodwin, *Friends of Liberty*, pp. 283ff.
48 The story is disposed of by Philp, *Godwins's Political Justice* (Ithaca, 1986), p. 105.
49 Most recently in *The Origins of Left-libertarianism*, P. Valentyne and Hillel Steiner (Palgrave, 2000).
50 William Ogilvie, *An Essay on the Right of Property in Land* (repr. In *Pioneers of Land Reform*, M. Beer (London, 1920).
51 Goodwin, *The Friends...* pp. 325–6.
52 There is a modern selection of Spence's writings, *Pigs' Meat* Geofry Gallup, (Nottingham, 1982) named after Spence's own twopenny periodical *Pigs' Meat, Lessons for the Swinish Multitude*, Daniel Isaac Eaton's periodical *Hog's Wash: A Salamagundy for Swine* also exemplifies this.
53 E.g. C. Wyvill, *Political Papers*, 6 vols, London, 1794–1804 (which contains minutes and correspondence from the activities of the Society of the Friends of the People) and, *Selections from the Papers of the London Corresponding Society 1792–1799*, ed. Mary Thrale (Cambridge, 1983).
54 Pathbreaking was *The Language of Politics in the Age of Wilkes and Burke*, James T. Boulton, (London and Toronto, 1963), and its logical complement *The Politics of Language 1791–1819*, Olivia Smith (Oxford, 1984).

55 *Rights of Man*, pp. 49, 64, 51, 80. Although radicals criticized Burke for his ornate rhetorical style Olivia Smith notes that he offended the prevailing neo-classical ideals and himself 'brought vulgar terms, arguments based on experience, and impassioned speech into political discourse'. *Politics of Language*, p. 39.

56 *Rights of Man*, p. 92.

57 *A Vindication of the Rights of Men*, Mary Wollstonecraft, in *A Vindication of the Rights of Men and A Vindication of the Rights of Woman* ed. Sylvana Tomaselli (Cambridge, 1995), pp. 5, 7.

58 TBS. *Rights of Man*, Part II, p. 236.

59 TBS. Hannah More, *Village Politics* (1792); reprinted in Hampsher-Monk, ed. *The Reaction to the French Revolution*, p. 196ff.

60 The identification of true atheists in eighteenth-century Britain is a difficult issue. However, some of the radicals (Daniel Isaac Eaton, for example) of the 1790s – and certainly their descendants – were quite explicit, not to say scatological, in their rejection of Christianity. See, e.g. *Radical Underworld: Prophets, Revolutionaries and Pornographers in London, 1795–1840*, Ian McCalman (Oxford, 1993), pp. 88ff, 202.

61 Thelwall republished Walter Moyle's *Essay on the Constitution and Government of the Roman State* under the provocative title *Democracy Vindicated* (Norwich, 1796). Claeys lists at least six titles relating to courses of lectures on public speaking, elocution, published by Thelwall in the first decade of the Nineteenth Century. Claeys, *Writings of John Thelwall*, pp. vi–iii.

62 *A Grammar of the English Language*, William Cobbett (1824), Dedication, Letter 1, Introduction (np.).

63 TBS. Spence's *The Real Reading Made Easy* (Newcastle, 1782) was followed by a phonetic version of his political utopia, Crusonia, which makes clear the author's regional roots: *A S'upl'im'int too thi Histire ov Robinson Kruzo being TH'I H'IST'IRE 'of KRUZONEA or R'O'INS'IN KRUZO'Z IL'IND* (Nuk'as'il, 1782, preface).

64 *The Diversions of Purley*, John Horne Tooke (New Edn., 1840). For a good discussion of the work see O. Smith, *Politics of Language*, Ch. iv, *passim.*

CHAPTER 7

Disconcerting Ideas: Explaining Popular Radicalism and Popular Loyalism in the 1790s

Mark Philp

This paper examines some of the assumptions that underlie our analyses of the popular radicalism and popular loyalism of the 1790s. It is centrally concerned with the relationship between political ideas and languages and political agency, but it focuses this concern on asymmetries in the explanations given of the different movements – asymmetries which have often derived from Whiggish assumptions about the steady progress of the democratic movement for political reform or Marxist influenced accounts of the rise of a working class movement. In discussing the explanations of radicalism and loyalism in the 1790s I also hope to shed some light more generally on the nature of radical movements, and the relationship between political theory, ideology and political practice. Both questions turn out to be integrally related to the issue of explanatory asymmetry.

I

In the 1960s and 1970s there was a rough consensus in British political science that working class support for Labour needed no explanation, whereas working class conservatism did. That is an explanatory asymmetry. It arises from the view that there is a natural class constituency for labour and a natural identification of class interests on the part of members of the working class with Labour, which makes working class toryism exceptional. Things have subsequently changed – although scholars disagree about by how much and since when – but leaving this aside, there is a similar asymmetry in many accounts of the 1790s. Consider, for example, E.P. Thompson's account of the development of working class consciousness allied to the reform movement:

> At the end of the decade (1820s), when there came the climactic contest between Old Corruption and Reform, it is possible to speak in a new way of the working people's consciousness of their interests and of their predicament as a class. . . . Given the elementary techniques of literacy, labourers, artisans, shopkeepers and

clerks and schoolmasters, proceeded to instruct themselves severally or in groups... here and there local Radical leaders, weavers, booksellers, tailors, would amass shelves of Radical periodicals and learn how to use parliamentary Blue Books; illiterate labourers would, nevertheless go each week to a pub where Cobbett's editorial letter was read aloud and discussed.... Thus working men formed a picture of the organization of society, out of their own experience and with the help of their hard-won and erratic education, which was above all a political picture. They learned to see their own lives as part of a general history of conflict between the loosely defined 'industrious classes' on the one hand, and the unreformed House of Commons on the other. From 1830 onwards a more clearly defined class consciousness, in the customary Marxist sense, was maturing, in which working people were aware of continuing old and new battles on their own.[1]

But contrast this with his account of popular loyalism:

... the old pretences of paternalism and deference, were losing force even before the French Revolution, although they saw a temporary revival in the Church-and-King mobs of the early nineties, the military display and the anti-Gallicism of the wars...the reciprocal relation between the gentry and the plebs...had lasted for a century.... For a hundred years they (the poor) were not altogether the losers. They maintained their traditional culture; they secured a partial arrest of the work-discipline of early industrialism; they perhaps enlarged the scope of the poor laws; they enforced charities which may have prevented years of dearth from escalating into crises of subsistence; and they enjoyed liberties of pushing about the streets and jostling, gaping and huzzaing, pulling down the houses of obnoxious bakers or Dissenters, and a generally riotous and unpoliced disposition which astonished foreign visitors, and which almost misled them themselves into believing that they were 'free'. The 1790s expelled that illusion, and in the wake of the experiences of those years the relationship of reciprocity snapped....We move out of the eighteenth century field-of-force and enter a period in which there is a structural re-ordering of class relations and of ideology. It is possible, for the first time to analyse the historical process in terms of nineteenth century notations of class.[2]

An asymmetry is implicit here. For Thompson, and for others, popular loyalism is a function of mechanisms of mobilization and public spectacle that were a staple part of the eighteenth century, in Church and King mobs or anti-Catholic riots; whereas popular radicalism represents something new, because it involves the articulate, intentional organization of members of the artisan and lower orders into associations dedicated to the discussion of political principles and to pressing the case for parliamentary reform. Moreover, popular loyalism is seen as an essentially unstable phenomenon, at times of stress easily eclipsed by grain riots or crimp riots, whereas popular radicalism sets an agenda for the participation of the lower orders in the representative institutions of British society that endures throughout the nineteenth century and provides an enduring basis (albeit expanded to include social and economic grievances) for a radical working class movement and an associated ideology. I have no wish to tie my case to Thompson, I think the underlying assumptions are extremely common in the literature. What I want to do, as systematically as possible in a brief paper, is to think through whether such asymmetries are justifiable in the 1790s.

II

We should be clear about the phenomena we need to explain. Loyalist activities include Church and King riots in the spring and early summer of 1791, the Paine burnings and hangings throughout England and Scotland in 1791–3 (especially in the spring and early summer of 1792); the extraordinarily successful loyalist movement of 1792–3; the widespread consumption of broadside ballads and cheap political tracts written expressly for a popular audience (both in 1793, and again with the Cheap Repository Tracts in 1795); the signing of loyal petitions and the sending of addresses to the king (in the summer of 1792, but also again in the autumn of 1795 after the attack on the King's coach in October); and the participation of members from a very broad section of the British social structure in the volunteer movement in 1797–8 through (with variations) to a peak in 1803–4, but continuing into the 1810s, and in the early nineteenth-century militias. Moreover, there has been a developing literature on the spread of popular support for the monarchy and popular patriotism and nationalism, from Colley and others, which sees the emergence in this period of a popular monarchy, rooted in a British nationalism which fundamentally changed the character of the relationship between the political system and the British people, and provided a popular patriotic discourse which saw Britain through the revolutionary wars and beyond as a united political nation.[3]

On the radical side we are concerned with the spread of reform societies and debating clubs, from 1791, in both London and in major provincial towns and cities; the development of an organized and articulate popular movement for reform, not least in the shape of the SCI, the LCS and other corresponding societies; the mass consumption of reform literature, especially Paine's *Rights of Man*; the petitioning of Parliament, for reform between 1791–3 and again in 1795 (over the Two Acts); the resurgence of a popular reform movement in the summer of 1795, with mass meetings and demonstrations; and its continuation, in increasingly covert activities through to the beginning of the nineteenth century. We should also include the activities of groups of those to whom Reid refers as infidels and political free-thinkers dedicated to moral and intellectual subversion, and an auxiliary force of lower-class religious enthusiasts who also sought the overthrow of the established order and who had met in a range of popular debating clubs until government repression reduced them to all but an incorrigible remnant.[4]

There is a further dimension of these movements. Both involved the widespread circulation of political literature and ideas, both treated their conflict as, in part, a conflict of principles, and both to some extent acted as forcing houses for the development of political ideas. Scholarly treatments of the political thought of this period have generally sought to show the continuities in political ideas with earlier languages and idioms of political thought – classical republicanism, country party traditions, mixed government, ancient constitutionism, both Hobbesian and Lockeian natural rights theories, Scottish political economy and even Filmerite defences of monarchy.[5] While there probably were exponents of such positions throughout the 1790s, the movements of this period cannot be seen as either straightforwardly adopting such ideas, nor as merely unfolding their practical implications or inherent logic. There is no unified ideology of reform or loyalism, and the commitments of those involved in popular politics, which are expressed in the pamphlets, statements and political activities of the period, should not be seen as relatively fixed views as to the kinds of reform or change they were concerned to bring about or resist. Rather, I have argued elsewhere both for the fragmentary character of radical thought (in particular) and for understanding the 'Revolution controversy', not as rehearsing well-established political doctrines, but as developing into a polarizing process in which substantive political doctrine was both quickly eclipsed and ultimately transformed by the demands of political rhetoric and in the course of which the agendas of the reform and loyalist movements were forged (for that generation).[6]

On this kind of account, popular radicalism in the 1790s was the outcome of a process of political contestation which began in the pamphlet press revolving largely, but not exclusively around Parliamentary circles[7] but which changed its character fundamentally into a practical political struggle for hegemony over the British people, a struggle in which they played an increasing part and during which the agenda of British politics underwent a profound change – in which the traditional picture of a balanced constitution became displaced by demands for mass political participation and the elimination of political privilege. In the process, the popular movement responded to government reaction by becoming both increasingly prepared to countenance more dramatic and, eventually, more violent methods of political activity, and increasingly marginalized, losing its broad popular base. And the same evolving character to loyalist organization and activity should also be recognized. The popular loyalist movement of the 1790s and beyond has a transformative effect on the way in which the political nation is conceived and represented in Britain. Despite its efforts to conserve a political and social order, its effect was to organize activity in a way that significantly extended the boundaries of formal and informal political participation. It is a very apt instance of Lampedusa's adage that 'if we want everything to stay as it is then everything has to change'.[8]

One feature of this account is that there is a more experimental and conditional connection between what people say and what they do and what they believe, than is usually given in accounts of political ideology. And one symptom of this is the 'strange bedfellows syndrome' – that Paine and Burke did not see in 1787–9 that they would be violently opposed on matters of deep principle within two years;[9] that Horne Tooke was prepared to associate and work with people whose political convictions were, at bottom, dramatically different from his (such as Hardy, Paine and Godwin); that Reeves was prepared to associate himself with a very wide range of responses to radicalism, ranging from the High Church Toryism of William Jones and the still more virulently anti-Jacobin John Bowles, through to the evangelically influenced moral reformers, such as Sarah Trimmer and Hannah More.[10] Such differences were ignored, not for tactical reasons, but because they appeared less salient than those which existed between those favouring reform and those resisting it. A further sign of the conditional character of ideology is the often strikingly diverse intellectual trajectories which individual ideological careers take in the period: Ritson's, from Jacobite to Jacobin; William Hamilton Reid, from writer of radical pamphlets and songs, through to loyalist snitch on the 'infidel societies', through to a reincarnation of his initial guise; Cobbett's move from reactionary patriot to radical reformer; and Henry Redhead Yorke's reverse course, whose radicalism took him to prison where he was converted to the loyalist cause in the arms of the jailor's daughter (a powerful incentive, although difficult for governments to replicate on a mass scale).

The shifting ideological commitments of participants and the fragmentary character of the ideological terrain, suggests both that we should not explain popular political activity as the unfolding of the implications of particular languages or discourses, and that the grounds for expecting symmetrical accounts of the two popular movements may be stronger than might initially be thought.

III

It is not altogether easy to locate the precise point at which asymmetry enters accounts, but we can move towards a clearer understanding if we take components that historical accounts generally combine in a complex interplay of causal explanation, narrative, *verstehen* interpretation and description, and press them so that they stand out more clearly than they would otherwise. This necessarily involves simplification and abstraction, but it helps us to appreciate the character of the differences between accounts – even if we might later want to question the value of the categories by which we achieve this. I want to distinguish between accounts which emphasize intentionality on the actor's part, and those which do not (usually by providing a causal account); and those which see the behaviour of those participating in popular loyalism as expressive of their fundamental interests and commitments, and those which do not. The distinctions are very rough and ready, but serve their purpose. They give us the following matrix:

	Intentional	Causal
Expressive	1.	2.
Non-expressive	3.	4.

To see how explanations might vary, compare accounts of crowd behaviour:

Cell 1 Accounts that see the crowd as the conscious agent of organized revolutionary working class, as in Sorel's General Strike; or as a conscious agent for a just allocation of resources, as in Thompson's Moral Economy.

Cell 2 Accounts that see the crowd as a process which expresses deep seated but poorly articulated fears and anxieties – as in Lefebvre's account of the 'panics' during the 'Great fear'.[11] Similarly accounts that associate crowd behaviour with objective correlates of scarcity, price rises, and so on, also combine the sense that there are causal process which nonetheless express certain fundamental concerns or interests of those who act.

Cell 3 The crowd as comprising rational individual agents within a larger process that is the aggregate of their actions (Granovetter's Threshold model of crowd behaviour[12]). We might also include accounts of crowds as paid mobs.[13] The behaviour in both cases is regarded as non-expressive in the sense that the intelligibility of the individuals' actions does not add up to an intentional account of the collective behaviour of the crowd, or to an account of the actions of the crowd necessarily being expressive of the interests of its members, even if their own actions are individually rational.

Cell 4 Structural accounts of, for example, Revolutionary Terror. Accounts of discursive frameworks, and of the controlling force of languages and ideologies. In extremis, LeBon's work on the crowd![14]

We can also categorize roughly some recent contributions to accounts of popular activity in the 1790s:

	Intentional		Causal	
	Loyalism	Reform	Loyalism	Reform
Expressive	1a. Dozier[15]	1b. Thompson	2a. O'Gorman	2b. Wells
Non-expressive	3a. Cookson	3b. Christie	4a. Coercion	4b. Reeves[16]

I should say something about the causal category. It includes accounts which treat the actions of agents as a result of forces, structural, economic, social or whatever, over which they have no control and from which they have little or no autonomy. Such explanations are becoming rarer and are increasingly linked to accounts of the way in which structural forces are mediated through meaningful social action. Nonetheless, there is a consistent theme in literature on popular political action that stresses either the irrationality of, or the structural grounds behind, popular political agency. I have also included accounts that suggest false consciousness and coercion as the ground for action. Clearly, to be coerced into doing something one must be free to do that thing, and one's behaviour might be regarded as intentional but non-expressive; however, while acknowledging the simplification involved in the matrix, I want to sustain a line between intentional action as purposive and not simply driven by exigencies that one cannot reasonably resist, and behaviour in which control effectively passes to another, or is analyzed as epiphenomenal of other features of the social, economic or political environment. I will say little about causal accounts; the main focus of my discussion will be on the contrasting assumptions underlying intentional accounts.

Although writers like Dozier take the Loyalist movement as a pure expression of the collective conservative will of the whole nation, and take expressions of loyalist sentiment at face value, loyalism is, in fact, a complex and evolving phenomenon, with the Church and King riots of 1791 and the Paine burnings of 1791–2 showing different patterns of incentives to the later loyalist associations, the petitioning movements and the rise of the volunteers and militia. Moreover, Dozier tends to under-estimate the range of motives people had for participating in loyalist activities and for shunning radicalism. Both prior to the Royal Proclamation in May 1792, but with greater energy subsequently, and with renewed vigour with the development of the loyalist associations of 1792–3, members of the gentry and the magistracy were actively involved in monitoring and, where possible, either prosecuting or shutting down all radical activity. Landlords were warned not to allow their premises to be used for radical meetings; booksellers and publishers were prosecuted; and lodging house keepers were expected to screen their guests, so as to keep out incendiaries and those of evil design. In Coventry, for example, the local Association issued a reward of fifty guineas for the 'discovery of persons distributing Hand Bills, pasting up papers, or giving away pamphlets of a seditious tendency' – to be paid on conviction.[17]

In collecting signatures for petitions, loyalist activists clearly intimidated many they canvassed by treating failure to sign as indicative of Painite leanings or French sympathies – hence the success in securing the signatures of leading Whigs and radical sympathizers. It is not difficult to believe that a similar process affected participation in Paine burnings. Given the structures of power within local communities, perceived non-compliance could threaten a working man with the loss of work, or custom. Moreover, the face-to-face character of petitioning and the organization of demonstrations would have communicated a clear sense of the costs of non-conformity.

Loyalism, therefore, undoubtedly increased the perceived costs of radicalism. It also provided incentives for participation – not least food and drink, time off from work and a degree of carnival! For example, at a meeting at Medlands near Exeter, one of Reeves's informants reported that 'a very respectable yeomanry (c40) whom with the clergy of the different parishes, din'd together, in one Room, and in another Room were assembled a great number of considerable Masters, whilst the house was surrounded by a numerous company of that truly useful class of persons, the day labourer, who were regal'd with the wine of the county (cyder) and join'd in chorus with those singing, God Save the King and other Loyal and constitutional songs'.[18] Paine burnings also combined a judicious mixture of threats and offers. O'Gorman's ongoing work on this widespread phenomenon – which takes place mainly between 1791–3, and is concentrated in the provinces, particularly the county towns of England, with Paine being ritually burned in effigy on something like 1,500 occasions – has emphasized their richness in symbolic and ritualistic elements and their attendance by a great many people from the lower orders of society. In an early version of his work he suggested that they could be seen as symptomatic of a spreading panic, deriving from French subversion and radical incendiaries (a cell 2 account).[19] Where his work is incontestable is in the weight it gives to the organized character of these events – they were often organized in incredible detail, with banners, costumes, procession routes and elaborately constructed effigies. But while this might provide evidence of the depth of the *peur* and the attempt to handle it through ritual, it also emphasizes what these affairs were not – namely, they were not riots.[20] The care over their orchestration clearly indicates a desire to avoid the uncontrolled exercise of mob violence. It is not difficult to see why this was so: the experience of the Gordon Riots, the example of France, long-standing experience of disruptive mob activity in elections, and fears that the rioters would run out of control and turn their hands against other institutions and individuals they resented, provide ample justification. Rather than encouraging riot, the explicit target was to anathematise an imagined radical project and to make loyalism the hegemonic performance.

The balance between threats and offers would differ in individual cases – but there is evidence of a good deal of both. Indeed, among some loyalists there was a recognition that they might have so increased the costs of non-participation that the Associations might *elicit* loyal performances from committed but prudent radicals. One writer draws Reeves's attention to 'Many persons being known to join in Associations who are inimical to the Present Government, either from malignant motives, or fearing to oppose the General Voice of the Country'.[21] This recognition was indicative of a general sense that the objective was not simply to elicit compliance but to ensure the allegiance of those involved.

Indeed, it is the fear that compliance is not backed by allegiance – that it is extremely fragile – that leads so many of those who write to Reeves to urge the Association to direct their attention to the lower orders:

> Although the coercive measures of administration may smooth the surface and keep down opposition for the present, yet if the common people are not reasoned out of their pleasing hopes of general equality, and opinions circulated to make them satisfied with Kingly government the consequences may hereafter be fatal to the constitution.[22]

Some correspondents wanted to do more than reason the poor out of their hope. Sarah Trimmer, for example, sought to give them a sense of belonging within the loyalist community: '. . .it strikes me that jealousies may arise and at least be created in the minds of many of them (the lower orders) at seeing their superiors uniting in bodies from which they are excluded'. The plan of association is incomplete in so far as it extends only to the middle orders. Involving the poor 'would give the poor a little of that *personal consequence* which is grateful to every human heart. They would consider themselves as *voluntary agents*, not as mere instruments to be used or not at the wile of their superiors – they would be stimulated to worthy actions by the idea that *individual merit* would not be overlooked.'[23]

Yet seeking their inclusion *was* not the same as achieving it and when radicals wanted to tease Reeves about his project, some did so precisely by emphasizing the fragility of popular loyalist performances:

> The Hampshire Sedition Hunters think it proper to acquaint their brethren at the Crown and Anchor; that last Monday their committee met – but having nothing to do – they ordered an effigy, for Tom Paine, to be made. . . (and) caused the mob to assemble to carry this effigy about the City. . . – the Mayor and one Alderman – being of a true Jacobite breed, gave money to the mob to Halloo – Church and King – and then to burn the effigy. . . N.B. we think it proper to inform you – that when the mob got drunk, some few did cry out – Tom Pain for ever – Tom Pain for ever, but they were very drunk. . . .[24]

Yet the desire to bring the people into loyalism undoubtedly had an impact. In the 1790s, popular loyalism changed the way in which political authority was exercised and supported in Britain. Participation in this movement to conserve 'enfranchised' (in a variety of ways falling short of the vote) many hitherto on the margins of the political culture or formally excluded from it. To that extent, the net effect of loyalism might be radically to change some individuals' relationship to the political (and sometimes social) world. Moreover, even if a wide range of motives might lead to initial participation in loyalism, the participation might itself have a reinforcing effect. Dundas, reflecting on the Scottish Volunteers in the 1790s commented:

> You will recollect many of the parts of this country which were most disaffected, but were insensibly cured of it by being enrolled under arms along with others of a different description. If on the other hand, they are not so associated, they become a prey to the intrigues of traitors and enemies, being debarred the privilege of bearing arms on the right side.[25]

Although Reeves's Associations had a very strong middle-class membership, suggesting that such participatory benefits were largely restricted to this class, in practice loyalism, volunteering and membership of the militia undoubtedly reached down to the poorer sections of society. Smith, in a study of the militia between 1807 and 1811 found that 51% of the men belonged to the 'artisan and shopkeeper' class.[26] Again, there were substantial incentives for such people to join – participation in the militia brought supplementary earnings, and provided immunity from the 'regular' militia. '. . .the clothing is a clear gain; and so is the shilling on Sunday, which forms the little sum to the poor man which may be freely spent on happiness in any shape'.[27] As to the volunteers: 'Its officers were often lesser men than the gentry who built their standing out of the lesser pickings of local influence and power. Its rank and file formed from the artisan and labouring poor could derive significant material benefit from their service'.[28] The total numbers of volunteers does not look huge, initially: 116,000 in 1798, 146,000 in 1801, but 380,000 in 1804. They made up around half of the home forces, rising to two-thirds in 1804. That gives Britain, with the militia, a total mobilized military force of over 800,000 – which is more than 1 in 5 of the total population capable of bearing arms (c:3.75m), which is a considerable proportion of the population.[29] It is over twice the size of the electorate![30] But does this mean that we should accept Dozier's perspective and see loyalism as an authentic expression of patriotic feeling on the part of the lower orders of society?

One complication in reaching such a conclusion is that the opposition between loyalists and reformers was an aim (and perhaps eventually an achievement) of loyalist propaganda, not a precondition for it. Patriotism had long been associated with reformist and oppositionist commitments and it is largely during the revolutionary war that it takes a distinctively conservative cast. Nonetheless, supporters of reform often continued to insist upon their loyalty to the king and constitution. Indeed, the London

Corresponding Society responded to the Royal Proclamation against seditious writing in May 1792 by concluding that the King could not but approve of their attempt to secure a perfect representation in Parliament. Moreover in the debates held at county and borough meetings called in the summer of 1792 to send loyal addresses to the crown, there was a good deal of public dispute about what loyalism means, with some understanding it as necessarily associated with the desire for reform.[31] What was true for 1791–4 also holds true for the later episodes of volunteering. Participation undoubtedly increased, and the sympathies of the mass, armed nation that was created were enlisted for the most part against the French. But the association of patriotic activity and anti-reformism, and of patriotism and mass participation, were temporary and conditional alliances. They required continuous promotion and they could, and did, break down – volunteers were unreliable when used for local policing (as during the food riots of 1800–1),[32] allegiance was often felt in strongly local terms, with a strong reluctance to serve outside the locality, and there were periodic difficulties arising from status issues between commanders and the lower officer corps. 'What was different about the national defence patriotism of the lower orders was the calculative, opportunistic attitude that was taken towards service by individuals and the collective opposition offered when service was believed to threaten general interests. Service, in other words, was overtly conditional'.[33] Indeed, the content of patriotism was 'constantly negotiable. with respect to the service that would be performed, the authority allowed officers, and the interests of individuals. On these loose terms patriotic commitment could happily coexist with all kinds of other loyalties.'[34]

On this account popular loyalism and patriotism does not seem adequately characterized as the authentic expression of a secure belief in the virtues of the status quo. But is popular radicalism any more authentic or deep-seated?

IV

Some care is needed in distinguishing different types of popular participation in reform activity, such as attending public meetings, joining corresponding societies, participating in debating clubs, and so on. We need to be careful because some activities which have implications for the direction the popular reform movement takes – such as food riots, crimp riots – and certain features of mass public activities – as when the king's coach was destroyed by a mob after the opening of Parliament in

October 1795 – may be driven by something other than radical intent. Behaviour may be the inarticulate expression of anger and frustration at events or a response to people's experience of hardship. But while this may be a feature of some of the activity, and may play a rather important role in some of the pressure on the government in 1795–6 and 1799–1801, it is not this activity that is seen as distinctive of the popular radicalism of the period. Rather, it is the organization of mechanics, tradesmen and shopkeepers, and of members of the literate middle orders, into societies committed to the political education of their fellow members of the public and to agitation for the reform of Parliament.

In understanding this activity we need to recognize, with much recent historiography,[35] that we cannot assume a direct causal connection between social location, the demand for political representation and a sense of common concerns or interests. It may be that certain social conditions would have certain natural correlates in class action, but I do not believe anyone could reasonably claim this for the 1790s. The issue, then, is whether there is some residual account that appeals to class interests.

The difficulty such an account faces lies not in its commitment to a conception of real interests (since these should not be dismissed *a priori*); rather it comes from connecting a story about real interests with one that shows why acting in certain ways (namely participation in radical societies) uniquely satisfies such interests – so that the actions, statements and commitments of participants are expressive of those interests rather than being tactically and conditionally allied to them – as I have suggested is plausibly the case for popular loyalism.

The very concept of commitment involves two distinct features: it involves a certain relationship between the individual's belief set and how s/he acts, such that the action is expressive of that belief set; but, with respect to political action and organization, we are also making the additional claim that the belief set is not simply a raw set of preferences, but involves adherence to some broad principles or political ideology that guides the agent's interpretation of the context with which s/he acts, and plays a major role in the agent's sense of self and his/her associated aspirations. That means we have to look at the way in which people's actions are mediated by representation, even if it also leaves it as a rather inscrutable matter of judgement as to how far those representations are in fact deep-seated commitments. A further dimension of activity that we must recognize concerns the individual motives that lie beneath collective action in politics. Individual acts of commitment usually take place within a broader context in which the agent identifies his fundamental interests both through representation and through identifying himself with others who subscribe to that set of representations and with whom that commitment is shared. Certainly, this is a feature of collective forms of political action, such as the radical movement in the 1790s. But it is a dimension that adds considerable complexity to any account of there being some collective real interests underlying participation in radicalism. It does so because one dimension of the process of commitment would seem inevitably to be a sense of how widely those involved believed their commitments to be shared (and shared by those whom their political ideas predicated as those with whom they had a common interest), or how widely they believed they could become shared (among that group). And in so far as they were not widely shared they would need some way of explaining this apparent lack of commitment in a way that did not then lead them to doubt the value of their own commitment and the legitimacy of their aims.

One way to take the argument, at this point, would be to identify the core constituency picked out by radical reformers in the 1790s and to see how far those who espoused radical principles could reasonably be said to have had a sense of a collective identity underlying their commitments. Although this seems to offer a solution to the asymmetry problem, I will suggest that it fails to do so and that we need to move to a second more fruitful account.

The difficulty with the idea of a core constituency, identified by the language of reform, and acting as a basis for collective self-representation and commitment, is that the way the core is identified under-determines the salience of its representation. In one sense those pressing for parliamentary reform were pressing for the cause of the majority – namely those excluded from parliamentary representation. This led many to think in optimistic terms, early on, about the ease with which reform could be achieved. By encompassing the majority the reform movement would effectively act as a voice for the people against an élite. Moreover, the fact that after 1782, the SCI, and from 1792, the LCS and a whole host of provincial reform societies were pressing for the adoption of the principles of 'ANNUAL ELECTED PARLIAMENTS, UNBIASED AND UNBOUGHT ELECTIONS, AND AN EQUAL REPRESENTATION OF THE WHOLE BODY OF THE PEOPLE',[36] must have seemed to give them a natural majority in favour of reform. A majority, which once it realized its weight would be able to recognize the truth in Hume's principle, that 'it is on opinion that government is founded',[37] and through it to put into practice

Paine's reading of Lafayette's comment: that 'For a nation to be free it is sufficient that she wills it'.[38]

Nonetheless, despite the apparent reasonableness of such a deduction there were a number of obstacles, both to the achievement of the aspiration and to recognizing its force as an aspiration. One set of obstacles blocked the formation of a sense of majority by dividing those who might have comprised it; another, blocked members of the lower orders from perceiving their common interests with their fellows. In the first case, although one way in which people might have recognized themselves as comprising a majority of society was in virtue of the narrowness of the franchise and their exclusion, this was a very local phenomenon, with considerable variation. Moreover, as O'Gorman has stressed, elections could be vigorous contests with extensive participation by those without the vote – and Paul Langford has suggested that some non-voters might well have had every justification for thinking of an extended franchise as a potential misfortune, involving substantial disruption of normal working activity.[39] Moreover, prior to 1792, the desire for inclusion was strongest among the more literate and educated middle classes – especially those with connections with the Dissenting community (since their exclusion was more pointed and extensive), who were practically involved in agitating for reform (and relief) both prior to and immediately after the beginning of the French Revolution. But that in itself did not create a sense of unity, since support for Dissent was not a majority issue, and those agitating for reform from a background in Dissent were by no means wholly in favour of the SCI demands for annual parliaments and universal manhood suffrage. Although those lacking the franchise were a majority, that, in itself, gave them no very strong reason for thinking and acting as a single body. Moreover, the divisions which took place in the early years of the Revolution Controversy, between moderate reformers and those pressing for more extensive changes, was sufficiently clear to ensure that no sense of a simple and united majority for reform could exist. And few people could have been in a position to think that they had nothing to lose by insisting that the demand for universal suffrage and annual parliaments was strictly non-negotiable. Indeed, there is a great deal of evidence to suggest that among members of the SCI in the 1780s and in the 1790s (most notoriously John Horne Tooke[40]), these shibboleths were markers in a negotiating process – few saw them as immediately attainable and many may have harboured doubts as to their ultimate desirability.

Indeed these problems were exacerbated for members of the lower orders interested in reform. For many such people, their political experience and their sense of the political order they inhabited was more a function of locality than otherwise, and they would have had little sense of the way in which their lives were systematically similar to or different from those in other counties or towns. This ignorance was recognized by the societies. Indeed, the very desire to correspond, which drove the first group of artisan reformers, was linked in part by trying to find out how far there were others elsewhere who shared, or could be brought to share, their understanding of their political condition. Although the 1790s saw the first great wave of provincial radicalism, it is plausible to argue that each local movement was shaped as much by local experience and events as by a sense that there was a broad national political agenda in which reform had to play a major part.

The lack of a clear and united majority is also partly a function of the political character of the reform movements of the period. Appeals to an economic and social base to the movements for reform were extremely rare: there was no clear, widely held sense that it was the artisan and labouring classes who produced the wealth of society, and no clear sense of exploitation which could be mobilized to create a sense of unity. Paine only begins to consider exploitation in *Agrarian Justice* – and then not in depth. Far more central for him is the engrossing of the national income through taxation by a monarchical government pursuing its private concerns through war, and although Spence makes a contribution to the theme he does so to a restricted audience. There was also no immediate identification with the needy – partly because the reformers included many people with a comfortable income or wealth, and partly because the 'Treadesmen – Shopkeepers and mechanicks'[41] who formed and sustained organizations like the LCS were neither the rural nor the urban poor. It is true that the language of exploitation is not entirely absent, nor is that of need:

> As our plan was *Universal Suffrage* and *annual parliaments*, the Society admitted journeymen treadsmen of all denominations into it – A class of Men who deserve better treatment than they generally meet with from those who are fed, and cloathed, and inriched by their labour, industry, or ingenuity.[42]

However, it is notable that this comes from Hardy's later account. The emphasis in the opening declarations of the Society is on the direct connection between representation and need:

> *Resolved*, – that in consequence of a *partial, unequal*, and therefore *inadequate Representation*, together with the *corrupt* Method in which Representatives are elected; *oppressive Taxes, unjust Laws, restrictions of Liberty*, and *wasting of Public Money* have ensued.[43]

The languages of exploitation and need begin to enter the reformers' armoury more pressingly as the cost of the war with France and the consequences of poor harvests begin to bite, at the beginning of 1795.[44] There is, however, some impetus to tackle issues of property and need earlier than this, in response to accusations by loyalists that the reformers were levellers in disguise. But, rather than producing a well worked-out set of causal processes, linking wealth, exploitation, need and the labour of the poor, the most common reaction is to deny that reformers have any interest in equalization of property. Part of Thelwall's *Rights of Nature*.. (1796) for example, is devoted to insisting that the idea of equalizing property was 'totally impossible in the present state of human intellect and industry'.[45] On the other hand, the poor were occasionally used to powerful rhetorical effect, especially by the more literary radicals, to attack the combination of wealth, power and privilege among the upper classes. Consider Holcroft's incensed comments to Windham:

> Who makes the laws ? The rich – Who alone can with probable impunity, break the laws? The rich – Who are impelled by want and misery to break them, and afterwards are imprisoned, transported and hanged? The poor – Who do the work? – The poor. Who reap the fruits? – The rich. Who pay the taxes? The poor for their labours pay everything. Who impose the taxes? The rich, whose luxury devours what the labours of the poor produce. On what do the rich feed? On the product of the poor's misery. On what do the rich ride? On the bent and broken back of the poor. . . .[46]

This is not a manifesto for revolution but, again, a series of rhetorical flourishes drawn out by Windham's suggestion that the war imposed no hardship on anyone. That the sense of exploitation is not greater is a function of the tendency to see current ills as a result of the corruptions of parliamentary representation rather than as indicative of deep-rooted structural inequalities.[47] These corruptions are sustained by 'a restless, all-consuming Aristocracy', 'treacherous and hypocritical statesmen', and by 'the venal oligarchy, (THE ONE HUNDRED AND SIXTY-TWO PROPRIETORS)' who have usurped the democratic branch of the constitution.[48] The design has involved abuses in the mode of election, the duration of parliaments and the perpetuation of corrupt property in decayed corporations. But once the problems of representation are resolved, the other evils of society, such as poverty will cease. Moreover, a very great proportion of the comments on the poor are comments on 'them', rather than on 'us'. That is, it is a concern that again divides the majority in terms of its self-identification, rather than uniting it. A further way in which the intensity of a collective identity and cause is vitiated is by the lack of any consistent sense of antagonism, to 'those of the higher ranks' – whom the corresponding societies welcomed but resisted putting in positions of influence, least it prevent 'the people exerting themselves in their own cause' by coming 'to depend implicitly (as formally) upon the mere ipse dixit of some NobleMan or great Man without the least trouble of examining for themselves. . . '.[49] The porous character of the reforming interest gives it both a degree of latitudinarianism towards those it admits and acknowledges as its fellows, and vitiates its capacity to root their political commitments in a consistent social identity.

In many respects this simply emphasizes Thompson's point about the political character of the project of poorer reformers, but in doing so it also undercuts accounts that look to the class interests of those involved. By taking a political view of the problem and of its solution, the reformers took as their allies an inherently unstable majority. Unstable, because while the aggregate interest was for the inclusion of the majority, individual incentives had no such collective dimension. But this did not mean that those who perceived their political exclusion as an injustice had no reason for seeking to unite with others – on the contrary, each clearly had a prima facie, but *ceteris paribus*, reason for uniting with others to change their representation. That is, it was a reason, but its force depended on a whole range of factors: the salience of that exclusion to the individual; a sense that the exclusion was shared by others in a way that gave them a common interest in challenging it; a sense that challenging it was feasible and its costs not prohibitive; a sense that he could not do as well or better elsewhere.

This may seem an odd way to describe the situation but it helps emphasize the extent to which members of 'the people' would have had a wide range of cross cutting interests and incentives (in which locality is a consistently under-estimated component). The broad convergence within the reform movement was on the wholly political character of their case – as opposed to social or economic (both of which played a central role in popular participation in the French Revolution). But, while one line between minority and majority was easy to draw (those with the vote and those without), there was little agreement on the issue of how the suffrage should be settled: that is, no ideological consensus either on the grounds for suffrage (rights vs utility vs prescription/tradition), or on whether or how it should be extended. On this account, then, membership of reform societies, participation in public meetings, and so on, might well have been as conditional for many radicals as it was for many loyalists.

Before I look at the second type of account we might give, I want to stand back a moment and look at the strategy of argument I have deployed. The preceding discussion resists the idea that a common set of real interests provided the basis for individual commitment and the unification of the reform movement, on the grounds that objective accounts of common interests are weak and difficult to connect with the way that individuals would have perceived their situation. For that reason, popular reformers' commitments might well have had the same conditional and tactical relationship to the radical ideas they were willing to subscribe to as was the case for loyalism. One possible response to this conclusion would be to claim that the failure of the project is largely a consequence of the very distinction between expressive and instrumental behaviour with which I began this paper. That is, that we should abandon that distinction, and simply accept that expressive commitment is itself either wholly idiosyncratic or largely illusory, and that political conflict is best understood in tactical terms. Since I don't find that picture attractive, let me suggest an alternative account.

V

This alternative account of radicalism avoids the concern with class interests and focuses instead on the dynamics of contesting exclusion. Members of the popular reform organizations that sprang up in 1791 and 1792 were largely excluded from the political system and were, in effect, making a bid for inclusion; a bid which drew forth fierce resistance. Part of the response to that resistance was for reformers' demands and attitudes to harden, with the reaction being regarded by many as further evidence of the urgency of reform, and of the need for thoroughgoing change; and in the face of that reaction, reformers' objectives often became seen as non-negotiable. That, in turn, hardened the reaction, which, in turn, further consolidated reformers' commitments.

But this story needs further development, not least because it implies that a process that forged commitment for the radicals on the one hand, might equally, and for the same reasons, have forged commitments for the loyalists on the other. I want to suggest, in fact, that there were four key elements in the process that differentially affected the reformers.

One difference between the conditional allegiance of popular loyalists and the commitments of popular radicals is that between going along with something (the status quo) and resisting it. In the opening stages of the decade, these differences were not huge for many participants – voicing objections to the system of representation in the company of others might be costless, or positively rewarding.[50] The situation changes as these actions gain a salience as a result of the actions and reactions of others – especially the government and local magistrates. The prosecutions for sedition (seriously underestimated in the standard work by Emsley[51]), would have been sufficiently widely known within their localities to bring those with reforming sympathies up sharp. So too would they have been brought up by Paine burnings, anti-radical mobs, Royal Proclamations, County meetings for loyal addresses, and so on. Different individuals at different times found their probably rather inchoate ideas and principles challenged, and were forced to reassess them to decide how far, and in what ways their views were dispensable, and how far they felt they had to affirm them as fundamental to their sense of themselves and their place in the world. By degrees, as they reacted to events, some came to define themselves as fundamentally in opposition to the status quo. And, over time, they had to face the issue of how far they were prepared to go in pursuing their commitments, and how far those commitments were forced to become intellectual in character, rather than being practically motivating. Loyalists were not confronted in the same way. Evidence of radical sedition might have confirmed fears of the activities of evil and designing men, as would the correspondence between reformers and the French Legislative Assembly and, subsequently, the Convention, and the later arrests for treason. But, confirming instances do not test belief in the same way as attempted refutation. Moreover, it is doubtful that many loyalists knowingly encountered radicals, save in the slogans they found chalked on doors, and the reports they received from loyalist pamphlets and broadsides. As a result they were not subjected to the same challenges, and consequently did not need to press their beliefs or test their commitments.

There is also a different internal dynamic in conformist and oppositional social movements. In the former case, there are few costs to professing one's commitment, or to seeking to influence the direction taken by the organization. Moreover, while those initially organizing the loyalist movements sought to mobilize loyal opinion, their ambition was a forked one: they wanted to mobilize and they wanted loyalists – on balance, their preference was for the former. As a result, within loyalist associations there could be a relatively broad and tolerant attitude to the views of participants who were, for whatever reasons, prepared to espouse their loyalty to King and country. The result was a relative degree of pluralism and tolerance and a reluctance to risk alienating one's membership. Among reformers, once reaction begins, the incentives are increasingly to mistrust outsiders and to shun publicity, with a corresponding tendency for one's commitments to harden and for internal disagreements to produce faction and splitting. In this case, what remnants of popular radicalism there were within the revolutionary cells of the United Irishmen, United Englishmen, United Britons, Spencians and others, had hardened into unconditional commitments.

A third related difference between the two movements lay in the detail of their respective programmes and in the relations between leaders and followers. The points are connected. The loyalist associations, and later the volunteers and militias, relied on a high level of upper and middle class initiative, their organizational form was essentially laid down by the associations' leadership, and their principles and commitments were set broadly by the idea of loyalty to the crown and a willingness to follow the leadership of the government. What was asked of supporters was support in that broad endeavour: while many middle class supporters also offered extensive advice and information, together with pamphlets, broadsheets and songs, the broader lower-order constituencies in, for example, the militia are unlikely to have been heavily involved in the ideological dimensions of their activities. In contrast, the reform organizations, as Gunther Lottes stressed twenty years ago,[52] were less led than collectively developed, with high levels of local participation and debate over both political principles and the practical organizational details of reform. This participatory dimension to the political agenda of the reform movement meant that members of the reform societies would have had an experience of arguing through and developing the details of their political principles that would have been in sharp contrast to loyalist meetings and would have, especially given the other conditions, ensured that those principles were forged as an ongoing process of developing commitment – a commitment which repression might silence without extinguishing.

The final difference between loyalists and radicals concerns the complications introduced by France. The popular reform movement arises, in part, out of the Revolution controversy and the assiduous circulation of its central texts, and France remained a central issue for reformers – becoming a bone of contention between supporters of moderate reform who distanced themselves from France after September 1792 and the popular organizations whose attitudes were unaffected by the September massacres, subsequently raising major issues of loyalty for reformers once Britain and France were at war. For many loyalists,

France simply conformed to its true colours as a traditional enemy, requiring mobilization and vigilance. But that could be achieved without thinking either that one was thereby necessarily mobilizing against reform in any of its colours, or that there was any justification for linking hostility to France to denying the legitimacy of its revolution or the principles it had initially espoused. Moreover, while such a position would generate suspicion towards groups who linked themselves to this traditional enemy, and might encourage fears of fifth columnists, fellow travellers and potential insurgents in the pay of foreign powers, the connection between such characters and popular reformers were pretty tenuous and largely failed to bear detailed scrutiny once brought before a court of law. In contrast, for reformers, France remained a complex point of identification – additionally complicated by their sense that the war against France was itself intended as a war against them. The various attempts to define the nature of the ideological links with France are evidence of the extent to which the radicals found their agenda framed by loyalism as either pro-French or pro-government and shows the way that they attempted to define a path in which reform remained an option. The difficulty with this was the extent to which, as opposition to the government was faced by more vehement reaction, reformers became persuaded that their own government was engaged in a conspiracy against their traditional liberties, with France as a pretext. On the one hand this offered an alliance with the respectable movement against the war among those whom Cookson has called 'The Friends of Peace'; on the other, as the decade wore on, it persuaded many that the only chance for effective resistance to growing domestic tyranny was to seek French support. From the summer of 1792, if not before, loyalism found it possible to tar radicalism with a broad French brush, and radicals were forced to work through the nature of their commitment to France and its implications often in considerable detail. That detail, however, often led to considerable latitude for French actions – not least because it was possible to explain them in terms of the exigencies faced by an embattled country, thrown into disorder by foreign interference, war, an internal history of long resistance to reform and the continuing effects of the remnants of despotism. Moreover, the growing sense that traditional national rivalry was being deployed against the liberties of the ordinary people, gave an added dimension to the reformers' understanding of the task facing them. It increased the scale of envisaged necessary reform, and the sense of the obstacles in its way, but it also increased the sense of urgency associated with the reform project.

In each of these four cases, we can see reformers as under pressure to work through their commitments in ways which simply did not apply to supporters of loyalism. Of course, while this account may show how initial dispositions to favour reform might be sharpened and hardened as the intellectual controversy of 1790 and 1791 becomes a struggle on the part of popular organizations to challenge their exclusion from the political system, it does not explain the origins of those initial predispositions. But, I would suggest, we can afford an extremely pluralist account of this – they certainly did not all come from the same source. They comprised the infidels, deists, free-thinkers, millennarians, Muggletonians, Swedenborgians, mystics, religious enthusiasts, dissenters, rationalists, disaffected working men, democrats, those who had gained some political education in the American War, hacks, reviewers and publishers, drop-outs from the gentry and aristocracy, literary enthusiasts for France, and so on, each of whom, in different ways, may have stumbled into the revolution controversy and found in it resonances of their own sense of exclusion, confirmation of the indefensibility of the aristocratic order, and intimations of the justice of their particular cause. Their origins are legion. What they came to share was an experience of forging their commitments, in part in company with others, in the debating societies and political organizations of the 1790s, and in part by coming to recognize the extent to which their beliefs were anathema to the existing order and by, nonetheless, continuing to affirm them. Doing so was doubtless assisted by their sense of solidarity with others, which could be generated by organizations, meetings and membership of societies, or could arise on the back of other activities, as Hardy had relied on when the first meeting of the LCS was held: 'After the business of the day was ended they retired as was customary for tradesmen to go to a public house and after supper conversation followed condoling with each other on the miserable and wretched state the people were reduced to, merely as we believed, from the want of a fair, and equal representation. . .'.[53] Even where there were such networks and a sense of solidarity, which was most likely in the larger urban areas, and principally in London – since these afforded a degree of anonymity and the opportunity for men of similar means and experiences to meet – these certainly could not insulate their members from the realization that they were in an increasingly precarious position. But the precariousness of their position and the shared sense of exclusion, for a period at least, encouraged them to overlook their differences – most notably on the question of religion, but also on aspects of the broader radical programme. For a period, roughly 1792–8 at least, there was a degree of unity on the principles of reform and the use of peaceful methods to those ends. Although membership figures for the reform societies fluctuated wildly in this period there was a core amongst whom a sense of the justice and significance of their cause took hold, leading them to take considerable risks and incur substantial costs, which became part of the inheritance and ballast of the popular movements of the 1790s. Thereafter, in the face of unremitting government attempts at suppression a much smaller collection of increasingly fragmented groups toyed variously with the organization of armed resistance, the encouragement of invasion, and further forms of sedition in a radical underworld.

VI

Three aspects of this story need further emphasis and elaboration. First, the practical consequences of the war with France were huge: on the one hand increasing suspicion of those who had tied themselves to the French revolution, and on the other spreading, from 1797 onward, a real fear of potential invasion which required extensive domestic mobilization. For those sympathetic to reform, the war with France, and the loyalists insistence that reformers were wild Jacobin enthusiasts, were seen as further indications that the ministry was pursuing a policy which would not only deny reform but would further load the people with excessive taxation and threaten English liberties. While for loyalists, the reformers' continued willingness to be associated with France, and their continuing pressure for reform confirmed their seditious intent and the dangers the constitution faced. What sustains the asymmetry between them, then, is that where it was possible for a broader public to go along with loyalism because it had significant benefits, relatively few costs (as the ability of volunteer regiments to refuse to serve outside of their county indicates), and was in practice a rather undemanding and tolerant creed, radicals faced the prospect of substantial costs for sustaining their commitment – and thereby had substantial incentives to review that commitment and its significance for them. Loyalists' commitments were broadly to king, constitution and country, and they were able to see reformers as tantamount to a foreign threat, which did not require refutation in detail so much as repudiation in general; in contrast, the radical societies became increasingly caught in a process of defining and defending their commitments in detail – feeling forced to tread warily to avoid prosecution for sedition, to repudiate the slurs of the opposition press, and to insist on their legitimate right to press for reform. And at each stage of this process a reinvestment in the commitment was required.

The second feature is the fact that this story about the forging of fundamental commitments is not harmed, in the way the class story is, by recognizing the huge diversity of oppositional groups which existed in Britain in the 1790s and which were only ever loosely linked together, nor by acknowledging the considerable differences in principles and aspirations among such groups. In their different ways they had come to define themselves as oppositional, and to regard that opposition as part of a common platform – even if, in some cases, the only thing they shared was being the target of government and loyalist attack. Popular loyalists could be half-hearted, hedging their bets, but radicals had to be firmly committed – albeit not necessarily committed to the same principles or ends.

The third aspect that bears emphasis concerns the ideological diversity of radicals, and the substantial difficulties that exist in reading some of the propaganda, ballads and squibs of the period – difficulties that arise from the local character of much propaganda, from its highly contextual nature, from the complex rhetorical techniques used to evade prosecution, and from the mix of highly adept and extremely clumsy contributions. Reeves himself mistook one of his letters as from a radical, not a loyalist; and failed to see that another was not a weak loyalist performance but an adept radical one. The Royal Proclamations, the prosecution of publishers, authors and booksellers, the hounding of chapmen and ballad singers, all served to heighten tension, and correspondingly to give publications a dramatically narrowed scope, but a correspondingly highly freighted and nuanced form. One associated feature is that much radical propaganda is increasingly dedicated to impropriety, lampooning, pornography and deriding the established political order and its members.[54] It was relatively easy to satirize and caricature the status quo – and it was often less risky and more effective: less risky because it could be more embarrassing to prosecute than ignore such publications because they parodied official and loyalist discourse and appealed overtly to values which the status quo purported to tolerate. Moreover, juries proved willing to tolerate less direct and more metaphorical attacks – as with Eaton/Thelwall's 'King Chaunticlere'.[55] Also, it was difficult to find a common language and set of interests which would unite the heterogenous mass of the people – especially difficult when the radicals faced loyalist appeals to popular patriotism and traditional distrust of and scorn for the French. Paine sought to do so, and in many respects had considerable success – in preparing Part Two of *Rights of Man* he claimed that he had 'so far got the ear of John Bull that he will read what I write – which is more than ever was done before to the same extent'.[56] But it is worth recognizing the limits of his success. While he achieved unprecedented circulation, he spoke in an idiom which was foreign to the traditional conception of the distinctive liberties of the free-born Englishman; his anti-monarchism was not universally popular and sat uncomfortably with some reformers' emphasis on restoring a balance between constituted powers; his proposals for welfare provision may have seemed attractive to some but it is likely that many would have resisted their non-local character, or would have preferred direct cuts in taxation. Moreover, while his writings fuelled the popular reform leadership and encouraged them to turn towards conventionism in pressing for reform, many among the leadership distanced themselves from substantial parts of the doctrine.[57] So much so that the willingness assiduously to circulate it seems to be best understood as on a par with the more satiric, lampooning and caricatural literature and prints circulated – they offered the frisson of thinking the unthinkable, of cocking a snook at those in authority and undercutting the pretensions of aristocracy – which, as Thompson points out, was a long-standing British popular tradition. We tend to read Paine for doctrine, but we probably understand his impact more adequately if we read him for 'attitude'. Horne Tooke found some bits of the book reprehensible, but reasoned that there were sections of the Bible 'which a man would not chose to read before his wife and daughters'[58] but his willingness to back its circulation was clearly based on his support for its effect, rather than for its doctrine. Finally, Paine's standing as a potential ideologue for radical reformers was seriously complicated by his views on religion (on which there were huge divisions among reformers – Priestley described the Age of Reason to Theophilus Lindsay as 'the weakest and most absurd, as well as the most arrogant of anything I have yet seen'[59] and later by his encouragement of the French invasion force (since defence of France was far from equivalent to welcoming a French invasion force[60]). While in many respects not an extremist – certainly if compared to those to whom he nearly fell victim in the French Revolution – Paine's universalism and his deism had a serious impact on his ability to offer a distinctive collective identity for a British radicalism.

This recognition of the difficulties facing those espousing reformist political principles invites a further conclusion. The loyalist anathematizing of so called 'republican principles' left reformers with a highly constrained form of political discourse – not that they could not think radically, but they were constrained to express their appeals to the public in as neutral a political language as possible. Hence the attractions of constitutionalism – to pretend a Burkean reverence for the constitution and to focus on less abstract justifications and less threatening targets within that framework. To this extent, one needs the greatest care in taking the official pronouncements of the radical societies as expressive of their fundamental commitments. There is, as I hope I have shown, every reason to think that we are dealing with an often unequivocal commitment to radical reform, but it does not follow that the language in which those aspirations were expressed fully captured the commitments of those who wrote and acted within the movement. If loyalist's lip-service is not expressive, because tentative and conditional; reformers' subscription to the idioms of constitutionalism is not expressive in a different way, because it is often tactical and rhetorical.

If this is right, then some asymmetry is permissible, but it needs to be engaged in with considerable care. It is not just a case of seeing radicalism as more expressive, we need to show in detail how the sense of fundamental interests and commitments becomes forged in the process of political dispute and action, and we need to recognize the refracted ways in which those commitments were subsequently expressed. In terms of our matrix there is a further conclusion that might be drawn. The extent of popular political mobilization in the 1790s was unprecedented: for many we are dealing with a novel experience of politicization – one that is common to every new generation but in this case had no traditional forms to structure and regulate it. Events led to different experiences of this politicization – some taking the direction of loyalism, others radicalism. But these were different experiences, with different consequences for people's sense of self and of their commitments, which suggests that the distinction between expressive and non-expressive is really one which evolves through the practical conflict of the period; it need not and should not be generated by an a-priori account of real interests.

VII

Does this account have implications for our understanding of radicalism? I think a number of things follow if we think of the popular reform movement of the revolutionary period as radical.

There is little or no unity of ideology among reformers – no wholeheartedly accepted radical programme, and no sense of the implications of holding one view necessitating other views. So if it is a radical movement it is not by virtue of a consistent ideology. That also means that the tradition of radicalism is not likely to be an ideologically consistent tradition. The 1790s may have borrowed from earlier periods, such as the Civil War and the Country Party opposition movement, just as later generations borrowed from the 1790s, but the borrowings do not establish the case for a consistent tradition.

If radicalism is not a matter of ideology, is it then a question of when certain ideas, and organizations and other manifestations are rendered radical? That is, is what makes something radical a matter of context – perhaps a combination of a system of social and/or political exclusion, on the one hand, denying access to positions of power and influence, or indeed, to positions of equal standing as citizens, coupled with a strategy of usurpation and its ideological elaboration on the part of those excluded? And is what gives a sense of a radical tradition a function of the family resemblances and overlapping memberships that exist between the groups excluded (the poor, the labouring classes, religious minorities, economically and physically exploited groups); and/or the grounds of their exclusion (denials of citizenship on the grounds of class, race, gender or sexual preference); and/or the strategies adopted for usurpation – the inversion of despised identities, the associated transformation in the sense of self and standing, the adoption of universalist principles to justify inclusion; and/or the nature and degree of resistance that they meet from the status quo? Indeed, in the latter case, is it in fact a feature of movements becoming radical that their attempts to secure their goals lock them into a struggle with the existing order in which both sides become more sharply defined and more antagonistic, with the consequence that the potential costs of concessions become exaggerated? If so, is what marks radicalism its outsider status – its lack of integration in the existing political and economic system and its increasingly confrontational attitude to that system, where those involved come to see their commitments as non-negotiable? If so, and this account seems to fit the picture of the 1790s that I have sketched, then it also becomes possible to see why some explanatory asymmetry can in fact be justified. Not by an appeal to real or class interests, but by recognizing the way that fundamental interests and commitments become forged in the process of political reflection and contestation.

ACKNOWLEDGMENT

My thanks for comments on earlier versions of this paper are owed to my fellow contributors, to Iain McCalman, Jon Mee and Martin Fitzpatrick, and to audiences at Hull and Cambridge Universities and the Humanities Research Centre at the Australian National University.

NOTES

1 E. P. Thompson, *The Making of the English Working Class* 2nd edition (Harmondsworth, Penguin, 1968) pp. 781–2.
2 E. P. Thompson, *Customs in Common* (Harmondsworth, Penguin, 1993) pp. 95–6.
3 Linda Colley, 'The Apotheosis of George III: Loyalty, Royalty and the British Nation, 1760–1820', *Past and Present* cii (1984), 97–129; also her, *Britons: Forging the Nation 1707–1837* (New Haven, Yale University Press, 1992) and Marilyn Morris, *The British Monarchy and the French Revolution* (New Haven, Yale University Press, 1998); David Eastwood, 'Patriotism and the English State in the 1790s' in *The French Revolution and British Popular Politics*, ed. Mark Philp (Cambridge, Cambridge University Press, 1991), pp. 146–68, H. T. Dickinson, 'Popular Loyalism in Britain in the 1790s', in *The Transformation of Political Culture: England and Germany in the Late Eighteenth Century*, ed., Eckhart Hellmuth (Oxford, Clarendon Press, 1990) pp. 503–33.
4 W. H. Reid, *The Rise and Dissolution of the Infidel Societies in this Metropolis* (London, 1800); I. McCalman, *Radical Underworld: Prophets, Revolutionaries and Pornographers in London, 1795–1840* (Cambridge, Cambridge University Press, 1988) p. 1.
5 Morris, *The British Monarchy and the French Revolution* p. 62.
6 Cf., Mark Philp, 'The Fragmented Ideology of Reform' in *The French Revolution and British Popular Politics* pp. 50–77; 'Vulgar Conservatism 1792–3', *English Historical Review* 110, No 435, February 1995, 42–69; 'English Republicanism in the 1790s' *J Political Philosophy*, 6(3) September 1998, pp. 235–62.
7 It is notable that Paine initially had thought it imperative to get the second part of the *Rights of Man* published at the end of 1791, when 'the town will begin to fill' with members of Parliament returning for the new session – although he failed for various reasons to do so. D. Hawke, *Paine* (New York, Norton, 1974) p. 238.
8 Cited in A. O. Hirschman, *The Rhetoric of Reaction: Perversity, Futility, Jeopardy* (Cambridge, Mass., Harvard University Press, 1991) p. 44.
9 See Thomas W.Copeland, 'Burke, Paine, and Jefferson' in *Edmund Burke: Six Essays* (London, Jonathan Cape, 1949) 146–89.
10 Cf., Emily Lorraine de Montluzin, *The Anti-Jacobins 1798–1800: The Early Contributors to the 'Anti-Jacobin Review* (London, Macmillian 1988), and Iain McCalman ed. *The Oxford Companion to the Age of Romanticism and Revolution* (Oxford, Oxford University Press, 1999).

11 Lefebvre clearly wished to down-play the irrational character of crowd behaviour during the Great Fear, in contrast to the work, for example, of Gustav LeBon. Nonetheless, the panics he describes are, while intelligible, at base, not rational or intentional, cf Georges Lefebvre, *The Great Fear of 1789: Rural Panic in Revolutionary France* (London, New Left Books, 1973 esp.p. 50, and Part III, p. 137–211 esp. 156–7.

12 Mark Granovetter, 'Threshold Models of Collective Behaviour', *American J of Sociology*, 83 (1978), pp. 1420–43.

13 As discussed at points in John Bohsetdt, *Riots and Community Politics in England and Wales 1790–1810* (Cambridge, Mass., Harvard University Press, 1983) and Nicholas Rogers, *Crowds, Culture and Politics in Georgian England* (Oxford, Clarendon Press, 1998).

14 Gustave Le Bon, *The Crowd: A Study of the Popular Mind* (New York, Viking, 1960). For theories of crowd behaviour see the judicious account in Rogers, *Crowds, Culture and Politics. . .*, chapter 1, and James Coleman's *Foundations of Social Theory* (Cambridge, Mass., Harvard University Press, 1990) chapter 9, especially his distinction between panics and hostile and expressive crowds. Clearly, in the light of these works we would be better off classifying types of crowd rather than trying to associate authors with a single type of crowd explanation. So 'moral economy' crowds need contrasting with hunger driven crowds, or panics, or élite-mustered crowds, and so on.

15 The sources for this include Robert R. Dozier, *For King, Constitution, and Country: The English Loyalists and the French Revolution* (Lexington, University Press of Kentucky, 1983); Thompson's comments on popular loyalism; O'Gorman's unpublished work on Paine burnings; Roger Wells, *Insurrection: The British Experience* (Gloucester, Alan Sutton, 1983) and *Wretched Faces: Famine in Wartime England 1763–1803* (Gloucester, Alan Sutton, 1988); John E Cookson *The British Armed Nation 1793–1815* (Oxford, Clarendon Press, 1997); and Ian Christie, *Stress and Stability in Late Eighteenth Century Britain: Reflections on the Avoidance of Revolution* (Oxford, Clarendon Press, 1984).

16 I am imputing to Reeves a rather similar view to that expressed by Dr Johnson, in *The False Alarm* (1770) and *The Patriot* (1774) *Yale Edition of the Works of Samuel Johnson*, vol X *Political Writings*, ed. D. J. Greene.

17 Bodleian Library, G.A. Warw. b. 292r.

18 British Library, Adds ms 16,924(29r).

19 *Some of* this work is pending. But see Nicholas Rogers 'Burning Tom Paine: Loyalism and Counter-Revolution in Britain 1792–3' *Social History* 32 (64), 1999, and his *Crowds, Culture and Politics* in *Georgian England* (Oxford, Clarendon Press, 1998), pp. 201–8.

20 This emphasis on the controlled nature of such loyalist demonstrations – they were not, for the most part, popular outbursts against radicals so much as carefully marshalled performances – can be recognized in reports to Reeves, such as British Library Adds ms 16,924 f, and f 112 when 'The last dying Speech and Confession of that infamous fellow Thos Paine who was hanged

and afterwards burnt this day here, many demonstrations of loyalty was shown upon the occasion and Fox's head was fixed on pain, with a bubble out of his mouth with these words: 'I will support thy doctrine to the utmost of my abilities, I only lament that we have not the original here'.

21 British Library Adds ms 16,924(134^{r-v}). See my 'Vulgar Conservatism 1792–3'.

22 British Library Adds ms 16, 927, (47v).

23 Letter from Sarah Trimmer, Adds m 16,923 f 47–50.

24 British Library Adds ms 16,928(5^{r}). Rogers, *Crowds, Culture and Politics* p. 209, treats this as a sincere loyalist account – but there are real grounds for doubt – not least the phrases' but having nothing to do', and 'true Jacobite breed.' Compare with other 'straight' accounts in the papers of burnings of Paine: 16,922(121^{r}-2^{v}), 16,923(67^{r}), 16,924(62^{r} (alongside Dr Priestley),112^{r}), and 16,928(7^{r}). One of Reeves' correspondents, T Hartley of Liverpool, accused republicans of 'artfully labouring to seduce people from the king: They know themselves weak in number, and therefore act by stratagem on all occasions – They are the first of all mixed companies to drink the 'King and Constitution,' but it is easy to discover by their *looks* and *motions* to each other that they do it in derision only.' 16,923 (f.85–6).

25 John Cookson, *The British Armed Nation*... pp. 67–8.

26 S. C. Smith, 'Loyalty and Opposition in the Napoleonic Wars: The Impact of the Local Militia 1807–15' D.Phil (Oxford, 1984), cited in Cookson, p. 89, note 76. See also Austin Gee, *The British Volunteer Movement 1794–1814* (Clarendon Press, Oxford, 2003) especially chapter 5 on the motivation for volunteering.

27 Cookson, p. 110.

28 Cookson, p. 91.

29 Cookson, p. 95.

30 Frank O'Gorman, *Voters, Patrons and Parties: The Unreformed Electorate of Hanoverian England, 1734–1832* (Oxford, Clarendon Press, 1989) p. 179.

31 See Marilyn Morris, *The British Monarchy and the French Revolution* p. 88. Equally, the letters to Reeves and the resolutions passed in the winter of 1792–3 hardly show a slavish devotion to Reeves' view of loyalism. Of course, as I discuss below, there is a problem in knowing how to read such assertions and ambiguities – whether they are ways of masking radical sentiment, or whether people genuinely did not see a desire for reform as incompatible with loyalty and patriotism. That the government and its loyalist supporters came increasingly to insist on this incompatibility suggests that they were trying to draw a line that others did not naturally draw.

32 See Cookson, *The British Armed Nation*, p. 237.

33 *Ibid*., p. 233. See also, the essays by Nicholas Rodgers, Katrina Navickas and Jon Newman in Mark Philp (ed.,) *Resisting Napoleon: The British Response to the Threat of Invasion 1797–1815* (Aldershot, Hants, Ashgate, 2006), chapters 2, 3 and 4.

34 Cookson, *The British Armed Nation*, p. 237.

35 Not least, with Gareth Stedman Jones, *Languages of Class* (Cambridge, Cambridge University Press, 1983).

36 *Selections from the Papers of the London Corresponding Society 1792–9* ed., Mary Thale (Cambridge, Cambridge University Press. 1983) p. 18.

37 David Hume, *Essays Moral, Political, and Literary* ed., E. F. Miller (Indianapolis, Liberty Press, 1987), p. 32.

38 Thomas Paine, *Rights of Man* in *Rights of Man, Common Sense and other Political Writings* ed., Mark Philp (Oxford, Oxford University Press, 1995) p. 96 and 172.

39 Paul Langford, *Public Life and the Propertied Englishman 1689–1798* (Oxford, Clarendon Press, 1991) p. 282.

40 See Christina and David Bewley, *Gentleman Radical: A Life of John Horne Tooke* (London, Tauris Academic, 1998).

41 Memoir of Thomas Hardy, cited in *Selections from the Papers of the LCS* ed., Thale, p. 7.

42 *Ibid.*, p. 8.

43 *Ibid.*, p. 10.

44 See David Eastwood, *Governing Rural England: Tradition and Transformation in Local Government 1780–1840* (Oxford, Clarendon Press, 1994) pp. 101–32.

45 See Albert Goodwin, *The Friends of Liberty: The English Democratic Movement in the Age of the French Revolution* (London, Hutchinson, 1979) p. 473.

46 *Ibid.*, p. 489.

47 Although it has recently been claimed that we can find in this period the beginnings of an understanding of this structural inequality which does not tie it to political representation. See Noel Thompson, *The Real Rights of Man: Political Economies for the Working Class 1775–1850* (Pluto Press: London, 1998).

48 London Corresponding Society's *Joint Address to the French National Convention, 27 September 1792*, reprinted in Goodwin, *Friends of Liberty* p. 502; W. Godwin, 'Essay Against Re-opening War with France' in M. Philp ed., *The Political and Philosophical Writings of William Godwin* (London, Pickering and Chatto, 1993) volume 2, p. 37; J. Thelwall, *The Natural and Constitutional Right of Britons* in G. Claeys ed., *The Politics of English Jacobinism: Writings of John Thelwall* (Pennsylvania, Pennsylvania State University Press, 1995) p. 31.

49 *Selections from the Papers of the LCS* p. 8.

50 As was mass participation in events celebrating French victories in, for example, November 1792. See for example the *Manchester Herald*, 1 December 1792.

51 Clive Emsley, 'An Aspect of Pitt's Terror: Prosecutions for Sedition during the 1790s' *Social History* 6, 2, May 1981; 'Repression, terror and the rule of law in England during the decade of the French Revolution' *English Historical Review* 100, 1985, 801–25. The most serious challenge to date to Emsley's

work is Steve Poole's 'Pitt's Terror Reconsidered: Jacobinism and the Law in Two South-Western Counties, 1791–1803 *Southern History* 17 (1995), 65–87. For the strategies and impact of the major trials for Treason see John Barell's magisterial *Imagining the King's Death: Figurative Treason, Fantasies of Regicide 1793–1796* (Oxford, Oxford University Press, 2000).

52 Günter Lottes, *Politische Aufklärung und plebejisches Publikum. Zur Theorie und Praxis des englischen Radikalismus im spätem 10. Jahrhundert* (Munich and Vienna, 1979; see also his 'Radicalism, revolution and political culture', in Philp ed., *The French Revolution and British Popular Politics.*

53 *Selections from the Papers of the LCS* p. 6.

54 My favourite contributions include Merry's *Wonderful Exhibition!!! Signor Gulielmo Pittachio: the sublime wonder of the world*, from the *Courier*, Friday Nov. 28, 1794, Lee's 'King Killing' and the *Admirable Satire on the Death, Dissection, Funeral Procession and Epitaph of Mr Pitt*, London, 1795. On the first see Jon Mee's, 'The Political Showman at home: Reflections on Popular Radicalism and Print culture in the 1790s' in *Radicalism and the Threat of Revolution: Essays in Honour of Malcolm Thomis* ed. Michael Davis (London, Macmillan, 2000), and his 'Reciprocal Expressions of kindness: Robert Merry, Della Cruscanism and the Limits of Romantic Sociability' in *Romantic Sociability* ed., Gillian Russell and Clara Tuite (Cambridge, Cambridge University Press, 2006); and on the second Mee's 'The Strange Career of Richard 'Citizen' Lee: Poetry and Popular Radicalism' in ed. Nigel Smith and Timothy Morton, *Radicalism in British Literary Culture, 1650–1830* (Cambridge, Cambridge University Press, 2002). See also, John Barrell 'An Entire Change of Performances?' The Politicisation of Theatre and the Theatricalisation of Politics in the mid 1790s' *Lumen* XVII(1998)11–50.

55 See Marilyn Butler (ed.), *Burke, Paine, Godwin and the Revolution Controversy* (Cambridge, Cambridge University Press, 1984) pp. 185–8.

56 *The Collected Writings of Thomas Paine* ed. Philip S Foner, (Secaucus, N. J., Citadel Press, 1948) volume 2, pp. 1321–2.

57 See T. M. Parsinnen, 'Association, convention and anti-parliament in British radical Politics, 1771–1848' *English Historical Review* 88, July 1973, 504–33, and E. C. Black, *The Association: British Extra-Parliamentary Political Organization, 1769–1832* Cambridge, Mass., Harvard University Press, (1963).

58 D. Hawke, *Paine p. 225.*

59 Franklyn K Prockhaska, 'Thomas Paine's *The Age of Reason* revisited', *J. Hist. Ideas*, Oct-Dec 1972, 33(4) 566.

60 See Alexandra Franklin and Mark Philp, *Napoleon and the Invasion of Britain* (Oxford, Bodleian Library, 2003) and the introduction to Mark Philp (ed.) *Resisting Napoleon: The British Response to the Threat of Invasion 1797–1815* (Aldershot, Hants, Ashgate, 2006).

CHAPTER 8

Henry Hunt's Peep into a Prison: *the Radical Discontinuities of Imprisonment for Debt*

Margot C. Finn

The question of continuity looms large in the historiography of nineteenth-century British radicalism. For decades, the mid Victorian years figured in the secondary literature as a 'profound caesura', a deep disjunction perceived to divide the robust radicalism of the French revolutionary and Chartist eras from the etiolated reformism of the late Victorian labour and socialist movements. But radical historiography of the modern era is now decisively shaped instead by the so-called 'currents of radicalism' thesis.[1] Where historians once saw a sharp break between the class-conscious politics of early nineteenth-century radicalism and the ameliorative reformism of the later Victorian period, the 'currents of radicalism' school posits a more continuous narrative of constitutionalist popular politics in which liberal, radical and even socialist tendencies are seen to have coexisted in a largely symbiotic relationship, rather than to have acted consistently in opposition to each other.[2] In this interpretation, populist appeals crafted to transcend both class rhetorics and economic conditions take pride of place, underpinning a continuous strand of radical activism that crossed socioeconomic divides and extended from the eighteenth into the twentieth century.

Recently, John Belchem and James Epstein have interrogated the role played in this debate over continuity by a central figure in the history of popular politics – the gentleman radical leader.[3] Gentlemanly radicals, these authors note, have served a central function in works that emphasize the continuities of the nineteenth-century radical movement. In the writings of scholars who otherwise evince disparate historical outlooks – Patrick Joyce, Eugenio Biagini and James Vernon, for example – the nineteenth-century gentlemanly leader functions as a human conduit of the radical populist tradition.[4] By interpreting men such as John Bright and William Gladstone as populist leaders rather than as liberal politicians, these historians have created a *terra firma* for radical continuity that stretches from at least the era of the French Revolution across the profound caesura of 1848 and the collapse of Chartism to the later Victorian period. 'No longer excluded or marginalized', Belchem and Epstein argue cogently of this approach, earlier 'popular demagogues like [Henry] Hunt and [Feargus] O'Connor, and the politics for which they stood, have been resituated within a longer narrative, placed in the radical mainstream where liberal values are seen as dominant and class-specific language and demands are either absent or of distinctly secondary importance'.[5]

Belchem and Epstein accept the existence of substantial overlap in the 'currents of continuity running from popular radicalism to popular Liberalism' and acknowledge the ways in which 'the style and rhetoric of gentlemanly leaders such as Bright and Gladstone facilitated the transition many working people made from Chartism to Liberalism and beyond'. But they also urge historians of radicalism to espouse 'a more highly qualified notion of continuity', one which attends more closely to shifts in 'the context of politics in action' over time. Viewed from this perspective, they argue, the popular constitutionalism of early nineteenth-century gentlemanly radicals such as Hunt and O'Connor can be seen to depart significantly from the political agendas later promoted by liberal politicians such as Gladstone and Bright. 'Articulated out of doors, as a claim on public space, constitutionalism provided Hunt and O'Connor with a vocabulary of open access and defiant independence . . . translating the crowd into an extra-parliamentary political force', they contend. 'For Bright and Gladstone, by contrast, constitutionalism became a self-selective language of acceptability, drawing aspiring new citizens away from the crowd into an enclosed culture of progressive improvement, party politics, and constituency organization'.[6] Alive to the discontinuities that marked radicals' persistent use of the constitutionalist idiom, this approach succeeds in capturing the very ambiguities, interruptions and inconsistencies in popular constitutionalism which arguably allowed radical traditions to emerge, evolve and persist throughout the long nineteenth century.[7]

This paper builds on Belchem and Epstein's arguments about the need to attend to change as well as continuity over time in gentlemanly radicalism. It does so by focusing on an episode in the history of popular politics in which both the disjunctions and the coherence of radical activism were conspicuously manifest. By exploring Henry Hunt's campaign to publicize the plight of imprisoned debtors in 1820–21, I draw attention to a political issue which had exercised English radicals since the seventeenth century. But Hunt's radical agitation, waged during his own imprisonment for sedition at Ilchester gaol, Somerset, in the aftermath of the Peterloo massacre, also marked a series of fissures in the history of radicalism and gentlemanly leadership. For as Hunt's efforts ultimately demonstrated, the mere availability of perceived ideological continuities within radical discourse did not ensure the continued salience of these discursive traditions within radical campaigns. In the months that followed the brutal repression of popular radicalism at St Peter's Fields, nineteenth-century popular leaders were eager to insert their own activities into a supposedly continuous pattern of radical activism with roots in the seventeenth century, espousing an invented constitutionalist tradition in which imprisonment for debt featured as an unproblematic focus of radical odium. But together, the changing composition of the prison population in the nineteenth century, the rise of disciplinary penal reform, the growing prominence of artisans in the radical leadership and the evolving trajectory of popular constitutionalism away from robust, often raucous and physical conflict toward the more 'enclosed culture of progressive improvement' described by Belchem and Epstein,[8] all combined to reduce the appeal of the imprisoned debtor as a symbol of radical oppression. In this context, Hunt's laboured investigation of the conditions suffered by debtors and other prisoners at Ilchester gaol – a histrionic and sexually explicit exercise in radical polemic publicized in radical tracts such as his *Peep into a Prison: Or, the Inside of Ilchester Bastile* – provides not only an optic for evaluating the shifting contours of gentlemanly leadership but also a case study in the broader transformation of nineteenth-century popular politics.

Medieval in its origins, arbitrary in its mechanisms and oppressive in its consequences, the practice of imprisonment for debt afforded prime material for radical critique. By empowering creditors to seize and detain their debtors without trial for extended periods, the legal processes of insolvency served for centuries to fill English prisons with a haphazard collection of debtor inmates – some truly indigent, some only temporarily embarrassed and others simply unwilling to meet their financial obligations. Until the Victorian era, the social composition of the debtors' prison was surprisingly eclectic, comprising gentlemen and labourers, professional men and artisans.[9] These civil prisoners, confined for extended periods in poorly maintained foundations with little official oversight, elaborated complex systems of self-government that brought a limited degree of internal discipline to institutions otherwise dominated by disorderly forms of male sociability. Allowing affluent debtors to live in seedy gentility while protecting their property from their creditors, the practices of imprisonment for debt subjected less fortunate insolvents (and their families) to extremes of poverty which were relieved only at episodic intervals by piecemeal parliamentary efforts to assist – and at times to liberate – the debtor inmate population.[10]

Antagonism to the system of imprisonment for debt, and concern to redress the oppressive tyrannies of prison conditions more generally, enjoyed a distinguished genealogy in the extended tradition of radical activism, of which nineteenth-century popular radicals claimed gentlemanly leaders such as Hunt and O'Connor to be the modern exemplars. Calls for stricter government oversight of venal prison officials were a commonplace of seventeenth-century radical critiques of English legal culture, and mounting concerns that arbitrary government would erode common-law protections of the subject lent added weight to established, generic objections to unjust confinement in the middle decades of the century. In the hectic years that surrounded the Civil War and Interregnum, prison conditions attracted the attention of a broad spectrum of political activists – many of whom, having suffered imprisonment for their own political beliefs and activities, possessed a vested, personal interest in this subject. Digger ideologues, despite their predominantly agrarian preoccupations, were careful to number imprisonment for debt among the 'wicked Laws' that constrained English freedoms. In a tract published in 1649, Gerrard Winstanley urged that 'prisoners that perish in prison by merciless Creditors & Jaylors . . . may not be meyd up, and starved, until they are poysoned there', and a Digger pamphlet of 1650 called upon Parliament to 'release all Prisoners for debt, that cannot pay their debts, and let the Prisons be for work-houses for the poor to make things for the fishing Trade. . .'[11] Leveller critics likewise waged a vociferous campaign from the fringes of political culture against the iniquities of profit-oriented and punitive imprisonment. Barebones Parliament, although unwilling to abolish imprisonment for debt altogether, did enact legislation in October 1653 that regulated gaolers' fees and subjected prison-keepers to a degree of judicial oversight.[12]

Published in 1646, John Lilburne's *Liberty Vindicated against Slavery: Shewing, That Imprisonment for Debt, Refusing to Answer Interrogatories, Long Imprisonment . . . Abuse of Prisons, and Cruell Extortion of Prison-keepers, are all destructive of the fundamental Laws and common Freedomes of the people* nicely illustrates the lines of seventeenth-century polemic against imprisonment for debt which were later to resonate with eighteenth- and nineteenth-century radical campaigns. Extolling Magna Carta, Lilburne argued from the premise that both common and statutory law were rendered null and void when they violated this foundation text of English liberties. Judged by this standard, contemporary prison practices such as the imposition of fees for foodstuffs and services by gaol keepers were not merely oppressive but actively illegal.[13] Imprisonment itself, as Lilburne – himself a former inmate of London's Fleet prison – reminded his readers by supporting his arguments with references to Sir Edward Coke's Institutes, was by law 'a keeping only for the bringing into tryall and judgment, but not a punishment or place of execution; for *a prison ought not to be imployed for punishing, but for the safe keeping of men* . . .'[14] Illuminated by this common-law perspective, the practice of imprisonment for debt represented a fundamental abrogation of the law by judges and lawyers, who by 'committing and detaining mens bodies for debt, discovered themselves to be Oath breakers, & betrayers of the Law wherewith they are intrusted . . .' The evils of this practice, Lilburne concluded, surpassed even the iniquities of Ship Money, 'for by the right of ship money, a man had but a small part of his goods unjustly taken from him; but by the false Judgement and executions against bodies of men for debt, Millions of people have been and are spoyled of their credits, callings, and Liberties, (which hath beene ever counted as the most precious Jewell belonging to the Commons of *England*) . . .'[15]

Lilburne's critique of gaol keepers' arbitrary powers over the imprisoned debtors in their charge was echoed by later seventeenth-century critics of the prison,[16] and was amply confirmed by gaol investigations conducted by reformers in subsequent decades. When a parliamentary committee led by James Oglethorpe conducted an extensive examination of the Fleet, the King's Bench and the Marshalsea prisons in 1729, it rehearsed again the trope of tyrannical oppression exploited in seventeenth-century polemic, exposing to public view prison officers' 'Barbarous and Cruell' treatment of debtor inmates 'in High Violation and Contempt of the Laws of the Kingdom'. Oglethorpe's committee found the Warden of the Fleet guilty of more than merely 'extorting exorbitant Fees' from debtor inmates. Known to discipline drunken and disorderly debtors by 'putting them in the Stocks', the prison-keeper had also made a practice of 'loading them with Irons, worse than if *Star Chamber* was still subsisting, and contrary to the great Charter, the Foundation of the Liberty of the Subject, and in defiance and contempt thereof, as well as of other good Laws of this Kingdom'.[17] In the Marshalsea, the Deputy Marshal had similarly failed to honour the constitutional protections afforded to freeborn English debtors.

In this institution, prison officers reportedly punished inmates by locking 'them up in the same room with bodies of debtors who have died', by restraining them with irons and by torturing them with thumbscrews.[18]

Conventions of representation such as these provided obvious material for prison inmates who wished to legitimate their activities by locating opposition to imprisonment for debt within a continuous 'current of radicalism'. In 1770, debtors in the King's Bench, London's largest debtors' prison, capitalized on this ideological potential in a series of attacks waged against the unconstitutional oppressions of their confinement. Led by the Scottish estate steward James Stephen, who had been imprisoned for debt in the King's Bench since 1769, a body of discontented inmates again resurrected seventeenth-century radicals' argument that the practice of imprisonment for debt violated Magna Carta and the common-law tradition.[19] Drawing inspiration from the legalistic tactics of the contemporary Wilkite agitation, Stephen actively deployed the instruments of the law to urge his claims. Having obtained a writ of habeas corpus to force a hearing before the court of King's Bench, he defied the presiding judges either to produce statutory justification for his imprisonment or to release him from confinement. The following months saw his rebuff by the court elicit continued, often riotous agitation against their incarceration by the debtors in the King's Bench. Together, symbolic efforts to break free of the prison, the destruction of prison property and attempts to restore order by stationing troops inside the prison walls rendered the King's Bench, in Joanna Innes's description, 'almost completely outside the prison officers' control' in 1770.[20] The eventual restoration of order through a negotiated settlement between the debtors and the court failed to end the agitation, serving instead to shift its focus from the law courts to Parliament, the institution to which imprisoned debtors continued to look for redress into the nineteenth century.[21]

Wilkes's imprisonment in the King's Bench in 1769–70 for his role in the general warrants controversy clearly lent added visibility to the King's Bench debtors' campaign at this time. But Wilkes's broader engagement with the politics of the prison also illustrates the potential liabilities of imprisonment for debt as a radical cause, presaging tensions within popular constituencies that were to resurface in the radical movements of the 1820s. In mobilizing petty tradesmen and artisans as radical activists, Wilkes cultivated an alliance with men who constituted both key victims and key exponents of imprisonment for debt. Linked alike to their customers and their wholesalers by extended circuits of credit, radical retailers were alive at once to the perils and the necessity of the debtors' prison, a circumstance that contributed to the tentative and opportunistic tenor of Wilkite criticism of the debt law.[22] As a gentlemanly radical par excellence, Wilkes himself often offered radical tradesmen more effective material for patriotic hagiography than for commercial sympathy. A notorious spendthrift, Wilkes was incapable of living within his substantial income and was dunned by creditors throughout his radical leadership. Political antagonists seized upon his financial situation in repeated efforts to discredit the radical leader's commitment to his artisan constituents. As John Sainsbury has demonstrated, adroit refashioning of Wilkite radical activities as patriotic contributions to the national wealth allowed Wilkes to feature in radical publications as a public creditor despite his conspicuous identity as a private debtor.[23] But critics understandably found this rhetorical sleight of hand unconvincing.[24] Successful in demonstrating the compatibility of campaigns against imprisonment for debt with radical rhetoric, Wilkes's activities thus also suggested the pitfalls that could attend gentlemanly leaders' exploitation of the debtors' prison in popular radical movements.

The efflorescence of increasingly broad-based popular agitation in the French revolutionary and Napoleonic eras nonetheless saw continued radical antagonism to the practice of imprisonment for debt. In the 1790s, the London Corresponding Society actively sought to recruit imprisoned debtors to the radical cause, successfully soliciting signatures from 200 inmates of the King's Bench for their petitioning campaign of 1793. Ultra-Jacobins active in the Hampden clubs of 1816–17 likewise continued to view imprisoned debtors as a natural radical constituency. As Edward Thompson noted of this activity, although debtors' prisons 'were places where spies might, on occasion, be recruited, they were also to a more important extent, finishing schools for Radicals, where the victims who languished under the punitive rigours of the laws of debt were able to read, to argue, and to enlarge their acquaintance'.[25]

Situated against this background, Henry Hunt's agitation on behalf of imprisoned debtors in 1820–21, at one level, illustrates the purchase of enduring 'currents of radicalism' within English popular politics. In the aftermath of the Peterloo massacre of 1819, Hunt was tried on a charge of unlawfully and seditiously assembling his followers at Manchester and received a sentence of two and a half years' imprisonment. Several other radical agitators were sentenced with Hunt at York, and the passage of the infamous Six Acts – legislation which sought to limit freedom of the press and to crush the mass platform – brought the remainder of the radical leadership into confinement by summer's end.[26] A shaken government dispersed these radical activists in a far-flung constellation of institutions: Samuel Bamford was imprisoned at Lincoln Castle, Richard Carlile at Dorchester prison, Hunt at Ilchester gaol. From these disparate outposts, the radical leadership struggled to maintain the allegiance of their increasingly demoralized supporters in the face of government repression and their own increasingly open disagreements over political strategy. Hunt's often bizarre behaviour at Ilchester – steeped in self-pity, nursed by his overweening narcissism and broadcast to the public through the serial publication of his *Memoirs* – contributed significantly to the divisive infighting that characterized this period of radical history.[27] Yet as John Belchem has argued, Hunt's 'egotistical prison writings, so readily dismissed as the demented outpourings of a blasted demagogue, are among his most important contributions to the radical movement'.[28] As a contribution to the history of radicals' engagement with imprisonment for debt, the importance of this episode in the history of popular politics is likewise central.

Like John Wilkes before him, the imprisoned Hunt ostentatiously promoted his image as a martyr for the people's liberties while self-consciously sporting the mantle of radical resistance to arbitrary power within the prison. As with Wilkes's advocacy of reform of the debt law, however, Hunt's association with the cause of imprisoned debtors was complicated by the dissonance that obtained between his gentlemanly proclivities and his popular allegiances. Hunt was initially spurred to action by the restrictions that Somerset magistrates and prison officers imposed on his privileged lifestyle within the prison walls, but he legitimated these efforts to increase his own well-being by integrating his claims as an inmate with a wider campaign to expose the iniquitous operation of arbitrary government within the gaol. The condition of criminal prisoners at Ilchester supplied Hunt with ammunition for this battle, but the unsavoury connotations of criminal confinement ultimately limited the rhetorical force of this particular line of argument. Imprisoned debtors, confined for safe custody rather than for criminal activities and identified as fitting objects of radical solicitude since the seventeenth century, unsurprisingly emerged as a particular focus of Hunt's solicitude in this context. His critique of conditions at Ilchester, disseminated by the radical press and in Hunt's vitriolic *Peep into a Prison*, forced both county and parliamentary investigations of the gaol in 1821. By playing an active role in each of these proceedings and publishing his own, highly partisan account of the parliamentary commissioners' findings in his *Investigation at Ilchester Gaol*, Hunt worked frenetically to keep his personal plight in public view while co-opting the inquiry for the wider radical movement.[29] The contours and the limitations of his campaign illustrate the shifting parameters of nineteenth-century radical leadership and ideology as well as the changing lineaments of radical antagonism to imprisonment for debt.

In key respects, Hunt's campaign at Ilchester drew upon established lines of radical polemic, self-consciously associating his imprisonment with the travails of earlier generations of gentlemanly leaders. Tracing his radical genealogy in the first instalment of his *Memoirs*, the imprisoned leader proudly added his name to the pantheon of early-modern patriotic heroes. 'Now, my friends and fellow countrymen, the writing [of] the history of my own life, during my confinement in a prison, will not, I trust, be considered presumption in me; because I follow the example of Sir Walter Raleigh and many other patriotic and eminent men who have gone before me', Hunt declared at the outset of his narrative. 'It may not be amiss to remind you that the brave and enlightened patriot *Prynne*, was imprisoned at Dunster Castle, in *this county* by the tyrant Charles the First. Prynne had his nose slit, and his ears cut off, for speaking and writing his mind; but it must not be forgotten, that he lived to see the *tyrant's head struck off*. . .'[30] Hunt's partisans outside the prison repeatedly drew upon this venerable current of radicalism in their efforts to maintain the gaoled leader and his plight in the public eye. Sung to the tune of 'Death or Liberty', the 'New Song for the Birth-Day of Henry Hunt Esq.' performed at a dinner convened by Oldham radicals in November 1821 thus predictably associated Hunt with Hampden, Sidney, Tell and Wallace.[31] Thomas Wooler, editor of the *Black Dwarf*, likewise invoked the memory of Stuart absolutism in endorsing Hunt's cause, warning readers that if the conditions of imprisonment at Ilchester were not ameliorated, 'the Court of King's Bench will become a *Star Chamber tribunal*. . .'[32]

Hunt's efforts to depict William Bridle, the prison-keeper at Ilchester, as a petty despot who exemplified the evils of arbitrary government worked alongside this series of historic associations, bolstering his campaign to claim the prison as a prime locus of the radical cause. His charge that the keeper routinely abused criminal prisoners – shackling inmates with onerous irons and blistering the heads of convicts as a form of punishment – figured in this analysis as an extreme illustration of the perils of absolute power. Seizing upon these incidents as a clarion call for 'a real, radical inquiry; an actual exploring of dungeons; an actual fitting of fetters', Hunt argued that Bridle was 'guilty of inflicting torture upon his prisoners . . . some chained neck and heals together, others with their limbs distorted. . .'[33] Substantiated, albeit on a much reduced scale, by the local and national investigations of conditions at Ilchester, these exaggerated charges against Bridle helped to lend Hunt's own imprisonment in the gaol an appropriately gothic colouration.[34] But as effective objects of radical sympathy, the convicted felons subjected to 'torture' at Ilchester possessed distinct liabilities. Described by Hunt himself as 'felons and convicts, house-breakers, forgers, coiners, and even . . . a man convicted of bestiality', Ilchester's criminal inmates offered Hunt little scope for sustained radical propaganda.[35] Indeed, it was precisely Bridle's insistence that Hunt could see his visitors only under the conditions accorded to convicted prisoners that galvanized the radical leader's campaign. 'Those who wished to speak with him were only permitted to converse with him through a DOUBLE GRATING, once in every twenty-four hours; and at the same period when the felons, and persons convicted of bestiality were permitted to converse with their associates', Wooler charged indignantly in the *Black Dwarf*. 'Mr. Hunt could not subject himself to this degradation. . .'[36]

It was in these specific circumstances that the condition of imprisoned debtors surfaced as an appealing radical cause in Hunt's campaign at Ilchester. Gesturing to established lines of radical polemic, Hunt's *Peep into a Prison* denounced the keeper's exaction of fees from impoverished debtors for the rental of prison beds and furniture – a practice earlier condemned as unconstitutional by Lilburne in 1649.[37] The burden of Hunt's campaign, however, lay significantly outside this tradition of argument. Antagonism to the practice of imprisonment for debt itself as a violation of common-law liberties was noticeably absent from his polemical critiques, and neither references to Magna Carta nor invocations of the Englishman's conventional birthright of freedom figured conspicuously in his writings. Rather, his determination to maintain his own personal comfort and gentlemanly perquisites shifted Hunt's polemical tact from common-law critiques of the arbitrary operation of the debt law to natural-rights defences of the conventional *privileges* accorded to debtors – as opposed to criminals – in the Hanoverian prison. This new emphasis on natural rights did not, in itself, represent a significant departure from the established conventions of nineteenth-century radical argument: by the early nineteenth century, natural rights were well integrated with more narrowly historical justifications of liberty in English radicalism.[38] The particular form that Hunt's natural-rights arguments assumed – as explicit defence of debtors' sexual rights within the prison – was, however, truly novel. Distinguishing his critique from the constitutionalist arguments of earlier radical antagonists of imprisonment for debt, Hunt's campaign at Ilchester also serves to illustrate the chasm that separated his brand of popular politics from the characteristic concerns and tactics of the popular liberal leaders of the later nineteenth century.[39]

Conventionally classified with civil prisoners such as debtors rather than with criminal inmates, late eighteenth- and early nineteenth-century imprisoned radical activists typically enjoyed wide latitude within the gaol. Like debtors imprisoned by common-law courts, political prisoners were understood to be confined only for 'safe custody'; their sentences were designed merely to confine (rather than actively to punish) their persons. In striking contrast to radical representations of the horrors of the debtors' prison, radicals' leaders' experience of imprisonment *qua* debtors was in consequence typically less than onerous.[40] Among Hunt's contemporaries, Richard Carlile at Dorchester and Samuel Bamford at Lincoln both benefited from this received practice in the aftermath of Peterloo. Carlile – whose wife and children joined him for extended periods of residence in the gaol – described his room as 'large, light, and airy' and expatiated in the *Republican* – which he continued to edit from within the prison's walls – on 'the enjoyment, nay the luxury, of hot and cold baths at pleasure...'[41] Bamford too was permitted to lodge with his wife for intervals during his confinement at Lincoln, and later described his 'comfortable quarters' within the Castle as 'remarkably clean, airy, and agreeable...'[42]

As a popular political leader and man of property, Hunt fully expected to enjoy similar conditions at Ilchester – as he had earlier in the century when confined in the King's Bench for his political activities.[43] By 1820, however, the changing composition of the prison population and the rise of disciplinary penal reform had begun to erode the foundations upon which this accommodating tradition of imprisonment had been built. Now serving to contain an inmate population in which criminal prisoners outnumbered debtors, English gaols were rapidly shedding the lax and disorderly practices and conditions associated with the debtors' prison.[44] At Ilchester, William Bridle's tenure as keeper had seen significant efforts to bring the gaol into conformity with this mounting national movement to refashion the prison as a site of orderly disciplinary confinement. Instrumental in introducing prison labour – the *sine qua non* of the new prison discipline – Bridle had also worked to segregate inmates into distinct classes according to their crime and status.[45] His efforts to enhance the prison's function as a site of retribution and reform by limiting the access of criminal and debtor prisoners alike to their friends and family members were fully consonant with this disciplinary impulse, in which the presence of women featured as a particular threat to orderly prison discipline.[46] Before Hunt's imprisonment, the local magistrates who established the prison's rules had endorsed these principles, prohibiting the wives of inmates from residing with their debtor husbands and barring them entirely from their husbands' private bedrooms.[47]

After an initial period of lenience, the Somerset magistrates chose to apply their new policy to Hunt, seeking to bring his treatment into conformity with the reformed rules for debtor and criminal inmates by relegating his family members to the common rooms and public spaces of the prison. A clear violation of established prison political etiquette and a sharp contrast to the conditions accorded to Carlile and Bamford, this policy decision was further exacerbated by the nature of Hunt's private life and by the magistrates' strict definition of 'wives' and 'family'. In Hunt's estimation, his longtime mistress, the married Mrs Vince, and his young ward, Miss Gray, were integral members of his family circle. (Both, to be sure, played a key role in helping to maintain Hunt's precarious mental balance throughout his career.) Neither woman, however, ultimately met the magistrates' definition of 'family', and both in consequence were repeatedly, if intermittently, excluded from Hunt's private apartments in the gaol.[48] Outraged by their removal, Hunt dispatched a barrage of insistent petitions to the sheriff and magistrates, and when this tactic proved unavailing transformed his private efforts to obtain redress into a public campaign against William Bridle's administration on behalf of his fellow inmates.

A reading of the public charges made in Hunt's *Peep into a Prison* and *Investigation at Ilchester Gaol* alongside the private diary he kept throughout the first year of his confinement illuminates the provenance, character and eventual limitations of his gentlemanly critique of debtors' deprivations. Far from rigorously eschewing contact with the despotic prison-keeper, as the *Peep* and the *Investigation* would later suggest, Hunt as a privileged gentlemanly prisoner had dined at Bridle's family table for the first weeks of his imprisonment. Maintaining friendly relations for months thereafter with Bridle's wife – who resided with her husband in accommodation within the gaol walls – the imprisoned radical leader enjoyed both convivial entertainment and political discussion at the Bridle residence. On 10 July 1820, Hunt recorded that he and Mrs Bridle had dined on 'a fine large Turbot [received] as a present from Mr. John Williams . . . in the name of the Radicals of Plymouth';

15 July 1820 saw William Bridle entertain Hunt after dinner by reading the *Courier* newspaper aloud; and Hunt described the meal he shared with the Bridles on 28 July 1820 as being a 'nice Shoulder of Mutton and Apple Pie which with the Vegetables were all well dressed & comfortable as usual'.[49] This halcyon phase of his imprisonment, which corresponded closely with the magistrates' initial willingness to allow Hunt to entertain Mrs Vince and Miss Gray in his private apartments, literally saw the radical leader enjoy the comforts of wine, women and song at Ilchester gaol. As his journal records, a pianoforte delivered to his chamber afforded Miss Gray an opportunity to demonstrate 'how very much improved both in her voice & playing' she had grown since Hunt's arrest, while together the gentlemanly radical's extended family consumed gifts from supporters that included bottles of wine and gin, a loaf of sugar, apricots, grapes and some 'nice ripe Pears'.[50]

The magistrates' decision to rescind these privileges and Bridle's willingness to enforce that decision, however, removed Mrs Vince and Miss Gray from Hunt's private quarters, precipitating his highly partisan investigation of Bridle's administration.[51] Initiated in the domestic sphere, this campaign insistently politicized the sexual immorality of the prison. Hunt's journal entries recorded not only Bridle's frequent absences from divine service, but also the increasingly visible tensions of the keeper's marriage. Here, although the record is murky at key points, there was evidently abundant salacious material at hand. An enquiry conducted at the gaol five years earlier had been provoked by a dismissed prison employee's charge that Mrs Bridle habitually and indecently consorted with her husband's prisoners. The litany of supposed abuses cited by Daniel Lake, formerly the prison task-master, had included plying prisoners with beer to induce them to sing for her house-guests, holding tea parties in the prison laundry with female convicts, conducting an affair with a convicted felon and unsuccessfully attempting to undress and seduce Lake himself. 'Mrs. Bridle Sir in her conduct is a disgrace to her sex', Lake had expostulated to a visiting magistrate. 'She admits other men into her Bed she even invites them'.[52] Although these charges had been dismissed as 'malicious and without Foundation' by the magistrates in 1815,[53] they clearly persisted in the institutional memory of the close-knit prison community. Already in July 1820, when Hunt recorded the absence of Mrs Bridle from the keeper's dining table he hinted darkly at an imminent divorce. The turnkey's wife, he noted in the journal, had informed him that Mrs Bridle's absence resulted from 'violent altercation & recrimination' occasioned by her sister-in-law's references to previous misconduct 'so gross that it would not admit of recapitulation. . .'[54]

Subsequent entries in the diary followed the Bridles' estrangement, temporary reconciliation and ultimate separation with keen interest.[55] Hunt – despite railing against their obvious contravention of the rule that prohibited female visitors from entering his rooms – clearly enjoyed Mrs Bridle's occasional forays into his personal apartments. Describing her as 'the most respectable and reputable person in the Jail', Hunt judged Mrs Bridle to be the aggrieved party in the marriage but, guided by tactical considerations, was initially careful to mask these sympathies from her husband. As he confided in his journal before this rupture, 'In my situation I wish to be friends with Both'.[56] When Bridle eventually enforced the magistrates' exclusion of Hunt's extended family from the prison, however, the gentlemanly radical abandoned this caution, and expanded his private, partisan support for Mrs Bridle into a public campaign to promote prisoners' sexual rights. His *Investigation at Ilchester Gaol* was silent about Mrs Bridle's alleged sexual misconduct, but repeatedly charged the keeper himself with having fathered children by female convicts employed as servants in his home.[57]

In this context, Hunt's public preoccupation with the violation of debtors' natural sexual liberties – as opposed to their constitutional freedoms – was (if highly self-serving) tactically astute. Neatly turning the tables on the gaol's administration, Hunt seized the high moral ground (which was denied to his own cause by his liaison with the married Mrs Vince) by claiming to defend the enjoyment of natural sexual rights by innocent married debtors. He pursued this strategy both by portraying Bridle as a moral reprobate unfit to govern the prison and, more broadly, by depicting the *reformed* debtors' prison itself as a fundamentally immoral institution which violated husbands' natural conjugal rights. Piously denouncing the private parties given by his former host as 'dissipated, drunken, gambling riots', Hunt in his *Peep into a Prison* expatiated upon the moral consequences of the exclusion of wives from debtors' private rooms mandated by the new disciplinary prison policies. A practice 'in opposition to the laws of God and nature', this 'most abominable and obnoxious restriction', Hunt revealed, had 'led to the most revolting scenes. Men are often surprised in the privy having connection with their wives, and such an occurrence on one of the tables of the tap-room has been of notorious frequency these many, many years'.[58]

In the official investigation that followed these revelations, Hunt expanded upon this theme with obvious relish, orchestrating a prolonged and masterly manipulation of trial procedure. By employing tactics that recall radical leaders' crafty defence strategies at state trials for sedition, Hunt shaped his probing examination and cross-examination of witnesses to elicit testimony designed to humiliate the prison administration while intimating his own superior moral standing.[59] Posing a succession of pointed questions to prison officers and prison inmates, Hunt extracted a wealth of explicit testimony on the sexual practices, sexual politics and sexual geography of the prison. Debtor Henry Child of Bath, imprisoned for debt for a year at Ilchester, responded frankly to Hunt's request that he detail how debtors and their wives contrived 'to have that connection together which God and nature had designed'. 'There was no other place but the privy, and [the] conversation room', Child testified. 'I have seen men and their wives go in and come out of the privy together. At one time I saw a man and his wife in that situation, which left no doubt of their being connected, or what was transacting between them.' Prodded by Hunt's prurient questioning, the shoemaker Nicholas Collard succinctly confirmed this evidence. 'Where had you connection with your wife?', Hunt asked the hapless debtor before the commissioners. 'In the conversation-room, that was the most private place, and [even] then I was liable to be interrupted every minute', Collard replied. For debtors who were unwilling to commit private acts in public places, Hunt's witness testified, visits to their bedrooms with their wives could be purchased for a fee, which was paid to the constables who guarded debtors' private quarters. Ranging from sixpence to a shilling per visit, this douceur was known colloquially as 'socket money'.[60]

In the wake of these developments, the Somerset magistrates bowed to the pressure of public scandal and the strictures directed against Bridle's administration by the government commission's report, and reluctantly agreed to modify their restrictions on spousal visitation. The new rules established for the prison in the summer of 1821 maintained the exclusion of wives from debtors' private quarters, but April 1822 saw the magistrates relent, ordering 'That the Debtors be Permitted to see their Wives in their Bed or Day Rooms during the day. . .'[61] Yet if Hunt's activities at Ilchester were arguably excellent political theatre and personal propaganda, as contributions to an extended radical critique of imprisonment for debt they were limited in both their aims and their achievements. Successful in reducing the severity of debtors' sexual privations at Ilchester, Hunt's peep into the prison was neither calculated nor capable of stemming the broader disciplinary tide which swept through the nineteenth-century debtors' prison.[62] In focusing on imprisoned debtors' natural sexual rights, indeed, Hunt had retreated from the ground occupied by earlier radical activists, who had used constitutionalist and common-law reasoning to denounce the practice of imprisonment for debt itself. Despite the small gains achieved by Hunt at Ilchester, the national trend toward restrictive, increasingly punitive confinement for debtors thus continued apace in the following decades, with little opposition from the popular radical movement and its leaders.[63]

Grandiose exercises in self-promotion, Hunt's *Peep into a Prison* and *Investigation at Ilchester Gaol* were nonetheless particularly appropriate political instruments for the imprisoned gentlemanly leader at this juncture in the history of radicalism. Denied access to the mass platform on which he had built his reputation as a tribune of the people, Hunt crafted a campaign that obviously complemented the prevailing concerns of popular politics outside the prison's walls. For Hunt's salacious public revelations of the conjugal deprivations suffered by supposedly innocent debtors at Ilchester meshed easily with the contemporary radical agitation on behalf of the beleaguered Queen Caroline.[64] Like the movement to support Caroline's battle for formal recognition of her legal status from her estranged spouse, Hunt's campaign employed sexual scandal and melodramatic narratives to legitimate and popularize a cause – in this instance, at heart his own forced separation from Mrs Vince – which initially appeared to possess little popular resonance. Within the prison's walls, Hunt's private support for the keeper's beleaguered wife replicated this public campaign, for the Bridles' marital troubles bore an uncanny resemblance to those of the royal couple. The distance that separated Hunt's private world view as a gentlemanly intimate at the Bridles' table and his public persona as William Bridle's radical antagonist in the *Peep into a Prison* was particularly conspicuous in this setting. Ironically indeed, William Bridle had played an active part in promoting Hunt's public affiliation with Caroline's cause in the weeks before his relations with Hunt had soured. Journeying to London in the summer of 1820 to deliver six female convicts to the hulks, the prison-keeper also willingly delivered an address supporting the Queen which had been composed by Hunt in Ilchester gaol.[65]

Although Hunt's obsessive preoccupation with his own personal affairs may go far to explain the limitations of his critique of the debtors' prison, the wider failure of contemporary radical activists consistently to espouse the cause of imprisoned debtors appears to have been rooted in broader trends that marked radical ideology and leadership in the nineteenth century. The conspicuous contrast between the financial resources enjoyed by gentlemanly radicals and the economic exigencies of less affluent radical leaders associated with small-scale trade was particularly significant in this regard.[66] Enmeshed in extended webs of credit with both their suppliers and their customers, shopkeepers and artisans were themselves particularly prone to suffer arrest for debt, and indeed composed the bulk of the insolvent inmates confined in early nineteenth-century debtors' prisons.[67] As the gaol correspondence of Richard Carlile suggests, the increasing presence of artisans and tradesmen within the radical leadership complicated the earlier, more legalistic and patrician interpretation of the debtors' prison as a site of unmitigated, tyrannical confinement. To a popular activist such as Carlile, whose precarious income derived from the profits generated from the sale of radical publications in a small shop kept by his wife in London and through a network of petty retailers in provincial towns, debtors were at once objects of radical compassion and potential agents of commercial ruin. During Carlile's incarceration at Dorchester, as he himself fell increasingly into debt to his suppliers, his efforts to extract payment from the radical activists who distributed his publications grew ever more urgent. By June 1824 he was reduced to bargaining for payment in kind: clothing, a watch and 'any quantity of Barnsley Linen' featured among the items he had requested in lieu of payment by March 1825.[68]

As government reprisals against radical leaders escalated, Carlile and other impecunious popular entrepreneurs were caught on the horns of a radical dilemma when they contemplated the practice of imprisonment for debt. Antipathy to the use of the law and the prison as a tyrannical means for securing contracts persisted in their political world view, but it existed uncomfortably alongside their rising hostility to the recalcitrant debtors who compromised the radical cause. Writing to Thomas Turton about the debts of Joseph Scholey, a radical tailor who retailed his tracts from a shop in Sheffield, Carlile expounded his philosophy of radical commercial credit. 'If you think that Mr. S. can and ought to pay me his Bill I shall proceed against him for its recovery, but if you think he cannot pay I have no desire to harass and imprison him', he wrote in November 1822.[69] By June 1823, a less forgiving attitude to debtors was interwoven with his continued recognition that a man such as Scholey 'may be honestly poor' and unable to pay his debts. 'If my agents would only keep up their payments, I should go on briskly; but I assure you, the larger part of them draw upon my patience as far as I can let them go', he complained to Turton. 'I do not know what these men think of themselves, but instead of being Reformers, I look upon them as worse than housebreakers; the villainy of robbing me under my present situation and difficulties is the worst kind of robbery that I can conceive, particularly by men who profess to be actuated by a desire for public good and public reform'.[70] Other popular leaders succumbed to just such pressures in these years, resorting to the law to recover debts from their fellow reformers. In 1825, Carlile reported that the radical editor of the *Black Dwarf*, Thomas Wooler, had taken legal action to seize goods in lieu of payment owed by a colleague whom William Cobbett had also threatened to imprison for his unpaid debts.[71]

If the exigencies of small-scale radical capitalism worked to erode popular leaders' traditional sympathies for imprisoned debtors, the growing purchase of respectability within the radical ranks also limited the potential of political campaigns crafted along the lines of Hunt's *Peep into a Prison* to mobilize sustained agitation against the iniquities of imprisonment for debt. As Anna Clark has argued, although sexual radicalism was conspicuous in the writings and activities of radical leaders in the 1820s and 1830s, it failed to win the allegiance of the wider working-class population.[72] Samuel Bamford's indignant commentary on Hunt's liaison with Mrs Vince in his *Passages in the Life of a Radical*, published in 1844, signalled an important shift in this regard.[73] To be sure, tolerance (and indeed enthusiasm) for gentlemanly leaders' sexual improprieties persisted in, and helped to animate, the Chartist movement, as the rakish Feargus O'Connor's devoted mass following amply demonstrated in the 1840s. But as Belchem and Epstein note in their analysis of gentlemanly radical leaders, the sexual standards of popular politicians shifted significantly thereafter. Conveying 'a very different image of manliness, more closely aligned with the eighteenth-century gentlemanly libertine', they argue, 'Hunt and O'Connor's reckless personal lives were in marked contrast to the bourgeois probities that characterized the public images of Bright and Gladstone's personal lives'.[74]

Indeed, the contrast between Hunt's and Gladstone's chosen sexual strategies can stand as a metaphor for the sea-change in gentlemanly leadership that marked the mid Victorian period. Where Hunt attempted to gain access to his openly acknowledged mistress by waging a salacious public campaign in defence of the sexual prerogatives of imprisoned debtors, Gladstone sought to curb his fascination with pornography and prostitutes through self-inflicted whippings conducted in the privacy of his own home.[75] Exemplary of the broader shift away from the raucous radical culture expressed through defiant crowd activity toward more enclosed and carefully orchestrated political movements, this contrast points to a salient discontinuity within the modern radical tradition. As a site for mobilizing radical passions, the debtors' prison boasted significantly less iconographic power in the early nineteenth century than it had in the Stuart age and the Hanoverian era. By cultivating the mass platform as the key instrument of popular constitutionalism and by promoting the electoral franchise as the platform's chief goal, Hunt had himself played a central role in this shift in the political geography of radical action. As a context for the practice of 'politics in action', the debtors' prison clearly suffered in this transition from disorderly to orderly popular radicalism. Sustained for over a century as the object of radical odium, imprisonment for debt faded from the popular radical conscience as unreformed prisons gave way to increasingly disciplinary penal institutions.[76]

The timing of this diminution of interest was, for a radical movement which increasingly claimed to speak for the working class, both ironic and unfortunate. For the practice of imprisonment by debt courts endured in England long after radical antagonism to the debtors' prison had faded from public view. Indeed, the practice of imprisonment for debt as perpetuated by the county courts from their foundation in 1846 until they relinquished the power to imprison recalcitrant debtors in 1970 was selectively aimed at small debts, and thus disproportionately imprisoned debtors drawn from the working classes.[77] In consequence, later nineteenth-century constitutionalist gentlemanly liberal leaders (whose popular politics – unlike the popular radicalism of O'Connor and Hunt – remained strictly inside the letter of the law) lacked not only these earlier leaders' personal experience of political confinement, but also their personal familiarity with the interior of the debtors' prison.[78] Declining to identify their cause with disorderly debtors and the riotous institutions which had historically housed them, these later gentlemanly leaders worked instead to shift the currents of English popular politics into more pacific, more liberal channels of political and economic reform.

NOTES

1 'Profound caesura' is Perry Anderson's telling phrase in 'Origins of the Present Crisis', *New Left Review*, no. 23 (January-February 1964), 33. The founding text of the 'Currents of Radicalism' thesis is Eugenio Biagini and Alastair J. Reid, eds., *Currents of Radicalism: Popular Radicalism, Organised Labour and Party Politics in Britain, 1850–1914* (Cambridge, 1991).

2 Classic statements of the older argument for radical discontinuity include E. P. Thompson, *The Making of the English Working Class* (London, 1963; 1968 edition) and Eric Hobsbawm, *Labouring Men: Studies in the History of Labour* (London, 1964). Gareth Stedman Jones's 'Rethinking Chartism', in his *Languages of Class: Studies in English Working Class History* (Cambridge, 1983), 179–238, provided a key transition text between the literature stressing discontinuity and that stressing continuity. For more recent works emphasizing (albeit in very different ways) populism and continuity, see Eugenio Biagini, *Liberty, Retrenchment and Reform: Popular Liberalism in the Age of Gladstone, 1860–1880* (Cambridge, 1992) and Patrick Joyce, *Visions of the People: Industrial England and the Question of Class* (Cambridge, 1991).

3 John Belchem and James Epstein, 'The Nineteenth-Century Gentleman Leader Revisited', *Social History*, 22, no. 2 (May 1997), 174–93.

4 Patrick Joyce, *Democratic Subjects: The Self and the Social in Nineteenth-Century England* (Cambridge, 1994); Biagini, *Liberty, Retrenchment and Reform*; James Vernon, *Politics and the People: A Study in English Political Culture, c. 1815–1867* (Cambridge, 1993).

5 Belchem and Epstein, 'Nineteenth-Century Gentleman Leader', 175.

6 *Ibid.*, 176–77.

7 For an important collection of essays which navigates between the radicalism-as-continuity and the radicalism-as-discontinuity standpoints and underlines the role of 'narrative instability and ambivalence' in maintaining the constitutionalist 'meta-narrative of English politics', see James Vernon, ed., *Re-Reading the Constitution: New Narratives in the Political History of England's Long Nineteenth Century* (Cambridge, 1996). The quotation is from Vernon's 'Notes toward an Introduction', 15. For my own earlier arguments about the shifting continuities of the radical tradition, see Margot C. Finn, *After Chartism: Class and Nation in English Radical Politics, 1848–1874* (Cambridge, 1993).

8 Belchem and Epstein, 'Gentleman Leader Revisited', 175.

9 Paul Haagen, 'Eighteenth-Century English Society and the Debt Law', in Stanley Cohen and Andrew Scull, eds., *Social Control and the State* (New York, 1983), 224–260, and *idem.*, 'Imprisonment for Debt in England and Wales' (PhD dissertation, Princeton University, 1986), 69–72 provide both an excellent introduction to the practice of imprisonment for debt and a discussion of the social composition of the debtors' prison. See also Margot C. Finn, *The Character of Credit: Personal Debt in English Culture, c. 1740–1914* (Cambridge, 2003), esp. 109–193.

10 For the disorderly self-discipline of unreformed debtors' prisons, see Joanna Innes, 'The King's Bench Prison in the Later Eighteenth Century: Law, Authority and Order in a London Debtors' Prison', in John Brewer and John Styles, eds., *An Ungovernable People: The English and Their Law in the Seventeenth and Eighteenth Centuries* (London, 1980), and John Bender, *Imagining the Penitentiary: Fiction and the Architecture of Mind in Eighteenth-Century England* (Chicago, 1987), 13–16, 26–33.

11 Gerrard Winstanley, *More Light Shining in Buckinghamshire* (1649), in George H. Sabine, ed., *The Works of Gerrard Winstanley: With an Appendix of Documents Relating to the Digger Movement* (Ithaca, NY, 1941), 638; *A Declaration of the grounds and Reasons, why we the poor Inhabitants of the Parish of Iver...* (1650), in Keith Thomas, 'Another Digger Broadside', *Past & Present*, no. 42 (February 1969), 65. Winstanley's experience with the debt courts predated his radical conversion: he became insolvent as a retail trader in the 1640s. See J. D. Alsop, 'Ethics in the Marketplace: Gerrard Winstanley's London Bankruptcy, 1643', *Journal of British Studies*, 28, 2 (April 1989), 97–119.

12 For the development of radical opposition to imprisonment in these decades, see Donald Veall, *The Popular Movement for Law Reform 1640–1660* (Oxford, 1970), 142–51.

13 [John Lilburne], *Liberty Vindicated against Slavery: Shewing, That Imprisonment for Debt, Refusing to Answer Interrogatories, Long Imprisonment, though for just Causes, Abuse for Prisons, and Cruell Extrtion of Prison-keepers are all destructive of the fundamentall Laws and common Freedomes of the people. Published for the use of all the Freeborne of England, whom it equally concerns by occasion of the House of Lords commitment of Lieut. Col. John Lilburn, close prisoner, first to New-gate, and next to the Tower. By a lover of his Country, and suffere for the common Liberty* (np., 1646), 104.

14 *Ibid.*, 7. After an initial period of solitary confinement, Lilburne's term as a political prisoner in 1638 had seen him mix freely with the other inmates of the Fleet, primarily a debtors' prison. His imprisonment is detailed in Pauline Gregg, *Free-born John: A Biography of John Lilburne* (London, 1961), 67–69, 73–74. For the medieval interpretation of imprisonment as an acceptable mechanism for pre-trial confinement but not of punishment, see George Rusche and Otto Kircheimer, *Punishment and Social Structure* (New York, 1939), 62.

15 Lilburne, *Liberty Vindicated*, 12–13.

16 See for example Marmaduke Johnson, *Ludgate, What It Is; Not What It Was* (1659), in *John Stow, A Survey of the Cities of London and Westminster and the Borough of Southwark*, 2 vols., 6th ed., (London, 1755), vol. 2, 694; Anon., *A Companion for Debtors and Prisoners, and Advice to Creditors in Ten Letters: From a Gentleman in Prison, to a Member of Parliament. Wherein, First, the Villianies and Indolencies of Bayliffs. Secondly, the Evil Practices of Jaylers and Pretended Solicitors, and Thirdly, the Irregularities of Prisons in General, Are Briefly Detected and Exposed* (London, 1699).

17 *A Report from the Committee Appointed to Enquire into the State of the Gaols of this Kingdom; Relating to the Fleet Prison* (London, 1729), 14, 2, 13. Oglethorpe's committee and its impact are discussed in Rodney M. Baine, 'The Prison Death of Robert Castell and Its Effect on the Founding of Georgia', in John C. Inscoe, ed., *James Edward Oglethorpe: New Perspectives on His Life and Legacy* (Savannah, 1997), 35–46.

18 *A Report from the Committee Appointed to Enquire into the State of the Gaols of This Kingdom: Relating to the Marshalsea Prison; and Farther Relating to the*

Fleet Prison (London, 1729), 8–9. For the King's Bench, see *A Report from the Committee Appointed to Enquire into the State of the Gaols of the Kingdom: Relating to the King's Bench Prison* (London, 1730).

19 For Stephen, see Merle M. Bevington, ed., *The Memoirs of James Stephen: Written by Himself for the Use of his Children* (London, 1954), esp. 84–102; for the early phases of this campaign, see esp. James Stephen, *Considerations on Imprisonment for Debt* (London, 1770). The abrogation of historic legal rights was a persistent theme in the writings of philanthropic prison reformers as well. See for example Josiah Dornford, *Seven Letters to the Lords and Commons of Great Britain, upon the Present Mode of Arresting and Imprisoning the Bodies of Debtors: Shewing the Inconsistency of it, with Magna Carta and a Free Constitution: with Observances on the Dragging of Debtors to Sponging Houses, and to Prisons in the first instance, before the Debt is proved, upon the bare Affidavit of the Vilest Character: and likewise some Remarks on the Fatal Effects of such Proceedings, on the Circumstances and Morals of Individuals* (London, [1786]).

20 Innes, 'King's Bench Prison', 290–98, citation from 295.

21 For the shift from the courts to parliament, see *ibid.*, p. 297, and Peter Lineham, 'The Campaign to Abolish Imprisonment for Debt in England 1750–1840' (MA thesis, University of Canterbury, 1974).

22 The broad contours of Wilkite radicalism as it related to debt are discussed by John Brewer, *Party Ideology and Popular Politics at the Accession of George III* (Cambridge, 1976), 163–200, esp. 174–80, and *idem.*, 'The Wilkites and the Law, 1763–74: A Study of Radical Notions of Governance', in Brewer and Styles, eds., *An Ungovernable People*, 128–71, esp. 138–39, 150, 153. The prominence of tradesmen among the population of imprisoned debtors is noted by Haagen, 'Eighteenth-Century Imprisonment for Debt'.

23 John Sainsbury, 'John Wilkes, Debt, and Patriotism', *Journal of British Studies*, 34, 2 (April 1995), 165–95. Sainsbury attributes Wilkes's continued ability to appeal to tradesmen-radicals to his 'success in representing himself as a patriot-hero as defined by classical criteria and imagery. This undertaking sought an inversion and transcendence of the conventional relationship between creditor and debtor. Wilkes, the incorrigible debtor, now became the nation's creditor when he returned in 1768, like a patriot hero of ancient Rome, to enjoy the public's favor.' (176).

24 See, for example, Robert Holloway, *A Letter to John Wilkes, Esq; Sheriff of London and Middlesex; in Which the Extortion and Oppression of Sheriffs Officers, with Many Other Alarming Abuses, Are Exemplified and Detected*...(London, 1771).

25 Thompson, *Making of the English Working Class*, 132, 692. Citation from 692.

26 John Belchem, *'Orator' Hunt: Henry Hunt and English Working-Class Radicalism* (Oxford, 1985), 118–119.

27 Samuel Bamford's recollections fully convey the intensity of the personal animosities generated by these developments. 'Hunt's tom-foolery excited my contempt', Bamford recalled astringently. 'Hunt at that time must have

been deranged – his vanity – his egotism were irrepressible, and I had now, and for ever after, done with his judgment.' Samuel Bamford, *Passages in the Life of a Radical*, 2 vols. (Manchester, 1844; reprint ed., London, 1967), 2:209.

28 Belchem, *'Orator' Hunt*, 133. Belchem's overview of Hunt's imprisonment (133–65) offers an excellent analysis of the tensions within radicalism at this time.

29 Henry Hunt, *A Peep into a Prison: Or, the Inside of Ilchester Bastile* (London, 1821); Henry Hunt, *Investigation at Ilchester Gaol, in the County of Somerset, into the Conduct of William Bridle, the Gaoler, before the Commissioners Appointed by the Crown* (London, 1821). For the official report of the inquiry, see *Report of the Commissioners Appointed to Inquire into the State of Ilchester Gaol*, Parliamentary Papers, 1822, vol. xi.

30 Henry Hunt, *Memoirs of Henry Hunt, Esq.: Written by Himself, in His Majesty's Jail at Ilchester, in the County of Somerset*, 3 vols. (London, 1820–21), 1: xvii, xix. The circumstance that Hunt's grandfather, colonel Thomas Hunt, was a Royalist, rather undercut this representation, but was finessed by Hunt's insistent allegiance to the legitimacy of resistance to tyranny. See *ibid.*, 21 ff.

31 'While thine shall be a deathless name,/Hist'ry a wreath for thee shall twine,/ With Hampden and with Sidney's fame,/With TELL and WALLACE record thine,/Let each Briton now with me,/Drink to "HUNT and Liberty."' Henry Hunt, *To the Radical Reformers, Male and Female, of England, Scotland, and Ireland*, 10 December 1821, 32. For a contemporary broadside linking Hunt to Hampden, Pym and Cromwll, see Finn, *After Chartism*, 36–37.

32 *The Black Dwarf*, 13 February 1822.

33 Hunt, *Investigation at Ilchester Gaol*, vii, 3.

34 The commissioners corroborated one instance of blistering, and one of excessive ironing. *Report from the Commissioners*, 9.

35 *Report of the High Sheriff and Magistrates*, 13–14.

36 *The Black Dwarf*, 13 February 1822. 'There are now persons confined in this jail for every species of crime in the catalogue of human depravity:–Some for rapes, some for *brutal assaults* upon *females*, one for BESTIALITY of the most revolting kind, some for *forgery*, for *house-breaking*, *manslaughter*, *murder*, &c. &c.-yet not one of these persons is prohibited from seeing his FEMALE friends upon the same terms, and at the same place that he sees his MALE friends...', Hunt complained. *To the Radical Reformers, Male and Female, of England, Ireland, and Scotland*, 21 October 1820, 7.

37 Hunt, *Peep into a Prison*, 6–7. In Lilburne's analysis, 'Keepers of Prisons should not have any colour or excuse, for exacting any thing from prisoners, who are in the custody of the Law, it is provided by for the Law, that all Prisons and Gaolers be the king for the publique good, to be made, repaired, furnished with all fitting accommodation, as beds, candlesticks, basons and chamber pots with other things needful, at the kings and publique charge...' Lilburne, *Liberty Vindicated*, 7.

38 For the compatibility of natural and historical rights in nineteenth-century popular radicalism, see for example Finn, *After Chartism*, 65–70.

39 For the role (and ultimate rejection) of sexual licence within the arguments of the broader radical movement, see Iain McCalman, *Radical Underworld: Prophets, Revolutionaries and Pornographers in London, 1795–1840* (Cambridge 1988), esp. 26–49, 204–231, and Anna Clark, *The Struggle for the Breeches: Gender and the Making of the British Working Class* (Berkeley, 1995), esp. 42–62.

40 'It was common practice to treat political prisoners as debtors,' Joel Wiener comments of this practice. 'Debtors could spend their own money on provisions and writing supplies and had unlimited visiting privileges.' Joel Wiener, *William Lovett* (Manchester, 1989), 72. Thomas Wooler endorsed this articulation, arguing that Hunt's 'sentence was merely that of *imprisonment*...' *The Black Dwarf*, vol. 6 (4 April 1821), 492.

41 *The Republican*, vol. 4, no. 2 (8 September 1820), 37. Carlile's imprisonment is detailed in Joel Wiener, *Radicalism and Freethought in Nineteenth-Century Britain: The Life of Richard Carlile* (Westport, Conn., 1983), 55–75.

42 Bamford, *Passages in the Life of a Radical*, 2: 171.

43 Hunt was first imprisoned in the King's Bench in 1800–1801, and confined there again in 1810 (Belchem, *'Orator' Hunt*, 21–22, 31–32). In Belchem's description, 'During his sojourn in the King's Bench in London he had enjoyed comfortable accommodation, good company, intelligent political debate, and the run of the key'. (134).

44 For an excellent overview of these developments, see Randall McGowan, 'The Well-Ordered Prison: England, 1780–1865', in Norval Morris and David J. Rothman, eds., *The Oxford History of the Prison: The Practice of Punishment in Western Society* (Oxford, 1995), 79–109. As McGowan notes, imprisoned debtors typically outnumbered criminal inmates in the eighteenth-century prison (81).

45 For Bridle's introduction of labour at Ilchester, see Hunt, *Investigation at Ilchester Gaol*, p. 135, and William Bridle, *A Narrative of the Rise and Progress of the Improvements Effected in His Majesty's Gaol at Ilchester, in the County of Somerset, between July 1808, and November 1821, under the Governance, Suggestion, and Superintendence of Wm. Bridle, Keeper: Being the First Part of His Exposition of, and Answer to, the Changes Lately Brought against Him by Henry Hunt, a Prisoner Confined in the Same Gaol* (Bath, 1822), not paginated, chap. 1. Outside the highly partisan evidence associated with the investigation, Thomas Fowell Buxton, a leading national figure in the prison reform movement, had commented favourably on Bridle's introduction of labour at Ilchester, claiming in 1818 that because of the inmates' employment 'there is no filth, no disorder, no tumult' within the prison. Thomas Fowell Buxton, *Appendix to the First Edition of an Inquiry, Whether Crime and Misery Are Produced or Prevented, by Our Present System of Prison Discipline: Containing an Account of the Prisons at Ilchester and at Bristol* (London, 1818), 11.

46 Margaret DeLacy's exemplary *Prison Reform in Lancashire, 1700–1850: A Study in Local Administration* (Stanford, 1986) details the broader implementation of disciplinary regimes for debtors and criminal prisoners in this period. See also Finn, *Character of Credit*, 152–93.

47 At the investigation of the gaol, Sir John Palmer Acland, a former chair of Quarter Sessions, testified that before Bridle's reforms debtors and their families lived in the prison 'men, women, and children altogether, so that in one year I took an account of 26 children running about the gaol, belonging to the parents within'. Hunt, *Investigation at Ilchester Gaol*, 135.

48 See Belchem, *'Orator' Hunt*, 134–37.

49 Henry Hunt Journal, 1820–21, Manchester Central Reference Library, MSF 923.2 H102, 10, 15 and 28 July 1820.

50 *Ibid.*, 31 July and 3, 4 and 8 August 1820.

51 The journal records an escalation of conflict with Bridle from 6 August 1820, when Hunt's visitors were required to leave the prison on Sundays during divine service. By 20 August 1820 Mrs Vince and Miss Gray were denied access to Hunt's apartments altogether.

52 For this earlier investigation, see the file of 'Papers Regarding Charges against William Bridle, Governor of Ilchester Gaol', Somersetshire Record Office, Q/Agi/9/1, esp. 'Substance of the Charges Preferred by Daniel Lake late Task Master of Ilchester Gaol against Mr William Bridle of the Same Gaol and Mrs Bridle His Wife'. Lake's comments were made in a letter of 19 February 1815 to the Reverend G. H. Coulson.

53 Ilchester Gaol, 9 March 1815: Minutes of the Investigation of Charges against the Governor, in Somerset R.O., Q/Agi/9/1.

54 Hunt Journal, Manchester Central Reference Library, 25 July 1820.

55 On 10 October 1820 he reported 'that Bridle & his Wife have made up their Quarrel & that they slept together for the first time last Night for 2 Months'; on 11 October he understood 'that Bridle & his Wife are kissing & cooing like Two Turtle Doves & it is quite like another Honeymoon'. 4 February 1821, however, saw Mrs Bridle 'packed off in the Night Coach to London', where her father resided.

56 Hunt Journal, Manchester, 28 July 1820. During a visit on 1 September 1820, Hunt sarcastically told Mrs Bridle 'we should be *hanged* for disobeying orders about Females coming to visit me'. Visits from Mrs Bridle to Hunt's apartments continued for months, and the two exchanged gifts of foodstuffs (a hare, a salmon, a brace of partridges), with Bridle himself often serving as an intermediary in the transactions throughout the autumn. See, for example, 1, 2, 14 and 15 September; 1 October and 27 November 1820.

57 Hunt, *Investigation at Ilchester Gaol*, 3.

58 Hunt, *Peep into a Prison*, 12, 7–8.

59 For radicals' negotiation and manipulation of criminal trial procedures, see esp. James Epstein, 'Narrating Liberty's Defense: T. J. Wooler and the Law', in his *Radical Expression: Political Language, Ritual, and Symbol in England, 1790–1850* (Oxford, 1994), 29–69, and *ibid.*, '"Our Real Constitution": Trial Defence and Radical Memory in the Age of Revolution', in Vernon, ed., *Re-reading the Constitution*, 22–51.

60 Hunt, *Investigation at Ilchester Gaol*, 73, 97, 92. Hunt's discovery of these practices in September from a debtor informant appears to have provided

a crucial inspiration for his *Peep into a Prison*. The entry for 4 September 1820 in his journal recorded his reaction to this information. 'Some go with their wives into the Necessary . . . others by a Signal by sticking a Fork into the Table, get all the other Men to leave the Room while they kiss their Wives &c &c &c Horrible! Horrible!!! mockery of morality . . . A peep into this Prison will be a good *specimen of morality* . . . These *moral Gentry* of Somersetshire have passed & sanctioned such proceedings as are revolting to human nature'.

61 *Rules, Orders and Regulations for the Government of the Common Gaol and House of Correction at Ilchester in the County of Somerset* (Taunton, 1821), 23–27, Somerset R. O., Q/Agi/10/3, and Magistrates' Book, Ilchester Gaol, 1821–44, 20 April 1822 (25), Somerset R. O., Q/Agi/7/3.

62 Belchem argues that Hunt's activities led not only to Bridle's dismissal but also to the prison's condemnation for demolition, and thus that 'in the history of prison reform, Hunt deserves an honourable mention'. (Belchem, *'Orator' Hunt*, 134). But this is an overly optimistic reading of Hunt's impact. Although Bridle was dismissed from office, the prison itself continued to operate until 1843. See Dunning, ed., *History of the County of Somerset*, 185.

63 The increasingly disciplinary character of debtors' confinement is discussed in greater detail in my 'Being in Debt in Dickens' London: Fact, Fictional Representation and the Nineteenth-Century Prison', *Journal of Victorian Culture*, **1**, no. 2 (Autumn 1996), 203–26.

64 For Queen Caroline and radical politics, see esp. Thomas W. Laqueur, 'The Queen Caroline Affair: Politics as Art in the Reign of George IV', *Journal of Modern History*, 54 (September 1982), 417–66, and Anna Clark, 'Queen Caroline and the Sexual Politics of Popular Culture in London, 1820', *Representations*, 31 (1990), 47–68.

65 For Bridle's role in transporting the address, see Hunt Journal, Manchester, 29 July and 9 August 1820. Both of the Bridles appear to have participated in the widespread public sympathy for Caroline. As Hunt noted on 23 July 1820, Mrs Bridle was 'very bitter against Men who use their Wives ill & was very pointed against the King & would not drink his Health which Bridle appeared to enjoy very much, as he laughed outrageously. If a Radical was to talk in this way he would be hung. But your Loyal people may say anything with impunity'.

66 This is not to suggest that gentlemanly radicals lacked financial concerns or were disassociated from commercial culture and indebtedness. Hunt, like Wilkes in the eighteenth century, was active in the entrepreneurial activities of the radical movement. He devoted considerable energy to retailing his 'Breakfast Powder', a substitute for coffee designed to allow his followers to abstain from excisable goods. Nor was Hunt immune from financial distress. But when pressed by legal costs (derived in part from the Investigation at Ilchester), Hunt's status as a landed proprietor allowed him to attempt to levy funds by distraining upon the tenants of his landed estate at Glastonbury. See Belchem, *'Orator' Hunt*, 139–40.

67 David A. Kent, 'Small Businessmen and Their Credit Transactions in Early Nineteenth-Century Briatin', *Business History*, 36, no. 2 (April 1994), 50.

68 For Carlile's descent into barter, see Richard Carlile to William Vamplew Holmes, 19 June 1824, 1 July 1824, 21 December 1824, and 23 March 1825, RC 389, RC 391, RC 402 and RC 402, Richard Carlile correspondence from Dorchester Gaol, Huntington Library, San Marino. He discussed his mounting debt of at least £300 in a letter to Holmes of 2 August 1824, RC 394.

69 Carlile to Thomas Turton, 21 November 1822, RC 434, Huntington Library.

70 Carlile to Turton, 23 June 1823, RC 437, Huntington Library.

71 Carlile to Holmes, 12 January 1825, RC 404, Huntington Library.

72 Clark, *Struggle for the Breeches*, 179–96.

73 'I could not but be sensible – though Hunt's self-love – which he was constantly disclaiming – blinded him to it – of the difference betwixt a man being indulged with the company of another man's wife', he commented of Hunt's determination to share his apartments in the prison with Mrs Vince. Bamford, *Passages in the Life of a Radical*, 2: 211–212.

74 Belchem and Epstein, 'Nineteenth-Century Gentleman Leader Revisited', 180.

75 H. C. G. Matthew, *Gladstone: 1809–1874* (Oxford, 1988), 90–95.

76 Benthamite radicals, in contrast to activists with a broader popular following, remained committed to the abolition of imprisonment for debt into the 1830s. See for example Runnymeade Secundus [pseud.], "A Follower of Bentham," *Magna Charta Shown to Have Been Violated; And Consequently, That Arrest and Imprisonment for Debt Are Illegal* (London, 1837), and Bruce Kercher, 'The Transformation of Imprisonment for Debt in England', *Australian Journal of Law and Society*, 2, no. 1 (1984), 69–74. Popular political activists continued to exploit their imprisonment in the Chartist movement, but by the 1840s had severed their association with imprisoned debtors. For O'Connor's politicization of the prison, see James Epstein, *The Lion of Freedom: Feargus O'Connor and the Chartist Movement* (London, 1982), 212–220.

77 For county-court imprisonment, see esp. Gerry Rubin, 'The County Courts and the Tally Trade, 1846–1914', in G. R. Rubin and David Sugarman, eds., *Law, Economy and Society, 1750–1914* (Abingdon, 1984), 321–48, and Paul Johnson, 'Class Law in Victorian England', *Past & Present*, no. 141 (November 1993).

78 The revival of liberal and socialist humanitarian concern for prison conditions, significantly, drew sustenance from the direct experience of imprisonment by men of the middle and upper classes in the late nineteenth and early twentieth centuries, from the imprisonment of Oscar Wilde to that of conscientious objectors in the First World War. See Victor Bailey, 'English Prison, Penal Culture, and the Abatement of Imprisonment, 1895–1922', *Journal of British Studies*, 36, no. 3 (July 1997), 285–324.

CHAPTER 9

Jeremy Bentham's Radicalism

F. Rosen

In 1998 the 250th anniversary of Jeremy Bentham's birth was celebrated, and among the numerous events held at University College London to mark the occasion was an exhibition of paintings, drawings and prints of Bentham or in some way related to him. It was the first attempt to collect and exhibit, where possible, all known representations of Bentham, and these were gathered together in an exhibition with a catalogue entitled *The Old Radical*.[1] When I first learned that this was going to be the title of the exhibition, I was somewhat puzzled, especially when told that this was a phrase that Bentham used to refer to himself.

The phrase would make perfect sense in a matter of fact way. When he wrote the words in 1823 at the age of seventy-five in a letter to Samuel Parr, he was both old and a radical.[2] But did he mean this or was he referring to his being a radical for a long time? If the latter, the remark is more problematic. He publicly declared himself to be a radical only six years earlier in 1817 in *Plan of Parliamentary Reform* where he promised in the full title of the work to show *The Necessity of Radical and the Inadequacy of Moderate Reform*.[3] But if he 'came out' as a radical in 1817, he wrote as a radical as early as 1809–10, as he clearly noted in *Plan of Parliamentary Reform*, and the manuscripts on radical reform bear these dates.[4] Furthermore, there has been considerable debate concerning manuscripts written at the time of the French Revolution which reveal Bentham's radicalism at this earlier period, and would make him an 'Old Radical' in an interesting way.[5] But in later years Bentham never discussed these earlier manuscripts, even though they were in his possession when he died.

One can thus argue that Bentham's political radicalism extended for more than forty years, at least from 1788–9 until his death in 1832, and this would amply justify the epithet, 'The Old Radical'. But as he did not refer to this earlier period, it must remain an open question if he was considering the length of time he subscribed to political radicalism. Furthermore, was political radicalism in the sense of an advocacy of a widespread suffrage, the secret ballot, annual parliaments, and the representative system the only kind of radicalism for which Bentham should be known? If radicalism means going to the root of a matter, perhaps Bentham was radical in his philosophy generally, and that may additionally have a bearing on the development of a radicalism in his political thought.

In an article entitled *Jeremy Bentham: From Radical Enlightenment to Philosophic Radicalism*, J. H. Burns attempts to chart the connections in Bentham's thought between his philosophical alignment with the Enlightenment and the later development of Philosophic Radicalism which J. S. Mill was to depict as: 'A radicalism . . . which is only to be called radicalism inasmuch as it does not palter nor compromise with evils, but cuts at their roots'.[6] Burns begins by clarifying what he means by 'Radical Enlightenment', and distinguishes his own view from that which holds that there was an alternative Enlightenment to what might be called the High Enlightenment. This alternative Enlightenment would question the unquestionable and speak the unspeakable, while at the same time, as Roy Porter has noted, 'parodying the refrains of the High Enlightenment in shriller or frowsier cadences'.[7] Burns tends to dismiss the distinction, at least for Bentham (rightly in my opinion), who might well belong to both camps. Bentham clearly aligned himself with the leading figures of the so-called High Enlightenment, but his writings on sexuality, for example, might be assigned to an alternative Enlightenment. But, for Burns, the Enlightenment generally is radical, and that radicalism is based on a number of elements such as the critique of religion which pervades much writing from Montesquieu and Voltaire to Bentham and many others, and the belief, strong in Bentham, that philosophy can change the world.[8]

This essay will examine both the political and philosophical dimensions of Bentham's radicalism and attempt to explore some of the interconnections between the two. It will also consider a variation of the traditional Marxist critique of Bentham's utilitarianism and will concentrate on E. P. Thompson's views of the extent to which Bentham's radicalism, as considered here, extended to the working class especially through his close friendship with the reformer, Francis Place.[9]

I

For what might at first glance seem a relatively straightforward topic, Bentham's political radicalism at the time of the French Revolution and his so-called 'conversion' or 're-conversion' to radicalism in 1809–10 has been in fact the subject of some debate.[10] No one doubts that in 1788–9 Bentham began to write about radical reform in France in the sense of near-universal suffrage, annual parliaments, the secret ballot and representative government, and that he also turned his attention at some point during this period to similar reforms in Britain. These views were never published, and it is not clear how much was known about them by other members of the Lansdowne circle with whom Bentham was actively working on a number of projects in attempting to influence the course of events in France. One reason for Bentham not publishing these manuscripts was that events were moving so quickly that new topics and concerns occupied his time. Bentham had met William Petty, Earl of Shelburne (created Marquis of Lansdowne in 1784) in July 1781, when Shelburne visited him in his chambers in Lincoln's Inn, asked to borrow a copy of *A Fragment on Government*, and invited Bentham to spend the summer at Bowood, his country house. Here Bentham met numerous leading politicians and thinkers and eventually worked closely with Etienne Dumont, who had become tutor to one of Lansdowne's sons in 1785, and the lawyer and politician, Samuel Romilly, whom he had previously met. Dumont and Romilly visited Paris for two months in the summer of 1788 where they met and cultivated Honoré Gabriel Riqueti, Comte de Mirabeau. Encouraged by Lansdowne, Bentham worked on a number of topics, including judicial organization ('Draught of a New Plan for the Organization of the Judicial Establishment in France', partly printed in 1790), legislative procedure for the new assembly (which became the 'Essay on Political Tactics', partly printed in 1791), and the panopticon prison project. Although this material was radical in the sense of containing new proposals that went to the roots of the points at issue, it was not of direct import for political and constitutional organization. Nevertheless, Bentham did write essays which contained such material, and this material seems to reveal an evolving position held by Bentham which eventually led to his advocating radical reform in France.[11]

In one of two recent papers, based on a consideration of this material, Philip Schofield has argued that up to the end of 1788, as evidenced in the 'Essai sur la Representation', Bentham's radical agenda was limited with regard to the extent of the suffrage. He excluded women, minors, the insane, non-readers, and proposed a qualification based on property that would enfranchise only ten per cent of the population, i.e. 2.5 million out of a population of 25 million.[12] Schofield speculates that at this point Bentham saw security of property as more important than political equality.[13] Nevertheless, in a few months in early 1789 when at issue was the whole French constitutional system, Bentham was willing to advocate in important manuscripts a more radical approach which excluded from suffrage only minors, the insane, and non-readers, but not women, and the property qualification was dropped. For this brief period Bentham saw no opposition between political equality and security of property in so far as the former did not entail equality of property.[14] Even though Bentham's proposals seemed highly radical, Schofield cautions against seeing them out of context: he concludes by noting that while favouring radical proposals for the election of the National Assembly, Bentham continued to support monarchical government.[15]

In the second paper Schofield considers the implications of these writings for radical reform in Britain. Here the material is even more fragmentary, and Bentham clearly was not tempted to develop his views on parliamentary reform more generally and extensively as he did later in *Plan of Parliamentary Reform*. Furthermore, the references to the existing system in Britain in the essays for France are often positive, as Bentham was usually recommending British practices to the French.[16] But Bentham proposed that the secret ballot, annual parliaments, near-universal suffrage (no property qualification), and a representative system should be adopted in Britain, though Schofield suggests caution here as well. He notes that while Bentham could envisage the abolition of the House of Lords, he did not advocate the abolition of the peerage and the form of government would remain a limited monarchy.[17]

Schofield's analysis of Bentham's unpublished writings at the time of the French Revolution differs from earlier studies in several respects. James Crimmins tends to see only one position taken by Bentham with regard to limitations on suffrage. In this respect he confuses matters somewhat in seeing (contrary to Bentham himself) the literacy qualification as limiting suffrage far more than the property qualification. More importantly, Crimmins seems unaware of how Bentham's views were evolving *during* the 1788–9 period in response to events in France.[18] When the possibilities of fundamental constitutional reform emerged with the formation of the National Assembly, Bentham seems most radical in his proposals, but at the same time Schofield cautions one to recall that Bentham did not adopt anything so radical as a republican agenda. Furthermore, Schofield has noted that Bentham's attitude towards the British constitution softened as early as the autumn of 1791 when he referred to the 'perfectibility' of the existing constitution, meaning its capacity for change and improvement.[19] What these and other examples used by various commentators suggest is that Bentham was working on several levels. On the one hand, his concern with political equality through a near-equal suffrage, the secret ballot and constituencies of roughly equal size follows from his understanding of the utility principle which was itself conceived as a distributive principle, and political equality in the senses advocated by Bentham was a way of increasing happiness in practice.[20] On the other hand, Bentham was an empiricist in the sense that concrete proposals had to take into consideration changing circumstances. What Schofield has reminded us, a thesis confirmed by Crimmins in his discussion of the 1793–5 writings,[21] is that Bentham was not a republican in this period, and even when he adopted republican institutions, it was not for the reasons given by earlier republican writers, that is to say, from a belief in natural rights or in a community of property. Bentham's intellectual pedigree is more directly from Montesquieu (even though Bentham rejects the separation of power as the basis of political liberty) and reflects Hume's emphasis on the secure ownership of private property.[22]

Discussions of the retreat from radical reform during 1793–5 have tended to concentrate on the extent to which Bentham abandoned his earlier commitment to radical reform. Materials are sparse and the most striking evidence is contained in a few sheets of jottings or 'rudiments' which have survived in the manuscripts.[23] It is difficult to determine the significance of these writings but it is fair to say that like many Englishmen and not a few Frenchmen, Bentham was considerably shaken by events in France and adjusted his sights accordingly, so that the existing British constitution appeared to have a permanence and utility that had not been apparent at the outset of the revolution when he was more willing to contemplate the radical reform of parliament. It may well be that Bentham had not rejected his understanding of the principle of utility which led in the direction of political equality, but he surely hesitated to translate that understanding into practice either publicly or even in his private writings. Although the sparsity of evidence tends to make any judgement of this period prove speculative, it seems that the difference between Bentham's writings in 1788–9 and 1793–5 is more than a matter of 'distance'. And that 'distance' cannot be wholly accounted for by the suggestion that Bentham was attempting at this time to have the panopticon adopted by the Pitt administration.[24] Although Bentham could easily adapt his principles to circumstances,[25] he did not show as much flexibility when it came to changing his principles so as to achieve acceptability in practice. In the latter case he was well aware of the limits of his ability to do so, an awareness that dogged many of his inventive proposals throughout his career.[26] As the events of the French Revolution unfolded, what was at stake, as Burns has written, was no mere Fabian retreat but a full-scale evacuation on the model of Dunkirk.[27]

However this material is interpreted, not much depends on it, except perhaps for Halévy's false view of the development of Bentham's radicalism which requires that this earlier period should be shown to be of slight importance in his account of Bentham's 'authoritarian liberalism'.[28] Most other commentators agree that when Bentham returned in 1809–10 to write in favour of radical reform, he was returning to principles he first developed in 1788–9, and even if he formulated these arguments differently in what appeared in *Plan of Parliamentary Reform*, the new formulation remained closely connected to his utilitarian philosophy. Nevertheless, to state this is not to deny that Bentham's later writings contain a development of radical ideas beyond any formulated at the time of the French Revolution, and without an appreciation of how far Bentham moved from this earlier period, it is not possible to grasp the full import of his mature theory of constitutional democracy, which was not only radical but highly original and innovative.[29]

Bentham's theory of radical political reform constitutes only one small part of his mature constitutional theory and might be encompassed (as it was) within his Election Code for the legislature.[30] But constitutionalism for Bentham meant more than the reform of elections to the legislature. Institutionally, Bentham's constitutionalism covered the whole of government including the electorate, public opinion, legislature, executive, judiciary, military and local government. Conceptually, it was both a theory of democratic political morality and political accountability. Philosophically, it was based on secondary principles, justified by the greatest happiness principle, concerned with increasing and extending competence in office and reducing the expense of government as a burden on the people. As a theory of government it placed as great an emphasis on the influence of public opinion as on the nature of the electorate as means to achieve accountable government, but at the same time granted ample powers to government so that it had no excuse to evade or avoid its tasks and responsibilities.[31]

Some of Bentham's ideas concerning administrative accountability were developed earlier and especially in the panopticon writings.[32] Nevertheless, the mature constitutional theory, written during the 1820s in the context of an attempt to draft a complete code of laws for a modern state, was not anticipated in his earlier writings on radical reform either in 1788–9, 1809–10, or 1817 when he published *Plan of Parliamentary Reform*.

II

Let us now turn to the legacy of the Enlightenment that also animated Bentham's radicalism. This topic too has generated some debate, though little has depended on unpublished manuscripts or inaccessible texts, but more on what various commentators believe the Enlightenment attempted to achieve and how Bentham aligned his writings to its achievements. Nevertheless, if Bentham's political radicalism was derived from earlier thinkers of the Enlightenment, it is worth considering which thinkers they were and of what this influence consisted.

Bentham credited Hume with first using the principle of utility (albeit in a vague way) in a foundational role[33] and made the curious remark in the early *Fragment on Government* (1776) that in reading Hume 'I felt as if scales had fallen from my eyes, [and] I then, for the first time, learnt to call the cause of the people the cause of Virtue'.[34] The remark is curious because one does not particularly associate Hume with 'the cause of the people', although Bentham eventually used the principle of utility to justify doctrines of radical reform and representative democracy. But it is arguable that Hume's empiricism (i.e. seeing virtue as it was manifest in society) and the related belief that government was based ultimately on opinion had great influence on the stress Bentham placed on the basis of obedience and sovereignty, the moral sanction, and public opinion and the public opinion tribunal.

There are numerous examples in Bentham's early writings where the influence of Hume might be detected. Bentham's rejection of the doctrine of the social contract and his conception of the basis of society as consisting of conventions or a 'habit of obedience' was clearly indebted to Hume.[35] When he considered the grounds for civil and political disobedience by a whole society, he did not look to rational criteria deduced from the principle of utility but to the violation of established constitutional conventions in a particular society. This was the 'common signal' for resistance.[36] Furthermore, when he considered self-regarding offences in *An Introduction to the Principles of Morals and Legislation* (1789) (henceforth *IPML*), he did not argue that such crimes (mainly sexual offences and an offence like suicide) carried no harm to others and should not be offences at all, but left such a determination to various countries to resolve through their own legislation.[37]

This deference to established conventions played an important role in Bentham's philosophy in two further respects. Firstly, in his account of the 'sanctions' which were used to bind an individual to the performance of given actions, Bentham included the moral or popular sanction, essentially the influence of public opinion, as an instrument separate from other sanctions, such as the political, which was an instrument clearly in the hands of the Legislator or other sovereign body.[38] In other words, the existence of public opinion in politics is assumed to have a separate existence to which the Legislator must respond. Bentham clearly warned the Legislator 'not to introduce, without a cogent necessity, any mode or lot of punishment, towards which he happens to perceive any violent aversion entertained by the body of the people'.[39] This warning included punishment clearly approved by the dictates of the principle of utility so that the Legislator must on occasion allow actions which were opposed to utility. As we shall see, the role of public opinion played a crucial role in Bentham's later radicalism.

The second manifestation of Bentham's deference to conventions occurred at the end of *IPML* where he considered if there were any proper limits to legislation in the ethical life of individuals. He started by assuming that private ethics and legislation had the same scope and object. Nevertheless, there were acts which should not be punished by legislation and should be left to the moral judgment of individuals in the community. Bentham believed that a clear line could be drawn between the spheres of private ethics and legislation so that in many fields of endeavour the task of the Legislator was simply to enable private ethics to operate more efficaciously.[40] He clearly was on the side of popular opinion as in the following remark:

> It may be observed, that with regard to this branch of duty, legislators have, in general, been disposed to carry their interference full as far as is expedient. The great difficulty here is, to persuade them to confine themselves within bounds. A thousand little passions and prejudices have led them to narrow the liberty of the subject in this line, in cases in which the punishment is either attended with no profit at all, or with none that will make up for the expense.[41]

In Bentham's later writings on representative democracy the role given to public opinion reflects this earlier inheritance from Hume. We shall examine these later developments after first considering the influence of a second figure from the Enlightenment, Claude Adrien Helvétius. Helvétius not only made the principle of utility an instrument of practice but also saw in the hands of the figure of the Legislator the tools to change society radically to advance the greatest happiness.

Bentham ranked the influence of Helvétius as second only to Hume and depicted the impact of *De l'esprit* in terms of the sun at high noon suddenly 'bursting forth' from behind a cloud. Writing in the third person, he continued:

> To this work Mr. Bentham has often been heard to say that he stands indebted for no small part of the ardour of his desire to render his labours useful to mankind on the largest scale, and for the energies he finds to persevere in them, and for the hope and belief that they would not be altogether fruitless.[42]

Helvétius gave Bentham the conception of the Legislator in whose hands, through law, the utility principle might be put into practice. 'He would trust everything to laws', wrote a contemporary of Helvétius, 'legislature is to be the God and conscience of mankind'.[43] Bentham adopted a number of key ideas which were first developed by Helvétius. First, he found there the view that all virtue could be based on utility – a view to which Hume never subscribed.[44] Second, Helvétius provided a number of hints regarding the analysis of language and the definition of terms, which Bentham used to create a new vocabulary of legislation, and a neutral vocabulary for the analysis of morality.[45] Third, Bentham was influenced by the idea of the Legislator, which seemed to give him the courage to attempt to become the 'Legislator of the World'.[46] The most important project in the final decades (though one envisaged early in Bentham's career and partially attempted) was his plan to construct a system of legal codes (penal, civil, procedural and constitutional).[47] So ambitious and determined an intellectual enterprise can be found in few other writers of the Enlightenment or in any other period; Bentham's belief that he could construct and implement such codes owed no small debt to Helvétius's conception of the Legislator who could change and mould human behaviour through law.[48]

Bentham was also attracted to Helvétius's tendency to simplify the account of morality and legislation he inherited from earlier thinkers. Helvétius was content to use pleasure and pain without qualification in his account of human action and to assume that human beings acted on the basis of their own self-interested pleasures and pains. The principle of utility was also adopted without qualification as the foundation of legislation and morality. Although Bentham did not follow Helvétius in a number of respects, especially in believing that not all behaviour was based on self-interest and that the analysis of pleasure and pain in Helvétius was severely limited, he was attracted to the clarity which Helvétius achieved through the simplification of the account of human action and the emphasis on the role of law in securing happiness.[49]

Although Helvétius claimed to be a disciple of Hume, a claim Hume rejected,[50] the views of both thinkers can be found in Bentham's philosophy and in his radical political theory. Bentham took from Helvétius his prescriptive theory of utility, parts of his critical theory of language, and especially the conception of the Legislator; in Hume he found in the idea of utility the empirical foundation of states, the importance of existing conventions and the independent role of public opinion. Although both Hume and Helvétius were radical in a philosophical sense and Helvétius was radical in a political sense in advancing republican ideas and a doctrine of equality,[51] neither attempted, as did Bentham, to explore the implications of the utility principle within a theory of radical politics. Although the views of Hume and Helvétius differed on crucial issues, and particularly on the role of the Legislator in society, Bentham managed to unite them in a new synthesis of philosophy and practical politics.

III

For Bentham, what moved anyone to action was the prospect of pleasure and the avoidance of pain. Pleasure and pain formed motives and motives were the basis of interests. Because we act from a multiplicity of motives, we have innumerable interests: some are common to virtually all people, while others are peculiar to individuals. One interest that most people seem to share is in security. We want to have the necessities of life and be able to secure whatever beyond these necessities we can acquire. Our interest in security, however, extends beyond immediate physical survival and surrounding ourselves with material goods. We want to be able to plan for the future and realize our plans and ambitions, and we look to society, law and government to assist us in achieving our aspirations.[52] A political system which does so is a source of great happiness, and Bentham became an advocate of a democratic political system when he realized that the hopelessly corrupt mixed constitution of Britain could not secure happiness. He thought that the former could do one thing that the latter could not. It could allow the citizens to have security against misrule by giving them the power to change their rulers without necessarily having to resort to revolution and the risk of civil war.

The machinery of representative government, the use of the secret ballot, annual parliaments, and a widespread suffrage would give a powerful incentive to the people to provide security for themselves against misrule. But such mechanisms, at the heart of the radical agenda, would not be sufficient because political power, in Bentham's view, always remained in the hands of ruling elites, however they were chosen and however easily they might be removed. They especially had the power to mislead and delude the people and to persuade them to act against their own interests.

Furthermore, their power gave them every incentive to rule corruptly and to profit at the people's expense. The people, however, had a number of institutions to bring to bear on government (including democratic government), and these were grouped roughly under the heading of the public opinion tribunal. First, Bentham regarded the press, and especially books and newspapers, as an important element in the public opinion tribunal, particularly in its capacity to act as a critical force in relation to government. At times Bentham seemed to rate freedom of speech, press and public discussion more highly than a democratic electoral system, as a force for good government. It is not just that such freedoms allowed increased rationality to enter the political arena. It was more the adoption of a critical perspective, which reflected other interests besides those which governments tried to pursue. At times these interests converged, as when government ruled in the interests of the people but at numerous other times they did not. The press could provide a record of where these interests diverged.

Second, Bentham placed much emphasis on the organization of government so that proper records were kept, full publicity was given to decisions and records, and what is now called freedom of information was established. Bentham delved deeply into such apparently uninteresting subjects as accounting practice, bookkeeping, records, etc., so that government would be as transparent as possible and serve a democratic polity. If there was to be a public opinion tribunal, it had to be able to obtain appropriate and accurate information.

Third, Bentham stressed the importance of bodies of ordinary people who would watch the actual functioning of government and played a critical role in its operations. The traditional institutional model was the jury in the judicial system. Bentham multiplied such groups, often informal ones, so that a popular element played an important role in numerous aspects of the administrative system.[53]

Besides these elements of the public opinion tribunal several others are worth special emphasis. One is Bentham's willingness to regard popular uprising or revolution as the ultimate sanction of the public opinion tribunal.[54] That he could see an enraged mob as part of this body is a useful corrective to the view that he regarded the press and public opinion as a somewhat utopian, rational force in society simply translating philosophical truths into democratic practices.[55] But if Bentham did not necessarily regard the actions of public opinion as solely a rational force in society, how could he argue that public opinion necessarily reflected or served the public interest?

The argument he developed was simple, though important. Bentham at times seemed to assert that *vox populi* was *vox dei*, and it was not always clear how he arrived at the view that whenever public opinion spoke-through books, newspapers, juries, public meetings and from anywhere in the world – it spoke for the public interest. His argument was hardly utopian, and no great testimony to human rationality. The people, he argued, lacked one feature possessed by rulers and politicians: power. They lacked the power to corrupt and delude, and hence they were more likely to represent the public interest than rulers. They could be fairly easily deluded and corrupted by rulers, and Bentham was fully aware of an all-pervasive false consciousness generated from a ruling establishment in Britain, which combined court, church, military, judiciary, lawyers and the government, and which led millions to act against their own interests and that of the public. But such false consciousness could never be complete, and the very existence of radicalism in Britain, despite widespread opposition and false consciousness, testified to that fact. It could not be complete because the people, however much they were lulled into complacency, retained powerful motives simply by being alive, to seek their own security, especially against the burdens of misrule, and they could do so by means of the public opinion tribunal which even the most powerful rulers could never ignore.

For Bentham, therefore, public opinion was the engine of reform. It acted directly on government and indirectly through the electoral system in a representative democracy. Though Bentham was 'radical', he did not extend his radicalism to giving the people the power to rule or to make important policy decisions. He rejected direct, participatory democracy. The people shared in politics and prevented misrule via the ballot and directed their rulers via public opinion. Even where he invoked resistance and revolution as an ultimate sanction, such direct action was limited and the new democratic regime was intended to be an indirect, representative system.

This brief account of Bentham's conception of public opinion and the public opinion tribunal is intended to show how he connected philosophical ideas with a conception of radical reform in politics. He established a close link between public opinion, happiness and truth, and without such a link, it is doubtful if so great an emphasis could have been placed on the role of the public opinion tribunal. The educated member of the public had a special role to play in Bentham's democratic polity. The most important elite in a representative democracy was not necessarily a ruling elite. To be a leader of public opinion, to receive the deference of the people due to one's intellectual ability and the clarity of one's thinking was no less an important achievement than ruling itself, and could be regarded as a qualification for ruling. In Bentham's ethics the exercise of effective benevolence, that is to say, to act habitually to increase the happiness of others was the highest of the virtues, and brought the individual happiness as well as contributing to that of others. The virtuous person also needed to know the truth in order to be successful.

For Bentham, the wealthy and educated members of society need not fear representative democracy, because they had much to gain from it. The experience of the United States had shown that a democratic system, however imperfect due to the exclusion of women from suffrage and the existence of slavery, posed no threat to security of property. The economic system most compatible with democracy would enable the wealthy to maintain and improve their position. But more importantly, from the ranks of the wealthy and educated came the elite which had most to give to political society. Their intellectual ability would continually clarify the ideas that underpinned the democratic regime. Their virtue would serve democratic ends. Bentham, himself, as 'legislator of the world', and the critic of fallacious reasoning in politics and philosophy, would represent the highest level of virtue, and the radicals, advancing reforms, operating in and out of government, serving the public good, would follow closely behind him.

IV

It might be argued that this positive account of Bentham's radicalism is somewhat flawed in that what is praised here is condemned in the Marxist critique of bourgeois ideology and shown by Marxists to be used to oppress and exploit the vast majority in society. An important example might be found in E. P. Thompson's *The Making of the English Working Class*. In the final section of that work, entitled 'Class Consciousness', Thompson takes great pains to distinguish utilitarianism, as among the worst aspects of bourgeois ideology, from the emergence of working-class consciousness and the trade union movement. In this account one of the most problematic characters is not the icon of middle-class radicalism, Bentham, who is wholly repudiated, but Francis Place, whose close contact with Bentham and James Mill is difficult to reconcile with his involvement in radical politics at the time of the French Revolution and later in the trade union movement. For Thompson, the famous tailor of Charing Cross, who rose to great prominence in the early nineteenth century, neither fits easily into middle-class radicalism due to his origins and some of his activities nor into working-class radicalism due to his association with Bentham and Mill. Consider one important paragraph on Place:

> The influence of Place was important, and we must come nearer to understanding the man. We have kept a watchful eye upon him throughout this study because, as an archivist and historian (of the L.C.S., of Westminster Radicalism, of the repeal of the Combination Acts) his bias has been gravely misleading. He has risen from being a journeyman breeches-maker into a prosperous shopkeeper and employer, and close confidant of Bentham and the Mills, and the adviser of M.P.s. From the early 1800s his emphasis has been upon the building of bridges between artisans and the middle class; he has lent his support to the Lancastrian schools movement and the Mechanics' Institute; his concern has been with the sober, respectable artisan and his efforts at self-improvement. But because he was so obviously a founding father of the Fabian tradition (and was taken uncritically as such by Graham Wallas) we should not see him just as a 'captive' of the middle class, nor should we suppose that he was incapable of taking up the most intransigent positions. On matters of free thought and expression he was still half a Jacobin; he had helped to publish the first edition in England of the *Age of Reason*, and even though he came to regard Carlile as a 'fanatic' he gave him a great deal of assistance in his earlier struggles. We have seen his fury at the oppression of 1817 and 1819, and the enormous application with which he was to work for trade union rights, even though his zeal for the cause of the unionists was curiously compounded with the political economy of M'Culloch. In intellectual terms, by 1818 he really was a captive of Bentham: he *learned* the doctrine of Bentham and the elder Mill rather than inquiring into them, and in his own writing he added almost nothing to them except the illustrative facts which he collected with such industry. But in political terms he was a force in his own right; he gave to the Utilitarians, not just a seat at

Westminster which was within his manipulation, but a point of contact with the world of the Radical tradesmen and artisans. The very fact that such a man could perform this role, both ideologically and politically, is a new phenomenon.[56]

Thompson, as we see, gives full credit to Place's significance in the development of working-class consciousness and recognizes that unless he provides a satisfactory explanation of Place's role in that development, his account of early nineteenth-century radicalism will be flawed. He rejects the view that locates Place at the core of British socialism as a 'founding father of the Fabian tradition'. As such, Place's 'bridges between the artisans and the middle class' as well as his political and ideological radicalism are not seen as the defining characteristics of British socialism but rather as revealing an unsatisfactory, almost schizoid personality. On the one hand, his contribution to political radicalism over many decades was enormous, but on the other hand the fact that he supposedly '*learned* the doctrines of Bentham and the elder Mill rather than inquiring into them' seems to suggest a deficiency either in his intellect or his personality generally, or, perhaps, both.

Let me suggest a different approach to one side of Place's complex character, that side connected with Bentham. Rather than seeing Place in a passive role, as being indoctrinated by Bentham and Mill, I tend to see him as a much more active figure in Bentham's life. If he did not lead Bentham to radicalism itself (Bentham had already arrived at that state before he met Place through Mill in 1813), he encouraged and led Bentham along the radical path. Bentham developed the view that increasing equality in society was an important element in enhancing security and that the way forward was a radical political agenda which would eventually lead to increased economic equality. If Place did not provide Bentham with these ideas (and I have no evidence either way), he surely encouraged them. He initiated and developed numerous contacts with radical activists and their journals through which Bentham's ideas might be circulated to a wider and different audience. For example, Thompson's paragraph about Place, which was quoted above, appears in the midst of a discussion of the *Gorgon*, edited by John Wade in 1818–19, in which in Thompson's words:

The *Gorgon*'s intellectual history is more exciting. It was an explicit attempt to effect a junction between Benthamism and working-class experience. It was not (as Place might have made it if he had captured it) an attempt simply to relay the ideas of the middle-class Utilitarians to a working-class audience. John Wade, the former journeyman wool-sorter who edited it (in 1818–19), was a man of originality and great application, who did not take his ideas on trust. In the result, the *Gorgon* seems not so much to accept these ideas as to wrestle with them: the enquiry is made – can Utilitarianism in the context of working-class experience be put to *use*?[57]

The laborious distinction between supplying 'the ideas of the middle-class Utilitarians' to a working-class audience (Place) and enquiry and wrestling with these ideas (by the former journeyman wool-sorter, Wade) is, I suspect, more the invention of Thompson's imagination than based on any concrete evidence. Thompson might not have known (as we now know from Bentham's *Correspondence*) that Bentham had probably provided funds for the *Gorgon*,[58] and if Place was unhappy with the *Gorgon*, it may well have been with the personality of Wade as opposed to any particular doctrines that Wade espoused. This was the case with Thomas Hodgskin, another working-class radical, whom Place introduced to Bentham probably in 1813 and who soon took an interest in Bentham's ideas and books. The acrimonious dispute between Place on the one hand and Joseph Clinton Robertson and Hodgskin on the other over the operation of the London Mechanics' Institution was over how best to organize its management. Place's insistence on the need to introduce wealthy patrons into the management of the society was more practical than ideological. Where he disagreed with Hodgskin over his ideas was mainly with Hodgskin holding a Godwinian belief in the possibility of society without government.[59]

Place's commitment to a radical agenda in politics and economics never wavered. He understood Bentham to have moved strongly in that direction, and realized how important an asset Bentham's support for various practical causes would be. Place was also a practical man who sought to create institutions and publications which could survive and found that he could work with Bentham to secure these ends.

Thompson is mistaken regarding Place on two counts. First, the assertion that Place was a 'captive' of Bentham is surely misleading and false. Even where Place used Bentham's ideas, as he did for his *Illustrations and Proofs of the Principle of Population* (1822), or when he helped to edit for publication Bentham's *Not Paul but Jesus* (1823), there was a good deal of interaction between the two friends.[60] Place would have found in Bentham's inventive mind and analytical skill important resources for his own work. He in turn provided Bentham with an outlet for his views, particularly on birth control which Bentham feared to make public under his own name. Place also provided access for Bentham to a wide variety of radical figures, contacts throughout the world, and a good deal of practical advice regarding tactics to be adopted in his various schemes for reform. Rather than seeing Place as a 'captive', it would be more accurate to see him as a good friend and colleague. Second, Thompson assumes, and his assumption operates as a rigid principle, that there was a middle-class utilitarianism which was wedded to classical political economy and Malthusianism and hostile to the sort of reforms that the working class would seek for itself, if it had the power and organization to do so. He applies this idea uncritically to Place's role in the development of working-class consciousness. The example of Place, however, should have suggested that the assumption was false. As he admits, Place 'was still half a Jacobin', assisted Carlile in his various struggles, worked for trade union rights, expressed anger at repression in 1817 and 1819, and his advocacy of birth control suggests a rejection of Malthusianism. Thompson fails to see that this side of Place was perfectly compatible with his friendship with Bentham who shared many of the characteristics admired by Thompson in Place. Thompson misses this obvious interpretation.

The reason he does so is only partly based on his use of Marx who saw utilitarianism mainly as a late-bourgeois ideology. Marx connected Bentham's writings with the period of the French Revolution and the development of large-scale industry.[61] This connection is incorrect and is probably based on Marx's limited familiarity with Bentham's writings. Though Marx most likely read Dumont's French recension, the *Traités de législation civile et pénale* which was published in 1802, he would not have been aware of the fact that these writings were completed in the 1770s and were more closely connected with the ideas of Montesquieu, Hume, Smith, Helvétius, Blackstone and Beccaria than with those of the period of the French Revolution. As we have seen, by the time of the French Revolution Bentham was willing to entertain radical principles and his thinking about the poor and about politics generally during this period reflected a very different range of concerns than in the 1770s, when his writings were restricted to legal and philosophical issues. Second, Marx seemed unfamiliar with Bentham's later radicalism and commitment to representative democracy. He may have known nothing of the alliance between Bentham and Place in extending radicalism to a working-class audience. Even though Thompson should have been aware of Bentham's radicalism, he goes beyond Marx in dismissing him not only as a bourgeois ideologist but also as a threat to working-class consciousness itself. This is especially puzzling in a massive book based supposedly on a thorough reading of original sources.

To explain Thompson's position, we might examine his earlier biography of William Morris, published in 1955, in which he compared Morris's idyllic utopia in *News from Nowhere* favourably with Stalin's post-war programme in the Soviet Union.[62] This material was omitted from a later edition published in 1976 to which he added a postscript to explain his earlier adulation of Stalin.[63] He admits there to allowing in the earlier edition 'some hectoring political moralisms, as well as a few Stalinist pieties to intrude upon the text' to which he adds: 'I had then a somewhat reverent notion of Marxism as a received orthodoxy, and my pages included some passages of polemic whose vulgarity no doubt makes contemporary scholars wince'.[64] He then writes that his disagreements with orthodox Marxism 'became fully articulate' in 1956.[65] *The Making of the English Working Class*, published in 1963, reflects this departure from orthodox Marxism (Stalinism), and what distinguishes it from traditional Marxism is its sympathy with the romantic tradition's critique of utilitarianism. In place of the heroic struggle of the proletariat to build factories, create wealth, improve housing and extend education – to realize Stalin's blueprint – one finds Thompson embracing a more conservative stance in opposing such reforms when they appear within middle-class utilitarianism on the grounds that they corrupt an authentic working-class consciousness. Where orthodox Marxism would see some links between utilitarianism, especially in the materialist version found in Helvétius, and early socialism,[66] Thompson considers these links as in effect a betrayal of working-class consciousness, and thus he elevates Wade, Hodgskin, etc. over Place. Unfortunately, this theoretical move makes him not only indifferent but also actively hostile to the links between middle-class and working-class radicalism. Among the most important of these links was that provided by Place in alliance with Bentham. Few non-Marxists have ever doubted the important link between Bentham's radicalism and British socialism,[67] and Thompson's achievement has been to attempt to use the romantic tradition and Marxist categories to obscure the link. The result has been an historically inaccurate account of the development of British radicalism and of the role of Bentham in it.

IV

To conclude, let me first summarize the argument thus far. I began by calling attention to Bentham's depiction of himself as 'The Old Radical', and considered in light of his career just what this meant. I called attention to his various incarnations as a political radical favouring near-universal suffrage, the secret ballot, annual parliaments and representative government in 1789 and 1809–10 before the publication of *Plan of Parliamentary Reform* in 1817. I then considered a different sort of radicalism in his thought, linked to Enlightenment philosophy and indebted to the earlier writings of Hume and Helvétius. An account of Bentham's emphasis on the importance of public opinion was advanced, and I argued that his emphasis on what he called the public opinion tribunal provided an additional and important dimension to the radical doctrines currently in force.

The question was then raised as to whether or not my account of Bentham's radicalism was simply a positive statement of what has been criticized and dismissed as bourgeois ideology in Marxist analyses of English radicalism, such as in E. P. Thompson's *The Making of the English Working Class*. I pointed out the extent to which Thompson failed to appreciate Bentham's later radicalism and the importance of his alliance with Francis Place in extending radical ideas to all classes, including the working class.

I want to end this essay by posing a question about connections between radicalism and the development of early liberalism in the 1820s to which part of my book, *Bentham, Byron and Greece*, was devoted.[68] The term, 'liberal', referring to a political doctrine, passed into the English language from the Spanish 'liberales' at this time and was eventually used as a term which seemed to overlap with that of 'radical'. The subtitle of Bentham's *Constitutional Code*, printed in 1827 and published in 1830, was *For All Nations and All Governments Professing Liberal Opinions*. Later in the century liberals would look back to earlier radicals and call them 'liberals', although these radicals may not have referred to themselves as 'liberals' at the time. My question is whether there were any differences in doctrine which accompanied the change in terminology. Did liberals stand for something different from radicals? In *Bentham, Byron and Greece* I noted that early liberals like John Bowring and Edward Blaquiere emphasized different issues from those of many British radicals. For example, they were more international in orientation and looked to the meliorating action of free trade, while the radicals seemed to concentrate on parliamentary reform in Britain. I want to suggest a further difference: radicals were for the most part an opposition force in British politics, and served as a true opposition in a regime where Whigs and Tories often colluded in maintaining corruption with its sinecures, pensions, etc., and nothing less than the threat of revolution would shift them from the corrupt abuse of power. Perhaps liberals did not see themselves as an opposing political force to the two main parties. As Bentham once put it (in a letter to Daniel O'Connell in 1829), those who were called liberals often included both Whigs and radicals.[69] The membership of the London Greek Committee, for example, brought together Whigs and radicals in their common support for the Greek struggle for independence. Bentham himself was happy as both an 'old radical' and as an icon of early liberalism.

NOTES

1 Catherine Fuller (ed.), *The Old Radical: Representations of Jeremy Bentham* (London: University College London, 1998).

2 Bentham to Parr, 17 February 1823, *The Correspondence of Jeremy Bentham*: volume 11 (1822-June 1824), ed. C. Fuller (Oxford: Clarendon Press, 2000), p. 209.

3 J. Bentham, *Plan of Parliamentary Reform in the Form of a Catechism, With Reasons for Each Article, Shewing the Necessity of Radical and the Inadequacy of Moderate Reform* (London: R. Hunter, 1817).

4 See *ibid.*, p. i, and Bentham Manuscripts, University College London, boxes cxxvi, cxxvii, cxxviii, cxxix(a), cxxx.

5 See E. Halévy, *La Formation du Radicalisme Philosophique* [1901–4], new edition, 3 vols., ed. Monique Canto-Sperber (Paris: Presses Universitaires de France, 1995), i. 151–87, 260–79, 314–21; ii. 5–37, 197–209; Halévy, *The Growth of Philosophic Radicalism*, trans. Mary Morris (London: Faber and Faber, 1952), pp. 120–81; Mary Mack, *Jeremy Bentham, An Odyssey of Ideas 1748–1792* (London: Heinemann, 1962), pp. 407–31, 440–3, 448–66; J. H. Burns, 'Bentham and the French Revolution', *Transactions of the Royal Historical Society*, 5th Series, 16 (1966), 95–114; J. R. Dinwiddy, 'Bentham's Transition to Political Radicalism', *Journal of the History of Ideas* 36 (1975), 683–700, esp. 683–4; M. James, 'Bentham's Democratic Theory at the Time of the French Revolution', *The Bentham Newsletter* 10 (1986), 5–16; J. R. Dinwiddy, *Bentham* (Past Masters) (Oxford: Oxford University Press, 1989), pp. 11–12; J. Crimmins, 'Bentham's Political Radicalism Reexamined', *Journal of the History of Ideas* 54 (1994), 259–81; P. Schofield, 'Jeremy Bentham, the French Revolution, and Electoral Reform' and 'Jeremy Bentham, the French Revolution, and Parliamentary Reform in Britain', unpublished papers presented at the Japanese Society for Utilitarian Studies conference, Zushi, and the Anglo-Japanese Research Committee meeting, Tokyo in September 1999. I am much indebted to Dr Schofield both for his scholarship in this field and for permission to refer to these papers in advance of his published work on Bentham and parliamentary reform. See *Utility and Democracy: The Political Thought of Jeremy Bentham* (Oxford: Oxford University Press, 2006).

6 *The Bentham Newsletter* 8 (1984), 4–14. The quotation from J.S. Mill on p. 12 is taken from a letter to Edward Lytton Bulwer, 23 November 1836, *The Earlier Letters of John Stuart Mill*, ed. F.E. Mineka, 2 vols. (Toronto: Toronto University Press, 1963) (*The Collected Works of John Stuart Mill*, ed. J.M. Robson, xii. 312).

7 Quoted by Burns, 'Jeremy Bentham: From Radical Enlightenment to Philosophic Radicalism', p. 4.

8 For Bentham's radicalism in relation to religion, see J. Crimmins, *Secular Utilitarianism: Social Science and the Critique of Religion in the Thought of Jeremy Bentham* (Oxford: Clarendon Press, 1990); P. Schofield, 'Political and Religious Radicalism in the Thought of Jeremy Bentham', *History of Political Thought* 20 (1999), 272–91; J. Crimmins, 'Bentham's Religious Radicalism Revisited: A Response to Schofield', unpublished paper presented to the International Society for Utilitarian Studies 2000 conference at Wake Forest University, March 2000 and published in the *History of Political Thought* 22 (2001), 494–500. For the view that philosophy can change the world, see the discussion of Helvétius below.

9 See E.P. Thompson, *The Making of the English Working Class* (Harmondsworth: Penguin Books, 1968), pp. 781–915.

10 See the references listed above at note 5.

11 See Dinwiddy, *Bentham*, pp. 5–6; F. Rosen, 'Jeremy Bentham', *New DNB*, forthcoming from Oxford University Press; the relevant volumes of the *Correspondence of Jeremy Bentham*: volume 3 (1781–1788), ed. I. Christie (London: Athlone Press, 1971) and volume 4 (1788–93), ed. A.T. Milne (London: Athlone Press, 1981). See also the editorial introductions to Bentham's *Political Tactics*, ed. M. James, C. Blamires, and C. Pease-Watkin (*Collected Works of Jeremy Bentham* henceforth *CW*) (Oxford: Clarendon Press, 1999), pp. xiii–xl, and *Rights, Representation, and Reform: 'Nonsense Upon Stilts' and Other Writings for the French Revolution*, ed. P. Schofield, C. Pease-Watkin, and C. Blamires, (*CW*), (Oxford: Clarendon Press, 2002). A version of Bentham's writings on judicial organization may be found in J. Bowring (ed.), *The Works of Jeremy Bentham*, 11 vols. (Edinburgh: William Tait, 1838–43), iv. 285–406. For panopticon, see Janet Semple, *Bentham's Prison: A Study of the Panopticon Penitentiary* (Oxford: Clarendon Press, 1993). See also F. Rosen, 'Jeremy Bentham on Slavery and the Slave Trade', *Utilitarianism and Empire*, eds. B. Schultz and G. Varouxakis (Lanham: Lexington Books, 2005), pp. 33–56.

12 Schofield, 'Jeremy Bentham, the French Revolution, and Electoral Reform', pp. 12, 16–17.

13 *Ibid.*, p. 17.

14 *Ibid.*, p. 20.

15 *Ibid.*, p. 22.

16 See Bentham, *Political Tactics* (*CW*), where one of his objects was to recommend the existing procedures in the British parliament to the French.

17 Schofield, 'Jeremy Bentham, the French Revolution, and Parliamentary Reform in Britain', pp. 7–13.
18 Crimmins, 'Bentham's Political Radicalism Reexamined', pp. 261–7.
19 Schofield, 'Jeremy Bentham, the French Revolution, and Parliamentary Reform in Britain', p. 13.
20 On the principle of utility as a distributive principle, see F. Rosen, 'Individual Sacrifice and the Greatest Happiness: Bentham on Utility and Rights', *Utilitas* 10 (1998), 129–43; in the context of these writings see the critique of Halévy in James, 'Bentham's Democratic Theory at the Time of the French Revolution', pp. 12–14.
21 Crimmins, 'Bentham's Political Radicalism Reexamined', p. 273.
22 See F. Rosen, *Bentham, Byron and Greece: Constitutionalism, Nationalism, and Early Liberal Political Thought* (Oxford: Clarendon Press, 1992), pp. 25–58.
23 See the discussion in *ibid.*, pp. 57–8. See also *Rights, Representation, and Reform* (*CW*), pp. lviii–lx.
24 See Crimmins, 'Bentham's Political Radicalism Reexamined', pp. 270, 272.
25 See, for example, Bentham, *Securities Against Misrule and Other Constitutional Writings for Tripoli and Greece*, ed. P. Schofield (*CW*) (Oxford: Clarendon Press, 1990), pp. 23–141, where he adapted his theory of constitutional securities to an Islamic state.
26 See Bentham's attempts to have his proposals for codification accepted in numerous countries, especially those in the common law tradition in *Legislator of the World: Writings on Codification, Law, and Education*, ed. P. Schofield and J. Harris (Oxford: Clarendon Press, 1998). See also F. Rosen, 'The Legislator, Constitutional Artifice, and Human Happiness', *Root Causes of Instability and Violence in the Balkans*, ed. A. Moulakis (Lugano: Martini Edizioni and Institute for Mediterranean Studies, 2005), pp. 34–53.
27 See Burns, 'Bentham and the French Revolution', pp. 95–114; and Mack, *Jeremy Bentham*, pp. 440–2.
28 See F. Rosen, 'Elie Halévy and Bentham's Authoritarian Liberalism', *Enlightenment and Dissent* 6 (1987), 59–76; *Bentham, Byron and Greece*, pp. 3–5.
29 See J. Bentham, *Constitutional Code, Volume I*, ed. F. Rosen and J. H. Burns (*CW*) (Oxford: Clarendon Press, 1983; F. Rosen, *Jeremy Bentham and Representative Democracy, A Study of the Constitutional Code* (Oxford: Clarendon Press, 1983).
30 See *Bentham's Radical Reform Bill, with Extracts from the Reasons* (London: E. Wilson, 1819); Bentham, *Constitutional Code, Volume I* (*CW*) p. 48 and n.
31 See Rosen, *Jeremy Bentham and Representative Democracy*; *Bentham, Byron and Greece*, pp. 59–76.
32 See L. J. Hume, *Bentham and Bureaucracy* (Cambridge: Cambridge University Press, 1981).
33 See Bentham, 'Article on Utilitarianism', *Deontology together with A Table of the Springs of Action and Article on Utilitarianism*, ed. A. Goldworth (*CW*) (Oxford: Clarendon Press, 1983), pp. 289–90; Bentham, *A Fragment on*

Government, ed. J. H. Burns and H. L. A. Hart (Cambridge: Cambridge University Press, 1988), p. 116.

34 Bentham, *A Fragment on Government*, p. 51n.

35 *Ibid.*, pp. 40–3, 51–2.

36 *Ibid.*, pp. 96–7, 102.

37 See Bentham, *An Introduction to the Principles of Morals and Legislation*, ed. J. H. Burns and H. L. A. Hart (*CW*) (Oxford: Clarendon Press, 1996), pp. lviii–lix, 277–8.

38 *Ibid.*, pp. 34–5 and n.

39 *Ibid.*, p. 183.

40 See *ibid.*, pp. 285–91. Cf. J. B. Schneewind, *The Invention of Autonomy, A History of Modern Moral Philosophy* (Cambridge, Cambridge University Press, 1998), p. 423.

41 Bentham, *IPML* (*CW*), pp. 290–1.

42 Bentham, 'Article on Utilitarianism' *Deontology* (*CW*), p. 325.

43 Elizabeth Montagu to Edward Montagu, 2 January 1759, as quoted in David Wisner, *The Cult of the Legislator in France 1750–1830, A Study in the Political Theology of the French Enlightenment* (Studies on Voltaire and the Eighteenth Century, no. 352) (Oxford: Voltaire Foundation, 1997), p. 5; on the idea of the Legislator in Bentham, see J. H. Burns, *The Fabric of Felicity: The Legislator and the Human Condition* (London: University College London, 1967).

44 Bentham, *A Fragment on Government*, p. 51.

45 *Ibid.*, pp. 123–4; see also *IPML* (*CW*), p. 102n.

46 See Bentham, *Legislator of the World* (*CW*); P. Schofield, 'Jeremy Bentham: Legislator of the World', *Current Legal Problems* 51 (1998), 115–47.

47 See Bentham, *Constitutional Code, Volume I* (*CW*), pp. xxxv–xxxix.

48 See Wisner, *The Cult of the Legislator in France*, p. 45.

49 See Bentham, 'Article on Utilitarianism', *Deontology* (*CW*), pp. 290–1, 325, 327.

50 See Hume to Adam Smith, 12 April 1759, *Correspondence of Adam Smith*, ed. E. C. Mossner and I. S. Ross (The Glasgow Edition of the Works and Correspondence of Adam Smith) (Indianapolis: Liberty Classics, 1987), p. 34.

51 See David Wootton, 'Helvétius: from Radical Enlightenment to Revolution', *Political Theory*, 28 (2000), 307–36.

52 See F. Rosen, 'Bentham and Mill on Liberty and Justice', *Lives, Liberties and the Public Good, New Essays in Political Theory for Maurice Cranston*, ed. G. Feaver and F. Rosen (London: Macmillan, 1987), pp. 121–38; P. J. Kelly, *Utilitarianism and Distributive Justice, Jeremy Bentham and the Civil Law* (Oxford: Clarendon Press, 1990).

53 For a fuller account of Bentham's emphasis on the role of public opinion and the public opinion tribunal, see Rosen, *Jeremy Bentham and Representative Democracy*, as index; P. Schofield, 'Bentham on Public Opinion and the Press', *Economical with the Truth: the Law and the Media in a Democratic Society*, ed. D. Kingsford-Smith and D. Oliver (Oxford: ESC Publishing, 1990), pp. 95–108.

54 See Bentham, *Security Against Misrule* (*CW*), pp. 122–4; Rosen, *Jeremy Bentham and Representative Democracy*, pp. 24–5.

55 For the view that Bentham placed too great an emphasis on rationality, see J.M. Robson, *The Improvement of Mankind: The Social and Political Thought of John Stuart Mill* (Toronto: Toronto University Press, 1968), p. 19.

56 Thompson, *The Making of the English Working Class*, pp. 845–6.

57 *Ibid.*, p. 845.

58 See *The Correspondence of Jeremy Bentham*, volume 9 (1817–1820), ed. S. Conway (Oxford: Clarendon Press, 1989), p. 249 and n.; volume 10 (1820–1821), ed. S. Conway (Oxford: Clarendon Press, 1994), p. 184. But see also G. Wallas, *The Life of Francis Place 1771–1854* (London: George Allen and Unwin, 1918), p. 204, a source which was known to Thompson.

59 See Rosen, *Bentham, Byron and Greece*, pp. 212–16. For a recent study of Hodgskin, see David Stack, *Nature and Artifice, The Life and Thought of Thomas Hodgskin (1787–1869)*, (Woodbridge Suffolk: Royal Historical Society and the Boydell Press, 1998). See also Wallas, *The Life of Francis Place*, pp. 112–13.

60 See Lea Campos Boralevi, *Bentham and the Oppressed* (Berlin: de Gruyter, 1984), pp. 106–12, 116–19. See also Dudley Miles, *Francis Place 1771–1854, The Life of a Remarkable Radical* (Brighton: Harvester Press, 1988), pp. 97–9, 119–20, 140–2; Mary Thale (ed.), *The Autobiography of Francis Place 1771–1854* (Cambridge: Cambridge University Press, 1972), pp. 5, 249–50, 288; Wallas, *The Life of Francis Place*, pp. 65–175.

61 K. Marx, 'Bentham', *Jeremy Bentham, Critical Assessments*, ed. B. Parekh, 4 vols. (London: Routledge, 1993), i. 386–90.

62 See E. P. Thompson, *William Morris, Romantic to Revolutionary* (New York: Monthly Review Press, 1961), pp. 760–1. The 1961 edition was a reprint of the original London edition.

63 E. P. Thompson, *William Morris, Romantic to Revolutionary* (New York: Pantheon Books, 1976), pp. 654–5, 769.

64 *Ibid.*, p. 769.

65 *Ibid.*, p. 810.

66 See, for example, Irving Louis Horowitz, *Claude Helvétius: Philosopher of Democracy and Enlightenment* (New York: Paine-Whitman Publishers, 1954), pp. 170–96.

67 See, for example, Roy Jenkins, 'Equality', *New Fabian Essays*, ed. R. H. S. Crossman (New York: Frederick A. Praeger, 1952), p. 69.

68 See Rosen, *Bentham, Byron and Greece*, pp. 3–5, 9–12, 125–43, 289–304.

69 Bentham to O'Connell, 10 November 1829, Bentham, *Works*, ed. Bowring, xi. 25.

CHAPTER 10

Religion and the Origins of Radicalism in Nineteenth-Century Britain[1]

J. C. D. Clark

ORIGINS: FROM 'RADICAL REFORMERS' TO 'RADICALS'

'Radicalism' was a specific ideology, first coined in England in the 1820s to express a fusion of universal suffrage, Ricardian economics and programmatic atheism. As such, it was only one of a range of new doctrines conceptualized at that time. Yet the history of radicalism, liberalism, socialism and conservatism has been equally obscured by two processes, themselves integral to the historical evolution of nineteenth-century ideologies. First, each began with a fairly clear and novel set of meanings which became diluted as more and more attempts were made to appropriate the original position and to steer it in new directions: so a term which was at its outset specific became steadily more imprecise and plural in its content. Second, the favoured term was projected backwards in time, and a spurious genealogy was invented in order to invest a newly coined doctrine with an air of timeless validity.[2] The most notorious capitulation to this need to find retrospective validation was perhaps Alexander Gray's book *The Socialist Tradition: Moses to Lenin*, but when first published in 1946 this exercise did not seem illegitimate. Gray was himself no hagiographer,[3] and was not consciously attempting to celebrate what he recorded: his book is evidence of the wide acceptance of assumptions about the timelessness of key categories. Only recently have such assumptions begun to be discredited.

The terms 'radical' and 'radicalism' were the main beneficiaries from this process of retrospective projection, and their timelessness was accepted into academic discourse. German historians applied the adjective 'radical' to the Reformation at least from the 1950s,[4] and that way of picturing this episode was given wide currency in English from George Williams's monograph of 1962.[5] The apparent validity of the term for the Reformation could only validate its usage for subsequent centuries. Despite debates over sixteenth-century phenomena, the category itself was strangely immune from historical challenge, so that even in 1991 one might read that 'Radicalism in the sixteenth-century Reformation first appeared in the stormy years of the movement in Germany and Switzerland'.[6] In the light of all that has happened in the methodology of intellectual history in recent decades, we can now see why such a sentence is the historical equivalent of the philosophical statement 'All square circles are French'. A sentence may be correct in grammar and syntax and yet convey no meaning. The use of anachronistic key categories merely creates a world of shadows and fictions in which no clear questions can be asked and no clear answers can be given. To ask whether the origins of English 'radicalism' can be traced in the 1640s or 1760s is to ask a question which is not wrong only because it is meaningless.

In locating 'radicalism' in the 1820s, we now adopt the conclusions of many specialized enquiries. It is no longer possible to see the 1760s as the key decade in initiating a novel phase in reform, or to see John Wilkes as a catalyst of a new ideology; no longer do we seek an English radicalism before Wilkes. We no longer see something called 'American radicalism' being born in these years through the communication to the colonies of a Commonwealth tradition, nor do we see the American revolution acting as the 'ideological midwife' of English reform.[7] We do not even see the intellectual groundwork of 'radicalism' being laid in Dissenting Academies. We appreciate that Thomas Paine did not call for universal suffrage,[8] and we do not credit him with creating 'Paineite radicalism'. We no longer see late eighteenth-century English society as swept by a transformative 'Industrial Revolution' which explains either the 'making of the English working class' or 'the rise of the middle class'.[9] Neither industrialization, nor class formation, nor popular protest will do. None of these things now suffices as an explanation of that specific ideology newly termed 'radicalism'.

Disorder and disaffection, alienation and marginalization did not await the formulation of the ideology of radicalism in the 1810s and 20s. Englishmen through the sixteenth, seventeenth and eighteenth centuries sometimes expressed the most profound antagonism towards their rulers, local or national, in Church or in State, in agriculture or in manufacturing, for a wide variety of reasons. Yet, even after this diverse experience, 'radicalism' was something new. Its conceptualization was a distinct and special episode that must be correctly located in the early decades of the nineteenth century, part of that wider and momentous process in which a whole vocabulary of political terms was coined, terms that quickly became basic to a new conceptualization of politics and society.[10]

In that conceptualization, the new ideology of radicalism did not spring at once into being, fully formed. Many of the component parts of radicalism can be found at earlier dates, but what counted in the conceptualization of this as of other ideologies was the novel and unpredictable assembly of those components. It was a process in which old usages survived and were added to, and transformed by new usages. 'Radical' had long been a familiar term in etymology, referring to the 'roots' of words, and this usage continued.[11] 'Radical' was familiar also in medicine. John Mudge offered a remedy which 'will immediately and radically cure a complaint very troublesome and fatiguing'.[12] This usage too continued.[13] 'Radical' in political discourse might therefore merely mean 'fundamental', without any implication of social levelling or reconstruction.[14] Samuel Johnson's usage was not new or controversial when he wrote that the American colonies 'were kept flourishing and spreading by the radical vigour of the Mother-country';[15] nor was Lord Stormont's in 1792 in extolling 'the radical beauties of the Constitution'. Paine quoted Stormont's speech to deny its substance, but he used the adjective in the same way to denounce 'the radical and practical defects of the system'.[16] William Wilberforce similarly claimed that man was 'tainted with sin, not slightly and superficially, but radically and to the very core'.[17] Even the noun did not have to signify membership of a group: in 1845 one Tory critic of Sir Robert Peel granted him the title, and predicted (rightly, as it happened) that Peel would subvert 'Conservatism'.[18]

This imprecision began to change with the formulation of the new doctrine of universal manhood suffrage by heterodox theologians, and its adoption as a practical political goal by their co-religionists in the late 1770s and early 1780s. Increasingly, the term 'radical reform' came to be applied exclusively to parliamentary reform.[19] It was in this sense that the Rev. Christopher Wyvill (whose theological opinions were scarcely orthodox) called for 'a radical reformation' in 1781, and the openly Unitarian John Jebb demanded 'a substantial and radical reform in the representation' in 1784.[20] In this sense 'Radical Reform' became increasingly reified, and acquired capital letters. In 1801, Christopher Wyvill called for 'nothing less than the attainment of such a redress of grievances, such a correction of abuses as may secure the future enjoyment of Liberty ... it ought to be a Radical Reform, on the Principles of the Constitution'. But John Cartwright's adherence to universal manhood suffrage would prevent the success of a national reform movement, urged Wyvill, since it would alienate 'the Rich'. 'This, I sincerely think, will be the consequence of consulting Theory alone'. Wyvill recommended Fox's solution, 'viz. to extend the Right of Suffrage to Householders not receiving alms':[21] this, presumably, still counted to Wyvill as a radical reform.

Neither the American nor the French Revolution was inspired at its outset by the idea of universal suffrage: the old diversity of meanings of 'radical' could continue. When the idea of universal manhood suffrage rose again to prominence in the years after 1815, Sir Walter Scott could observe in 1819 that '*Radical* is a word in very bad odour here, being used to denote a set of blackguards a hundred times more mischievous and absurd than our old friends in 1794 and 1795'.[22] 'Radical' was now a shorthand for 'Radical Reformer', and the clearest and most extreme definition of that term was 'a believer in universal manhood suffrage'. Even so, the substantive 'radical' was not, and had never been, synonymous with a doctrine soon to be coined: radicalism.

Not all usage was equally exact, however. The old senses of 'radical' in medicine or etymology meant that many men could still try to appropriate the term. In 1835 even a heterodox churchman could do so: Jonas Dennis, congratulating himself on his 'voluntary sacrifice of professional emolument' in his 'consciousness of personal integrity, and persuasion of divine approbation' in his task of detecting 'radical errors, ecclesiastical and sectarian', that is, faults in the doctrine of the Church of England. Dennis wrote as an opponent of Catholic Emancipation and the repeal of the Test and Corporation Acts to protest that the Church of England was 'a solitary instance of a religious community deprived, through crooked state policy, of the exercise of its unalienable right to efficient synodical assemblies', as a result of which, 'heresy, scepticism and infidelity, are encouraged and diffused to a terrific extent'.[23] Another author in 1820, who believed that the 'mill-stone' of the national debt was 'the sole cause of the public distress', proposed a national lottery and encouragement for 'domestic fisheries' to reduce it:[24] this was his 'radical' solution, one which clearly had nothing to do with 'radicalism' in its extensive later meanings and expressed no sense of alienation from the social order.

In popular discourse, then, the key terms were often inexact, and open for appropriation. One journal, launched in 1833, announced that 'our principles are most decidedly liberal, radical and Christian . . . It shall be our endeavour to make the *Truth* as agreeable as possible to all classes and parties.'[25] Out of the diversity and imprecision of daily usage, a new doctrine, 'radicalism', nevertheless emerged, and came to be seen as a reified actor on the national stage in what was eventually characterized as the 'age of ideologies'.[26] Radicalism was not a timelessly applicable category, nor did it have such close functional equivalents in earlier centuries that the term can be used in disregard of its specific subject: it was a concept freshly minted in the early nineteenth century. If, as is argued here, that process of conceptual innovation can be dated and analysed, 'radicalism' can be recovered as a valid term of historical analysis.[27] Such a recovery will show us not only what the phenomenon was, but also why it is merely a solecism to invoke the term in any period before the phenomenon existed.[28]

ENEMIES: THE ANTI-JACOBIN CONTRIBUTION

Both the friends and the enemies of fundamental reform took part in shaping the emerging concept in the years after 1815. The enemies tended to look to the recent past, and to argue for a fundamental affinity between the radical reform of their own day and the revolutionary Jacobinism of the 1790s; they tended to counter the disturbances of the postwar period in the same way that they had resisted revolution in the 1790s, by arguing that radical reform was synonymous with religious infidelity, and that it could only be effectively countered at local level by a return to Christian piety.

This strategy was present as early as the 1790s. For the satirical poet George Huddesford (1749–1809), 'radical reform' was evidently a synonym for 'Jacobin reform'. He denounced both in classically learned doggerel verse:

> As, when "Revenge Timotheus cried,"
> And maudlin Greeks electrified,
> His strains inspir'd ferocious joy,
> And zeal to level and destroy:
> Such furious joy the Factious feel,
> Such transports of destructive zeal
> Inflame the disaffected swarm,
> At sound of Radical Reform.

Such men, claimed Huddesford, looked to the day

> When Jacobin Reform uncheck'd
> Shall take its radical Effect![29]

This anti-Jacobin idiom can be traced in recognizable form from the 1790s at least to the 1820s, and survived in the novels of John Galt (discussed below) to 1832. Within this idiom, a satire of 1820, combining visual images with political verses, emphasized the identity of the radical and the Jacobin: the slogans of 'Universal Suffrage' and 'Liberty or Death' on the banners of the mob were held to lead directly to mob violence, summary execution, the destruction of Magna Carta and the Bill of Rights, and an assault on the three-columned temple of King, Lords and Commons.[30]

One friend of the constitution tried to use the new term in its defence. 'The term Radicals is commonly applied to all who wish to destroy or infringe on the constitution', he argued; what the ministers were proposing to do to Grampound[31] earned them that title. Successive constitutional milestones had guaranteed that constitutional rights would not be taken from the people without their consent, but 'it remained for the present days of Radicalism to advance a contrary doctrine: a complete revolution in our constitution is now about to take place, not by consent of the people, but by the efforts of a Radical Ministry'. They could claim no mandate from the people for such a change, since the electorate numbered only 400,000 in a nation of 18,000,000, and since 300 of the 489 English MPs were nominated by 'proprietors or patrons of Boroughs'. The constitution needed 'that reform . . . which alone can save the country from Radicalism', namely the end of the 'borough system'.[32]

Another observer relied on the theory that 'nations, like animals and vegetables', passed through the stages of origination, maturity, reproduction and annihilation in calling for 'extraordinary, judicious, and decisive measures' to rejuvenate a Britain which had quite possibly 'passed her meridian'. He was no friend to what was generally called '*a radical Reform*', however, which he saw as synonymous with 'anarchy, or a general pillage'. His argument was that 'too little attention has hitherto been paid to the encouragement of virtue', and his amateur schemes, devoted to that end, culminated in a defence of the constitution against 'the Catholic claims'. Not that he was against parliamentary reform: only, the franchise in the hands of so many of 'the lower orders', as it currently was, encouraged dissolute lives. The solution was the representation of 'interests, rather than individuals'.[33]

Satirical narratives in the anti-Jacobin tradition could dwell on the ignorance of ordinary people about the precise beliefs and proposals of the radical reformers, as in a cottage conversation between Jenny and Hannah:

> [Jenny]: 'there's to be great doings in London, to-day. Hunt and all the patriotics are to meet in Spa Fields, and get things to rights abit; so my husband and a few friends are spending the day at the Anchor, to drink success to the good cause.' [Hannah]: 'What cause, Jenny? What are they to meet for? And what are they going to set to rights?'

[Jenny]: 'Why, I can't tell you all the particulars, Hannah; but they are going to order it so, that every body shall have plenty of work and plenty of bread'.[34]

The unspecific promise of radical reform had its practical advantages. In 1819, 'Britannicus' was aware that

there have risen up men, from amongst the lowest of the people, who rend the air with clamours in favour of a remedy which they represent to be abundantly competent for the removal of all our evils. This much boasted specific is *Radical Reform* – a thorough change in our whole political system – a complete renovation of our civil and ecclesiastical establishments.

His practical instance of this was France during the Revolution.[35] Real reformation, insisted Britannicus, could only come from a return to religion: this constituted the only effective 'Radical Reform'. His opponents, by contrast, had a secular analysis:

The Reformers assert that our distresses are the result of immoderate taxation – taxation occasioned by extravagant expenditure – extravagant expenditure upheld by political corruption. Their summary method of cure, therefore, is to strike, as they conceive, at the root of corruption, by establishing *Annual Parliaments and Universal Suffrage.*

The result of this could only be 'universal anarchy' and general impoverishment. Scripture taught that 'war, and famine, and pestilence ... are dispensations of Providence by which rebellious nations are chastised': the only remedy was 'true religion'.[36]

Those who wished to urge Biblical morality (prudence, thrift, delayed marriage) on needy labourers as a means of raising the 'subsistence wage' could see themselves as recommending a 'radical reform' in the old sense: a reform of human nature.[37] It is easy to read such moral tracts as simplistic and condescending if their sophisticated economic underpinning (Malthus, Chalmers) is overlooked. Whatever their economic analysis, such men were generally led to a particular view of the recent political origins of the problem. According to John Harford, a leading Evangelical, in 1819, Richard Carlile's republication of *The Age of Reason* during his trial, and newspaper reports of the proceedings, 'have given, of late, an unusual currency to the name and to the opinions of Paine. The Radical Reformers are also grown bold enough to acknowledge him as their Apostle and their Idol'. Outlining Paine's career up to the publication of *Rights of Man*, Harford concluded: 'It is impossible to overlook the striking resemblance which exists between the Revolutionists of 1793, and the Radicals of 1819. – They all belong to the same family, and are wedded to the same principles'.[38]

Now as then, there was a plan for elections to a Convention which would bypass Parliament. 'The whole system of 1793, and that of 1819, are equally founded on Thomas Paine's doctrines of the Rights of Man':

> not only in their general system of proceeding, but in almost every minute particular, the Radicals of 1819 are copyists of the Revolutionaries of 1793. The same inflammatory language belongs to both. With both, kings are tyrants, religion a fable, its zealous friends hypocrites and knaves, the rich, plunderers of the poor, all employers oppressors, rebellion another name for patriotism, and the assassination of those whom they deem the enemies of their cause, the acme of public virtue ... As to the scheme of universal Suffrage and annual Parliaments, a notion borrowed from Paine, which is the watchword of this party, it is so triumphantly absurd as hardly to justify a serious refutation.[39]

Paine was the clue to the true nature of the Radicals, argued Harford: 'For some time we heard only of "universal suffrage" and "annual parliaments," and were left to guess the ultimate objects of the party; but the whole truth is now displayed in a broad day light, and the evidences of a deliberate conspiracy to overturn the government are no longer wanting'.[40]

Perhaps significantly, Harford did not use the term 'radicalism': his interpretation of 'Radical Reform' was backward-looking, and he did his best to identify it with Jacobin revolution. For Harford not radicalism but 'Modern Infidelity, with Faction and Revolution in his train, is the grand enemy whom we have to oppose'.[41] He did not appreciate those newly-emergent features which were to provoke the conceptualization of a new ideology. His preoccupations were those of the activist Evangelicals with whom he associated.[42] He was preoccupied not with *Rights of Man* but with *The Age of Reason*. The 'one great and impassible barrier' to the success of Paine's schemes, insisted Harford, was 'the influence of Christianity'. It was a 'pillar of national principle and happiness', since the Bible 'teaches its disciples on the same principle that they serve God to honor the King'. What the nation needed was a religious revival, 'a RADICAL REFORM, such as the world has never yet seen'.[43]

Harford was undiscriminating in his denunciations. Many of the points to which he objected were no part of Paine's teaching. The undoubted attachment of Paine to natural rights had not logically entailed universal suffrage[44] or a hostility to employers as such. Harford's tract was mostly concerned with retailing scandalous biographical information about Paine and stories of the horrors of the French Revolution; he said little about the exact points of connection between Paine and the radical reformers, which was his central claim. Harford's object was to disparage the radicals of 1819 by asserting an obvious identity between them and the irreligion and threats of revolution of the 1790s. The differences were important, however. Although Carlile did indeed republish Paine's Deist tract *The Age of Reason*, and although it obtained a wide currency, it is suggested here that radicalism was novel and important in adding an economic analysis of debt, taxes and distribution to the natural-rights and Deistic agendas of the 1790s, an economic analysis which then came to dominate and obscure the others in a context not of deism but of atheism.

The emergence of that economic agenda will be examined below. The anti-Jacobins were rightly sensitive, however, to one central aspect of radicalism's economic component. The Christian message was embodied in the Church, but this institution had an earthly dimension and presented a material target. 'We have long had our *radical reformers*', wrote one pamphleteer, 'foretelling instant and inevitable ruin to the State ... This is not reformation – it is revolution'. He specified its targets: 'Retrenchment is the plea; confiscation is the object – confiscation of all appropriated revenue – subversion of all established institutions. And church revenue, and the church establishment, are the first, marked, objects of aggression'. He suggested a series of agrarian reforms to mitigate the burden of tithes.[45]

What came to preoccupy radical reformers, it seems, was not just taxes in general, but tithes in particular;[46] not merely property in the abstract but Church property and landed estates, the nexus of squire and parson. This was not dictated by existing alignments, since anti-Jacobins did not ordinarily define themselves for agriculture and against industry: before Ricardo, they were more able (despite Godwin's attack on 'landed inequality') to see land and manufactures as complementary rather than antithetical. In one pamphlet, 'a manufacturer' was presented as advising his radical reformer son that his son's favourite writings 'contain nothing new. The same fallacies have been often used and detected.' But 'You think, no doubt, that the wise and sagacious authors of them have just now discovered, that the Bible is false, and the Government is wicked; and that the one ought to be burnt, and the other overturned without delay'. The author bracketed 'Infidels, and pretended Reformers' together and refused to see anything new in the world after 1815. The Christian message, he argued, contradicted the claim of the perfectibility of government and the equality of property which were basic to 'Radical Reform'.[47] This perspective was not wrong, but it was too limited. It omitted the way in which pre-existing elements were being brought together in a crucial process. New ideas, and new terms to describe them, arrived together.

THE LIFE-EXPERIENCE OF THE RADICAL: 'NATHAN BUTT' AND SAMUEL BAMFORD

Not all who were sceptical towards radical reform entertained as static a view of its nature as did the anti-Jacobins. One shrewd observer in particular implied a theory of its development over time which deserves to be tested against the evidence. John Galt[48] was better known for his minor classic, *Annals of the Parish* (1821), a penetrating exposure of Scots foibles through the genre of the fictional autobiography, but this remarkably prolific author had an insight into politics also. In the early 1830s, he returned to the *genre* in which he had recorded his biggest success. *The Member* (1832) concerned the adventures of a Scots nabob, MP for the aptly-named borough of Frailtown. *The Radical* (1832) was a similar satire on the life of the fictitious 'Nathan Butt', depicted as dedicating his autobiography to Lord Brougham as a man who had released 'property from that obsolete stability into which it has long been the object of society to constrain its natural freedom'.

Butt recounted with pride his struggles, from his infant years, against 'misrule, the lot of all, under the old system': he began with a story of how, as a baby, he had bitten his grandmother, who had tried to intervene to stop him from strangling a kitten: it was emblematic of 'the divine right of resistance'. Punishment for stealing apples while a schoolboy confirmed 'my abhorrence of coercive expedients in the management of mankind'.[49] Butt rationalized his conduct: 'It was not the sordid feelings of the covetous thief that drew me into that enterprise; but an innate perception of natural right'. Chastisement by his father, after being expelled from school for leading a rebellion, 'gave me both black and blue reasons to resent the ruthlessness of that false position in which children and parents stand, with respect to each other'. In the family as elsewhere, maintained Nathan Butt, 'the impulses of nature are justly acknowledged as superior to all artificial maxims and regulations'. Such a young man was a natural admirer of the French Revolution: 'It was delightful to contemplate the triumphs of liberty among them, and how they hallowed their cause with blood'.[50]

The ascendancy of Napoleon, who betrayed this revolutionary promise, made Butt and his fellow-radicals 'shrink back into ourselves, and seek to obscure our particular opinions by a practical adherence to the existing customs of the world – errors and prejudices which we never forgot they were'. His marriage was tolerable, though marred by a family quarrel over the baptism of his child when he made public his belief that there was nothing in religion 'beyond the ingenuity of those who in different ages had invented its several rites, as a mode of levying taxes for the maintenance of their order'. Napoleon's restoration reawakened his public hopes; but 'the battle of Waterloo blighted my expectations; and with a sick and humbled heart, I acknowledged that the cause of philanthropy was, in consequence, suspended'.[51]

Nevertheless, after 1815, 'the rumours which then began to rise of discontents in the manufacturing districts, assured me that the great cause still lived, and that the candle, though low in the socket, was not extinct'. When the violence of these mass meetings failed, the radicals turned to argument. 'Nothing could be more galling to the latent indignation of the country, than that so many should enjoy the fruit of the taxes – should revel in elegance, or wallow in opulence, on the hard-won earnings of the industrious poor; and we took up this obvious truth as our theme'. Fortunately, Butt could exploit what he sensed was an important social change going on around him: 'an ebb or subsidence of anxiety for the interests of posterity, – an ancestral error in the feeling of patriotism or public spirit, which occupied a high station in the minds of our predecessors'. This now came to include the question of property. Butt was not completely unhappy at the prospect of postwar distress: 'Radicalism thrives by it and the general world is turned more towards the question of permitting property to continue in such large masses'.[52]

Butt now began to advocate 'the breaking into pieces of the great masses of property' as a way of alleviating beggary. Rents, not taxes, were the root cause of distress, and the solution called in question 'the existence of that class or order called "landlords"'. It was at this point in the novel that Galt placed Butt's refusing to hear the deathbed request of his uncle and business partner from the Presbyterian clergyman who had attended the deceased: 'Were all men to treat the members of the privileged orders [of priesthood] as I have done, the nuisance of being troubled with them would soon be abated'.[53]

Butt's political goals were still outlined by Galt in highly generalized terms, 'nothing less than the emancipation of the human race from the trammels and bondage of the social law; although, certainly, I did abet rational undertakings to procure parliamentary reform, as among the means by which my own great and high purpose might be attained'. Parliamentary reform was evidently a means to an end, and not the only means at that.[54]

The truth is, that the [parliamentary] Reformers and the Radicals are two very different parties. It is not impossible – and I say so, having studied their predilections – that the former may hereafter amalgamate themselves with the Whigs and Tories, which the latter never can. Radicalism is an organic passion, and cannot be changed in its tendencies; it goes to the root of the evil that is in the world, and discerns that, without an abolition of the laws and institutes which it has been so long the erroneous object of society to uphold, the resuscitation of first principles can never be effected; and nothing less than that resuscitation will be satisfactory.

Reformers sought 'a moderate measure of amendment in things that have fallen into abuse'; Radicals sought 'a new system – a revolution'. Butt now realized the quite different nature of the two groups. The same conclusion was impressed on him when he was elected to Parliament in time to support the 1832 Reform Bill: he as a radical urging it forward merely as the prelude to future reforms which would finance poor relief out of 'the parks, palaces and grandeur of the aristocracy', a reformer arguing against Butt that 'we should be thankful and content' with whatever could be obtained.[55]

Galt was a brilliant satirist: his novel is evidence for the perception of the phenomenon by a friend of the old order from the perspective of 1832 more than for the historical trajectory of the phenomenon itself. Nevertheless, his satire suggests some important hypotheses. Radicalism, in this account, was not a clearly conceptualized ideology from the 1790s or earlier. It had its antecedents, instead, in ideologically unspecific Jacobin aspirations of limitless progress and human perfectibility. Nevertheless, this disposition began to acquire clearer shape in the world from 1815, as Galt began to sense the radical reformers' impatience with both 'Whigs' and 'Tories',[56] and as the theme of the levelling of property, and the breakup of great landed estates, became more prominent in the radicals' agenda.[57] The theological element was nevertheless present throughout: as Butt's friend Mr Cobble, the Reformer, tells him: 'you behold evil in all things'.[58] What Galt did not record, or seek to satirize, was Butt's encounter with a new and clearly-defined ideology: 'radicalism' did not present itself to Butt as a school, with a philosopher as its patron saint; but it acquired its parliamentary impact as 'knife and fork questions' rose to practical prominence. Life also could imitate art. When John Stuart Mill founded a group to propagate his philosophy, he called it the Utilitarian Society, borrowing the term from John Galt's *Annals of the Parish*, 'in which the Scotch clergyman, of whom the book is a supposed autobiography, is represented as warning his parishoners not to leave the Gospel and become utilitarians'.[59]

From fiction, we return to authentic testimony. It suggests that Galt was not wrong in discerning an element of individual emancipation in 'radical reform'. One tradesman recommended that position to his fellows through an autobiography whose leading theme was 'the spirit of independence against wrongs . . . the spirit of independence against sufferings of a poor deserted child, a defenceless orphan'.[60] The same life-experience informed the memoirs of Samuel Bamford,[61] a work designed to record 'some of the most remarkable and interesting events which took place in the manufacturing districts of Lancashire, and other parts of England, during the years 1816 to 1821'.[62]

An underlying theme of his book was how much the radical agenda had changed in his lifetime. Looking back, Bamford recorded the resolutions of the twenty-one Hampden Clubs of the area around Manchester, held in the neighbouring small town of Middleton on 1 January 1817:

> resolutions were passed declaratory of the right of every male to vote, who paid taxes; that males of eighteen should be eligible to vote; that parliaments should be elected annually; that no placeman or pensioner should sit in parliament; that every twenty thousand of inhabitants should send a member to the house of commons; and that talent, and virtue, were the only qualifications necessary. Such were the moderate views and wishes of the reformers in those days, as compared with the present: the [secret] ballot was not insisted on as a part of reform. Concentrating our whole energy for the obtainment of annual parliaments and universal suffrage, we neither interfered with the house of lords; nor the bench of bishops; nor the working of factories; nor the corn laws; nor the payment of members; nor tithes; nor church rates; nor a score of other matters, which in these days have been pressed forward with the effect of distracting the attention, and weakening the exertions of reformers

– who would all, he argued, stand much more chance of success in a House of Commons elected on universal suffrage.[63] Yet since Bamford's memoirs covered only the years 1816 to 1821, they offered no systematic account of the broadening of the reformers' agenda that this retrospect identified. It is open to argument that that extension into the field of the redistribution of property came when the agenda of universal suffrage, familiar since the 1780s, was linked in an explosive way with that most sensitive issue of Church reform. No single individual did more to make that connection than Bentham.

FROM 'RADICAL REFORM' TO 'RADICALISM': JEREMY BENTHAM AND THE REV. JAMES MILL

It was Bentham above all who provided a term, 'radicalism', in a setting in which men were open to a definition. The French visitor Louis Simond had been surprised in 1810 to find

> the great number of people in the opposition; that is, those who disapprove, not only the present measures of ministers, which have not been of late either very wise or very successful, but the form and constitution of the government itself. It is stigmatized as vicious, corrupt, and in its decay, without hope or remedy but in a general reform, and in fact a revolution.

He divided people into three categories in this respect: 'whigs, tories and absolute reformers'. Their categorization would be easy, 'for there are a few principal topics, which, like cabalistic words, it is enough to touch upon, to know at once the whole train of opinions of those with whom you speak'.[64] Simond's 'absolute reformers' were, within a decade, to see themselves as 'radicals' expressing a position which was recognizable when identified as 'radicalism'. In that process, Bentham's 'deep-rooted hatred, not only of revealed, but also of natural religion'[65] was fundamental.

Yet because Bentham founded so powerful a school, the nature of his achievement was identified, over succeeding decades, largely in the secular and utilitarian terms which the school itself dictated. It is this later assumption which must be dispensed with if a properly historical account of the origin and conceptualization of radicalism is to be established. The first category to be rejected is, of course, 'philosophic radical' itself. Elie Halévy began the first chapter of his classic study with the birth of Jeremy Bentham in 1748; only in an aside did Halévy disclose that the term 'Philosophical Radicals' did not begin to be used of a group until some fifteen years after Bentham's conversion to universal suffrage, and authorship of *Radicalism not Dangerous*, in 1820.[66] As William Thomas has now shown, the term 'philosophic radical' was coined by John Stuart Mill in 1837 in reaction against what he then perceived as the narrowness of the ideas of Bentham and James Mill.[67] Far from explaining the phenomenon, the term itself becomes a subject for historical explanation. Consequently, the idea that one might write 'a continuous or comprehensive history of a body of ideas called philosophic radicalism, utilitarianism or Benthamism' must be rejected: the scholarly conclusion is, rather, 'the variety both of theoretical outlook and of political response within the group'.[68]

Bentham's own early intellectual formation therefore assumes much greater importance, for the later term 'radical' does not explain it. This formation was obscured in the nineteenth and twentieth centuries, not least by the pious Unitarian John Bowring's omission of Bentham's virulent writings against religion from the 1838–43 collected edition of Bentham's *Works*.[69] Nevertheless, Bentham's crusade against the Church, its liturgy and its teachings in the years 1809–23 can be traced back to his own loss of faith in an Oxford where subscription to the Thirty-nine Articles was a central public affirmation of identity and soon became the centre of controversy.[70]

Bentham dated his revulsion from the Church, and the loss of faith in its teachings, to the expulsion of six Methodist undergraduates in 1761.[71] Later, in London in c. 1773, Bentham drafted (but left unpublished) contributions to the controversy of 1768–74 over the subscription required of Oxford and Cambridge undergraduates. In 1774 appeared a translation of Voltaire's *Le Taureau Blanc*, with a lengthy Preface by Bentham himself (again anonymously) which expressed not merely scepticism at formal Biblical exegesis but a blasphemous hostility towards the claims of Christianity as such to historical veracity.[72] Already, then, in this work and in the manuscripts on subscription, conventional religion had been cast as the enemy of mankind in a way which fully anticipated Bentham's published writings of 1817–23.

The subscription controversy arose at the time when Bentham was drafting his attack on the man who had emerged as the leading Anglican defender of the nexus of Church and State, Sir William Blackstone. In his anonymously-published tract of 1776 attacking Blackstone's *Commentaries*, Bentham singled out as the very first passage to which he objected Blackstone's paragraphs on the Dissenters, a passage inspired, according to Bentham, by 'the first transport of a holy zeal'; the youthful critic cited in his support the tracts by the Dissenters Priestley and Furneaux which seized on Blackstone's harsh account of the laws against nonconformity.[73] In 1790, Bentham wrote to congratulate the Unitarian Duke of Grafton for his anonymous pamphlet attacking the establishment, Bentham condemning 'the tyranny exercised by the church over the consciences of men' and 'its pernicious influence on the public morals'.[74]

These expressions of belief were, however, private. Bentham was remarkably reticent in public, and in published work, about his religious opinions. As late as 1831 he acknowledged that he had concealed his irreligious opinions from a Calvinist reformer, pretending to be committed merely to 'universal toleration'.[75] In one case, the *Traités de législation civile et pénale* (Paris, 1802), Bentham's editor Etienne Dumont excised his patron's 'plea for atheism' and softened many other irreligious passages.[76] There seems little doubt that Bentham knew that the massive commitment of English society to Christianity, whether within or outside the Church, would mean a damaging reaction against him if his views became known. It might even mean prosecution.

The fragmented nature of Bentham's published work during his lifetime has generally been ascribed to his self-absorbed pattern of working, for he often abandoned a good project before its completion for a better. Much of the delay in publishing his writings on Christianity is, however, explained by the legal penalties still enforced against views as extreme as Bentham's, and by the government's anxious response.[77] In 1809, the failure of the Walcheren expedition and a wave of satire against the army and its commander, the Duke of York, was met with a series of prosecutions for seditious libel. Bentham's attention was drawn to the system of picking more reliable men to serve on the 'special juries' used in these cases; he denounced the system in *The Elements of the Art of Packing*, a work revised for him by James Mill.[78] While the book was being printed, the publisher became alarmed, and halted work. Bentham consulted the reformer and MP Sir Samuel Romilly, who advised that the Attorney General, Sir Vicary Gibbs, would certainly prosecute. So the printing was finished in 1810, but the book was not openly sold until 1821 (although it had some private circulation). Similarly Bentham's *Plan of Parliamentary Reform*, drafted in 1809, was not published until 1817; *Swear not at All*, an attack on the use and nature of oaths, was printed in 1813 but not published until 1817.[79]

The most legally sensitive of issues was still religion, and it was here that Bentham's writings came to centre after he became interested in the subject of judicial procedure in 1802. In 1809, he began drafting a work entitled 'Church', part of his critique of English institutions: this grew in size and proliferated, resulting in works published between 1817 and 1823[80] which have been characterized as a campaign to extirpate religious beliefs and practice as a necessary precondition of the establishment of a utilitarian society. For powerful philosophical reasons, Bentham was an atheist, and, for him, law and religion were inextricably linked.[81] A society in which Christian belief was widespread would presumably resemble the society in which Bentham actually found himself: to arrive at his ideal form of society through the action of innumerable individual pursuits of utility, it was necessary that those individuals understand pleasure in atheistic terms.

Atheism could be made explicit in Bentham's writings, although these had normally to be published under pseudonyms. It was, however, implicit in all of his writings, especially those which dealt with a legal system which still claimed that Christianity was a part of it.[82] After John Stuart Mill finally edited and published Bentham's *The Rationale of Judicial Evidence* in five volumes in 1827, John Henry Newman commented: 'Mr. Bentham made a treatise on Judicial Proofs a covert attack upon the miracles of Revelation'.[83] For Bentham, therefore, a commitment to reform in law and administration had co-existed throughout his life with hostility to orthodox Christianity and to the Church. It was this integral role of Bentham's theological views that the positivist and anticlerical Halévy obscured.[84] In the late 1810s, however, Bentham took three steps of basic importance. He began to publish his irreligious works; he became converted to universal suffrage; and he coined the term 'radicalism' to describe his position, the ideology which identified the precise agenda or targets for utilitarian reform. Universal suffrage as a political goal was not new: it had originated in the 1760s and 1770s, but among a small group of heterodox dissenting intelligentsia.[85] Bentham relocated its premises within atheism, and this was to give it a far larger social constituency in the urban-industrial society which now began to develop.

These doctrinal changes were reflected in the evolving language of politics. Halévy thought the expression 'radical reform' had 'first been in fashion for a time round about 1797 and 1798, when Fox and Horne Tooke, derided by the *Anti-Jacobin*, had come to an agreement in order to demand a "radical reform" ... Then the expression seems completely to have disappeared and does not occur again before about 1810 ... The adjective *radical* and the substantive *reformer* are used henceforward with increasing frequency ... But it appears that it was not until 1819 that the adjective Radical was used, by an abbreviation, as a substantive'. Halévy related this to the publication in 1817 of Bentham's *Plan of Parliamentary Reform, in the Form of a Catechism*, an event which led to his co-operation with Sir Francis Burdett, and Bentham's adoption of the goal of universal suffrage.[86]

It was in the same year that he met James Mill that Bentham had drafted what was later published as *Plan of Parliamentary Reform*; perhaps he was influenced by his Scots disciple.[87] Bentham was undoubtedly frustrated at official resistance to reform and alienated from the government in 1809–10, but he was not thereby converted to 'radicalism':[88] there was no such pre-existent position to which to convert except universal suffrage. Yet Bentham was not yet an exponent of that doctrine: it seems that his conversion to the opposition in 1809–10 arose from his adoption of the belief that 'abuses in the law and abuses in parliament were symbiotic'.[89]

Bentham's draft *Plan of Parliamentary Reform*, which Cobbett refused to print in his *Register* in 1810, did not then include universal suffrage among its goals:[90] the secret ballot, not a universal franchise, was as yet Bentham's key device. Although he favoured a 'uniformly large' electorate in each constituency, that electorate was to be controlled by a property qualification, and this was only one of many political reforms primarily designed to check a malevolent monarchy.[91] From a wide franchise, envisaged by Bentham in c. 1790, it was a quantum leap to 'virtual universality of suffrage' in 1817. Bentham's development in politics and religion owed much to co-operation and discussion with a needy but forceful disciple whom he met in 1808, James Mill. The evidence does not establish that either converted the other;[92] nevertheless, they had important commitments in common, and probably encouraged each other in similar directions in the next decade.[93]

The young James Mill (1773–1836), son of a shoemaker, had gained his start in life through the patronage of Sir James Stuart, who intended to help his protégé become a Presbyterian minister. Mill indeed read theology at the end of his course at Edinburgh University (1794–7) and was licensed to preach in 1798, but failed to obtain a parish; in about 1807–11 he lost both his vocation and his faith, and soon became as ardent an atheist and anticlerical.[94] His thought, however, never lost its 'strongly moralistic element': 'He may have come to reject belief in God, but some form of evangelical zeal remained essential to him'.[95] His censorious disapproval of the clerical and patrician elites of the England in which he struggled to make a living as a journalist, often disguised for tactical reasons, only became more embittered with time.[96] Although Mill's *Essay on Government* (1820) was reticent about precisely what he sought in the realm of parliamentary reform, his views on that topic in 1817–18 have been rightly described as 'very radical, not to say apocalyptic'; they included universal suffrage.[97] This, and Mill's covert atheism, has led one scholar of Mill's unpublished papers to stress 'the well concealed contents of his private thoughts'.[98]

Bentham's public interventions in 1817–23 were part of a wider pattern. In the late 1810s, the disaffected intelligentsia often returned to the question of the existing state of parliamentary representation as the major barrier standing between them and the implementation of their schemes. It was in these years that the idea of 'radical reform' became sharpened and acquired an identity as 'radicalism', an ideology combining a central commitment against revealed religion and the Church of England with critiques of the Church's main props: the unreformed Parliament, the monarch and the landlord.[99] This reignition of the reform agenda coincided with a renewed wave of prosecutions for blasphemous or seditious libel, beginning in 1817,[100] and a renewed government campaign against subversive political association that culminated in the 'Six Acts' of 1819.

In 1817, Jeremy Bentham cast his tract advocating parliamentary reform 'in the Form of a Catechism'. Its Apocalyptic quality was precisely the reason why he rejected 'moderate reform' in favour of 'radical ... reform': 'reform or convulsion,' he insisted: 'such is the alternative'.[101] England was compared with the predicament of France under the restored monarchy: there, 'the wardrobe of the Holy Virgin will be supplied with a new gown, and every prison in the country with a new set of torture-boots and thumb-screws'. Bentham defined himself against a social system of nobility, of corruption and sinecures, of endless and unnecessary war, the whole personified in the person of a monarch, whose nature was 'to draw to himself in the greatest quantity possible'. This constituted a system:

> And here we have one *partial*, one *separate*, one *sinister* interest, the *monarchical* – the interest of the ruling *one* – with which the *universal*, the *democratical* interest has to antagonize, and to which that all-comprehensive interest has all along been, – and, unless the only possible remedy – even parliamentary reform, and that a radical one, should be applied, – is destined to be for ever made a sacrifice: – a sacrifice? – yes: and, by the blessing of God, upon the legitimate and pious labours of his Vicegerent [the king], and the express image of his person here upon earth, a still unresisting sacrifice. Omni-presence, immortality, impeccability – equal as he is to God, as touching all these "attributes" (ask Blackstone else, i. 270, 250, 246, 249), – who is there that, without adding impiety to disloyalty, can repine at seeing any thing or every thing he might otherwise call his own, included in the sacrifice?[102]

In this predicament, the 'ultimate end' was not merely improvement, but 'political salvation', namely 'democratical ascendancy' via 'virtually universal suffrage'. Bentham's definition of this omitted only idiots, infants and those incapable of 'exercising it to the advantage either of others or of themselves'; it included women.[103] In another pamphlet, Bentham attempted to explain his proposal:

Universal Suffrage, Annual Parliaments, and *Election by Ballot.* – At Public Meetings, these are the words commonly (it is believed) employed, for expressing the essential features of Radical Reform.
Another expression, however, there is, which in some respects seems to afford a promise of being more apposite. This is – *Secret, universal, equal, and annual suffrage*; or say, *Secrecy, universality, equality, and annuality of suffrage. Suffrage* is the common subject, to which all these qualities are referable: it presents a bond of union, by which all these elements may, in our conception, be knit together into one whole.

Bentham rebutted an accusation: 'Under Radicalism, all property, it is said, would be destroyed'; clearly this was not the case in Pennsylvania. There, 'for these forty years, radicalism has been supreme: radicalism without Monarchy or Aristocracy: radicalism without control, and not any the slightest shock has property there ever received'.[104]

Bentham's *Plan of Parliamentary Reform* (1817) was swiftly followed by a related and much larger work, extending to 759 pages, a pertinacious assault on the legal framework and the doctrine of the established Church.[105] Bentham prefaced it with an explanation: the former work had given 'a sort of sketch . . . of one of the two *natures*, of which our constitution, such as it is, is composed, viz. the *temporal* one. In the present work may be seen a portrait of the other nature, viz. the *spiritual* one'. The sketch in 1817 had been 'a miniature'; the attack on the Church was 'more particularly delineated' in his new volume.[106] Bentham candidly recounted his own intellectual formation as a churchman; the clergymen among his ancestors; the daily devotions 'in every part accordant to the rites of the established Church'; his father's membership of a club in which he was the only one not to be a clergyman of the Established Church; his own disillusion with Oxford at the expulsion of Methodist undergraduates. Bentham likened the proceedings against them to the Inquisition. At that moment, 'that affection which at its entrance [to Oxford] had glowed with so sincere a fervor, – my reverence for the Church of England – her doctrine, her discipline, her Universities, her ordinances, – was expelled from my youthful breast'. In 1818, Bentham devoted himself to proving that the Church's Catechism was 'a bad substitute' for the Bible, and a system of education based on that Catechism, that of the National Society, was an '*Exclusionary System*', dedicated to promoting '*Prostration of understanding and will*', in other words, 'slavery'.[107] Persuaded by his review, Bentham announced the 'utter rottenness' of the Anglican 'system of Church Government' and its 'complete ripeness for dissolution'.[108] It was an inflammatory work, and internal evidence suggests that James Mill may have had a hand in its composition.[109]

Why did Bentham now openly commit himself to universal suffrage, and publish *Church-of-Englandism* over his own name? The agitation for reform in the nation was growing; mass unrest might seem to point to an impending crisis, in which Bentham might at last intervene to effect. The Home Secretary, Lord Sidmouth, moved to press magistrates to bring prosecutions for blasphemous and seditious libel. It was in this gathering crisis that Bentham's *Plan of Parliamentary Reform* (1817) and *Swear not at All* (1817)[110] appeared. We know that *Church-of-Englandism* had been held back. Bentham had shown the draft of *Church-of-Englandism* to Romilly, seeking reassurance. Romilly was appalled: many passages seemed blasphemous and open to prosecution; he advised restraint. Yet, in three highly-publicised trials (17–19 December 1817), the bookseller and freethinker William Hone was acquitted on three counts of blasphemous libel.[111] At last, it seemed, the tide of public opinion on religious freedom had turned. Bentham could come into the open, and in 1818 *Church-of-Englandism* was released for sale. Yet if Bentham thought the danger over, he acted too soon. Prosecutions of Richard Carlile for blasphemous libel began in January 1819, and he was convicted in October.[112] Bentham and his circle had a crusade against orthodox religion still to fight.

Not only James Mill, but others of Bentham's inner circle shared this interest, though with a quickly-reasserted caution. George Grote[113] heavily edited, or reworked, a set of Bentham's manuscripts to produce a volume entitled *Analysis of the Influence of Natural Religion on the Temporal Happiness of Mankind*, published in 1822 and ascribed to 'Philip Beauchamp'.[114] Its publisher was listed as Richard Carlile, who, already in prison for a similar offence, may have been seen as immune from further prosecution. The book professed not to deal with the truth or falsehood of natural religion, but claimed to show that it was 'the foe and not the benefactor of mankind', so calling in question whether 'any alleged revelation' was sufficient to 'neutralise the bitterness' of natural religion's 'fruits'. Natural religion alone 'invariably leads its votaries to ascribe to their Deity a character of caprice and tyranny'; it 'must produce the effect of encouraging actions useless and pernicious to mankind, but agreeable to the invisible Dispenser'. Since epistemological scepticism was normally directed against revelation, and often assumed an inherent benevolence in natural religion, this was a shrewd strategy. The tract culminated in a denunciation of the clergy, who, it demonstrated, 'cannot fail to be animated by an interest incurably opposed to all human happiness'; moreover, 'between the particular interest of a governing aristocracy and a sacerdotal class, there seems a very peculiar affinity and coincidence – each wielding the precise engine which the other wants'.[115] It has been rightly observed that Bentham's critique, despite its disavowals, here extended beyond natural to include revealed religion also. Bentham's unpublished manuscripts went much further, to the complete extirpation of all religion. In this he came close to abandoning the central axiom of utilitarianism that each man is the best judge of his own interests.[116] But it was essential that he do so if utility was not to mean what it meant in the works of Archdeacon William Paley: that man naturally pursued an idea of the good implanted in him by God. In such a universe, as Sir William Blackstone had explained, the institutions of government and society could claim an authority quite independently of the personal preferences of individuals.

Meanwhile, Francis Place, a supporter of universal suffrage, annual parliaments, the secret ballot and republicanism, was organizing another set of manuscripts on which Bentham had been working since c. 1815 into a work published in 1823 as *Not Paul, but Jesus*, claiming as author the equally fictitious 'Gamaliel Smith'.[117] Here, in print, Bentham now turned to revealed religion. The book argued that 'all the mischiefs, which have been imputed to the religion of Jesus' were the result of Paul's teaching doctrines opposite to those of his master, and doing so from 'inducements of a purely temporal nature'. Chapter XVI summarized Bentham's conclusions: '*Paul's Doctrines Anti-apostolic. – Was he not Anti-Christ?*' He answered clearly: 'here is an Antichrist, and he an undeniable one'.[118] Despite Place's editorial role, only the first third of the work was printed (it still ran to 403 pages). Bentham's request that the rest be published after his death was ignored, and Bowring suppressed it.[119]

In 1819–20, Bentham wrote (but left unpublished) a defence of his pamphlet *Bentham's Radical Reform Bill*. It was, as he made prominently clear, an attempt to rescue radicalism from the destructive criticism of Tories and Whigs alike, and from the charge that 'radical reform' would mean 'a general destruction of property'. This was logically impossible, showed Bentham (to his own satisfaction). The fear rested only on the assumption of the 'consummate excellence' of the government, the 'consummate depravity' of subjects – 'the supremely ruling *one* [the king], sharing with the Almighty in his attributes, as Blackstone, who enumerates them expressly, assures us he does; those in authority under him a little lower than the angels; the subject-many devoid of reason, and in shape alone differing from beasts . . .'[120]

Bentham carefully rehearsed the examples of America since the Revolution, and the Volunteer Movement in Ireland during the American revolutionary war, to prove his claim: 'Radicalism not Dangerous . . . democratic ascendancy has nothing dangerous in it'. Remove the church, the king, the aristocracy – the evil forces in society – and all the rest, including its institutions, the pre-eminence of the social elite, and private property itself, could remain unchanged. Bentham in his formal pronouncements sought in this way to limit both his analysis of the problem, and his solutions. In recent years,

> In our Islands, the distress has had two causes: the deficiency of [economic] demand as in the United States for produce, and that excess of taxation which has been produced by vicious constitution and misrule. The misrulers place it of course, the whole of it, to the commercial account; no part to the financial and constitutional: but the people, who not only feel but see what the taxes are, as well as in what state the constitution is, are not to be thus blinded.

The solution therefore was that offered by 'the features or elements of radicalism', namely '*secrecy, universality, equality, annuality* of suffrages'.[121]

Yet if radicalism had not already contained so potentially powerful a redistributionist threat, Bentham (and others) would not have had to labour so hard to deny it. The redistribution of property had been a theme never wholly absent in Christian thought, especially since the Reformation, and derived from the interpretation of Genesis. Patristic commentators like Ambrose and Augustine had expounded God's grant of the world to mankind in common. Some more recent commentators claimed that this implied an equal grant to men in the present. John Locke encountered this position as a possible corollary of his argument for the natural equality of man by creation, and had to devise elaborate theories of property to account for and excuse the wide inequalities of wealth in his own society.[122] It was nevertheless possible to cite Locke's doctrine of property in an egalitarian sense, and this usage recurred in works like William Ogilvie's anonymous *An Essay on the Right of Property in Land* (1781) and George Dyer's *The Complaints of the Poor People of England* (1793).

Locke was not a necessary source, however, since all reformers could much more obviously appeal to Scripture. Paine's ideas of the equality of 'natural' rights and the legitimate redistribution of landed estates via punitive taxation were equally based on creation: 'every child born into the world must be considered as deriving its existence from God. The world is as new to him as it was to the first man that existed, and his natural right in it is of the same kind'. Paine proved his point by quoting Genesis.[123] A sermon by Richard Watson, Bishop of Llandaff, entitled *The Wisdom and Goodness of God, in having made both Rich and Poor* provoked Paine to publish *Agrarian Justice*, which proceeded from the argument that 'It is wrong to say that God made *Rich* and *Poor*; he made only *Male* and *Female*; and he gave them the earth for their inheritance'.[124]

The dependence of Locke's argument on premises about God's intentions was well understood, however. Thomas Spence, the most consistent advocate of the redistribution of land,[125] linked Locke's *Two Treatises* with Leviticus in 1793.[126] Spence's father was a member of a fundamentalist sect, the Glassites; he himself was inspired by the firebrand Presbyterian minister James Murray.[127] In 1797, he praised Paine's *Agrarian Justice* for its use of Locke and its invocation of the Biblical teaching that 'God hath given the earth . . . to mankind in common', but went far beyond Paine's limited proposals.[128] At his trial in 1803, Spence invoked Locke and the Bible once more to support 'this my Millennial Form of Government'.[129] It may indeed be that Spence's 'millennium was secular',[130] but it may also be doubted how secular such an idea can become. Before 'radicalism' and 'socialism', there were few secular sources of powerful imagery. Charles Hall, author of *The Effects of Civilization on the People in European States* (London, 1805) and sometimes wrongly classed as an early socialist, similarly 'seemed to have found more inspiration from the Old Testament than any other source' for his plans to give labourers access to land.[131]

It is, of course, conventional to trace mid seventeenth-century projects for material redistribution (as with the 'Digger' Gerard Winstanley) to theological roots, to posit an hiatus for more than a century thereafter, and to treat redistributionist ideas in the early nineteenth century as self-sufficiently secular in nature.[132] Although this is not the place for a full investigation of the subject, this explanatory scheme now seems ripe for re-examination. If radicalism was formulated following a religious critique of landed inequality, it is understandable that this critique should have carried over to be one element of the new but secular ideology. It was not, however, a preoccupation of that quintessentially urban intellectual Bentham himself: the priest, not the landowner, was his target.

Nevertheless, as socialists were soon to argue, general economic redistribution beyond the issue of land was not central to radicalism. If it was not, however, the question becomes harder to answer: how did the 'radicalism' of the 1820s differ from the phenomenon of the 1790s so widely (though inaccurately) called 'Jacobinism'? An answer, at least in outline, now begins to emerge. Jacobinism was normally premised on natural rights, although not because it was drawn from any deep knowledge of natural rights theory; its enthusiasm about the rights of man was inseparably linked to Deism, that worship of a Supreme Being that shaded so easily into the 'religion of humanity'. Radicalism (although it sometimes used the rhetoric of abstract rights and the rhetoric of historic constitutional liberties) was normally intellectually premised upon utilitarianism, which in Bentham's famous phrase regarded natural rights theory as 'nonsense upon stilts'. It too was firmly atheist, since atheism was (as Bentham well knew) a necessary precondition of the sorts of reform he expected from utilitarianism. Radicalism was, moreover, both utilitarian and atheist in a context created by Ricardian economics, that essential theoretical constituent of the critique of the old order of squire and parson.[133] Radicalism was, therefore, far more powerfully redistributionist than Jacobinism ever became. And yet the targets of radicalism were still highly selective, as another new ideology was now to demonstrate: socialism.

RADICALISM VERSUS WHIGGISM AND SOCIALISM

It was not only the anti-Jacobin idiom which stood outside radical reform and acted to promote its self-definition; other self-consciously reformist traditions also came to be contrasted with radical reform as it developed into radicalism. Whigs, too, had their agenda, and despite long years in the wilderness it was their hour, not the radicals', which came in 1830.[134] As radical reformers increasingly inclined to distrust the Whigs for the covert limitations the Whigs placed on their intentions, radical reformers found themselves threatened from 'the Left' as the new ideology of socialism itself found a way of explaining why even radicalism was too limited. For 'socialism' too was conceptualized in these years, considerably earlier than is often supposed. Socialism did not stand on the shoulders of radicalism; it was defined over against it. Most notably, where radicalism was generally irreligious, socialism was frequently driven by Christian ideals of community.[135]

In these circumstances radicals began to extend their genealogy backward in time, where even Paine's intellectual horizon in the 1790s had extended only as far back as the sanitized Whig triumph of 1688.[136] In 1819, the first issue of the periodical *The Radical Reformer* set out its creed:

> Impressed with a deep sense of the awful situation of the country, and convinced that an ignorance of, and *contempt* for the NATURAL RIGHTS OF MAN, are the sole causes of the corruptions of government and public grievances, some admirers of the genuine principles of the Constitution have come forward to lay the foundation of the present work.

This did not entail novelty, however, for the authors sought to locate themselves within a tradition, 'what Algernon Sydney called "THE GOOD OLD CAUSE"'.[137] Natural rights, and an appeal to an historical constitutionalism, were still present among radical reformers; ahistorical utilitarianism did not at once sweep the board. Nineteenth-century radicals went on to construct a genealogy for radicalism which ignored religion and stressed patriotism to reach back to the Levellers, but that is another story.

Even the most strident of the radical reformers could still profess a scrupulous respect for most forms of private property. Richard Carlile, in Dorchester jail from November 1819 to November 1825, conducted an extensive and influential publicity campaign that scarcely touched on issues of redistribution.[138] Only on the land question did Carlile adopt a redistributionist scheme with an explicit acknowledgement of Thomas Spence: in *The Republican* for December 1822 he explained how the products of industry were private and could not be taxed, but land was public property, held only conditionally by the landlord, and subject to taxation considered as 'a rental, or a payment from those who hold to those who do not hold'.[139] Henry Hunt, another champion of universal suffrage, annual parliaments and the secret ballot, took a similar position. His newsletter *To the Radical Reformers* was written from 'Ilchester Jail', or as he finally called it, 'Ilchester Bastile', from 1820 to 1822.[140] Hunt used it to review the issues of the moment and incite indignation over the Queen Caroline affair, the anniversary of 'the Manchester massacre', the treatment of prisoners. In the midst of his endless and strident invective, Hunt indeed professed that 'The Radicals have always said, and honestly said, that they want nothing new, they only want the constitution; and a reformed House of Commons, chosen by the *whole people*, would at once restore that constitution'; 'rational liberty' could only be brought about 'by holding all private property sacred and inviolable'. As Hunt replied to an address from 'the Committee of Female Reformers of Manchester', 'Be but the friends *of Universal Suffrage* united, then our tyrants will fall and you will be free'.[141]

Assurances like these did not always persuade a wider audience. The author of the homiletical tale *Will Waver* evidently saw the first and main threat of radical reform in 1821 to be the expropriation of the squirearchy and the division of landed estates. Almost equally prominent was the theme of the fictional village radical Jem Gudgeon's irreligion: 'I would have a man use his reason, and not be priest-ridden; I would have him follow his nature, and not a parcel of lies, invented by the priests to keep folks in order'.[142] Christian apologists, although sensitive on this point, were also aware that radical reform had acquired an economic theory from Ricardo which systematized a widely-held critique (seen, for example, in Cobbett) in which high taxes to fund an enormous national debt were identified as a prime cause of poverty, and in which rent was identified as an unjustified extortion by what Ricardo in 1817 defined as 'the unproductive class', the landlords.[143] Even John Harford, though preoccupied by what he saw as the lasting legacy of Thomas Paine, identified the preoccupations of 1819. 'The DEBT, the DEBT, is now the hue and cry of the whole party', he wrote of the radicals.[144]

A new journal, *The Radical*, posed in its first issue of 1831 the question 'What is a Radical?' and answered it:

> a Radical is one who, impatient of enormous taxation imposed by a set of tax-imposers, over whose rapacity he has no control, is determined to procure a remedy for such a foul disease. He is acquainted with the cause: he is aware that it is the present system of government by which the irresponsible, almost self-elected, aristocratical *Few* contrive to exclude the *Many* from the deputation of Representatives to the Assembly where the taxes are imposed; he is desirous of *eradicating* such a monstrous, unjust, detestable system: he is conscious that a Whig or *partial* remedy will prove insufficient for a cure; he honestly proclaims every quack, pretended remedy to be inefficacious; he is not such a fool as to imagine that a *partial* or *moderate* dose of political medicine will relieve the People. If a man has a fever, he must be cured *radically*, not *partially* or *moderately*. On the same principle the honest political physician will prescribe a course of medicine which will go to the *radix*, or root of the national disease. He will physic, purge, bleed, – he will ERADICATE, – he will be a RADICAL.
>
> This is a *radical*, efficacious, certain, safe cure. Recipe: –
>
> EVERY MAN (*not incapacitated by crime or extreme ignorance*) A VOTE IN ELECTING A REPRESENTATIVE in *the Assembly where the Laws are made*.[145]

In 1820–2, Henry Hunt stressed the consistent hostility of the Whigs towards the radicals. The Whigs had not been libertarian in their legislation 'in 1807, when they were last in power; and what has been their conduct ever since? have not many of them, upon all occasions, joined the minister to make laws to put down the radicals'?[146] Certainly, the Whigs shied away from universal suffrage, and many of them were hesitant about any measure of parliamentary reform in the first three decades of the nineteenth century.[147]

By the time the Whigs achieved power in 1830 and found themselves unexpectedly united behind a parliamentary reform bill, the position of the radicals had moved further still. For them, universal suffrage was now even more clearly only a means to an end. After its ringing opening declaration in favour of the franchise for all, *The Radical* specified its grievances: the tax on newspapers; unemployment; tithes; the death penalty; the question of distribution:

> An abundant harvest will not suffice to alleviate efficaciously the cruel sufferings of the poor man; for it is not the *insufficiency* of *produce* which reduces him to misery and famine – it is its *unjust distribution*. The poor man often dies of hunger, not on account of there being no bread to eat, but because he, who prepares it, has none to eat!
> The working-man has it not in his power to buy sufficient bread for his family, because all the instruments of labour are subject, under the name of *rent*, &c., to enormous subtractions made for the profit of the *do-nothings*; so that, these deductions being effected, there remains for the unfortunate labourer out of the produce of his labour, but a scanty and insufficient portion.[148]

Despite its attempt in its first issue to be most things to most men, the new journal *The Truth* displayed what was by 1833 one hallmark of the radical position: it included as its leading principle the claim that, since 'nature . . . gives to all an equal right to the soil', the great landed estates should be broken up.[149]

This was the undisguised message for an audience presumed to be sympathetic. For the parliamentary classes, the nature of radicalism could still be described in minimal terms. In 1830, the *Westminster Review* placed the question of the franchise first in its discussion of radical reform. The anonymous author reassured his readers: 'Let no man be startled at the term radical; does any man but the guilty, desire a reform that is not radical? 'Radical' means that which shall do something effectually; and 'not radical' means not doing it at all. Does any man go to a doctor, and ask for a cure that is not radical?' It followed that

> the time cannot be far off, when the middle classes, and those of the highest who are not entered of the plot, will come forward to join their influence to the cause of the starving poor . . . The time will come when rich and poor will combine to make every man eat out of his own dish; and the actual agent in this cruel

operation, will be a radical reform in what is called the commons house of parliament.[150]

Thanks not least to the crises surrounding the Reform Act, by the 1830s 'the Radical party' had been reified as an actor in parliamentary elections.[151] Yet no sooner was this identity established than, in the same decade, another new ideology, socialism,[152] began to define itself over against radicalism.[153] In 1835, Robert Owen's socialist weekly *The New Moral World* recorded a meeting of the London 'Great Radical Association' and briefed its readers on the contrasting principles of the radicals. 'These are, – "universal suffrage, equal representation, annual parliaments, vote by ballot, and no property qualification" '. Radicals were 'informed that the *root* of the evil by which they are oppressed and enslaved, is not in the constitution of the monarchy, not in the constitution of the House of Lords; no, these are only *branches* of the root; but the root itself, is in the constitution of the House of Commons'. This was all very well, argued the Owenite, but how would it help?

We will suppose that the new Parliament was assembled, elected according to these new arrangements, and that they immediately proceeded to make the monarchy elective, or to determine to have a President, who should be satisfied with a salary of 5000 *l.* per annum; that they would abolish the House of Lords, or make that an elective body; that they would separate the church from the state, abolish tithes, and make the voluntary principle, for the support of the clergy, the law of the land; that they would annihilate the pension list, and abolish all useless places and sinecures; disband the standing army; and, in short, reduce the expenditure of the government of this country to a level with that of the United States; supposing all this accomplished within the space of the next two years, – and few of our Radical friends calculate upon a more rapid accomplishment of their wishes, – we then again enquire to what extent the condition of the labouring population will thereby be improved?

A reduction of public expenditure would throw many labourers out of work;

and this would go on, until the wages of labour would be reduced to the same relative scale as at present; that is, *to the mere subsisting price*; which, as the political economists tell us, is the natural reward of labour: and, notwithstanding all this change, therefore, in two years after, the industrious classes would find that they were just in the same state as before.[154]

By 1838, another observer could contrast socialists and radicals even more sharply:

Embracing in its objects the political equality and self government aimed at by the Radicals, the scheme of the Socialists superadds a new principle of morals, and a new system of marriage, the destruction of priestcraft, and community of property. The means too proposed by the latter for the accomplishment of their views, vary essentially from those which have been adopted, or contemplated to be used, by the Radicals.

The radicals were not homogeneous, he acknowledged; 'a large section are favourable to, at least, the economic views of the Socialists, and seek political power merely as an effective instrument for removing the competitive principle from society'.[155] But the views of the 'anti-Socialist section' of the radicals could be listed:

The purely political Radicals say that through the following gradations, beginning with universal suffrage as a first step, might be reached the maximum of human liberty and happiness.
First. A really responsible, justice-loving, and cheap government.
Second. A relieving of the people from the ascendancy and dominion of any religious sect, and the government from all care about religion.
Third. A good education for every citizen; the removal of all fiscal restraints from, and the utmost possible extension of, knowledge.
Fourth. An equal chance of participation in all state honours and emoluments.
Fifth. An equitable, simple, and comprehensive code of laws, impartially, cheaply, and readily administered.
Sixth. The abolition of private property in the soil.
Seventh. The suppression of all other monopolies, and the utmost possible freedom, both local and national, given to the competitive principle.
Eighth. An unexceptionable circulating medium.[156]

Samuel Bower's eight components of radicalism were highly generalized, or unobjectionable, or utopian; some were already familiar, even dating back several centuries. What was new was the way in which this list of aims had been fused together, given a unity and a coherence by the existence of a view of man. For the secular, free-standing, omnicompetent individual, the Church and the institutions of society that claimed a divine sanction were the barriers to the maximization of utility. How far would this programme go? Would this critique condemn the squire as well as the parson? Some radicals, but not all, extrapolated their analysis of the unreformed political system and of the origins of the national debt to include reform of landownership, but others did not. Bower added a footnote to his sixth point concerning land:

This has not been found a place in the programme generally given to the public. Some, however, of the most honest and fearless of the Radicals have shown the institution of private property in the soil to be what it really is, namely, an evil of the first magnitude, and one the abolition of which must be an early fruit of the political enfranchisement of the people.[157]

There was much in this of which the socialist Bower approved; but 'the system of individual competition', he argued, would still preserve 'the classification of society into master and servant, and richer and poorer'. This would in practice 'destroy the assumed political equality'.[158]

By the late 1830s, then, distinctions between the creeds of radicals and socialists had been drawn with some clarity. Radicals could perceive Chartist disorders as proof that the diagnosis offered by radicalism was a correct one. One radical insisted that 'Our grievances, in short, are, – Enormous Debt, and habitual Extravagance disabling us from paying it'. Since 'The interest of the Debt is defrayed by heavy taxes laid on the poor', this was the grievance on which 'all the rest turns' argued Francis Newman, a professor at the new University of London. 'As long as it exists, it is morally certain that poor men will become disaffected to the existing constitution as fast as they gain political information'.[159] Socialists, by contrast, 'located the cause of working-class misery within economic activity and no longer thought of political corruption (the debt and taxes) as the cause of poverty and inequality. Their attention was less on the owner of land than on the owner of capital, less on the farm, the landless, and the unemployed than on the factory and the working poor'.[160]

Although radicalism expanded far beyond its starting point, it had never expanded as far as to include this socialist agenda. Socialism and radicalism were henceforth alternatives, competing for the allegiance of a mass audience. They were not, however, unchanging ideologies. With the passage of time, they developed, notably by the steady elimination (at least in the eyes of the intelligentsia) of the theological element in their origins, and with the substantial assimilation of many elements of radicalism (anti-imperialism, financial reform, religious pluralism) by the Liberal party.[161] By the late nineteenth century, this process of amnesia was largely complete. Viewed from Balliol College in the 1880s, it seemed that

> The old Radical creed may be summed up in three words – justice, liberty, and self-help. To obtain justice and liberty they believed all classes should be admitted to the suffrage; to promote self-reliance they believed that every restriction on trade should be abolished, that labour and commerce should be as free as the winds. Two things are observable in this creed, the intense dislike of the old Radicals to State interference, and their complete faith in the people.[162]

But this was only part of the story. 'Radicalism' had begun life as an ideology intended to negate the 'old society': in order to do so, it had to propound a new view of man which replied to man as he was. Universal suffrage was not a self-evident idea for the secular utilitarians. In the eighteenth century it took its rise within Arianism and (especially) Socinianism, theologies which carried to the most articulate theoretical extreme Dissent's idea of the individual as free standing, with immediate personal access to God. As such, the appeal of universal suffrage in Socinianism rather than Paine's Deism was, at first, narrowly framed and strangely limited. It was only when an alliance was forged between universal suffrage and utilitarianism that 'democracy' understood as individual agency could become a potent force. The conceptualization of 'radicalism' was a key to the forging of that alliance, but the secular world to which radicalism appealed was not self-generated. The secular ideologies of the nineteenth century emerged only out of a profound engagement with religion. Their conceptualization did not prove the emancipation of modern man from his past. On the contrary, they showed how profoundly shaped by his past he was even in the act of seeking to escape from it.

NOTES

1 For comments on a draft I am grateful to Victor Bailey, Stewart Brown, James Burns, Richard W. Davis, Jacob Ellens, Gareth Stedman Jones, William Thomas and Anthony Waterman.

2 For nineteenth-century radicals' later construction of a tradition extending back to Hampden, Pym and Cromwell, see Günther Lottes, 'Radicalism, Revolution and Popular Culture: An Anglo-French Comparison', in Mark Philp (ed.), *The French Revolution and British Popular Politics* (Cambridge, 1991), pp. 78–98; Margot C. Finn, *After Chartism: Class and nation in English radical politics, 1848–1874* (Cambridge, 1993), pp. 35–7. By contrast, the actual 'influence of Levellerism on subsequent radical-democratic movements' was only 'subtle and somewhat oblique': F. K. Donnelly, 'Levellerism in Eighteenth and Early Nineteenth-Century Britain', *Albion* 20 (1988), pp. 261–9, at 261. In recent scholarship, older assumptions of the secular, functional continuities of seventeenth- and eighteenth-century reform movements have everywhere broken down.

3 Alexander Gray, *The Socialist Tradition: Moses to Lenin* (London, 1946; 4th impression, 1963) was a careful and critical study of 523 pages. Gray (1882–1968) had been a civil servant for sixteen years before taking the chair of political economy at Aberdeen in 1921; he held a chair at Edinburgh from 1935 to his retirement in 1956, and also wrote *The Development of Economic Doctrine* (1931). For service on many government boards and commissions, he was knighted in 1947. In the preface to *The*

Socialist Tradition (p. v) he recorded his personal dislike of Marx, Lassalle and Rousseau.

4 See Adolf Laube, 'Radicalism as a Research Problem in the History of Early Reformation' in Hans J. Hillerbrand (ed.), *Radical Tendencies in the Reformation*, special issue of *Sixteenth Century Essays & Studies* 9 (1988), pp. 9–23. Laube cautioned: 'A more detailed analysis of the problem of radicalism indicates that "radical" does not so much refer to a substantive content as to an adjectival quality' (pp. 10–11). More extensive cautions are expressed by Hans J. Hillerbrand, 'Radicalism in the Early Reformation: Varieties of Reformation in Church and Society', *ibid.*, pp. 25–41.

5 George H. Williams, *The Radical Reformation* (Philadelphia, 1962).

6 Michael G. Baylor (ed.), *The Radical Reformation* (Cambridge, 1991), p. xi. For the persistence of this methodological vice of anachronism in some quarters see, for example, Eric Heffer (ed.), *Cromwell and Communism: Socialism and Democracy in the Great English Revolution* (London, 1980); Isaac Kramnick, *Republicanism and Bourgeois Radicalism: Political Ideology in late Eighteenth-Century England and America* (Ithaca, New York, 1990); Gordon S. Wood, *The Radicalism of the American Revolution* (New York, 1992). Cf. George L. Cherry, *Early English Liberalism: its emergence through Parliamentary action, 1660–1702* (New York, 1962); Martin Seliger, *The Liberal Politics of John Locke* (London, 1968); Ruth Grant, *John Locke's Liberalism* (Chicago, 1987).

7 J. C. D. Clark, *The Language of Liberty 1660–1832* (Cambridge, 1993).

8 Paine's remedy for political ills was what he described as 'the representative system', not universal suffrage. Although well aware that 'not one person in seven is represented', his remarks on the franchise were few and perfunctory, referring to taxpayers' practical involvement with government and the collective role of 'the people' rather than to the ontological status of individuals: Thomas Paine, *Letter Addressed to the Addressers, on the Late Proclamation* (London, 1792), pp. 27, 39, 48, 57–8, 67–8. In *Rights of Man*, Paine was content with the property qualification in the proposed French constitution; by *Dissertation on First Principles of Government* London, 1795) he argued to reduce the property qualification to zero in 'the system of representative government' (pp. 8, 22, 30); in neither case did he begin with the individual, as Price and Priestley had done, but rather with the principle of equality. For the origin of the doctrine of universal suffrage in Socinianism rather than Paine's Deism see J. C. D. Clark, *English Society 1660–1832* (Cambridge, 2000), chapter 4.

9 For a recent attempt to invent a long genealogy for class formation see P. J. Corfield (ed.), *Language, History and Class* (Oxford, 1991). For a later chronology and different analysis, see Clark, *English Society 1660–1832*, chapter 2. The evidence presented here does not bear out claims that radicalism was intrinsically related to class formation: David Nicholls, 'The English Middle Classes and the Ideological Significance of Radicalism, 1760–1886', *Journal of British Studies* 24 (1985), pp. 415–33;

Edward Royle, 'The language of class and radicalism', *History Review* no. 29 (December 1997), pp. 38–42.

10 For the process as a whole, see Clark, *English Society 1660–1832*, 'Keywords'. This essay is not an attempt to construct an ideal type but to explain the degree of coherence in a newly-coined doctrine. A prosopographical study would be needed to determine how many reformers subcribed to 'radicalism'. Clearly, too, political terms like this are no sooner propounded than they begin to be claimed, or repudiated, for tactical reasons. As we shall see, that was the case with the older term 'radical reformer'. It should be emphasised at the outset that it is not being argued here that all, or even most, reformers were atheists.

11 E.g. John Ward, *Four Essays upon the English Language ... To these is subjoined A Catalogue of the English Verbs, formed thro their Radical Tenses* (London, 1758); [John Murdoch], *A Radical Vocabulary of the French Language* (London, 1782); John Jamieson, *Hermes Scythius: or, The Radical Affinities of the Greek and Latin Languages to the Gothic* (Edinburgh, 1814); *A. Thibaudin's Proposed Original System for a Radical, Universal & Philosophical Reform in the Spelling of Languages* (London, [1842]).

12 John Mudge, *A Radical and Expeditious Cure for a recent Catarrhous Cough* (London, 1778).

13 E.g. J. F. Dieffenbach, *Memoir on the Radical Cure of Stuttering, by a surgical operation*, trans. Joseph Travers (London, 1841).

14 E.g. William Spence, *The Radical Cause of the Present Distresses of the West-India Planters Pointed Out* (London, 1807).

15 [Samuel Johnson], *Taxation no Tyranny; an Answer to the Resolutions and Address of the American Congress* (London, 1775), p. 23.

16 Paine, *Letter Addressed to the Addressers*, pp. 8, 33.

17 William Wilberforce, *A Practical View of the Prevailing Religious System of Professed Christians ... contrasted with Real Christianity* (London, 1797), pp. 26–7.

18 *Sir Robert Peel the Greatest Radical of the Age, and the Best Friend of O'Connell* (London, 1845).

19 Clark, *English Society 1660–1832*, chapter 4; Derek Beales, 'The Idea of Reform in British Politics, 1829–1850', *Proceedings of the British Academy* 100 (1999), pp. 159–74, for the general restriction of the term 'reform' to parliamentary reform. Joanna Innes kindly showed me the text of her unpublished paper, 'The Idea of Reform in English Public Life, to 1830'.

20 John Disney (ed.), *The Works ... of John Jebb* (3 vols., London, 1787), I, p. 194; Christopher Wyvill, *Political Papers* (5 vols., York, 1794–1804), I, p. 341.

21 [Christopher Wyvill], *A Letter to John Cartwright, Esq.* (York, 1801), pp. 4–5.

22 Sir Walter Scott to Thomas Scott, 16 October 1819, in H. J. C. Grierson (ed.), *The Letters of Sir Walter Scott* (12 vols., London, 1931–7), VI, p. 2.

23 Jonas Dennis, *Church reform, by a Church radical, comprising a Review of the Thirty-nine Articles* (London, 1835), pp. iii-v.

24 *Thoughts on a Radical Remedy for the Present Distresses of the Country* (London, 1820), pp. 8, 21.

25 *The Truth. A Weekly Radical Christian, and Family Newspaper*, vol. 1, no. 1 (10 February, 1833), pp. 1–2.

26 In this essay I offer an account of the emergence of a coherently-defined doctrine out of diverse earlier usages, and its subsequent re-diversification. For a study which adopts a loose definition of radicalism and which consequently focuses on the diverse practical commitments of the individuals involved see Eileen Groth Lyon, *Politicians in the Pulpit: Christian Radicalism in Britain from the Fall of the Bastille to the Disintegration of Chartism* (Aldershot, 1999). This work seeks to make a case for the salience of religion in reforming movements, and so neglects the role of irreligion in the conceptualisation of that particular variety of reform that came to be called 'radicalism'.

27 Its imprecision in current scholarship is often acknowledged. Writing a survey of the subject before the recent reinterpretation of the long eighteenth century, two historians had been compelled to preface their study with the warning: 'The word "radicalism" has so many meanings that as a concept in historical analysis it is practically useless ... To impose coherence on this evidently vague topic is misleading. There is no clear picture of tributaries feeding into a main stream which can then be followed to the estuary and the sea': Edward Royle and James Walvin, *English Radicals and Reformers 1760–1848* (Brighton, 1982), pp. 9–10. Cf. Richard L. Greaves and Robert Zaller (eds.), *Biographical Dictionary of British Radicals in the Seventeenth Century* (3 vols., Brighton, 1982–4): 'The term "radical" as we use it is confessedly an anachronism for the seventeenth century' (I, p. vii). No more adequate definition of the term was offered in Joseph O. Baylen and Norbert J. Gossman (eds.), *Biographical Dictionary of Modern British Radicals* [1770–1914] (4 vols., Hassocks, 1979–88).

28 It will therefore be clear that that twentieth-century hybrid, 'bourgeois radicalism', is a double solecism.

29 [George Huddesford], *Bubble and Squeak, a Galli-maufry of British Beef with the Chopp'd Cabbage of Gallic Philosophy and Radical Reform* (London, 1799), pp. 41, 43. Timotheus, statesman and general, incited the Athenians in 358 or 357 BC to expel the Thebans from Euboea. Huddesford quoted Dryden's *Alexander's Feast*, Act II: 'Revenge, revenge, Timotheus cries,/See the furies arise,/See the snakes that they rear,/How they hiss in their hair,/And the sparkles that flash from their eyes!'

30 *The Radical-House which Jack would build* (2nd edn., Exeter [1820]). This was a reply to the pamphlets of William Hone; for whom, see below.

31 Electoral malpractice in the borough of Grampound had reached such a level in the 1818 election that the ministry was finally shamed into legislation to remove its right to return two Members. The ministry wished to transfer that right to Yorkshire.

32 *An Address to The Ministerial Radicals, and a call upon all who love the constitution, and are anxious for its preservation in that state in which it was delivered by our forefathers to the House of Brunswick, by one of the middle class of the people* (London, 1820), pp. 1, 17–18, 27. The author was evidently an Evangelical who objected to the ministers for swearing, blaspheming, and breaches of Sabbath observance (p. 22).

33 *Hints for Radical Reform, on Principles of Equity. By Amor Patriae* (London, 1821), pp. 1–3, 46, 51–2.

34 *The Radical Reformists. A Narrative, adapted to the Present Times* (London, n.d. [? 1816]), p. 4.zz

35 *Radical Reform, the Only Remedy for the Disorders of our Country; or, Observations on the Changes Necessary both in Church and State. By Britannicus* (London, 1819), pp. 4, 6.

36 *Radical Reform, the Only Remedy*, pp. 8–10, 15.

37 E.g. *Radical Reform: or a Better Cure for Poverty and Distress, than Burning Corn Stacks and Destroying Thrashing Machines. A Dialogue* (Doncaster, 1831).

38 John S. Harford, *Some Account of the Life, Death and Principles of Thomas Paine, together with Remarks on his Writings, and on their intimate connection with the avowed objects of the Revolutionists of 1793, and of the Radicals in 1819* (Bristol, 1819), pp. v–vi, 17.

39 Harford, *Principles of Thomas Paine*, pp. 17–19.

40 Harford, *Principles of Thomas Paine*, p. 73.

41 Harford, *Principles of Thomas Paine*, p. 81.

42 John Scandrett Harford (1785–1866). Son of a Quaker banker, he converted to the Church after the death of his brother in 1804. He became a zealous supporter of the Church Missionary Society and the Bible Society, and was a close friend of Hannah More and William Wilberforce. He succeeded to his father's estates in 1815, and acted as J. P., deputy lieutenant and high sheriff for his county.

43 Harford, *Principles of Thomas Paine*, pp. 22, 82. Part of his tract was taken up with a defence of the veracity of Scripture.

44 See above, n. 8.

45 *Hints to Radical Reformers, and Materials for True* (London, 1817), p. 3.

46 For primarily social and economic studies of this phenomenon, which nevertheless capture its virulence and wide extent, see Eric J. Evans, 'Some Reasons for the Growth of English Rural Anti-Clericalism c. 1750-c. 1830', *Past & Present* 66 (1975), pp. 84–109, and idem, *The Contentious Tithe: the Tithe Problem and English Agriculture, 1750–1850* (London, 1976). Resentment against tithes had, of course, been evident earlier without alone engendering 'radicalism': cf. Margaret James, 'The Political Importance of the Tithes Controversy in the English Revolution 1640–60', *History* 26 (1941), pp. 1–18.

47 *A Letter from a Manufacturer to his Son, upon Radical Reform* (London, [?1815]), pp. 1–3, 13.

48 John Galt (1779–1839), a Scot who pursued a career in England. Unsuccessful in a series of business ventures, he turned to writing and

can in some ways be compared with that other ministerial supporter, Sir Walter Scott.

49 [John Galt], *The Radical. An Autobiography* (London, 1832), pp. iii, 5, 16.
50 [Galt], *The Radical*, pp. 17, 25, 55, 61.
51 [Galt], *The Radical*, pp. 75, 79, 92.
52 [Galt], *The Radical*, pp. 93, 98, 106–7, 109.
53 [Galt], *The Radical*, pp. 111–2, 121.
54 [Galt], *The Radical*, p. 132.
55 [Galt], *The Radical*, pp. 132–3, 193–4.
56 [Galt], *The Radical*, pp. 99–104.
57 [Galt], *The Radical*, pp. 111–12.
58 [Galt], *The Radical*, pp. 133–4.
59 J. S. Mill, *Autobiography and Literary Essays*, ed. John M. Robson and Jack Stillinger (Toronto, 1981), p. 81; William Thomas, *The Philosophic Radicals: Nine Studies in Theory and Practice 1817–1841* (Oxford, 1979), p. 2.
60 George William Downing, *An Address to the Independent Livery of London, on the Advantages to be Derived from a Radical Reform in the Commons House of Parliament* (2nd edn., London, nd [?1818]), p. 4.
61 Samuel Bamford (1788–1872). Son of a Methodist who was converted away from Christianity by Paine in the 1790s. Himself a weaver, poet and political organiser, he opposed violent means and became a special constable during the Chartist disturbances. Present at the Peterloo incident, he was convicted of conspiracy to incite a riot and imprisoned for a year; he then withdrew from politics. Martin Hewitt argues that Bamford's 'religious beliefs were a crucial source of his radicalism ... his anti-clericalism was deep-rooted' and virulent as late as 1859: 'Radicalism and the Victorian Working Class: the Case of Samuel Bamford', *Historical Journal* 34 (1991), pp. 873–92, at 880, 884.
62 Samuel Bamford, *Passages in the Life of a Radical* (2 vols., Heywood, [1841–2]), I, p. 3.
63 Bamford, *Passages in the Life of a Radical*, I, pp. 10–11.
64 [Louis Simond], *Journal of a Tour and Residence in Great Britain, During the Years 1810 and 1811, by a French Traveller* (2 vols., Edinburgh, 1815), I, p. 36.
65 Vernon F. Storr, *The Development of English Theology in the Nineteenth Century 1800–1860* (London, 1913), pp. 383–94, at 384. Storr, like other theologians, did not establish connections between Bentham's religion and his politics, and Storr's insights were generally overlooked by later historians of religion. They tended to treat the Benthamites' irreligion as a reason for passing them over, preferring to focus on the more congenial John Stuart Mill: cf. Bernard M. G. Reardon, *Religious Thought in the Victorian Age: A Survey from Coleridge to Gore* (2nd edn., London, 1995), pp. 198–200.
66 Elie Halévy, *The Growth of Philosophic Radicalism*, trans. Mary Morris (London, 1928; 2nd edn., 1934), p. 264. Nowhere else in the work did Halévy mention, let alone explore, the emergence of this concept.

J. H. Burns, 'Jeremy Bentham: From Radical Enlightenment to Philosophic Radicalism', *The Bentham Newsletter* 8 (1984), pp. 4–14, sought to place Bentham more exactly in his setting but without defining and locating these key terms.

67 '. . . it looked as if the Whig government which had passed the Reform Bill would let the reform movement flag unless a united body of radicals goaded it on. A name was needed which would be a rallying point without becoming another sectarian label'. Thomas, *Philosophic Radicals*, p. 1.

68 Thomas, *Philosophic Radicals*, pp. 1, 4.

69 Professor J. H. Burns reminds me that the edition was left incomplete because of the publisher's financial difficulties, and more research is needed into this question. Nevertheless, it seems fair to say that the next generation of Bentham's followers understood his canon as one hardly concerned with religion.

70 The fullest and most perceptive investigation of Bentham's religious views is now James E. Crimmins, *Secular Utilitarianism: Social Science and the Critique of Religion in the Thought of Jeremy Bentham* (Oxford, 1990). This able study does not, however, examine the nature of 'radicalism' or draw the connections between religion and politics proposed here. In arguing for the chronological and conceptual priority of men's religion in explaining their politics, I am retaining a model first developed in my *English Society 1688–1832* (Cambridge, 1985).

71 For Bentham's Oxford years (1760–4) and the controversy of 1773, see J. E. Crimmins, 'Bentham's Unpublished Manuscripts on Subscription to Articles of Faith', in *British Journal for Eighteenth Century Studies* 9 (1986), pp. 33–44 and idem, *Secular Utilitarianism*, pp. 115–28. For this culture at Oxford, and its requirements, see J. C. D. Clark, *Samuel Johnson: Literature, religion and English cultural politics from the Restoration to Romanticism* (Cambridge, 1994) and *idem.*, 'Religion and Political Identity: Samuel Johnson as a Nonjuror' in Jonathan Clark and Howard Erskine-Hill (eds.), *Samuel Johnson in Historical Context* (London, 2002).

72 James Steintrager, 'Morality and Belief: the Origin and Purpose of Bentham's Writings on Religion', *The Mill News Letter* 6, no. 2 (Spring 1971), pp. 3–15. Steintrager concluded that 'A strong opposition to religion was built into the very fibre of his utilitarian system almost from the very beginning in 1768', p. 7.

73 [Jeremy Bentham], *A Fragment on Government* (London, 1776), p. xvi; Clark, *English Society 1660–1832*, chapter 3.

74 Bentham to Grafton, c. 7 September 1790, in Alexander Taylor Milne (ed.), *The Correspondence of Jeremy Bentham*, IV (London, 1981), p. 201.

75 Bentham to Francis Place, 24 April 1831, in Graham Wallas, *The Life of Francis Place, 1771–1854* (London, 1898), p. 82.

76 Halévy, *Philosophic Radicalism*, p. 520. *Traités de législation* was not published in England until 1864, although it began to appear in the USA in 1830. Halévy included this insight in an appendix; his text gave the

misleading impression that Bentham's writings on religion were merely opportunistic, provoked by the controversy over rival school systems in the late 1810s: cf. Steintrager, 'Morality and Belief', p. 7; Crimmins, *Secular Utilitarianism*, pp. 165–81.

77 For legal action against such phenomena see William H. Wickwar, *The Struggle for the Freedom of the Press 1819–1832* (London, 1928); Joel H. Wiener, *Radicalism and Freethought in Nineteenth-Century Britain: The Life of Richard Carlile* (Westport, Conn., 1983); Olivia Smith, *The Politics of Language 1791–1819* (Oxford, 1984); Clark, *English Society 1660–1832*, chapter 5.

78 Jeremy Bentham, *The Elements of the Art of Packing, as applied to Special Juries, particularly in cases of Libel Law* (London, 1821). 'Libel' included the religious offence of blasphemous libel.

79 Alexander Bain, *James Mill. A Biography* (London 1882), pp. 98, 101–2, 108, 127; Stephen Conway (ed.), *The Correspondence of Jeremy Bentham*, VIII (Oxford, 1988), pp. 26, 37, 60–1, 93–4, 430.

80 *Swear not at All* (1817); *Church-of-Englandism and its Catechism Examined* (1818); *Analysis of the Influence of Natural Religion on the Temporal Happiness of Mankind* (1822); *Not Paul, but Jesus* (1823).

81 James E. Crimmins, 'Bentham's Metaphysics and the Science of Divinity', *Harvard Theological Review* 79 (1986), pp. 387–411; *idem.*, 'Bentham on Religion: Atheism and the Secular Society', *Journal of the History of Ideas* 47 (1986), pp. 95–110; *idem.*, *Secular Utilitarianism*, pp. 161–4 and passim.

82 Clark, *English Society 1660–1832*, p. 492.

83 John Henry Newman, *Discourses on the Scope and Nature of University Education* (Dublin, 1852), p. 132.

84 'At bottom, in Bentham and James Mill anticlerical and democratic opinions were confused . . .': Halévy, *Philosophic Radicalism*, p. 294.

85 Clark, *English Society 1660–1832*, chapter 4.

86 Halévy, *Philosophic Radicalism*, pp. 261–3.

87 Thomas, *Philosophic Radicals*, p. 33.

88 I differ here from the argument of J. R. Dinwiddy, 'Bentham's Transition to Political Radicalism, 1809–10', *Journal of the History of Ideas* 36 (1975), pp. 683–700. Although learned and illuminating, this article did not examine the category 'radicalism'.

89 Dinwiddy, 'Bentham's Transition', p. 688.

90 Recent scholarship has urged that Bentham's unpublished papers show that he was strongly led in the direction of universal suffrage by the logic of his utilitarianism as early as c. 1788–90. For an overview, see James E. Crimmins, 'Bentham's Political Radicalism Examined', *Journal of the History of Ideas* 55 (1994), pp. 259–81. Yet the evidence so far presented suggests that Bentham's priority in c. 1788–90 was to secure good government by procedural means rather than to begin with individual entitlements to the franchise. Nor would such a conversion in c. 1788 explain the conceptual innovations in the late 1810s and early 1820s examined here.

91 Halévy, *Philosophic Radicalism*, p. 259; Dinwiddy, 'Bentham's Transition', pp. 690–1.

92 Cf. Crimmins, 'Bentham's Political Radicalism', pp. 274–81. This ante-dating of Bentham's conversion to democracy to c. 1790 appears to neglect the emergence of religious questions to prominence in Bentham's thought in the years c. 1808–17.

93 Robert A. Fenn, *James Mill's Political Thought* (New York, 1987), pp. 30–3, argued that Mill's loss of faith owed much to conversations with Bentham.

94 Bain, *Mill*, pp. 22, 32, 88–9. In 1818, Mill was approached to be a candidate for the chair of Greek at Glasgow University: he declined, among other reasons being unwilling to subscribe to the Westminster Confession of Faith that the post required: *ibid.*, pp. 166–8. For Mill's atheism, see Crimmins, 'Bentham on Religion', p. 99. 'The Established Church in England was virtually Mill's *bête noire*': Fenn, *Mill's Political Thought*, p. 89. The extent of Mill's determination to transform the Church was only revealed at the end of his life in his article 'The Church, and its Reform', *The London Review* 1 (July 1835), pp. 264–304: Fenn, loc. cit., pp. 89–93; Bain, *Mill*, pp. 381–8. It was quickly followed by his equally revealing article 'Aristocracy' in *The London Review* for January 1836: Bain, *Mill*, pp. 399–403. For an element in Mill's intellectual formation that may have struck a chord with Bentham see Clark, *English Society 1660–1832*, pp. 159–60.

95 Thomas, *Philosophic Radicals*, pp. 99–100.

96 Even Bentham, according to Bowring's report, said of James Mill that 'His creed of politics results less from love for the many than from hatred of the few': Bain, *Mill*, p. 461.

97 Thomas, *Philosophic Radicals*, pp. 124–7, 133–4. For Mill's deliberate concealment of his 'profound radicalism' in this area, see Fenn, *Mill's Political Thought*, pp. 108–27.

98 Fenn, *Mill's Political Thought*, p. iv.

99 Cf. Wiener, *Carlile*, pp. 21–2, 24, 26, 63–5, 101–19.

100 Richard W. Davis, *Dissent in Politics: The Political Life of William Smith, MP* (London, 1971), pp. 190–203.

101 Jeremy Bentham, *Plan of Parliamentary Reform, in the Form of a Catechism, with Reasons for each Article, with an Introduction, shewing The Necessity of Radical, and the Inadequacy of Moderate, Reform* (London, 1817). The work consisted of a 337 page introduction to a 'Catechism of Parliamentary Reform' of 52 pages. In the Introduction, Bentham paid tribute to John Cartwright as 'the worthy father of radical reform' and commended the late Duke of Richmond for championing universal suffrage in 1780 and 1783: his pamphlet, urged Bentham, could be bought from William Hone's book-shops (*ibid.*, pp. xxxix, clii). Perhaps Bentham owned a copy of *The Bill of the late Duke of Richmond, for Universal Suffrage, and Annual Parliaments* (London: W. Hone, 1817).

102 Bentham, *Plan of Parliamentary Reform*, pp. ii, vi, xviii–xix.

103 Bentham, *Plan of Parliamentary Reform*, pp. xxxvi–xxxvii, lviii, xciii, 9.

104 [Jeremy Bentham], *Bentham's Radical Reform Bill, with extracts from the reasons* (London, 1819), pp. 1, 8–9.

105 Jeremy Bentham, *Church-of-Englandism and its Catechism examined* (London, 'printed, 1817: published, 1818'). This work includes *The Church of England Catechism Examined*, separately paginated. Perhaps the high price, 20s., helped shield it from legal action.

106 Bentham, *Church-of-Englandism*, pp. x–xi.

107 Bentham, *Church-of-Englandism*, pp xi–xii, xv, xix, xxxv–xxxvi, xliii.

108 Bentham, *Church-of-Englandism*, 'Church of England Catechism', pp. 194–5.

109 Thomas, *Philosophic Radicals*, p. 36.

110 In the 'Advertisement' to this work, Bentham explained that he was induced to publish by 'the addition so lately made of the scourge of religious persecution to the yoke of despotism': Crimmins, *Secular Utilitarianism*, p. 151.

111 Thomas, *Philosophic Radicals*, pp. 31, 42. Hone's works included *The Late John Wilkes's Catechism of a Ministerial Member* (1817); *The Political Litany* (1817); *The Sinecurist's Creed* (1817); *The Political House that Jack Built* (1819); *The Right Divine of Kings to Govern Wrong!* (1821), etc. Unusually, Hone's journey led in the opposite direction. He converted to Christianity in 1832, and was received into the Church in 1834: Smith, *Politics of Language*, pp. 154–201, at 174–5. For Hone's trials as a formative influence on 'Carlile's evolution as a radical freethinker' see Wiener, *Carlile*, p. 24.

112 For his republications of freethinking classics see Wiener, *Carlile*, pp. 35–6. Bentham tried to persuade Carlile to accept free legal representation, but he refused: *ibid.*, p. 45.

113 George Grote (1794–1871), heir to a banking firm. A Freethinker, he was introduced by Ricardo to Mill and by Mill to Bentham. Grote's first pamphlet, published anonymously, was *Statement of the Question of Parliamentary Reform* (London, 1821), which argued for virtually universal suffrage.

114 Crimmins, *Secular Utilitarianism*, pp. 207–26.

115 [Jeremy Bentham, ed. George Grote], 'Philip Beauchamp', *Analysis of the Influence of Natural Religion, on the Temporal Happiness of Mankind* (London: R. Carlile, 1822), pp. iv–v, 16, 35, 128–137.

116 James Steintrager, 'Language and Politics: Bentham on Religion', *The Bentham Newsletter* 4 (1980), pp. 4–20, at 10–11. Grote evidently omitted this material from the published version.

117 Place claimed editorship in a note on his copy, now in the British Library: Halévy, *Philosophic Radicalism*, p. 544; Crimmins, *Secular Utilitarianism*, pp. 227–53.

118 [Jeremy Bentham, ed. Francis Place], 'Gamaliel Smith', *Not Paul, But Jesus* (London: John Hunt, 1823), pp. v–vi, xiv, 366, 372.

119 Steintrager, 'Morality and Belief', p. 11.

120 Jeremy Bentham, *Radicalism not Dangerous*, in John Bowring (ed.), *The Works of Jeremy Bentham* (11 vols., Edinburgh, 1838–43), III, pp. 599–622, at 600, 609. This was the work's first publication.

121 Bentham, *Radicalism not Dangerous*, pp. 612–3, 616.

122 [John Locke], *Two Treatises of Government*, ed. Peter Laslett (Cambridge, 1988), I, s. 6; II, ss. 25–6, 34, 36, 50.

123 Thomas Paine, *Rights of Man: Being an Answer to Mr. Burke's Attack on the French Revolution* (London: J. S. Jordan, 1791), pp. 46–7.

124 Thomas Paine, *Agrarian Justice opposed to Agrarian Law* (2nd edn., London [1797]), pp. v–vi, 12, 16, 29: 'Land ... is the free gift of the Creator in common to the human race'.

125 T. M. Parsinnen, 'Thomas Spence and the Origins of English Land Nationalization', *Journal of the History of Ideas* 34 (1973), pp. 135–41.

126 John Dunn, 'The politics of Locke in England and America in the eighteenth century', in John W. Yolton (ed.), *John Locke: Problems and Perspectives* (Cambridge, 1969), pp. 45–80, at 68–9, quoting Thomas Spence, *The Rights of Man as Exhibited in a Lecture* (4th edn., London, 1793), pp. 23–4.

127 Thomas R. Knox, 'Thomas Spence: The Trumpet of Jubilee', *Past & Present* 76 (1977), pp. 74–98. For Murray see Clark, *Language of Liberty*, pp. 31, 124–5, 267, 329–31.

128 Thomas Spence, *The Rights of Infants* (London, 1797), p. 3.

129 Dunn, 'The politics of Locke in England and America', pp. 68–9, quoting *The Important Trial of Thomas Spence* (London, 1803), pp. 59–60.

130 Knox, 'Spence', p. 98.

131 Thomas A. Horne, *Property Rights and Property: Political Argument in Britain, 1605–1834* (Chapel Hill, 1990), p. 235.

132 Gregory Claeys, *Machinery, Money and the Millennium: From Moral Economy to Socialism, 1815–1860* (Princeton, 1987), pp. 8–9. The most clearly secular critique of landownership in the 1790s was that of William Godwin. Yet Godwin's atheism, like James Mill's, took its intellectual shape as a result of their abandonment of their careers as Nonconformist ministers: Clark, *English Society 1660–1832*, pp. 404–6. It is suggested here that Bentham and Mill were more influential in formulating a new doctrine in the 1820s than Godwin had been in the 1790s. Godwin's problem was that his doctrine undercut all private property; Ricardo's strength was that his was directed against the landlord.

133 For the role of Ricardian economics in negating the Anglican model of the social order see Clark, *English Society 1660–1832*, chapter 2.

134 For a rehabilitation of the Whigs and of Whiggism from the perspectives imposed on them by students of utilitarianism, especially Halévy, see William Thomas, 'L'utilitarisme et le libéralisme anglais au début du XIXe siècle', in Kevin Mulligan and Robert Roth, 'Regards sur Bentham et l'utilitarisme', *Recherches et Rencontres* 4 (Geneva, 1993), pp. 39–58.

135 Constraints of space prevent anything more than a brief consideration of the relation of radicalism to socialism: this deserves a study in itself.

136 For Richard Carlile invoking the 'Norman Yoke', Wat Tyler and Oliver Cromwell in these years see Wiener, *Carlile* pp. 30 n. 10, 31 n. 23, 116 n. 11.

137 *The Radical Reformer, or People's Advocate*, vol. 1, no. 1 (15 Sept. 1819), pp. 1–2.

138 'Carlile's radicalism, as it developed from the pressure of events in the early 1820s, was essentially preindustrial. It was not directed against the inequalities of the new economic system ... nor did it consciously appeal to the class feelings of poor people ... Carlile ... blamed the "traditional" enemies of the poor ... kings, lords, taxgatherers, fundholders, magistrates, and, above all, clergymen. They were the appropriators of the soil and of common property'; as Carlile wrote, '"Property holding tempered by the elective principle" would be allowed to flourish': Wiener, *Carlile*, pp. 101, 104–5. Wiener identifies Bentham's collaborator Francis Place as one man who encouraged Carlile towards full atheism in these years (ibid., p. 111).

139 Horne, *Property Rights and Poverty*, p. 227.

140 Henry Hunt (1773–1835). A parliamentary reformer since at least 1806, he lost money in a series of farming ventures and gravitated to the circle of extremists by the time of the Spa Fields meeting in 1816. In 1818 he stood for election at Westminster on a platform of universal suffrage, the secret ballot and annual parliaments. For his role in organizing the mass meeting at St Peter's Fields, Manchester, he was sentenced to two years' imprisonment in 1820. John Belchem's *'Orator' Hunt: Henry Hunt and English Working-Class Radicalism* (Oxford, 1985), explains Hunt's politics chiefly as 'democratic constitutionalism' via mass political mobilization.

141 Henry Hunt, *To The Radical Reformers, Male and Female, of England, Ireland and Scotland*, (1 July 1820; '40th day of the 2nd year after the Manchester Massacre', pp. 3–4; 23d Day, 2d Month, 2d Year ... p. 7). Hunt distanced himself from Carlile's atheism, but Hunt's diverse reforming enthusiasms lacked unity, and he was not a leader in the formulation of radicalism.

142 *Will Waver, or Radical Principles. A Tale* (Oxford, 1821), pp. 3–7, 22.

143 Although a distinction between 'productive' and 'un-productive' workers can be traced back at least to Adam Smith, it became polemical, and lost its technical meaning, after Ricardo.

144 Harford, *Principles of Thomas Paine*, p. 73. Denunciations of the national debt led some radicals like Cobbett into openly anti-semitic remarks about financiers: W. D. Rubinstein, 'British Radicalism and the "Dark Side" of Populism', in Rubinstein, *Elites and the Wealthy in Modern British History* (Brighton, 1987), pp. 339–73, at 350–5. The degree to which xenophobia and racialism were integral to early English radicalism, or part of racially unspecific denigration of groups outside Cobbett's ideal rural society, deserves further study.

145 *The Radical*, no. 1 (20 August 1831), p. 1.

146 Henry Hunt, *To The Radical Reformers* (1st Day, 3rd month, 2nd year ...), p. 20.

147 Clark, *English Society 1660–1832*, chapter 6.

148 *The Radical*, no. 1 (20 August 1831), pp. 1–3.

149 *The Truth. A Weekly Radical Christian, and Family Newspaper*, vol. 1, no. 1 (10 February, 1833), pp. 1–2.

150 [Thomas Peronnet Thompson], *The Article on Radical Reform. From the Westminster Review, no. XXII, For January 1830* (London, 1830), pp. 2–3, 8, 10. Thompson (1783–1869), an army officer, took up politics on his return from India in 1822 and soon associated himself with the circle of Bentham. In 1829 he became the owner of *The Westminster Review*, and wrote for it prolifically over the next seven years.

151 E.g. Thomas Doubleday, *A Letter to the Radical Reformers of Newcastle upon Tyne, on the Late Election and its Attendant Circumstances* (Newcastle, 1835), p. 10.

152 Arthur E. Bestor, Jr., 'The Evolution of the Socialist Vocabulary', *Journal of the History of Ideas* 9 (1984), pp. 259–302; G. de Bertier de Sauvigny, 'Liberalism, Nationalism and Socialism: The Birth of Three Words', *Review of Politics* 32 (1970), pp. 147–66, at 163–4; Gregory Claeys, '"Individualism", "Socialism", and "Social Science": Further Notes on a Process of Conceptual Formation, 1800–1850', *Journal of the History of Ideas* 45 (1986), pp. 81–93.

153 For the relations between socialism and radicalism in this period see especially Gregory Claeys, *Citizens and saints: Politics and anti-politics in early British socialism* (Cambridge, 1989), chapters 1–4.

154 *The New Moral World*, no. 50 (10 October 1835), pp. 396–7.

155 Samuel Bower, *The Peopling of Utopia; or, the Sufficiency of Socialism for Human Happiness: being a Comparison of the Social and Radical Schemes* (Bradford, 1838), pp. 3–4.

156 Bower, *Peopling of Utopia*, p. 4.

157 Bower, *Peopling of Utopia*, p. 4.

158 Bower, *Peopling of Utopia*, p. 5.

159 Francis W. Newman, *An Appeal to the Middle Classes on the Urgent Necessity of Numerous Radical Reforms, Financial and Organic* (London, 1848), pp. 4–5, 13. Not everything was immediately referred to economics. In 1832 Thomas Hodgskin invoked Lockeian natural rights arguments to contest the Benthamite case for inequalities of private property: Dunn, 'The Politics of Locke in England and America', p. 69; Horne, *Property Rights and Poverty*, pp. 237–43. Hodgskin was chiefly concerned with land.

160 Horne, *Property Rights and Poverty*, p. 234.

161 'Carlile, the prophet of a counter-hegemonic ideology of infidel-republicanism, was also the harbinger of the mid-Victorian *rapprochement* between radicalism and liberalism': Belchem, *Hunt*, p. 7. For the later evolution of the position see especially Miles Taylor, *The Decline of British Radicalism, 1847–1860* (Oxford, 1995).

162 'Are Radicals Socialists?' in Arnold Toynbee, *Lectures on the Industrial Revolution in England* (London, 1884), p. 204.

CHAPTER 11

Joseph Hume and the Reformation of India, 1819–33

Miles Taylor

In August 1831 Joseph Hume, the radical MP for Middlesex, introduced a little-known amendment to the reform bill. He proposed that nineteen extra MPs should be added to the House of Commons for the colonies (four for British India, eight for the Crown Colonies, three each for British America and the West Indies, and one for the Channel Islands). All those eligible for jury service would constitute the electorate in these colonies, and their chosen representatives would sit in Parliament for a guaranteed three years. Somewhat surprisingly, Hume's amendment was supported, not by his radical or Whig colleagues, but by a rather motley collection of ultra Tories: the Marquis of Chandos, Sir John Malcolm and Sir Charles Wetherell amongst the most prominent of those who seemed to have little problem with extending the vote to thousands overseas whilst resisting the £10 franchise at home.[1] Less surprisingly, the amendment was defeated, and although the Duke of Richmond tried to press it on his cabinet colleagues later in the year as they drafted the third version of their reform bill, the attempt to introduce direct representation of the colonies was unsuccessful in 1832, just as it had been when advocated sixty years earlier by principled Whigs such as George Grenville, and as it was later in the nineteenth century when put forward by cunning Tories such as George Curzon.

Hume's amendment, however, is more than a curious footnote to the history of parliamentary representation. It is an indication of how proximate a number of important turning points in Britain's imperial history were to the reform of parliament in 1832. The passage of parliamentary reform in Britain coincided with tithe reform in Ireland, slave emancipation in the West Indies, retrenchment in colonial armed forces across the globe, and with the renewal of the East India Company's Charter.[2] On closer examination still Hume's amendment reveals how intertwined parliamentary reform had become with the whole question of the government of India. Hume's principal support for his amendment in 1831 came from old Indian hands: from Sir John Malcolm, the former Governor of Bombay, and from Sir Charles Forbes, a leading Bombay merchant. Although other colonial interests were prominent in the campaign for direct colonial representation – above all the planters of the West Indies, whose nominal chief was the Marquis of Chandos – it was the India interest for whom colonial representation became an overriding concern. Indeed, the reform bills of 1831–2 provoked an unusual degree of excitement in British-Indian society more generally, especially in Bengal. Protest meetings were held in Calcutta when the Lords rejected the third bill, in London prominent Calcutta reformers such as Ram Mohan Roy waited anxiously for the Lords' decision, and as the reform debates were moving towards their climax during the spring and early summer of 1832, the unreformed Parliament was completing its last significant task: inquiring into the renewal of the East India Company's Charter.[3] The Select Committee on the East India Company's affairs, appointed in January 1832, was one of the largest parliamentary committees ever constituted, comprising 71 MPs. By day they heard evidence for and against the renewal of the Company's charter, by night many of them lined up on different sides of the reform question. This chapter surveys some of the reasons why it was that India came to loom so large in the reform of Parliament in 1831 and 1832.

It does so by looking, in the main, at Joseph Hume (1777–1855). For Hume was an old Indian hand as well. He had served as a surgeon in the East India Company's navy at the turn of the century. During the Maratha wars of 1802–6 he had occupied the lucrative posts of paymaster and postmaster in one of the Bengal native regiments. And on his return to England in 1808, with a fortune estimated at £40,000 he became a proprietor of East India stock, and for over twenty years was one of the leading voices of reform in Indian affairs – from the backbenches of the House of Commons, and to a far greater extent from the floor of East India House, where proprietors met four times a year to discuss the Company's affairs. Hume's Indian career and his participation in the Company's affairs have been altogether neglected by his biographers. Hume is nowadays mostly remembered as a somewhat dour Scot, whose dogged and pedantic questioning of government finance, usually late into the evening – sustained on his feet, apparently, by eating pears – kept the Commons sometimes amused but mostly bored for the best part of 35 years until his death in 1855.[4] Although he was associated with the 'philosophic radicals' around Bentham, Hume is not usually thought of as a fellow intellectual, nor is he associated with any particular shift in the development of English political thought.[5] This is an oversight, for his Indian dimension reveals him in a very different light – concerned with retrenchment, but much more preoccupied with what he and his colleagues defined as 'liberalism': judicial reform, so-called 'native' education, free trade and, above all, a free newspaper press. Hume occupied a prominent position as a conduit between merchants, officials, soldiers, judges and residents of Bengal, and the Company and Parliament at home.[6] These groups were predominantly British in origin, but as the 1820s passed Hume also became something of a spokesman for Anglo-Indian (mixed-race) and Indian reformers (principally Hindu) as well. He was an embodiment of the principle of virtual representation as far as Calcutta was concerned, and in this respect his career in the 1820s serves as a case-study of how the momentum for reform of the British state – and in particular, the ending of civil disabilities – was coming from far beyond the metropole.[7] By the late 1820s, Hume and his friends, together with agents despatched from Bombay and Calcutta, were pushing their campaign for the reform of the government of India out of East India House and into the English provinces and up into Scotland. By 1829 they had lit a spark on one issue – free trade to China – which began to mobilize merchants and manufacturers who within a few months added parliamentary reform to their list of demands. This chapter commences by looking at the Indian career of Joseph Hume. Then it turns to Hume's role in debates over Company policy in the 1820s, and then finally considers the public campaign against the renewal of the Company's Charter, which took place on the eve of parliamentary reform.

I

Joseph Hume worked for the East India Company for twelve years. He made a lot of money in India, and never lost his faith in the Company as a vehicle of benign modernization. Hume graduated from Edinburgh University in 1797, where he had studied anatomy, midwifery and chemistry, and he promptly joined the Company's naval service as a surgeon. Like many other enterprising Scots (and English), Hume clearly went into the Indian medical service with a view to enriching himself. Years later he defended the system of allowances or advances which enabled surgeons to retain the surplus of their annual budgets. Such bounties, Hume claimed in 1829, 'were the *stimulus* to embark, and their best consolation while abroad', allowing enterprising and hardy men eventually to return to England though, as he put it, 'God knew that few enough lived to realize their hopes'.[8] In 1796 Hume joined a Company ship, appropriately named 'Hope', as surgeon and made several voyages during the following three years, before entering the Bengal service of the Company as assistant surgeon in August 1799.[9] As a ship's surgeon he mixed philanthropy with good business, successfully increasing his allowance by treating not only the Company's officers and soldiers, but the lascars on board as well.[10] And later in Bengal in 1804 he was allowed by the Company to distribute for sale a medicine for liver complaint, which he himself had developed, throughout the Company's territories, free of freight charge. He also invented a way of keeping gunpowder dry, again something he exploited commercially.[11] In Bengal Hume was attached to the 13th Native Infantry under the command of Lt. Colonel Peregrine Powell.[12] The 13th – or 'Poel-ki-Paltan', as it was nicknamed – played a key role in the second Maratha war (1802–4), defeating the Rajput prince Shamshir Bahadur at the battle of Caspah in 1804. In 1803 Hume served as assistant surgeon in the hospital at the regiment's Chanar rock fortress in Mirzapur, along the Ganges valley, and the following year, probably because of his acquired fluency in Persian and Hindustani, he was made paymaster for the regiment, now serving in the Bundhelkhand, the conquered territory lying between the Ganges and the Yamuna rivers. For this purpose Hume was given an allowance of around 210 rupees per month (about £20). But it was in 1805 that Hume's real opportunity for lucre arose, when he was made postmaster, or dakmaster, for the whole of Bundhelkhand, a position he occupied until his return to England in the summer of 1808. Postmasters arranged the relay system of horses or palanquins which transported people or mail over the vast distances of northern India. Postmasters in India occupied an important strategic position, especially from the turn of the century onwards, when the Company suppressed the native dak system, and brought in its own postmasters. Communicating with villages and public functionaries all the way along the main arterial routes, knowing who was travelling where and when, and able to intercept the mail if need be, postmasters were often the best means of surveillance maintained by the Company. These were also highly lucrative positions, as postmasters charged their passengers at a rate of one shilling a mile.[13] It was probably by these means that Hume came by his Indian fortune. On his return to England he embarked upon a tour of England and Scotland, and then one of the eastern Mediterranean. By 1811 he had invested in £3000 worth of Indian stock, thereby becoming a proprietor, and in 1812 he bought himself a seat in Parliament, although he only remained there a few months.[14]

Back in Britain Hume quickly identified with the campaign to open up the Company's trade monopoly, possibly with a profiteer's eye on the commercial opportunities that would ensue. Along with others he pressed Parliament to throw open shipping contracts in the Company's tea trade with China to competition from private shipowners.[15] In 1813 he made a drawn-out attack on the high salaries being paid to Company directors, accusing the Court of endorsing too great a 'liberality'.[16] Like many returning nabobs, Hume clearly had his sights set on a Company directorship. He cultivated friendships carefully, and fell in love judiciously – in 1815 marrying Mary Burnley, the wealthy daughter of a proprietor of East India stock, thereby acquiring not only more of a stake in the Company, but also a nice stake in the country. Burnley Hall, near Great Yarmouth, became his provincial home for the next forty years. Hume's social ascent, however, did not take him to the peak of Company influence. He never became a director, and seems to have given up the pursuit after his campaign of 1813.[17] It was later put to him that his failure to do so was due to the fact that proprietors felt there were far too many Scottish directors already,[18] but it probably owed more to his increasing prominence as a free-trade critic of the Company's affairs. Whatever, there is little to suggest in Hume's Company dealings that before 1818 or so he was anything other than a Scot on the make and Indian take, an accusation that was often made in the 1820s.

But in 1818 Hume re-entered Parliament, this time as MP for Aberdeen, and it was from this point on that his views as an Indian reformer began to cohere. In one of his first (of many) speeches in the new Parliament, in March 1819, he spoke up for reforming the administration of justice in India. Poor policing, expensive litigation, long delays between arrest and trial and lack of uniformity between the presidencies meant that, he argued, 'the administration of justice in the whole of Europe did not cost so much as . . . in the British dominions of India'.[19] Hume's speech was not only noteworthy for the fact that he raised the issue of judicial reform in India – a topic which, as we shall see, was of recurrent importance throughout this period. But particularly interesting was his comparison between European states and British India. And of even more significance was the eulogy with which Hume ended his speech on that occasion. He praised the recent publication of Mr Mill, a book 'which contained so many accurate statements and so much clear reasoning, that it could not fail to be eminently beneficial'. The analogy with Europe and the reference to James Mill supply important clues as to the contexts in which Hume's views on India were taking shape.

Hume and James Mill were close friends, having attended as small boys the Montrose Academy at the same time – Mill was four years senior to Hume. When Hume settled in London on his return to England in 1808, he became a frequent visitor to Mill's Queen Square, Westminster, residence. Through Mill, Hume met Bentham and also London artisan radicals such as Francis Place, with whom he collaborated over, initially, the educational projects of Joseph Lancaster, but later and more famously, repeal of the Combination Acts in 1825, and the establishment of the Parliamentary Candidate Society in 1831. For all their collaboration, Place did not think highly of Hume, finding him 'devoid of information' and only making his friendship because Mill insisted that he might be worked on with favourable results.[20] But Hume proved much more than a utilitarian stooge in his views on India. There was a considerable difference between the indictment of East India Company policy offered by Mill and Hume's faith in Company rule. Hume knew Mill best before he became poacher turned gamekeeper, that is, before he joined the East India Company in 1819 as Assistant Examiner. Until that point, Mill had been a fierce critic of Company policy in India, fiercer than his *History of British India* (1817), in which the narrative stops at 1805, actually suggests. Mill's *History of British India* is, of course, renowned as a blueprint for the western, utilitarian modernization of India (and also an attack on the Anglican *ancien régime* at home) – a rebuke to a generation of 'Oriental' scholars such as William Jones and policy-makers such as Cornwallis and Hastings who had, according to Mill, exaggerated the efficiency of traditional Hindu law and administration, turned a blind eye to arcane religious practices and overstated the vibrancy of Bengal literary culture.[21] But in the dozens of articles which James Mill wrote between 1802 and 1818 for reviews such as the *Eclectic*, the *Edinburgh*, the *Monthly* and the *British*, there was a far more sustained assault on the East India Company itself, and it is this commentary with which Hume was probably most familiar.

In his articles on India for the reviews, which appeared with a particular intensity in the years surrounding the renewal of the Company's Charter in 1813, James Mill advocated the opening-up of Company territories to European commerce and colonization. It was impossible, Mill argued, for India to be governed from Britain. To the problem of distance was added the potential for corruption of parliament by Indian patronage. What was needed instead was government on the spot: a 'simple form of arbitrary government, tempered by European honour and European intelligence'. Perhaps, Mill suggested in 1810 – apparently in all seriousness – one of the royal family could be made a hereditary Emperor of Hindustan, and encourage the settlement of the country by Britons, who could then staff the judicial and administrative system.[22] Mill also castigated the drift of Company policy since 1793, by which more and more territory had been annexed, at increasing military cost and against the wishes of either Parliament or the Board of Control. Revenues from India were now (by 1813) outstripped by the costs of military occupation, and the English taxpayer was subsidizing it all, unknowingly for the moment, but not forever: Mill warned in 1815 that '[T]he people of England may by false representations be led on to support misgovernment in India with their own substance, till the poverty and degradation of this country be the deplorable result'.[23] In other words, India under Company rule was not a source of wealth to England, as many imagined. Unreformed, it was a burden, slowly crippling the polity at home.

Mill's critique of the Company, developed in the decade or so before he joined its salariat, found echoes in some of what Hume was to argue from 1819 onwards. Like Mill, Hume supported the European colonization of India, the end of the Company's trade monopoly and judicial and administrative modernization. But Mill's cricitism of Company policy also serves as a counterpoint to Hume's stance on several issues. Unlike Mill, Hume never became a great supporter of the Anglicization of the Indian judiciary and administration. As we shall see, he remained firmly in the 'Orientalist' camp, when it came to discussing education, and he proved more muted on issues such as *sati* than one might expect. Nor did he ever doubt the ability of the Company to be an agent for the moral reform of India. He did not swallow the radical line of some of the scholars and sycophants who gathered around the ageing Bentham, that imperium in India was imperilling liberty at home. This was a view that could be found, for example, in the *Westminster Review*, in which writers such as John Bowring advocated colonization of India and the transfer of rule from the Company to the Crown.[24] Hume remained a Company man. He was of course a proprietor. Unlike Mill and his acolytes he also believed that the Company had done a great deal of good. Hume felt that just as the forces of liberalism were gaining ground in Europe after 1815, so too were they under Company rule in India.

Hume saw Company rule in his lifetime not as an inefficient dictatorship no better than its Mughal predecessors, nor even as a wise despotism of the sort advocated by James Mill. Rather, he believed that, especially after 1813, there had been 'disseminated throughout that country, the enlightened views and liberal principles which had lately been gaining such progress throughout Europe', as he told the House of Commons in 1825.[25] And this brings us to the second context, alongside that of Mill's influence, which needs to be taken into account in any understanding of Hume's views on India. Hume saw India as analogous to Greece, or to Portugal and Spain, that is, countries of antique culture and civilization, which had thrown off religious and monarchic oppression and embraced liberal development. He had himself travelled in Greece and Egypt, and other parts of the Ottoman empire, and like many of his generation, being swept up in the philohellenism of the romantic era. Hume was encouraged in his viewing India through a European lens, by his association in the East India Company with Lord Byron's chums, John Cam Hobhouse, and especially with Douglas Kinnaird and Leicester Stanhope (the future 5th Earl of Harrington). The involvement of this merry crew in the politics of Greek independence is of course well-known. Bentham's fastidious plans for a Greek constitution; Stanhope and Byron's madcap soldiering in the Gulf of Pastra in 1824; Bowring, Hobhouse and Hume's shady role in the London-based Greek committee's raising of money to support the Greek cause in 1825 – have all been carefully documented.[26] But what has been overlooked is how the some of them – principally Hume, Kinnaird and Stanhope – were at the same time involved in what they called 'liberal' reform in India. Indeed, their reputation as Indian reformers predated their support of the Greek cause. This chapter now looks at Hume, his friends and their role in East India Company politics in the 1820s in more detail.

II

Until 1823 Hume remained a faithful though not uncritical supporter of Company rule in India. He had of course welcomed the breakup of the Company's monopoly on trade in 1813, and he continued to advance the cause of further free trade in the Indian and south-east Asian subcontinent. Hume resumed his friendship with John Crawfurd, like him an Edinburgh graduate and veteran of the Company's medical service and the Maratha war of 1803–5. Crawfurd had gone on to serve as trade envoy in Java and Siam and been part of Britain's government in Singapore; he was recognized as an authority on the commercial resources of the whole region.[27] Crawfurd returned to England in 1824 and Hume supported him in his call for opening up trade in the Indonesian archipelago.[28] Hume also became a sort of mini-clearing house for Company officials, soldiers and widows wishing to press their claims for promotion, compensation, pensions and other forms of redress on the Directors. There was one cause Hume advocated with particular enthusiasm in the early 1820s – the training of Company servants in proficient Hindustani. Hume befriended and became a vocal supporter of John Gilchrist, another former Company surgeon and Benthamite freethinker who was employed by the Company on an *ad hoc* basis to provide instruction in Hindustani, and of Sandford Arnot, who, following his deportation from Bengal, set up the London Oriental Institution, where he lectured on the Hindustani language and, less helpfully perhaps, Indian cookery.[29] At East India House Hume led a concerted campaign to ensure that all cadets were fluent in Hindustani before they left Haileybury, the Company college set up in 1818. In general, Hume disapproved of Haileybury (although his own son, Allan Octavian Hume, was sent there in the 1840s). Instead of creating a liberal elite, Haileybury was moulding a clinical despotism. As Hume put it in 1823, the Company college was 'educating a set of young men on an exclusive system, as a distinct class or sect . . . afterwards sent out to India, without an opportunity of having been afforded them of imbibing English sentiments and feelings.'[30] But Hindustani education aside, Hume was generally approving of Company rule. He revered the Marquis of Hastings, Governor of Bengal between 1813 and 1822, and he trusted George Canning, the President of the Board of Control from 1816 to 1822.[31]

In 1823, however, Hume's view of Company rule in India began to change markedly. The Marquis of Hastings left India in 1822, recalled under a cloud for approving a loan from the merchant house of Palmer and Co to the prince of Hyderabad. Into his shoes, temporarily, stepped John Adam, his secretary, who acted as Governor of Bengal in 1823, until the arrival of Lord Amherst, who then remained Governor until 1828. Between them, in the eyes of Hume and others, these two men – Adam and Amherst – turned back the clock in India, returning British dominion to the days of despotic and unaccountable government. One of the first things that Adam did was to revoke the licence of the *Calcutta Journal*, an English language newspaper, and deport its editor, James Silk Buckingham and its sub-editor, Sandford Arnot. With its regular criticism of Indian officials Buckingham's paper had been trying the patience of the Bengal government for some time, although Hastings' administration had resisted prosecuting him for libel, on the interesting advice of the Advocate-General, to the effect that a Bengal jury would view such a prosecution as, in his word, 'despotic'.[32] But Adam went further, not only deporting Buckingham, but bringing in a new Press Ordinance which was approved by the Calcutta judges in March 1823, and which effectively censored and shackled the Bengal press. Buckingham was deported in April, and the *Calcutta Journal* eventually had its licence withdrawn the following November.[33] In a public letter Adam defended his action, claiming that newspapers such as Buckingham's *Calcutta Journal* served only a mischievous purpose. They did not inform or enlighten the public, for in British India, there was no 'public' to inform. Adam undertook this action, later endorsed by Amherst and by Lord Liverpool's cabinet, partly on the advice of Sir John Malcolm, who, in a long memorandum written before his departure from India in 1822, warned that a free press in India would spread 'insubordination, contention, & disaffection, if not rebellion', especially amongst the Anglo-Indian community, that is the descendants of European men and Indian women, who staffed the quill-wielding local bureaucracy.[34] Significantly, Malcolm attributed the whole licentiousness of the press to the independence of the judiciary in Bengal, which since the 1790s had proved headstrong and defiant in the face of the Bengal government.

Here we have in miniature many of the issues which were to dominate subsequent discussion of Indian affairs both in Britain and in Calcutta, and, to a lesser extent, in Bombay, down to 1832. The revocation of press licences in Bengal raised a series of questions. What legal rights did Englishmen have in India ? By whom should Englishmen be judged in India – the Company, a jury of their peers, or by juries which included so-called 'native' members ? Who constituted the public in the three Presidencies, when the Company itself had the final say on who could settle and pursue trade there ? Were self-styled 'Indo-Britons' – the offspring of mixed marriages – part of the public or not ? What rights did they have ? What local check was there on the government of the Presidencies ? How independent could the judges presume to be ? As the news of Buckingham's deportation and the new Press Ordinance trickled back to England, Hume and his allies amongst the Court of Proprietors were fairly sure of the answers to such questions. From the summer of 1824 onwards Hume, Stanhope and Kinnaird, sometimes supported by Charles Forbes, used the proprietors' quarterly meetings to raise questions about the treatment of the *Calcutta Journal* in particular and the freedom of the press in general. Stanhope took up Buckingham's cause, likening him to Burke, Cornwallis, James Mill and the Marquis of Hastings, and promising to put his case before Parliament, 'where every man was entitled to seek redress; no matter of what colour, the whole of the inhabitants of India were virtually represented in the Parliament of this country'.[35] Hume was less enamoured of Buckingham, mindful of the fact that, as he put it, everyone who came into contact with Buckingham seemed to suffer. But he was convinced of the principles involved in the case, which he set out in two speeches to the Court of Proprietors in July and December 1824.[36]

In these speeches Hume refused to accept the axiom that India could only be governed by a despotism, a despotism which necessarily included proscribing the freedom of Englishmen who settled there. Before 1765, he argued, the government of India was 'undoubtedly a despotism', but, since then, courts of justice and the press had been established. Executive power in India remained paramount and irresistible – '[t]he proconsuls of ancient times never enjoyed greater power than their Governors in India did' – but it had been tempered by a free press, that 'potent engine', both in Britain and India for checking 'the most arbitrary tyranny'. Moreover, suppressing the press in Bengal, according to Hume, would have the effect of putting a halt to the diffusion of 'liberal and enlightened principles', such as those propagated by the numerous Bible societies, educational foundations and orphanages which had been set up in Calcutta. Indeed, societies such as these suggested that there was indeed a 'public' in India, which was expanding to draw in Indians as well. Here Hume cited the example of Ram Mohan Roy and his newspaper which was campaigning against 'idolotary'. In turning its face against this growth of enlightened opinion, Hume argued, the Company was acting like the Pope, or the kings of Spain and Portugal who had recently imposed similar restrictions on the press. Hume ended his second speech of December 1824 on a warning note, citing a 'foreign writer' – probably either Say or Sismondi, whose analyses of British India in the mid 1820s were well-known to Hume – to the effect that 'in every country of Europe where a free press existed, commotions were exceedingly rare; but, that where the press was destroyed, seditious meetings, or rather meetings for the recovery of public liberty, were extremely frequent'. What is particularly significant here is that Hume made no distinction between the governance of Britain and the governance of India. Both had the potential for despotism – Hume referred to the House of Commons as a 'tyranny having the exterior forms of a regular constitution' – both required a free press to check that possibility. Hume also disputed the the presumption – one shared by James Mill – that the 'public', or what we might call civil society along the lines of a European enlightenment model, was absent in India. Admittedly, Hume's definition of the 'public' in this instance seems restricted to the white

Anglican community of Calcutta, (although it is arguable, given his usual hostility to religious proselytizing, that this was a tactical argument). His colleague, Leicester Stanhope, certainly had only an exclusive and limited sense of the 'public'. In a letter to Jeremy Bentham in 1825, in which he praised Buckingham, Stanhope suggested that the readers of Buckingham's newspaper 'comprise almost the whole Indian public'.[37]

Over the next two years, events in India served to expand the identity of the Indian 'public' described by Hume and other liberal proprietors. In the early part of 1825 news began to reach London of a mutiny at Barrackpore, involving the Bengal 47th native regiment in the previous December, when soldiers destined for the war in Burma, having already marched 1000 miles, refused to go any further. 140 were shot dead and another 160, attempting to flee the bullets, were also killed.[38] The Calcutta press was not allowed to report the incident, and to concern over the freedom of the press, was now added grave disquiet at the whole system of rule associated with Lord Amherst, who had declared war on Burma, and who was having to redeploy rapidly hundreds of regiments from the north-west frontier and the conquered territories of the interior for the long haul eastwards. Hume brought up the Barrackpore incident at the Proprietors' meeting of March, 1825 and managed to gain enough support in the Court for a sustained campaign calling for Amherst's dismissal. This campaign included the highly unusual step of some Proprietors, including Hume, Kinnaird and Forbes, organizing a public meeting in London to voice their criticism. Hume also bombarded the Directors with private letters calling for the Court of Proprietors' meetings which discussed Amherst's policy to be made special and therefore extraordinary occasions, and for full discussion of Buckingham's case.[39] Both the Directors and the Board of Control seriously considered the recall of Amherst over the delay in publishing the papers relating to Barrackpore, but then dropped the idea.[40] Hume castigated Amherst for approving the high-handed action of Edward Paget, the commander of the regiment. Any governor worth his salt would have at least made enquiries about the troops' grievances, just as, Hume later told the Commons, '[s]ome years ago, in this very metropolis, harmony had been restored by similar means of remonstrance and conciliation'.[41] There was also a wider lesson to be learned. For Hume and Stanhope the connection between freedom of the press and the mistakes of military command was clear-cut. When the official papers on the incident were finally put before the Court in 1826, Hume suggested 'that where the evils suffered by military men were pent-up and concealed, the effect had often been a terrible convulsion, which led to the downfall of nations... therefore he deeply regretted the silence which was imposed upon the press of India'.[42]

Hume responded to Amherst's governorship, which even he was conceding by 1825 showed that Company rule did amount to 'a system of despotism', by reverting to his usual call for greater independence to be given to the judiciary, but now also demanding a widening of the composition of juries. In May 1825 he argued in the Commons that all Indian judges in the King's courts should be appointed for life, not as a sinecure, but to stop them being removed at pleasure.[43] In 1825 Hume was particularly exercised over the attempts of Amherst and Adam to remove Edward West, one of the Bombay King's court judges, from his position, due to the too great a leniency he was reported to have shown to Indian offenders. The following year, much to the liberal proprietors' delight, the Bombay judicial bench ignored the subservience of their brethren in Calcutta, and refused to pass a restrictive Press Ordinance.[44] Hume also began to campaign, mainly in parliament, for inclusion of mixed-race and native Indians, at a judge's discretion, on grand juries in the three Presidencies, as had been introduced in Ceylon, something he pressed on the cabinet in March 1826. The secretary to the Board of Control, Charles Williams Wynn, trotted out the usual reply, to the effect that no complaints had been received from India complaining about the exclusion of natives from juries there.[45] The obvious implication was that India lacked public opinion, therefore the judicial system was safe in the hands of the white governing class.

By 1826 Hume was clearly at the limits of the uses to which the Court of Proprietors, and, to a lesser extent, the Commons, could be put as forums for the reform of abuses in India. Hume remained adamant throughout this whole period that it should be the Directors and the Proprietors who discussed and decided Indian affairs. 'That Company [and not Parliament]' he told the Court in December, 1826, 'were the sovereign of India, and ought not to allow, while they possessed that power, any others to exercise it for them; if they did they might be assured they would lose it forever'.[46] But the Company, in its treatment of the press in Calcutta, its refusal to condemn Amherst and Paget and in its apparent undermining of judicial independence in both Bombay and Calcutta, seemed, in Hume's view, bent on not doing its job properly. From this point on – 1826–8 – Hume began to hint that pressure would have to be brought from outside the Court of Proprietors and indeed, from outside the Commons, if the Company were to reform itself before the Charter was up for renewal in 1832–3.[47] Hitherto, Hume's career as an Indian reformer mirrored his career as an English reformer – bringing about discrete policy changes by working persistently behind the scenes, avoiding publicity, using private contacts and influence, as well as sheer weight of assembled evidence. Now he was advocating going public in order to reform India, a shift in attitude which was paralleled by his decision in 1830 to forsake a small Scottish burgh, and contest a populous London constituency – Middlesex – where, outside of the City of London, East India Company proprietors were thickest on the ground. In doing so, Hume was absorbed into the public campaign for the reform of Indian government, which became linked into the wider issue of parliamentary reform at home.

III

By the late 1820s, the East India Company was in dire financial straits. The combination of a landholding system which yielded low revenue together with a bloated civil administration, and a constantly expanding frontier, requiring more garrisons and ever-more volatile mixes of indigenous troops, guaranteed the pushing of Indian retrenchment to near the top of the agenda for the cabinet by 1828.[48] In that year Sir Robert Peel warned the Duke of Wellington that the Company was not far off insolvency.[49] Bentinck was sent out to replace Amherst as Governor of Bengal, and got downsizing off to a belated start, and Sir John Malcom returned to India with a similar remit as Governor of Bombay. But by then, many merchant houses in India had been hit by the splash-back from the English banking crisis of 1825–6, and many Indian residents were objecting to the increasingly draconian forms of indirect taxation brought in by Amherst and his successor Bentinck in order to bale out the fiscal crisis. Back in Britain, the prized Chinese trade, monopolized by the Company, was looked on by prominent merchants in several ports – principally Glasgow, Hull and Liverpool – as a fair alternative to American and European markets which were becoming increasingly competitive. So when Hume and his liberal friends amongst the Court of Proprietors began to go public, there was something of a ready-made audience, both in Bengal and parts of Britain, for public criticism of the Company.

In India the spark which ignited the campaign was local reaction to the new Stamp Act, brought in towards the end of 1827 – a uniform duty on all public documents, be they newspapers, legal materials, vital registration papers, etc. Mindful of what John Adam, the acting Governor of

Bengal had declared in 1823, i.e., that there was no Indian public, critics in Calcutta now had a field day, arguing logically that if there was no public, then how could its publications be taxed. One pamphlet, written in Calcutta, but published in London, declared that '[t]his shadow of a public has started into life – it moves for itself – it is become a remonstrating and petitioning body, conscious of its rights, calmly bent upon obtaining them...'[50] The British merchants of Calcutta appointed John Crawfurd as their agent in Britain, and he promptly set about alerting newspapers and of course, his old friend Hume, with the effect that Calcutta's opposition to the Stamp Act received wide coverage in London – the *Examiner* newspaper, for example, noted how the Calcutta pamphlet recalled the rhetoric of the days of Benjamin Franklin and American independence.[51] Crawfurd also wrote a series of pamphlets, advocating colonization and a break-up of the Company's monopoly; on behalf of the Calcutta merchants he began to look to the British provinces for support – metropolitan London being deemed too much under the sway of Company influence.[52] In his turn to provincial support Crawfurd was joined and overtaken by James Silk Buckingham, the deported editor of the *Calcutta Journal*, now resident in London and publishing the *Oriental Herald*. In new year 1829 Buckingham, deeply aggrieved over his treatment by Adam and Amherst, began a lecturing campaign throughout England and Scotland, ostensibly giving talks on his experiences of India and the near east, but as it turned out using the tour as a platform for attacking the Company monopoly on trade and settlement. During the course of 1829 Buckingham visited Liverpool (on several occasions), Birmingham, Bristol, Hull, Manchester, Whitby, Glasgow and other Scottish towns.[53] What happened after one of Liverpool lectures was fairly typical. A separate meeting had been organized to discuss the merits of petitioning Parliament for ending the Company's China trade monopoly. Prominent local merchants of all shades of political and religious opinion, for example, John Gladstone, William Ewart, William Rathbone and Thomas Thornley, all supported the idea. Then some speakers at the Liverpool meeting passed from considering the affairs of the Company to a wider attack on the 'boroughmongering' House of Commons which for so long had propped up the East India monopoly.[54] Thus, in the spring and summer of 1829, long before Thomas Attwood began to assemble the Birmingham Political Union, the demand for parliamentary reform was beginning, in a piggy-back fashion, within the agitation against the renewal of the East India Company's Charter.

By 1829 Hume found himself joined in the Commons by more supporters of free trade in India and China, including William Whitmore, a Shropshire ironmaster, who in 1832 became one of Wolverhampton's first MPs. And Hume, naturally enough, became the figurehead, alongside Whitmore, Charles Forbes and James Mackintosh, for the anti-Company petitions which came into the Commons by the dozen during 1829 and 1830. Many of these petitions included the Company's inability to suppress *sati* as one of its many failures. In the Commons Hume also continued his campaign for reforming the judicial system, by widening the composition of juries.[55] This cause was given a great boost when the Bombay government finally lost all patience with its judges and forced the removal of one of them, John Grant. In the new year of 1830 details of Grant's treatment began to emerge, leaked to the Calcutta newspaper, the *Bengal Hurkara*, and then passed on (allegedly by Hume) to the *Times*. Lord Ellenborough, the Tory President of the Board of Control was revealed to have written to John Malcolm, the Governor of Bombay, that the only way to treat wayward judges like Grant, was to deal with them as one would a 'wild elephant', training it into submission by making it walk between two tame elephants, ie the Board of Control and the Governor. Ellenborough's letter caused a furore, clearly revealing what many critics had suspected, that the Company had no time for an independent judiciary.[56] The 'wild elephant' episode, it might be said, was the straw which broke the camel's back. Hume raised the issue of Grant's treatment in the Commons on 5 February 1830 almost as soon as Parliament reassembled and four days later Wellington's government appointed two Select Committees – one in the Commons and one in the Lords – to inquire into the Company's affairs with particular reference to the China trade. Within a year these committees had dovetailed into the much larger committee which deliberated over the renewal of the Company's Charter. Within a year too, Wellington's government had fallen, mainly because of its poor record on retrenchment, and the Whigs had come in; many of the same merchants, manufacturers and ex-Company employees who had gathered to hear and cheer Buckingham during 1829, now turned their attention to parliamentary reform.

IV

And so we come full circle. When Joseph Hume stood up in the House of Commons in the middle of August, 1831 and made his amendment to the reform bill, calling for colonial representation, he did so not as an extreme radical or zany utilitarian, as he is often caricatured, but as a veteran of twenty years of East India Company politics, and, increasingly in the 1820s, the virtual member for the empire. The franchise which Hume suggested for the empire – a jury qualification – was potentially an extensive one, especially given that Hume had campaigned for overhauling the composition of Indian juries and giving them a native or at least mixed-race element.[57] His notion of who constituted the public in India had been greatly expanded by the events of the 1820s that this chapter has described. Hume's conception of citizenship in the empire broadened just as the question of the franchise at home was beginning to be debated by Parliament. Not surprisingly, some of those East India Company proprietors who supported his amendment, such as Sir John Malcolm, insisted that MPs for India be elected by the holders of Company stock and no-one else. They did not share Hume's notion of an Indian public. But it is important to recognize that Hume's amendment was, in many respects, a defensive move, an admission of the failure of the East India Company to reform itself. Had the Company properly conducted its affairs by listening to its Court of Proprietors, then its sovereignty over the government of India would not have been questioned and the possibility of colonial representation or indeed intervention by any institution other than the Company would not have arisen. In that sense, Hume belonged in the anti-reform camp, insofar as he wished to uphold the established rights of a chartered company, just at the moment when Parliament was attacking corporations all round. But just as the value of its stock barely kept par after the mid 1820s, so the Company's reputation suffered as well. The treatment of the press in Calcutta, the 'wild elephant' affair of Ellenborough and Malcolm, and the sheer weight of revelations about the Company's parlous revenues all fuelled widespread public opposition to renewal of the Company's charter. Hume would rather have dealt with these problems literally in-house, but with noisy and embittered friends such as Crawfurd and especially Buckingham, that proved impossible. Their campaign against the Company's monopoly on trade and settlement threw a shaft of light on the 'boroughmongering' and 'rotten' state of parliamentary representation, demonizing the East India MPs in much the same way as West Indian proprietors became targetted by the anti-slavery campaigners. In this sense imperial interests were very much part of the system of 'old corruption' that came under attack in 1831–2. One effect of this was that the East India interest in the Commons was cut by a third between the general election of 1830 and that of 1832, so that when the Charter came up for renewal in Parliament in 1833, the Company's advocates were far fewer.[58] Hume himself played an important part in the inquiries into the Company's Charter, serving on all three of the Commons' Select Committees between February, 1830 and July, 1832, including a long stint on the busiest part of the inquiry – the Finance and Accounts sub-committee of 1832.[59] Somewhat inadvertently Hume the Indian liberal had helped paved the way for English radical reform.

Hume welcomed the main terms of the Company's renewed Charter, agreed to by Parliament in July 1833. The Company lost its monopoly of the China trade and the territorial revenues of India were transferred from the Company to the Crown. Political power was retained by the Company and the Board of Control, but the Governors' powers became hedged in by a strengthened higher judiciary and by the provision of advisory councils. Hume opposed Buckingham's (now MP for Sheffield) insistence on abolition of the Company, but he did call for future renewal of the Charter at ten not twenty year intervals, for greater native representation on the new councils and for some permanent members of the Board of Control.[60] What happened next – the Whig and utilitarian experiment in India under Bentinck, Macaulay, Dalhousie and the rest – is of course well-known, or at least much better known than the tale told here.[61] Of much of it, Hume would have disapproved – policy made in England not India, the drive towards Anglicization in education and administration, the roughshod treatment of native princes. True, his old Byronic pal from the early 1820s – John Cam Hobhouse – was President of the Board of Control in the Whig administrations of the 1830s and 1840s, but Hume's time as an Indian reformer came to a close. By the late 1830s Hume had got rid of most of his India stock, and although he was active in defending the claims of the deposed Rajah of Sattara in 1848–9, and although he spoke out against the activities of Sir James Brooke in Borneo in 1853, his days became spent in arguing for English not Indian retrenchment, and for the civil liberties of London artisans rather than Bengal merchants, Company officials and native Indians.[62] Hume, in other words, became the radical reformer of legend. But, as this chapter has atempted to demonstrate, he reached that destination via a long Indian liberal detour. As Hume told the Court of Proprietors in April 1833, he considered that 'India had been, through all its difficulties, a source of great moral if not of pecuniary support to England', whereby the British might manage their dominion in a more liberal manner than had been achieved by other European powers such as the Spanish, Dutch or the French.[63] Moreover, Hume's campaigning on behalf of imperial subjects, whose civil rights were more precarious overseas than they were at home, is an important reminder of how the reform of the British constitution in the late 1820s and early 1830s was not only a product of the banking houses of Birmingham, the dinner table of Holland House, or the taverns of Covent Garden. It was also made in India.

ACKNOWLEDGMENT

An earlier version of the chapter was given to the 'Reconfiguring Britain' seminar at the Institute of Historical Research, London. I would like to thank all those who commented on that occasion. I am particularly grateful to Peter Marshall and Jon Wilson, whose expertise on Bengal proved especially valuable.

NOTES

1 *Hansard*, 3rd ser. vi (16 August 1831), cols. 110–42.
2 For a fuller discussion see my 'Empire and parliamentary reform: the 1832 Reform Act revisited' in A. Burns & J. Innes (eds.), *Rethinking the Age of Reform: Britain 1780–1850* (Cambridge: Cambridge University Press, 2003), pp. 295–311.
3 *India Gazette* [Calcutta], 10 April 1832, pp. 2–3; Sophia Dobson Collet, *The Life and Letters of Raja Rammohun Roy* (1900; revised edn., Calcutta, 1962), pp. 331–4; C. H. Philips, *The East India Company, 1784–1834* (Manchester, 1940), ch. 10; Philip Lawson, *The East India Company: A History* (London, 1993), pp. 157–8.
4 Ronald K. Huch and Paul R. Ziegler, *Joseph Hume: The People's MP* (Memoirs of the American Philosophical Society, vol. 163, Philadelphia, 1985) includes the bare minimum on Hume's service in India, whilst Valerie Chancellor, *The Political Life of Joseph Hume, 1777–1855* (privately printed, London, 1986), pp. 14–16 is more expansive.
5 Alexander Bain, *James Mill: A Biography* (London, 1882), pp. 76–7; Graham Wallas, *The Life of Francis Place, 1771–1854* (London, 1898), pp. 183–4. See also: William Thomas, *The Philosophic Radicals: Nine Studies in Theory and Practice, 1817–1841* (Oxford, 1979), where Hume has an occasional walk-on part.
6 Hume's biographers have been handicapped by the loss of his personal papers in a fire. But he bequeathed a huge collection of pamphlets – over 1000 separate items – to the library of University College, London, many containing his own marginalia and accompanied by correspondence. Sixteen volumes of this hitherto neglected source are comprised of pamphlets devoted

to Indian affairs, principally before 1833, and together with the debates at East India House, they provide the basis for this chapter.

7 In the early 1830s Hume also acted on behalf of settlers in Upper Canada, and was sounded out as agent for Prince Edward Island in 1841: Phillip A. Buckner, *The Transition to Responsible Government: British Policy in British North America, 1815–50* (Westport, Connecticut, 1985), pp. 28–9, 44–5n. He was also a vocal supporter of settlers in the Cape during the 1820s: A.V. Millar, *Plantagenet in South Africa: Lord Charles Somerset* (Cape Town, 1965), p. 221. For a broader picture of Anglo-Indian culture in Bengal in the 1820s, see: P. J. Marshall, 'The Whites of British India, *1780–1830*: a failed colonial society', *International History Review*, 12 (1990), 26–44, esp. 31–5.

8 'Debate at East India House' [hereafter EIH Debates] (16 Dec. 1829), *Asiatic Journal* 1 (Jan-April, 1830), pp. 53–4.

9 DG Crawford, *History of the Indian Medical Service, 1600–1913* (2 vols., London, 1914), ii, p. 78.

10 Hume to Court of Directors, Bombay Public Consultations, 7th May 1800, Oriental & India Office Collection, British Library, London, [hereafter OIOC], F/4/89.

11 East India Company, Court of Directors Minutes, 20 June 1804, 18 July 1804, OIOC, B/139.

12 East India Company, Personal Records, OIOC, O/6/17, p. 323; *East India Register and Directory*, 1804–8. For Powell, see the entry in V. C. P. Hodson, *List of Officers of the Bengal Army, 1758–1834* (4 vols, London, 1927), iii, pp. 563–4.

13 C. A. Bayly, *Empire and Information: Intelligence gathering and social communication in India, 1780–1870* (Cambridge, 1996), pp. 58–60; M. Fisher, 'The East India Company's "suppression of the native dak"', *Indian Economic & Social History Review*, 31 (1994), 319–26; 'Travelling by dak', *Asiatic Journal* (May-August, 1833), pp. 181–4.

14 East India Company, Stock Ledgers E-K (1807–18), OIOC, L/AG/33. For Hume's early career in the House of Commons, see the entry in R. G. Thorne (ed.), *The House of Commons, 1790–1820, IV: Members*, G-P (London, 1986), pp. 262–5.

15 Hume later claimed he petitioned Parliament over this issue before he became an MP (EIH Debates, 21 Dec. 1825, *Asiatic Journal*, xxi (Jan. 1826), p. 123), but there is no evidence of this petition in the Commons Journals. In June 1810 the Company's shipping monopoly was subject to some reform.

16 *The Speech of Mr Joseph Hume at East India House on the 6th of October 1813, upon the motion for an increase of the salaries of the Directors of the Company* (London, 1813), pp. 6–7, 10–19, Hume colltn., UCL, 112/3.

17 Robert Chambers (comp.), *Biographical Dictionary of Eminent Scotsmen* (5 vols, revised edn., London 1875), iii, p. 311. In 1818 Hume confessed to a friend seeking patronage that he was 'not on a footing with any Director

to whom with propriety I could at present apply.': Hume to George Sinclair, 20 October 1818, Sinclair Mss, National Archives of Scotland, Edinburgh, vol. 8.

18 EIH Debates (20 Dec. 1820), *Asiatic Journal* xi (Jan., 1821), p. 98.

19 *Hansard*, xxxix (16 March 1819), col. 1003.

20 Wallas, *Life of Francis Place, 1771–1854*, pp. 183–4.

21 Eric Stokes, *The English Utilitarians and India* (Oxford, 1959), ch. 1; George D. Bearce, *British Atiitudes Towards India, 1784–1858* (Oxford, 1961), pp. 65–78; Javed Majeed, *Ungoverned Imaginings: James Mill's The History of British India and Orientalism* (Oxford, 1992), ch. 4; Nigel Leask, *British Romantic Writers and the East: Anxieties of Empire* (Cambridge, 1992), pp. 87–8.

22 [James Mill], 'Affairs of India', *Edinburgh Review* xv (April, 1810), pp. 155–6.

23 [James Mill], 'Tytler's Political State of India', *Eclectic Review* iv (Oct. 1815), p. 318. Mill cited Hume's speech of June 1814 as evidence of how parlous the Company's finances were: Mill, *History of British India* (10 vols, London, 1817), v, pp. 22n, 25n.

24 [John Bowring], 'Colonization and commerce of British India', *Westminster Review*, xi (Oct. 1829), 326–53.

25 *Hansard*, new ser., xii (24 March 1825), col. 1169.

26 Douglas Dakin, *British and American Philhellenes during the war of Greek Independence, 1821–33* (Thessaloniki, 1955). For Stanhope in particular, see: F. Rosen, *Bentham, Byron and Greece: Constitutionalism, Nationalism and early Liberal Pooitical Thought* (Oxford, 1992), ch. 8, esp. p. 148.

27 For Crawfurd, see: Nicholas Tarling, *Imperial Britain in South-East Asia* (Oxford, 1975), pp. 50–1, 90–6; Jane Rendall, 'Scottish Orientalism: from Roberson to James Mill', *Historical Journal*, 25 (1982), 43–69.

28 *Hansard*, new ser., xi (17 June 1824), col. 1447.

29 For Gilchrist's earlier career in India, see: David Kopf, *British Orientalism and the Bengal Renaissance: the Dynamics of Indian Modernization, 1773–1835* (Los Angeles, Calif., 1969), pp. 31, 83–4. Hume later referred to Gilchrist 'as honest a Man as I ever knew': 'Portrait of J.B. Gilchrist' [n.d.], Hume papers, National Library of Scotland, Edinburgh, Acc. 11, 638.

30 EIH Debates (18 Dec. 1822), *Asiatic Journal*, xv (Jan., 1823), p. 161; cf. EIH Debates (19 Dec. 1821), *ibid.*, xiii (Jan., 1822), pp. 79–83

31 EIH Debates (4 April 1821), *ibid.*, xi (May, 1821), p. 483; EIH Debates (29 May 1822), *ibid.*, xiv (June, 1822) p. 66.

32 'Extracts from a Public General Letter concerning the Calcutta Journal' (28 May and 25 June 1819), Adam papers, OIOC, Mss Eur F109/51.

33 M. K. Chanda, *History of the English Press in Bengal, 1780–1857* (Calcutta, 1987), ch. 25.

34 'Minute of a meeting of Liverpool, Canning, Wynn, the Chairman, Deputy Chairman and members of the Secret Committeee of the East India Company' (1 March 1823), Amherst papers, OIOC, Mss Eur F140/63; Sir John Malcolm, 'Memorandum' (12 April 1822), *ibid.*, F140/63.

35 EIH Debates (18 Jan. 1826), *Asiatic Journal*, xxi (Feb. 1826), pp. 261–2. See also Stanhope's *Sketch of the History and Influence of the British Press in India, containing remarks on the effects of a Free Press, etc* (London, 1823). Buckingham also sought out aid from John Bowring: Buckingham to Bowring, 2 Sept. 1823, cited in B.M. Sankdher and I.B. Roy, 'James Buckingham, East India Company and a plan for the future government of India: a study of sources', *Indian Historical Records Commission: Proceedings* 44 (1976), p. 240.

36 EIH Debates (23 July 1824), *ibid.* (Sept, 1824), pp. 270–85; EIH Debates (22 Dec. 1824), *ibid.* (Jan. 1825), pp. 65–75.

37 Stanhope to Bentham, n.d. [1825], British Library, Add. Ms. 33,546, fols. 58–9.

38 For the Barrackpore mutiny, see: Douglas M. Peers, *Between Mars and Mammon: Colonial Armies and the Garrison State in India, 1819–35* (London, 1995), pp. 170–5.

39 East India Company, Court of Directors, Minutes, 6 Dec. 1825, 7 Dec. 1825, OIOC, B178; *British Interests in India: Resolutions of a Meeting held 28th December 1825* (1826), Hume colltn., UCL, 114/7; *Hansard*, new ser. (2 Feb. 1826), col. 62, *ibid.* (6 Feb. 1826), col. 100.

40 Williams Wynn to Amherst, 22 Dec. 1825, Amherst papers, OIOC, Mss Eur 140/107.

41 *Hansard*, new ser., xvi (22 March 1827), col. 1323.

42 EIH Debates (26 July 1826), *Asiatic Journal*, xxii (Sept. 1826), pp. 335–7.

43 *Hansard*, new ser. xiii (13 May 1825), cols. 586–7.

44 P. Dawtrey Darvitt, *Bombay in the Days of George IV: Memoirs of Edward West, Chief Justice of the King's Court during its conflict with the East India Company* (London, 1907), ch. 12.

45 *Hansard*, new ser. xv (20 March 1826), cols. 107.

46 EIH Debates (20 Dec. 1826), *Asiatic Journal*, xxiii (Jan. 1827), p. 174.

47 *ibid.*, p. 174; *Hansard*, new ser., xviii (25 March 1828), col. 1343.

48 Peers, *Between Mars and Mammon*, chs. 7–8; Seema Alavi, *The Sepoys and the Company: Tradition and Transition in Northern India, 1779–1830* (Delhi, 1995), pp. 8–9.

49 Peel to Wellington, 18 Aug. 1828, *Despatches, Correspondence and Memoranda of Field Marshal Arthur, Duke of Wellington (1827–28)* (8 vols., London, 1871), iv, p. 632.

50 *An Appeal to England Against the New Indian Stamp Act* (London, 1828), pp. xii-xiv, Hume colltn. UCL, 111/3.

51 *Examiner*, 2 March 1828, pp. 130–1. For Crawfurd's mission: *Report of the Proceedings at a General Meeting of the Inhabitants of Calcutta, on the 15th December, 1829* (Calcutta, 1829), Hume colltn., UCL, 108/7, pp. 8–10. In April, 1828, Crawfurd sent Hume a copy of the anti-Company *Report of the Liverpool East India Association* (Liverpool, 1828), *ibid.*, 108/8. Crawfurd later lobbied the government direct: Crawfurd to Huskisson, n.d. [1830], BL, Add. Ms., 38,743, fol. 302.

52 [John Crawfurd], 'Indian taxation of Englishmen', *Edinburgh Review* 47, (Jan. 1828), 134–84; Crawfurd, *The Chinese Monopoly Examined* (London, 1829); *idem.*, *View of the Present State of Free Trade and Colonization of India* (London, 1829), Hume colltn., UCL, 108/9.

53 J. S. Buckingham, *History of the Public Proceedings on the Question of the East India Company Monopoly* (London, 1830); Ralph E. Turner, *The Relations of James Silk Buckingham with the East India Company, 1818–36* (Philadelphia, PA, 1930); *idem.*, *James Silk Buckingham, 1786–1855: A Social Biography* (London, 1934), pp. 238–45; D. Eyles, 'The abolition of the East India Company's monopoly, 1833' (unpublished PhD thesis, Edinburgh, 1956), pp. 144–8.

54 *Oriental Herald & Colonial Review*, xx (1829), p. 501.

55 Between 1829 and 1833 261 petitions were presented to the Commons, protesting against the Company's monopoly, and 201 to the Lords: Eyles, 'Abolition of the East India Company's monopoly', p. 215; William Whitmore, *Substance of a Speech . . . on Trade with the East Indies and China, 14th May 1829* (London, 1829). For the petitioning campaign over sati, see: Lata Mani, *Contentious Traditions: The Debate on Sati in Colonial India* (Los Angeles, Calif., 1998), pp. 23–4; Clare Midgley, 'Female emancipation in an imperial frame: English women and the campaign against sati (widow-burning) in India, 1813–30', *Women's History Review* 9, (2000), 95–112. For Hume on jury composition, see: *Hansard* new ser., xxii (5 June 1829), col. 1754.

56 *Times*, 28 Jan. 1830, p. 2; entries for 28 Jan. and 29 Jan., 1830 in *A Political Diary, 1828–30, by Edward Law, Lord Ellenboorough* (2 vols., London, 1881), ii, pp. 39–40. Grant sent his own account of the episode to Hume later in the year: *Memoir by the Honourable Sir John Peter Grant Kt. of the reasons which induced him to resign his commission of one of His Majesty's Puisne Justices of the Supreme Court of Judicature, Bombay* (Bombay, privately printed, 1830), Hume colltn., 117/10; Dawtrey Darvitt, *Bombay in the Days of George IV*, ch. 17; J. W. Kaye, *The Life and Correspondence of Major-General Sir John Malcolm, GCB, etc* (2 vols London, 1856), ii, pp. 525–40.

57 Judicial reform in Bengal continued to be brought before Hume's attention during 1832. On moving to Calcutta from Bombay, John Grant kept Hume informed of judicial affairs there. He complained to Hume of the 'altered state of this Bar . . . it is quite certain that the natives are afraid of entering the Supreme Court' and hoped that the new government in Britain would take care to select better judges: Grant to Hume, 23 March 1832, Brougham papers, UCL, Ms. 18, 123.

58 Philips, *The East India Company*, ch. 10; Eyles, 'Abolition of the East India Company's monopoly', pp. 217–36.

59 *Report of the Select Committee on the East India Company's Affairs (Finance and Accounts): Evidence*, British Parl. Papers (1831–2), x (Pts. 1–2).

60 *Hansard*, 3rd ser., xix (10 July 1833), col. 498, (12 July 1833), cols. 618, 629, (16 July 1833), cols. 666–7. In supporting the transfer of the revenues to the

Crown Hume did, it should be noted, propose better terms of compensation for proprietors than were being offered: EIH Debates (22 April 1833), *Asiatic Journal*, n.s. xi (May-Aug., 1833), pp. 145.

61 Bearce, *British Attitudes Towards India*, ch. 6; Stokes, *English Utilitarians and India*, passim; Lynn Zastoupil and Martin Moir (eds.), *The Great Indian Education Debate: Documents Relating to the Orientalist-Anglicist Controversy, 1781–1843* (Richmond, 1999); S. C. Ghosh, 'Bentinck, Macualay and the introduction of English education in India', *History of Education* 24 (1995), 17–24; Jacob Thiessen, 'Anglo-Indian vested interests and civil service education, 1800–58', *Journal of World History* 5 (1994), 23–46.

62 East India Company, Stock Ledgers E-K, (1837–49), OIOC, L/AG/45. For Hume's campaign on behalf of the Rajah of Sattara, see: Hume to Hobhouse, 19 Oct., 1848, 20 Nov. 1848, 28 Nov., 1848, 1 Jan. 1849, Broughton papers, OIOC, Mss. Eur. F213/19, pp. 56–9, 64; Hume, *A Letter to the Right Honourable the Earl of Malmesbury . . . Relative to the Procedings of Sir James Brooke . . . in Borneo* (London, 1853).

63 EIH Debates (22 April 1833), *Asiatic Journal*, n.s. xi (May-Aug., 1833), pp. 137–8.

Afterwords

Afterword: Radicalism Revisited

Conal Condren

Nothing expresses the precarious modality of historiography more than worries about the historian's vocabulary. What might seem to be matters of 'mere' semantics, housekeeping, sectarian infighting or signs of intellectual under-employment, may be much more than any of these. Although historians do not enjoy a specialized and insulating vocabulary, they do have a variable sense of being engaged in a distinctive activity. This means that while they can borrow from elsewhere to enrich their work, by doing so they risk eroding or reforming their awareness of disciplinarity.

One can identify two problematic sets of relationship for historiography: the discourse of neighbouring academic disciplines and subject areas, such as anthropology, economics and psychology, and the forms of discourse of daily moral and social commitments. The history of historiography may be seen as an interplay between these webs of association. None of them are totally entrapping, or amenable to neat patterns of change, but they make it difficult to see any static essence of intellectual integrity to which all historians adhere, or towards which they have struggled. Certainly a concern with anachronism provides a robust thread of continuity, but it remains an underdetermined criterion of judgment and demarcation. Additionally, its saliency is more clearly tied to the narrative and descriptive functions of historiography than to the explanatory. As these are easily entangled the results can be decidedly messy: little wonder that when evoked in criticism, accusations of anachronism can seem suggestive of double standards or lack of reflexivity.[1] Historiography then, is best identified less in terms of achievements, shared paradigms, as they were once called, or a doctrinal credo, than by a configuration of attitudes, revealed and negotiated precisely when historians focus on the mere semantics of their own discourse.

It is this issue that holds the present volume together. And it is possible to divide the essays into two fairly neat groups. There are those dealing with times in which the nouns 'radical', as a political actor, and 'radicalism' can be found flourishing like mushrooms, so raising questions concerning scope, meaning and force of words actually used, or when not used overlooked or displaced. They exist, in Russellian terms, as part of the historian's object language. And there are those dealing with the time in which the noun 'radicalism' did not exist, and it, like 'radical', as a political actor rather than a root, must needs be sown by the historian, in the interests of historiographical mediation, re-descriptive interpretation or explanation; it is part of the historian's meta-language. As a whole, the essays are about a presence whatever its meaning, or an absence construed as a presence by reading back from later usage or across from patterns of metaphorical association. It is the latter group, the contributions, by Alford, Borot, Burgess, Greaves and, near the perimeter, Philp, Hampsher-Monk and Clark that, in Richard Hooker's terms form the 'battel ground' for the following reflections.[2] For the questions raised by them are important and extend to the nature of politics and historiography themselves. How and in what ways can it make historical sense to talk of radicalism and its variant forms (radical as adjective and noun) and in respect to what delineating paradigmatic vocabulary (conservative, reactionary, liberal, traditional) and what whole syntagma of relationships, progressive, marginal, innovatory, reformist, extreme, moderate, subversive and so on? Can it, as Richard Greaves argues, be usefully purged of its modernizing penumbra of associations to render it if still technically, at least harmlessly anachronistic? Is it, as Glenn Burgess claims, a partial misdescription for the religious construction of politics? What are the specific dangers of relying on it? If, as Hampsher-Monk suggests, radicalism was a fragmented force, a linguistic counter-factual in the 1790s why do we need to construe it even as present? Conversely, what are the consequences of trying to dispense with it?

Barely a generation ago, while words like 'left' and 'right' were being recognized as anachronistic, potentially misleading and so at least needing to be contained in 'scare quotes', the abstraction radicalism was hardly noticed. Rather, the presupposed phenomenon it labelled was the focus of attention. Radicals were important, though usually marginal, their actions and attitudes being taken to be a major explanatory force in historical, especially political and social change. Radicalism was thus a potent category of analysis, framed by the similarly important, though undeniably less exciting phenomenon of conservatism. It was a force, it had a history and alleged traditions of radical political theory and practice attracted possibly disproportionate attention given the number of people apparently belonging to them. The Russellian categories alluded to above of object and meta-language, may not always be viably distinguished, but there is little doubt that the persistent confusion between them when historians wrote about radicalism detracted from the value of a good deal of work.[3]

Matters began to change, I think, after J. C. Davis's first critical exploration of radicalism in early-modern Britain. This raised the crucial question of what might be involved in establishing a model for successful radical change in a traditional society.[4] Although, historiography being the sprawling beast that it is, some still proceed as if such questions have never been asked, far less of what was assumed of radicalism, above all political radicalism, can now be taken for granted. Over the last fifteen years or so, the words 'radical' and 'radicalism' have increasingly appeared in the ambivalently protective and subversive inverted commas that so often signal the guttering presence of half-dead semantic stars.

It is vital here to stress the looseness of the abstraction radicalism, for it captures the multivalence illustrated in this volume. Most obviously, one must distinguish it in the context of different sets of historically specific relational terms such as Jacobinism, socialism, antinomianism and Lutheranism. This, however, leads to broader point that because of its generality, radicalism may be injected into quite different discursive contexts. The predominant notion of political radicalism may have nothing but a loose association of historiographical ideas with philosophical or scientific radicalism. To allude to one unfortunate title, we might create a quite specious sense of paradox and surprise by seeing Thomas Hobbes as *A Radical in the Cause of Reaction.*[5] The general descriptor, 'radicalism' may thus blur important distinctions, or create the impression of some underlying phenomenon, of a *zeitgeist* working its way from politics to formal logic and architecture. It is for this reason that portmanteau terms like radicalism taken to a world in which they did not literally exist need to have their differing, slippery and sometimes obfuscating functions made clear.

First, radicalism has been used for what can be construed as a distinct intellectual and emotional force: it marks an ideology or a doctrine, and so may be some relatively coherent social phenomenon to which people can be committed and which might explain their actions. This, albeit none too precisely, may be called dispositional or doctrinal radicalism and is important to understanding Bentham, as the essays by Clark and Rosen demonstrate. It is largely this sort of radicalism, I think, which Hampsher-Monk argues failed as a language of politics in French

Revolutionary England. Overwhelmingly, such doctrinal radicalism has been seen in terms of political dispositions and principles, amounting to hostility to tradition, the status quo, and exhibiting faith in the possibility of a new and better society and so is apt to presuppose a progressive structure to social time. It was this that a generation or so ago was taken to be a fairly continuous tradition in English politics and which Colin Davis constructively questioned. It is this that is the major casualty of Jonathan Clark's essay. Secondly, radicalism may refer to a contingent social grouping of frustrated exclusion, which may be called alienated radicalism. It is this that Mark Philp pinpoints and such an understanding is drawn on also by Richard Greaves in his attempt to reserve a neutral sense of radicalism for those disaffected with the status quo. Thirdly, there is what might be called simply extremity radicalism, the term predicating actions, policies and arguments considered untoward, in some way immoderate and surprising. Our sense of extremity radicalism may be a function of contextual ignorance, but in principle, it is difficult to see how we can dispense with some such notion.

There are, I shall argue, inherent or potential problems with all senses, but it is best to begin with the most ecumenical point. Any of these uses might be merged or confused. Indeed, a characteristic of the literature devoted to radicalism has been the creation of a coherent phenomenon by running them together. There might not be a specific doctrine, but from the consequences of social interaction, historians have been apt to assume an underlying disposition towards dissatisfaction with a perceived status quo and a desire to create something new. From this point it has been easy to elide the different senses of radicalism as varying manifestations of the disposition. All radicals being on the side of the future has been the crucial thing; their putative existence puts a little bit of us in the past and a little bit of them in the present. The radicals have seemed to stand at the fundamental nexus of historical significance and contemporary relevance.

This leads directly to a further point, quite simply that the radical family of words and its neighbours originated in political polemic and edification and has retained in mutated and sometimes muted form a practical moral and political vibrancy, thus tying historiography to its own origins in political commitments.[6] There is no doubt that one reason for the persistence of the vocabulary of radicalism in historiography is to maintain this relationship, justified in two complementary ways: that the historian should be a participant in political debates, and/or that the use of such words renders history more intelligible beyond the realms of professional discourse. I don't want to take up such issues of intellectual casuistry directly (they are not much apparent in this volume), it is simply to be noted that in them lies a rationalization for the erosion of historiographical conventions of argument and standards of proof. There is sometimes the implicit rider, the Matthew gambit, that those who wish to dispense with radicalism in historiography are actually hostile to radicalism in a political context. Those who are not with me are against me. But with due respect to the New Testament, this is bad logic that does not in any case correspond to the complexity of the historiographical situation. Many who do not see themselves as committed to political radicalism or 'left-wing' or 'progressive' politics have been quite happy with the terminology of radicalism in historiography; some who do don't use it.

One crucial problem beyond political affront is that we are not having to cope in any of the senses identified above with an isolated term and its cognates, but with a relational sub-field of our political vocabulary which, complex and variously loaded as it is, has slipped into historiography only partially to be domesticated by established historicist concerns for the minimalization of anachronism. It is this that has led recently to some historians continuing to use the term sometimes in scare quotes perhaps because they see how radical are the consequences of doing without such language. As I have suggested before, we might, then, have reached the point hypothesized by Quine when dealing with natural languages: we know a translation is inadequate, but it will have to do.[7] The problem is a genuine one, only I don't think we have really reached it with radicalism.

The point can be made by the emergence of my own purely contingent interest in the issue. Some years ago I was asked to participate in a political theory seminar on conservatism. It was chaired by a senior colleague who, although avowedly conservative, was happy to adopt a radical position if students too easily agreed with him. The educational aim was provocation, the unhistorical presupposition was that the political world pivoted on such a distinction. On the reading list was an anthology called *The Conservative Tradition*, a sort of titular companion to *The Radical Tradition*. Reading *The Conservative Tradition* made us wonder whether there was any such thing. The problem was not generated by or lay with radicalism per se (a word hardly mentioned in the book) but with the historiographical validity of the dichotomy of which it was a defining part. It was this that had been cosmically projected to suggest over-arching (or underlying) conceptual phenomena well beyond the contemporary world in which, undeniably, words like radical and conservative remain important. Even now, however, this dichotomy is neither exhaustive of modern political dispositions nor discriminate and stable. Radical has conceptual space in the context of further allied terms, reactionary, liberal, moderate, left, right, centre and progressive, and European and North American associations differ markedly. As Rosen concludes his essay, when we are talking about Bentham's radicalism, one problem lies in delineating it from liberalism. As Clark argues in his, the central Benthamite distinction is between radicalism and socialism.

Most of these terms adjacent to radicalism have been suitable candidates for reification; any might give spurious universal significance to local preoccupations. When first forced to confront their slippery uses, it became clear to me that the place of such terms in historiography might be driven largely by contemporary political commitments and the need to invent traditions to service them. But the prominence of these dichotomous 'isms' might also be sustained by the industrial and economic nous of capitalist publishers. Recent work on the mechanisms by which canonic literatures are created suggests a symbiotic relationship between academic empire building and the commercial interests which can help advance careers, so creating an image of energetic study on widespread and important literary movements.[8] In a much weaker sense and without suggesting any such industrious networking, it is understandable that established evocative terms should provide focal points for publishing titles and blurbs. How much this explains the continuance of the vocabulary of radicalism is impossible to tell; but it is certainly the publishing perception that Antinomians don't sell, radicals do.

For all that, I had certainly underestimated the historiographical cum political commitment to radicalism as a coherent phenomenon. I had not seen what Alistair MacLachlan has explored, the extent to which historiographical narrative can come close to political allegory and that the need for a radical tradition in English historiography was tied to the disintegration of the belief in the British Civil Wars as the first in a series of modernizing revolutions. This collapsed into the capacious claim that the whole civil war, even the early-modern period had been revolutionary in its consequences, a retreat from any helpful understanding of causation. This in turn has withered into the conviction that at least the radicals tried, they showed us an alternative way.[9] Awareness of the radical tradition authenticates and keeps before us significant political choice, although if Burgess is right, it is exactly this that is wrong. For some, then, much more has been at stake than cauterizing an unselfconsciously and over-extended sector of the historian's vocabulary; it has been a matter of what sort of political activity is possible and legitimate. Not fully realizing the depth of political commitment led me to underestimate the impact of my first delivered paper on this subject. The cunning plan was to cut an ecumenical swathe through a communal carelessness by citing as many examples as I could from the work of my expected audience. I succeeded only in dividing it into those who talked to me after and those who didn't.[10]

Given that this volume displays quite different functions for the radical family of words, there is probably no one answer as to what we can do with it; and the preceding essays have certainly refined my rather dismissive views, in one way making them more austere, in another less so. I had isolated extremity radicalism as innocent and largely unproblematic; but in fact, extremity radicalism can be an insufficiently discriminate notion. Luc Borot's valuable essay on Overton gives a clear impression of radicalism as standing in opposition to moderation. In the sixteenth and seventeenth centuries however, the whole vocabulary of moderation was unstable and contested, so it hardly makes for reliable points of contrast or agreement.[11] Borot is clearly aware of the need for some definitional care here, but despite initial attempts there is a double sense of moderation as flexibility, and as mainstream, or disciplined action. Thus extremity radicalism may mean unwavering and adamantine, or extreme in behaviour. Interestingly, each possibility may draw on the differing metaphorical associations of *radix*, the root, so seeming to present a unified concept: extremity radicalism suggests the firmly rooted and also the need to prune back to the root, or even to root out.

Neither sense, however, is necessarily distinguished from conservatism and may easily enough be conjoined with an appeal to tradition. As the 'root and branchers' made clear in their rhetoric of reform for the English church. They wanted to root out episcopacy which had taken too firm a hold, so pruning back to purity the authentic church. Or consider The Levellers: 'Because we would have the dead and exhorbitant Branches pruned, and better sciens grafted, therefore we would pluck the Tree up by the roots. Yet thus we have been misconceived...'[12] Fancifully abridged, 'don't call us radicals', to which the reply has been, 'we don't believe you. We need you to be radicals'. Yet, to call them radicals, even qualified as extremity radicals, hardly does justice to the nuances of their claims, as Burgess's essay outlines. They insist, conventionally enough that any government is better than none and they are rooted very firmly in a world in which justifications for action are best tied to conservation. They express not a radicalim as such but what may be called an extremity casuistry of conservation – in extremis you may innovate to conserve. It is a familiar rhetoric of justification ('spare the rod and spoil the child', 'be cruel to be kind'), its salient features being the paradoxical affirmation of a valued end through means that are accepted to be questionable.

Indirectly, Borot's usage raises difficulties for Richard Greaves's attempt to neutralize radicalism, and indeed use it as a means to cope with the highly prejudicial vocabulary of political positioning in seventeenth-century argument. Radicalism as a general classifier for all contemplating extreme action against the Stuarts, retains its positive twentieth-century associations with directional innovation. In previous discussions I had certainly underestimated justificatory appeals to innovation and Greaves's argument provides independent evidence to support this criticism.[13] But innovation is no simple marker for 'radicalism'. Characteristically, justifications for innovation were made by Needham and Sidney, are further examples of the extremity casuistry of conservation.[14] The advocacy of innovation is not antithetical to but, cloaked in a sense of conservation, it accepts that previous innovations (those of papacy, espiscopacy and royal aggrandisement) had been a cause of evil. It is also a defensive attempt to deflect the force of a normally odious term. All of this means neither that innovation marks a radicalism opposed to conservatism, or moderation, nor that there is any inconsistency in a writer by turns appealing to the need to innovate and the need to conserve against the innovations of others. Yet Greaves brings together under one heading much material that affirmed traditionality and accused the Stuarts of innovation. Further, some of this material is evidence of extreme action but not necessarily an unwavering position.

Greaves is surely on strong ground to say that the intended consequences of extreme behaviour would have meant the overthrow of the Stuart monarchy, so bringing about a new situation. Yet this remains a tenuous justification, I think, for the label 'radical'. This is partly because identification by consequence is a touch arbitrary; it is, more importantly, a classificatory move which obscures or ignores the very point at issue, namely the language of justification which remained largely tradition centred, even when innovation was evoked. The new situation (and all situations are in some sense new) might have been in the justificatory argot of the time a restoration, reformation or return. On all sides, the issues of late Restoration politics were shaped by a powerful awareness of a traumatic past and, as it were, of unfinished business, a sense, as Hampsher-Monk correctly states, that survived in England to the end of the eighteenth century, for the French Revolution was mediated by understandings of the meaning and potentialities of an authoritative past.

And so, hardly surprisingly, pervading all the 'radical manifestoes', to say nothing of the work of people like Sidney was a heady mixture of appeals to restoration and reformation against the innovations of the regime alongside a casuistic mitigation of innovation in the name of primordial values and purer societies.[15]

It is important then, to distinguish a present regime or situation, a status quo, from tradition, reformation from transformation and innovation from change or progress, for much of the evidence mustered by Professor Greaves maintained that the present regime was not traditional, the Reformation was threatened and customary property was at risk, perhaps by the greatest of innovations, a transformation to Catholicism which had been perilously close in the recent past, and because of the same ruling family and its new counsels. Such possible changes were anything but a reformation as the case of Sidney and his associates makes abundantly clear. For such people, violence was a justifiable last resort to protect what had been achieved.[16] The classifier 'radical' remains too porous a term to capture the evidence, whilst its use still illustrates the problem of mis-description Davis and I initially confronted, the misfit between the justificatory rhetorics of tradition and the historian's sense of what is innovatory or will have radical consequences. In a word, 'radicalism', requires that we overlook the seventeenth century use of terms like reformation and innovation, their implications and associations and replace them with our own. Both Borot and Greaves are sensitive to the difficulties in dealing with seventeenth-century political and religious nomenclature, but I remain more skeptical than either about how much can be read from the pragmatic structure of what survives. In so far as we might use the word innovation and its cognates as a set of markers for what we call radicalism, we are identifying a widely available but rarely used rhetoric of emergency in a tradition-centred society, little wonder that, in Hampher-Monk's and Philp's terms it remains 'fragmented'. As this rhetorical and casuistic status is insufficiently recognized across the whole literature addressed to tracing the history of radicalism, it is difficult to see what can be construed concerning underlying or implicit political identities and the interplay of historical narrative and explanation.

Greaves's evidence, however, is wonderfully diverse, and he is careful and surely correct not to impute any core doctrine of radicalism; and it was doctrinal radicalism, rather than my own under-specified extremity radicalism that I argued was so distorting when transported into the early-modern world. As the problems here so easily flow through to adjacent uses of the word, the case bears a minimal restatement. William S. Connolly has argued that descriptions do not involve the merely ad hoc labelling of phenomena, but the imposition of a cohesive perspective.[17] His point is not one of inescapable logic for isolated terms can be taken from one discursive framework to another and be effectively assimilated. This, however, requires very stable conceptual relationships in the new environment, exactly what we do not have in historiography. It also requires what we have never had in the literature on early modern radicalism, a comprehensive delineation of what it does not mean when taken from its conventional network of associations. In the absence of this care, because radical hunting has carried so many modern expectations, the whole structure of earlier argument has been, I argued, misunderstood and systematically misdescribed through the more accessible political vocabulary of a post-French revolutionary world the use of which imposed an unduly modernizing perspective.[18] To provide a crude synopsis: in a world in which most people attempted to co-opt rhetorics of tradition, 'radicalism' ended up largely as our description of the strained exploitation of such idioms of conservation.[19] As Robert von Friedeburg has recently remarked of European *politica* writing in general, it was meant to be 'an *ars conservandi* in times perceived to be troubled'.[20] There seemed, and still seems to me, to be the following explanatory possibilities for our persistently reading against the grain of the *ars conservandi* of English political discourse: Either we didn't recognize the place of words like restore, reform, return, in a justificatory rhetoric of tradition and a fortiori not notice that words like innovation and newness were predominantly prejudicial; or we did not find the use of such language convincing as expressions of the customary; or we had been persuaded by hostile contemporaries that these arguments were not properly at one with authentic tradition. And sometimes this was inadvertent as we did not notice the terms in which hostility was couched. Such possibilities fit well enough with Colin Davis' perceptive remark that in the seventeenth century we find not so much radicals as people having radical moments: they are, I argued, apt to be moments of mishap.[21] In short, seventeenth-century radicalism was largely the progeny of careless if enthusiastic history. The gist of this I think still stands and has recently been re-enforced by evidence of which I was ignorant.[22]

Moreover, what I did not do was to take account of the possibility of alienated radicalism, a condition of frustrated exclusion, which may slide into extremity radicalism as either producing extreme reactions to a given set of circumstances and/or exhibiting positional inflexibility.

Mark Philp makes a strong case for a need for a concept of alienated radicalism around the time of the French Revolution. There may be indirect support to be drawn from Kedourie's thesis, that early nationalistic doctrines in all their passionate extremity were developed by and attractive to the over-educated and marginalised of post-French Revolutionary Europe.[23] But in such contexts, and Professor Greaves's turbulent Restoration may by extension be one of them, the predicate radical is not only dependent on an expressed sense of frustration but also upon the historian's preceptions of centrality. From the nineteenth century the historian can at least simply ask if radicalism was used in this sense; before then, it is a considerably more tendentious issue. If this alienated radicalism may result in extremity radicalism, the work of the Marian exiles Ponet, Goodman and Knox may provide the most likely examples; it may also just as plausibly result in highly conventional and flexible responses. John Humphrey, for example, was persistently frustrated at being excluded from the Church of England after he left it in 1662. But from then until his death in 1719 he presented a persona of compliance and support in the hope of a policy of comprehension that would welcome him back in his clerical office. Once these possibilities are taken into consideration there is no warrant for a rescue of the radical tradition, or the refashioning of a hagiography of radicals, (Knox and Goodman would be among the elect), neither of which, of course, Philp attempts. The result is more likely to be a fragmented history of casuistic moments, shared by the otherwise most unlikely of fellow-travellers.

Similarly, once such variations are entertained, the use of the word radical invites the use of its delineating neighbours, (conservative, moderate, liberal, reactionary) to capture what in one way or another radical excludes. We are back with the problem of importing into the description of a pre-French Revolutionary world a whole intrusive vocabulary from later times. Neither does alienated radicalism account for figures who, at the centre of things, embark on dramatic policies: Pope John XII and Bismark and Mrs Thatcher, to say nothing of Alford's instigators of the Association of 1584 or Charles II's cuddling up to his cousin Louis. These would have to be radical in a different sense. Given such variables housed under the accommodating auspices of 'radicalism', we may have additional arguments for doing away with the terminology wherever we can, especially if we are concerned with reaching rather than misleading a wider audience.

Burgess' subversive exploration of the central case of civil war radicalism raises additional issues. He leaves my arguments intact with respect to the anachronistic abridgment of seventeenth-century discourse; but, he suggests, beyond politics one can find future-minded and doctrinally-based figures who fit some of the criteria that might justify the label radicals. The somewhat Davisonian irony is that these are non-political millenarians whose sense of time and change, makes them look decidedly dated and even apolitical. Much of what we call radicalism, argues Burgess, is what seems in part to be an inadequate understanding of a religious construction of the political. Where a quite different facet of an under-specified radicalism is apparent in politically central actors such as the Levellers, we are confronted again by the pervasive use of rhetorics and casuistry of traditionality. Irrespective of issues of avoidable anachronism, the use of the portmanteau radicalism, he concludes simply, blurs important lines of intellectual and social demarcation.

These are important arguments, not least for their far-reaching implications concerning the distinction between the political and non-political, on which he has written incisively in a different context.[24] Most significant here is the distinction between the political and the religious. God was known to work in mysterious ways, *Flavit Javhe et dissipati sunt*, according to the medal commemorating the dispersal of the Armada in 1588. Sir Henry Spelman's *History of Sacrilege* shows that one did not have to be a 'radical' to accept a pretty thorough infusion of God's ways with the whole history of human endeavour.[25] An appeal to God and what might be done, or had to be done at the due time, could be casuistic mitigation for violence. As Willie Lamont has argued, reading the map of Revelation for knowledge of the Last Days could be central to political action or inaction.[26] Harry Vane was probably seen as too dangerous to live because of the possibility of converting mystical theology into violence.[27] Overall, a strong if variable sense of the theological colours civil war discourse and it raises the question of whether those Burgess has isolated as seemingly radical because of their perception of time and change were really only making explicit what in different contexts many would have accepted. Christian time was lineal, so those who feared the consequences of explicit escatology might have inflicted what we have seen as radicalism upon those who expressed it. Burgess valuably insists on distinguishing people lumped together as radicals, so constituting a mythic identity of radicalism. To allude to Hampsher-Monk's argument and its problems, shortly to be addressed, Burgess reveals a radicalism sufficiently fragmented to deny the plausibility of its reification. If so, I think this is right, but to distinguish in terms of the political and its religious construction, is to point to something both unstable and negotiable. The alacrity with which seventeenth-century people claimed God was working through them, or others soon to come, might even suggest a hermeneutic lifeline for those who would risk decoding eschatology into political doctrine and re-asserting a radical tradition. His argument, then, makes imperative the one thing we do not have, a thorough mapping of the political in seventeenth-century England. In the meantime his conclusions are bound to sound paradoxical, that those who look most radical, might best not be called that. The argument leaves us with the imponderable: if what we have called radicalism was a religious construction of the political, what in the seventeenth century does a non-religious construction look like?

It might appear that the most difficult issue concerns the identification of radicalism as a cohesive intellectual phenomenon on the eve of the invention of the neologism. The closer we come to the invention or a metaphorical translation of a term, the more acute seems the question of whether the concept came first. There remains great appeal in Nietzsche's dictum that the name-givers are the great originals for they make us see what was already before us.[28] Once William Thoms had invented 'folklore', a cohesive industry grew up.[29] Once Tourette's syndrome was identified, 'touretters' were seen everywhere.[30] Once Bentham had invented 'radicalism' and provided himself with a lineage from Hume (the conservative?) and Helvetius, it is easy to see the word as what Bentham himself warningly called a 'certificate' for a prior phenomenon.[31] And there is indeed a danger of mystification if recognition of the organizational potential of language is wedded to theories which presuppose language to have a predominantly representational or certifying function. Ogden and Richards posited a triangular relationship between words, phenomena and concepts; and although such triangulations make sense of some word use in the context of the informational functions of language, in general it encourages the reification of a conceptual realm for words to represent.[32] This remains a problem endemic to *Begriffsgeschichte*, despite its extraordinary care in diversifying our sense of contexts for word use. Hence the problem of radicalism might be construed as replacing the label, finding a less formally anachronistic term for the phenomenon, or, as Greaves argues, purging it of its modernizing associations to capture the phenomenon more historically.

To assume, however, that radicalism is merely an infelicitous or reformable descriptor for what must already be in the evidence is to miss the point; the issue is whether the phenomenon is created by the act of assigning a name, or through a new classifier's reorganization of the evidence. In either case, it is a matter of whether we are dealing in a strict sense with a weak performative in the context of the expressive and creative functions of language. A number of Hampsher-Monk's comments on language seem to me to point independently in this direction. As I've suggested, the act of labelling is, in any case, more than a matter of singular substitution, the noun radical and the covering term radicalism remain Trojan horses taking with them a whole delineating subset of the vocabulary, a descriptive perspective and its multiple associations into an alien past; it is precisely this which marks the shift from the informational to the creative. So, in the name of representing something from the past, we end up re-presenting our own semantic and conceptual world in it.

There are many reasons for the reification of conceptual realms but simplistic views of language remain of importance. Concepts, however, need not be treated in a way that encourages bypassing the material evidence. Characteristically, when historians use the word concept, it is to signal a high tolerance of semantic substitution under the auspices of a given concept expression. The term concept may be seen minimally as a meta-locution, from the concept of the indefinite article to the concept of the divine.[33] We can, I think, treat concepts not as independent things, constituting a sphere analogous to the material whose history in any literal sense can be written, or to which the historian has independent access, but as generalized shorthands for more specific standardized patterns of word use.

The word atom, for example, has survived in use since antiquity. Yet, to state the obvious, it does not refer to *the* concept of the atom; the conceptual functioning of the word is understood to be theory dependent, and we can recognize theory dependency by the sorts of terms (molecule, particle, quark and so on) that enable the word atom now to have a particular conceptual status. Moreover, even over the short time-span of the twentieth century we can see a serious change in the conceptual functioning of the word atom precisely because we can identify theory dependency through the new semantic neighbours that 'atom' has acquired (consider heavy water, H_2O_2) and with these we can talk meaningfully of sub-atomic physics. Ignoring the specific configurations of words, allowing each to have a discrete conceptual status easily encourages the projection of a theoretical object creating the illusion of historical discovery analogous to an archaeological find. Yet, when historians may be said to have discovered a concept, it is usually because they have been able to offer a redescription that makes better historical sense of the evidence they already have; it reorganizes more coherently, suggestively and less anachronistically than had been possible beforehand. The argument has been that the concept of radicalism makes poorer historical sense of what we have and not perceiving the specific semantic constraints on the word radical has facilitated seeing it as a marker for the phenomenon of 'radicalism' in a way that in Scott's terms 'parochializes' the past.[34] It is not unlike assuming an unchanging concept of the atom. It is only this sort of confusion that has sustained the illusion of a cohesive radical tradition irrespective of whether the projected object is extremity, alienated or doctrinal radicalism. Concomitantly, it has encouraged the view that the word can be saved for the historian by acts of isolated definition bringing usage into alignment with the phenomenon taken as a given.

This brings me back to the configuration of words immediately before and after the French Revolution as it is here that the methodological difficulties of dealing with radicalism are most acute. The tensions in Hampsher-Monk's suggestive argument become most instructive and for this reason can be dwelt upon disproportionately to the chapter's merits. It takes the concept of radicalism to be important in helping to explain the non-happening of an English radical revolution. It is a little like the dog that didn't bark in the night. If, to crib Wittgenstein, the limits of my language are the limits of my world, I may not be capable of coherent radical action if my language is inadequate to the purpose. The radicalism of eighteenth-century England was, argues Hampsher-Monk, only fragmented, and so could not perform as French radicalism did. As Hampsher-Monk is clearly aware, it is difficult to theorize about revolutions that do not happen, more troublesome still to write histories of their non-eventuality. The issue here is how far assuming the pre-existence of the phenomenon of radicalism beguiles us into asking questions that can't really be answered: how helpful is it to rely on a concept of radicalism to explain, as it were, its absence as revolutionary activity?

The essay is ingenious and insightful but seems to gain some of its theoretical force by conflating rather different senses of language. First, there is the presuppositional importance of natural languages, which has given rise to the logical non-issue of agency versus imprisonment within the limitations of 'my world'.[35] Second, there is the looser, more figurative notion of political theorizing as made up of distinguishable languages, an analytic device famously associated with J.G.A. Pocock. Sometimes in the literature this has become interchangeable with more conventional talk of ideologies, sometimes more helpfully it refers to contingently if commonly interconnected patterns of vocabulary actually used. Hampsher-Monk, for example, points to languages of natural rights, corruption, ancient constitutionalism and religion as all being available in the eighteenth century and depicts people as choosing between them. One problem brought about by the convergence here of object and meta-language is to avoid giving the impression that to act, the eighteenth-century English had first to have read their Pocock. Another is that even if these are languages, and not simply *topoi*, one can hardly point to people choosing between them as counter- evidence to claims of linguistic determinism which concern language in the first sense; the people Hampsher-Monk deals with were all writing English, some were fluent in French. Then there is radicalism: it certainly is not a language in the first sense, and though alluded to as a language in the second, it seems to have failed and been fragmented, either as ideology or cohesive vocabulary. It is, however, difficult to see how radicalism is a language in the Pocockian sense, as unlike custom, natural right, religion or corruption, it was not yet in the vocabulary as a point of focus. Thus, does the non-performance of radicalism, a claim presupposing a phenomenon's existence, actually attest to a non-existence? Night there was, to be sure, but was there a dog in the first place? Hampsher-Monk posits that although axes might cut off heads, only words abolish monarchy, on the grounds, I take it that to do X one first needs a word for X.[36] If so, one would have thought that the word radicalism would be a precondition for its success or failure in doing anything. There seems little to be gained by reifying a non-performing radicalism, so creating a problem that needs then to be explained. Especially in an argument so emphasizing language, it is puzzling that the phenomenon of radicalism should be taken for granted despite its absence in language. The late eighteenth century did, however, see markedly changed resonances for words in the ambit of innovation and it is such shifts in language, (consider reform in the context of progress, improvement, originality) that encourage the conceptual reification of radicalism that anticipates only a little and yet reconfigures quite a lot.

Hampsher-Monk saliently refers to people attempting to change the language through which they work. His point is central and Clark has shown just how important it is to recognize Bentham as such a linguistic reformer, if we are to historicize radicalism. His was the certificate that made possible the problematic back-projection of the phenomenon. Radicalism, Clark argues, as doctrine, a concept term, was precisely an expression of something self-consciously new, part of a creative Benthamite performance of ideological positioning, for which a neologism was totally appropriate. As the particular nexus of early nineteenth-century political (and one can say without anachronism) ideological battles has sunk from view, radicalism has gradually had its meaning dissipated. Initially the expression of a utilitarian atheism, quite distinct from socialism, radicalism became merged with concepts of socialism as some of these also became non-Christian, agnostic or atheistic, and with liberalism. The consequence is that not only does a doctrinal radicalism mis-describe the pre- nineteenth-century world, it also becomes so generalized as to lose what is distinctive about the nineteenth century. The neologism makes the point that we might expect from the dramatic enrichment of European political vocabulary from around 1790–1820, that doctrinal radicalism, and a putative language of radicalism has a history that is discontinuous with and independent of other meanings associated with radical. To reiterate, the transformation of the European political vocabulary in that thirty-year period was not just a matter of new wine into old bottles; new words and the relationships between them amounted to a different way of seeing things politically. The history of radicalism and its immediate semantic neighbours begins, as I suspect does the history of ideology (one of those terms) during the same traumatic years.

I have stressed the importance of semantic and pragmatic relations in identifying words functioning conceptually. By direct extension one can then ask, if we move towards dispensing with the word radicalism, or at the least make clear what we are not talking about when using it, what consequences might there be for phenomena conventionally predicated radical? If the world is not naturally divided into radicals and non-radicals such as conservatives, reactionaries or moderates we are in a better position to distinguish strategic uses of shared language from what we might simply assume to be familiar doctrinal fissures beneath it.

The conjunction of radicalism with republicanism in early modern Britain might be a significant case in point, although the following illustrative comments must be taken as tentative and provisional. The two terms are certainly closely associated historiographically if not historically;[37] and each exhibits all the features of underdetermined content and dubious explanatory status identified by Höpfl as typical of 'ism' terms.[38] Several of the essays in this volume (those by Borot, Alford and Greaves) explore or touch on this conjunction by using reference to republicanism to elucidate radicalism. Republicanism in early modern Britain has largely been seen as radical by default, oppositional and marginal in a monarchical context of rule. Despite John Pocock's insistence that republicanism is a language not a programme, it has been reduced to the more programmatic aspects of language use and prematurely narrowed to non-monarchical forms of government. So our attitudes start generating problems: on the surface, the fewer the republicans we find the more marginal and suggestively radical they can seem, for surely to entertain a world without monarchy in such a society has in some sense to be radical? Yet we look a little closer, find open recognition that the Israelites fared better under judges than kings, and admiration for Venice as a model for modern government and the republicans seem less radical by their swelling numbers. The more 'republicans' we find, the more problematic their status seems to be. And it is too easy to conclude that because republicans seem to be everywhere, because England was for so long what Collinson has called with studied paradox a monarchical republic,[39] there is something odd or incipiently antimonarchical and endemically radical about English political culture. We might end up in the eighteenth century with a sense of surprise to discover that the radical and republican fellow-travellers are the tories, travelling 'leftwards'.[40] Little wonder that Hampsher-Monk is led to raise the question of radicalism's non-performance when faced with the French Revolution. That the conjunction of terms creates this sort of puzzle in the evidence, is a possibility likely to occur only late in the reasoning process.

As recent work is making more apparent, however, English political discourse inherited an extensive notion of the *respublica* from medieval and ancient sources that could happily include a monarchical element. This taking different forms, complicates reference to monarchy as a litmus test for republicanism. The monarchical element might be an executive principle, or a person; and that person have an elected, or an hereditary office. In all cases authority might be variable. As a result, it is not so difficult to see how the literate in sixteenth-century England could write of their own polity in persistently Ciceronian terms, construing their commonwealth to be monarchical, their monarchy a form of republic.[41] Given the absence of hostility to monarchy per se, we do need to consider what republicanism might have been about, not least because as Alford's essay shows, the overt need to defend Elizabeth called forth a rhetoric of association and bonding that looks decidedly republican. The corollary of this, as Scott points out, is that we cannot see sixteenth and early seventeenth century England as having 'a purely monarchical mind-set'.[42] Such dichotomies arise later, and to read them back into Elizabethan and early Stuart England, is not just, as he intimates, anachronistic, it is to mistake a contingent feature for a defining essence.[43] It is to narrow seventeenth-century perceptions of political possibility to our own. So, to put the matter another way round, what is it that we questionably call 'republicanism'?

An ideal of good government was central to any notion of a republic. It was concerned with problems of appropriate participation, the virtues and conditions needed for this, most specifically, with secured liberties, properties as established rights, the rule of law and the public good (which obviously is not the Habermasian public sphere of which historians are latterly in hot and fruitless pursuit). As such, republicanism was a vocabulary of approbation and appropriation. Not surprisingly, it is found coalesced with the pervasive vocabulary of the *ars conservandi* (traditionality, reform, recovery, restoration), which was similarly positive in its connotations. These collocated vocabularies carried with them concomitant terms of distribution, accusation and warning, most prominently licence, luxury, arbitrary rule, self-interest, private interest (not the private sphere either), corruption, slavery, tyranny, oppression, innovation, destruction, party and faction. In short, we are left with a battery of descriptors providing the negative delineation of 'republican' and conservatory virtue. It is true that under the pressures of argument, perhaps leakage from natural philosophy, and certainly during the Commonwealth period there was some casuistic acceptance of innovation or attempts to elide it with reformation, so blunting its accusatory force. Other words too, (such as liberty, licence, private interest, luxury and party), would have their emotional resonances and rhetorical roles altered. This qualification aside, we are not dealing with neutral terms or the identifying ideolects of parties. We would have to look long and hard (beyond stage caricature) to find anyone claiming to be in favour of anything other than a care for the commonwealth and the public good, a love of law and liberty and the protection of just participation, and instead to be about the businesses of novelty and new fashion, new counsels, the promotion of slavery, oppression and arbitrary rule. The contours of republicanism have been firmed up and reified either by historians forgetting that expressions like tyranny and slavery were highly prejudicial (admittedly difficult) rebellion and arbitrary rule, no less so (surprisingly easy); or simply by a willingness to take sides with a curious inadvertence. So, when David Hume wrote with studied paradox that modern monarchies could be praised as once only republics could, he was at once subverting the value of party divisions, referring to Britain as a 'free government', and re-affirming the primacy of notions of good government, specifically a rule of law, in any polity.[44]

Moreover, in a world without bureaucracies, in which humble parish officials were elected or selected by lot, and were answerable to parish communities, social organization can look inherently and quite conventionally 'republican'. In early modern Britain there was, as Borot remarks, a permeating civic ethos. As participation was a necessity of survival, the hard facts of social life gave an immediacy to what we call classical republican discourse. England might not have been a city state, but it was city-centred and every village was to an extent self-governing. Even the village constable, church warden, or scavenger had liberties of office necessary for the job in hand, and could be accused of being arbitrary if seen to be officious, or accuse others of arbitrariness, corruption, oppression or tyranny if unduly interfered with.[45] Not surprisingly as Borot makes clear, public presence and well used traditions of petitioning were forms of sanctioned participation irrespective of the franchise – a most unreliable guide to civic participation. In short, the language of active responsibility and the protection of liberties necessary to sustain it might have nothing necessarily radical about it in any sense of the term. This incidentally, casts light on a major conclusion drawn by Gregory Claeys, that Mary Wollstonecraft's radicalism lay in challenging the distinction between public and private spheres of virtue. But this is a distinction that was only in the uncertain process of being firmed up in the late eighteenth century; the need to challenge it has become almost the sine qua non of respectable western liberal feminism since then. Her apparent challenge is, in short an affirmation of her place in the pedigree. Yet, at the least, Wollstonecraft was still in touch with a world in which any distinctions between public and private had to be negotiable and were mediated by a pervasive vocabulary of good and bad government, of office holding and its abuse. The family could still be seen, and probably was predominantly seen as a microcosm of the polity. This meant that husbands and fathers could be tyrants and oppressors, like constables and kings. Wollstonecraft exploits this republican *habitus*, to allude again to Borot, giving us a very Platonic notion of justice: in taking public offices to themselves, men were guilty of a form of *pleonexia*. Wollstonecraft's argument is almost inescapably republican but I am unclear as to the way in which it helps to call it radical.

In this way, for large tracts of time, or in some evocations of it at any time, what we have isolated as the language of 'republicanism', or italicize with the exclamatory adjective 'radical', may have been only a particular use of a shared vocabulary of social survival, an abridgment of organizational necessity. This is what we might expect if we are indeed dealing with a 'language' in Pocockian terms, with a characteristically associated, relatively stable but diversely employable sector of the vocabulary.[46] What is sometimes seen as a radical republican ideology might be the frustrated and perhaps strained employment of common linguistic currency usable by anyone justifying their conduct, or wishing to attack others. In this light, there may be further value in Mark Philp's argument when applied not just to radicalism but to an adjacent notion of republicanism.

Be this as it may, republicanism seems to have been fashioned into an ideologically distinctive shape by what has been overlooked or taken for granted. It is remarkable how resilient has been the sort of lineal structure of commitment found in Foxe's 'Book of Martyrs'. As Borot has shown, it provided a model for Leveller persuasive practice and, of course, the Levellers became central to a secularized martyrological radical tradition. In the same idiom has been a broken line of republican heroes, Cicero, Machiavelli, Milton, Marvell, Harrington, Neville and Sidney. This lineal structure has helped create an illusion of a doctrinal continuity sustained in an ambiance of hostility. In short, there has been a tendency to create a cohesive phenomenon by mistaking a shared and contested language of combat for the constitutive vocabulary of opposing group identities to which are attached fitting emblematic figures. Thus seventeenth-century politics is fashioned on the structural analogy of twentieth-century ideological positioning.

Once the nexus of radicalism and republicanism is uncoupled, it is easier to see what might otherwise be screened out, that, as Borot notes, mainstream, defensive and popular tracts such as the *Eikon Basilike* use a republican rhetoric. So the reader is assured that Charles acted in the people's interest, and for the good of the commonweal.[47] He, being a man of reason, law, and loving the proper participation of his parliament, had found himself confounded by a faction which, dominating parliament, tried to dictate and command his duty.[48] And so sensitive is he to tyranny, that he warns his son to use his prerogative to soften the rigours of the law rather than relentlessly following the letter, which is a tyranny of office. We may not believe any of this. If, as Christopher Wortham has informally expressed it, Charles was the Basil Fawlty of the seventeenth century, we probably shouldn't any more than Milton did in *Eikonoklastes*; but it shows us clearly what was an important vocabulary of justification. It is, then, not surprising that, as David Norbrook has suggested, we can find few voices absolutely hostile to monarchy before the civil wars; we can even find the odd one that associated the execution of Charles I with a restoration.[49] This arguably stretches the rhetorics of traditionality to their limit and in a way analogous to the *Eikon Basilike's* exploitation of the language of the commonweal. With hindsight we are on the cusp of a significant change, but it is very much with hindsight.

Overton's *A Remonstrance* is an intimation of what is to come, arguing that since the Norman Conquest kings have been the greatest oppressors and questioning that it is 'impossible for any Nation to be happy without a King'.[50] It was, however, probably only after the execution of Charles and the establishment of a new regime appropriating the mantle of a commonwealth and having to massage accusations of innovation into necessity, that a decisively non- or anti-monarchical republicanism really hardened and gathered force, for example, in Marchamont Nedham's *Mercurius politicus* (1650–3) and then in Algernon Sidney's *Court Maxims*, c.1665. These far more than Overton's remarks, provide relentless attempts to co-opt the whole language of good government to a form virtually by definition excluding monarchy. From about the same time the term commonwealthsman which had been used to mean one who belongs to or serves the interests of the polity was becoming tarnished with regicidal associations as Charles II's more determined supporters tried to collapse good government into his rule, bad government into that innovatory commonwealth which had been erected on the corpse of his father. We may have, in short, an oddly Gibbonesque conjunction of opposed polemical interests leading in the same direction, to a bifurcation of the notions of commonwealth and monarchy couched in doctrines of institutional integrity and appropriateness.[51] This doctrinal distinction as Greaves clearly shows, could afford very stark alternatives by the late Restoration. But if we go back to before the period he discusses, it seems that there is nothing natural or pre-ordained about the doctrinal development, and its absence looks to be odd in and before c.1649 only if we continue to assume a fixed prior republican ideology to give bespoke doctrinal clothing to England's 'radicals' so encouraging the expectation that anti-monarchical republicans are progressives, royalists reactionaries or vice versa.

With such trajectories that largely ignore contemporary language for our own conceptual expectations, networks of justification for judgments about underlying sincerity, form for content, we make it hard to isolate crucial issues of language change and social group formation and make it very difficult to explain why even in the early eighteenth century, the proscribed and marginal tories should be the ones appealing to the vocabulary of republicanism, voicing hostility to corruption, so conspiring to look 'radical'.

If, to put it with radical extremity, there is plausibility in such a hypothesis, disengaging a nonexistent political radicalism from a ubiquitous and protean, or motherhood republicanism, there are two immediate consequences. First, we can ask how and when a shared vocabulary became doctrinally oppositional, and in opposition to what, rather than assuming ab initio that a certain use of a vocabulary must correspond to an ideological division. This is to say, it might be possible to start afresh with a history of republicanism, as Jonathan Clark has shown how we must start afresh with a history of radicalism, as an ideological position.

Second, we can give a sharper edge to the triumphalist treatment of the rise of representative democracy; representation which contingently went hand in hand with the development of state apparatus for effective rule may also have gone hand in hand with participatory decline.[52] Being enfranchised might not in all cases have been a simple enhancement of status. For some, it might have foreclosed on other conventional forms of political behaviour, or been substituted for them. It may be that those most interested in enfranchisement were those who were able to buy themselves out from the burdens of participation but wanted some compensation. There may be, in short, some parallel between the rise of representative government in England and the earlier decline of the medieval communal republics. At the very least, such an hypothesis suggests some much needed complexity for the familiar and largely whiggish accounts of the triumph of constitutional modernity.

Irrespective of these hypotheses, the closure of one set of historiographical issues through the reform of the historian's vocabulary can only open up new questions and new ways of seeing things. A neat conclusion perhaps, for the foregoing essays show by degrees just how it is possible and how difficult it can be. Dealing with language, Wittgenstein remarked, is like trying to mend a cobweb with one's fingers, the historian's language is no exception.

NOTES

1 One recent example, Roy Porter, *Enlightenment: Britain and the Creation of the Modern world* (Allen Lane: London, 2000), cf pps 9–13 with 30–33.

2 Richard Hooker, *The Laws of Ecclesiastical Polity* (Dent: London, 1965 edn.), 5.3.4.

3 The methodological problems here not only go deep into historiography, but also into neighbouring fields of enquiry. Francis West has discussed the confusions between explanatory models and evidence to be explained in, 'The Colonial History of the Norman Conquest', *History*, 84 (1999), pp. 219–236. Jo-Anne Pemberton has commented on the reification of forces and processes in international relations, 'Towards a new world order: a twentieth century story', *The Review of International Studies*, 27 (2001), esp. pp. 26–27.

4 J.C. Davis, 'Radicalism in a Traditional Society: The Evaluation of Radical Thought in the English Commonwealth, 1649–1660', *History of Political Thought*, 3 (1982), pp. 193–213; see also J.C.D. Clark, *Revolution and Rebellion: State and Society in England in the Seventeenth and Eighteenth Centuries* (Cambridge University Press: Cambridge, 1986), pp. 97–103.

5 Arnold A. Rogow, *Thomas Hobbes: A Radical in the Service of Reaction* (New York, 1986).

6 The point has been carefully elaborated with respect to the continuity of misleading language in discussing the 'radical' Athenian democracy of the 5th century BC and its more 'moderate' successor. See Paul Millett, 'Mogens Hansen and the Labelling of Athenian Democracy', *Polis and Politics: Studies in Ancient Greek History*, ed. Pernille Flensted-Jensen, Thomas Heine and Lene Rubinstein (Museum Tusculanum Press: Copenhagen, 2000), pp. 342–352.

7 See Conal Condren, *The Language of Politics in Seventeenth-Century England* (Macmillan: London, 1994), p. 142.

8 David Simpson, *The Academic Post-Modern and the Role of Literature* (Chicago, 1995). I am grateful to Professor Evelyn Ellerman for drawing this to my attention.

9 Alistair MacLachlan, *The Rise and Fall of Revolutionary England* (Macmillan: London, 1994), esp. pp. 298–325. His argument is principally an historiographical one and does not entail that there was nothing revolutionary about the Civil Wars.

10 'Radicals, Moderates and Conservatives in Early-Modern Political Thought: A Case of Sandwich Islands Syndrome?', *History of Political Thought*, 10 (1989), pp. 525ff., was first given as a paper at the Australasian Historians of Medieval and Early Modern Europe Conference, Auckland in 1987.

11 Peter Lake, 'Joseph Hall, Robert Skinner and the Rhetoric of Moderation at the Early Stuart Court,' Lori Anne Ferrell and Peter McCullough eds., *The English Sermon Revised: Religion, Literature and History, 1600–1750* (Manchester University Press: Manchester, 2000), pp. 167–185.

12 John Lilbourne, William Walwyn, Thomas Prince and Richard Overton, *A Manifestation*, 1649, in D. Wolfe ed., *The Leveller Manifestoes of the Puritan Revolution* (Frank Cass: London, 1967), p. 391.

13 See Jonathan Scott, *England's Troubles: Seventeenth-Century Political Instability in European Context* (Cambridge University Press: Cambridge, 2000) pp. 233–236.

14 Scott *Ibid.*, p. 235, who overlooks this in the process of refreshing his radicals.
15 See for example, Jonathan Scott, *Algernon Sidney and the Restoration Crisis, 1677–1683* (Cambridge University Press: Cambridge, 1991), pp. 26–49, 265.
16 Scott, *Algernon Sidney*, pp. 266–7.
17 William S. Connolly, *The Terms of Political Discourse* (Robertson: Oxford, 1983 edn.), pp. 10–40.
18 'Radicals, Moderates and Conservatives'; and *The Language of Politics*, 5.2–3.
19 *The Language of Politics*, 5.10.
20 Robert von Friedeburg, 'Reformed Monarchomachism and the genre of the political in the Empire: the 'Politica' of Johannes Althusius and the meaning of hierarchy in its constitutional and conceptual context', *Archivo della Ragion di Stato*, 6 (1998), p. 138.
21 J.C. Davis, 'Review' of R. Greaves and R. Zaller, eds., *A Biographical Dictionary of British Radicals in the Seventeenth Century* (Harvester: Sussex, 1982) in *Political Science*, 37 (1985), p. 172
22 Tim Cooper, 'The Antinomians Redeemed: Removing some of the 'Radical' from Mid-Seventeenth-Century English Religion,' *The Journal of Religious History*, 24, 3 (2000), pp. 247–262; and at length, *Fear and Polemic in Seventeenth-Century England: Richard Baxter and Antinominanism* (Ashgate: Aldershot) 2001; see also Lotte Mulligan and Judith Richards, 'A 'Radical' Problem: The Poor and the English Reformers in the Mid-Seventeenth-Century', *The Journal of British Studies*, 29 (1990), pp. 118–46; Paul Millett, 'Mogens Hansen and the Labelling of Athenian Democracy', pp. 337–362.
23 Eli Kedourie, *Nationalism* (Hutchinson: London, 1962), ch. 1–2.
24 Glenn Burgess, *The Politics of the Ancient Constitution: An Introduction to English Political Thought, 1603–1642* (Macmillan: London, 1992), pp. 115–78.
25 Sir Henry Spelman, *The History and Fate of Sacrilege, Discover'd by Examples of Scripture, of Heathans, and of Christians; from the Beginning of the World, continually to this Day* (1632?, 1698), edited with Introductory essay by Two Priests of the Church of England (Joseph Masters: London, 1846, 1853).
26 William M. Lamont, *Richard Baxter and the Millennium* (Croom Helm: London, 1979)
27 David Parnham, *Sir Harry Vane, Theologian: A Study in Seventeenth-Century Religious and Political discourse* (Associated University Presses: London, 1997), e.g. pp. 265–9.
28 Friedrich Nietzsche, *La Gaia Scienza, Werke* (Munich, 1963) vol.**2** para 63.
29 William Thoms, 'Letter', in *The Athenaeum*, no. 982, 22 nd August, 1846 reprinted in Richard Dorson, ed. *Peasant Customs and Savage Myths: Selections from the British Folklorists* (Routledge, Kegan Paul: London, 1968) vol.**1**. pp. 52–4. I am grateful to Averil Condren for this point.
30 Oliver Sacks, *The Man Who Mistook His Wife for a Hat* (Pan Books: London, 1985), pp. 87–9.
31 Jeremy Bentham, 'Table of the Springs of Action' (1815) cited in Dwight Bolinger, *Language, The Loaded Weapon* (Longman: New York, 1983), p. 5.

32 C. K. Ogden and I. A. Richards, *The Meaning of Meaning* (Routledge: London, 1923).

33 *The Language of Politics*, Introduction, pp. 16–17.

34 Jonathan Scott, *Harry's Absence: Looking for My Father on the Mountain* (University of Victoria Press: Wellington, 2000), pp. 191, 206.

35 Both system and agency in language are mutually preconditional. That is, an agent uses a system as a necessary means of saying anything, the system is a necessary abstraction from agency. Only sometimes do I get the impression that Hampsher-Monk has fallen foul of a false dichotomy. It is a variation of the fruitless disputes in social theory over the primacy of methodological individualism versus holism.

36 The proposition, like Wittgenstein's famous proposition about the limits of 'my world', may be tautologous or fallacious. There may be a confusion here between ontology and predication, between X and words being the necessary conditions for talking about something as X. There may not be a problem if dealing with performatives as opposed to constatives in a strict Austinian sense; but Hampsher-Monk is using performative in a familiar and much looser manner to capture people acting on their world through words, performative embraces deliberative rhetoric, the point of using language, as Hobbes put it, being to get something done. There are substantial differences between saying I cannot place a bet without having the verb to bet (strict performative); and saying there can be no revolution because I don't have the word for it. So the limits of my language are strictly only the limits of my world if we are talking about my perceptions of and choices in it. This is tautologically true and all the more reason in the interests of elucidating such choices, not to inject radicalism into a world limited by its absence.

37 See, for example, the following nevertheless excellent studies, David Norbrook, *Writing the English Republic* (Cambridge University Press: Cambridge, 1999) ch.1; Markku Peltonen, *Classical Humanism and Republicanism in English Political Thought, 1570–1640* (Cambridge University Press: Cambridge, 1995); and Jonathan Scott, *England's Troubles*, pp. 75–80; 233–9.

38 Harro Höpfl, 'Isms', *The British Journal of Political Science*, 13 (1981), pp. 1–17.

39 Patrick Collinson, 'The Monarchical Republic of Queen Elizabeth I', *Bulletin of the John Rylands Library*, 69 (1987), pp. 394–424.

40 Linda Colley, 'Eighteenth-Century Radicalism Before Wilkes', *Transactions of the Royal Historical Society*, 5th series, 31 (1981), p. 8 and p. 14.

41 Collinson, 'The Monarchical Republic'; Peltonen, *Classical Humanism*, ch.2.

42 Scott, *England's Troubles*, p. 79; *The King's Answer to the Nineteen Propositions* (1642) does make a contrast between a monarchy and a republic, like Venice, but proceeds to muddy institutional waters with Polybian mixed government theory.

43 Scott, *Ibid.*, p. 79.

44 David Hume, 'Of Civil Liberty', in *Essays*, ed Knud Haakonssen (Cambridge University Press: Cambridge, 1994), pp. 56–7.

45 For a thorough and timely discussion of these themes see Mark Goldie, 'The Unacknowledged Republic: Office-holding in Early Modern England', in Tim Harris ed., *The Politics of the Excluded, c1500–1850*, (London: Palgrave, 2001), pp. 154–194; also Patricia Crawford, 'The poorest She': women and citizenship in early modern England' in Michael Mendle ed., *The Putney Debates, 1647* (Cambridge University Press: Cambridge), pp. 197–218.

46 J. G. A.Pocock, 'The Concept of Language and the metier d'historien: some considerations on practice' in Anthony Pagden, ed. *The Languages of Political Theory in Early-Modern Europe* (Cambridge University Press: Cambridge, 1987), pp. 19–21.

47 *Eikon Basilike*, 1649, pp. 2, 79–80, 239.

48 *Ibid.*, p. 79.

49 Norbrook, *Writing the English Republic*, p. 16.

50 Richard Overton, *A Remonstrance of Many Thousand Citizens* (1646) in D. Wolfe ed. *The Leveller Manifestoes of the Puritan Revolution* (Frank Cass: London, 1967), p. 115.

51 In *The Decline and Fall* Gibbon suggests that both early Christians and their persecutors had an interest in claiming Christiantity was a very large and widespread sect, but by such agreement it does not follow that it was.

52 Goldie, 'The Unacknowledged Republic', pp. 153–4, 183–4.

Afterword: Reassessing Radicalism in a Traditional Society: Two Questions

J. C. Davis

INTRODUCTION

The most obvious functionality of radicalism is that it challenges the status quo, whether in its language, legitimations, objectives, institutions, processes, dispositions of power or achievements – or all of these. These are, after all, the instrumentalities of governance, of rule, and it is, at one end of a spectrum or the other, the transformation of rule which radicalism seeks.

Such an apparently unexceptional statement, or definition, belies the problems immediately confronting the historian. The essays in this collection circulate – sometimes explicitly, sometimes implicitly – around two of the most important of these problems or questions. The first concerns the transformation of rule implicitly envisaged by radicalism and the ambivalent status which attaches to it. Is it a question of substance or imagination, of fact or of fiction and might there be continuous histories of either of these? Should radical ideas, groups, movements and actions be depicted as existing in a 'real' world and is their history to be juxtaposed in counterpoint with the hard 'facts' of political, legal, constitutional, social and economic history? Yet, as an alternative to the status quo, radicalism appears to shift from the real world to the imagined, from reality to ideality, from description to fiction. But, of course, we also recognize that realities are themselves constructed and, in some sense, imaginatively constructed. Indeed some historians of radicalism have claimed a capacity, in specific forms of it, to see beneath the illusions of power, the fictions of the status quo and to grasp the 'realities' of exploitation underpinning and, at the same time, obscured by them. In what sense, then, are the fictions of 'reality' distinguished from those of 'radicalism'? What is their relationship with the hard substance of 'reality'? When, historically, does it make sense to insist on the demarcations between the radical and the established and between fact and fiction in their advocacy and defence?

Almost as an extension of this first question, the second asks what language we, as historians, may legitimately use to describe the moments, or possibly the tradition, of depicting or attempting the transformation of rule. There are those, as these essays make clear, for whom the use of the term 'radical' to describe appeals or actions attempting the transformation of rule before 1800 would be a form of crass anachronism. Such a discrimination in the application of the labels of 'radicalism' implies a discontinuity, in the history of self-consciousness about the transformation of rule, profound enough to inhibit us from envisaging a history of 'radicalism', in thought or action, capable of spanning the sixteenth to the twenty-first century. The question of language therefore raises the question of tradition or of a history capable of spanning the *moyenne durée.* While the transformation of rule and the question of language may be linked for the historian of radicalism, confusing the two rapidly produces an unhelpful stalemate. As Richard Greaves perceptively suggests here, strict reliance on contemporary usage as a guide is vitiated by contemporaries' common relish for languages of extreme partisanship,[1] but the problem has other dimensions.

This essay, therefore, will discuss the fictions and the substance of aspirations to transform the nature of rule and the associated question of language. In the limited detail which space will permit, I explore possible answers to these problems in interpreting some seventeenth-century radicals. Finally, and far too sketchily, I engage with the themes arising out of current historiography which, it seems to me, such answers must confront.

I. TRANSFORMATION OF RULE

Was it possible for people in England before 1800 to envisage the transformation of rule or did they live in a society capable of embracing vicissitude but not transformation? Was early modern political culture inescapably one of *restauratio* rather than *innovatio* or *transformatio*?

The first issue here is that of the possibility in the past of moments of a self-conscious intention to transform substantially (or envisage the transformation of) the nature of rule. This means not simply the replacement of one set of rulers with another but the transformation of the disposition of legitimate claims to rule and/or of the processes and institutions of rule. As Luc Borot suggests, the radical must be more thoroughgoing than other oppositionist movements.[2] How far back into the English past can we reasonably claim that there were such moments of substantial radicalism? A second issue is whether such moments may be seen as linked in a self-conscious tradition. Glenn Burgess, in his introduction to this volume, points out a number of problems with the passing-of-the-baton approach to the history of radicalism. One is that the nature of this baton may be perceived in markedly different ways by different generations. Another, developed further in Burgess' essay, is the fundamental discontinuity between the approaches to transformation of a confessional society and those of a secular society. A third, as we have seen, is the problem of a discontinuous language and the question of implicit anachronism in applying the language of 'radicalism' to a world innocent of such terminology. We may add to this, more generally, the contested historiography of transformation in the English past. In the late eighteenth century, there was, as Ian Hampsher-Monk observes, a yawning interpretative chasm between Richard Price's insistence that the Convention Parliament of 1688 established a revolutionary tradition and Edmund Burke's view that the Convention had denied itself the authority to act de novo.[3] Such divergent claims were, of course, made in the pursuit of wider political arguments. There may be some justification for the view that an historically sensible history of radicalism might only be possible without such political pre-engagements, but we also have to acknowledge that amongst the motives for the study of the history of radicalism is the political. Minimizing the abuse of the past and maximizing the intellectual legitimacy of our enquiry may, however, be dependent on asking appropriately focused questions and observing some possible pitfalls.

In 1982 I was arguing for a more careful and more politically neutral identification of radical ideas and movements in early modern England by focusing on the functional requirements which radicals might expect of their radicalism: the delegitimation of the status quo, the legitimation of an alternative to it and the envisaging of a transfer mechanism capable of bringing about the desired transformation.[4] The burden of my argument was to identify the difficulties inherent in articulating a radical/transformative vision, without resort to divine agency, in mid seventeenth-century England. That those difficulties were overcome, albeit by fewer 'activists' than was commonly supposed,[5] required and still requires some explanation. I would now put the question from a slightly different angle, looking this time at what political radicals might envisage transforming rather than at what the required building blocks of such transformation might be. I suggest three broad targets:

1. the nature of the institutions, procedures and processes of rule (civil and/or religious); that is to say of the perceived characteristics and implications of government/governance;
2. the relationship between government and society;
3. the nature of society and social relationships and therefore of those mechanisms or cultures which can effectively govern it.

These three 'targets' may be almost invariably interlinked. To transform the nature of rule invariably impinges on the relationship between rules and ruled, government and society. A more direct intervention in the relationship between state and society may involve changes in government procedures or institutional arrangements. Social transformation will almost inevitably involve changes in government and in the relationship between it and society. The historiography of the Reformation over the last thirty years has emphasized the interpenetration of all three aspects. The English Reformation is now seen as a much more radically transformative set of aspirations than the royal and legislative will that tore apart that shibboleth of constitutional and political conservatism, Magna Carta. Its radicalism witnesses transformative institutional, procedural and process change in government, drastic and highly contested change in the relationship between government and society, and profound social change both in the reality of substantial economic transfers and in the aspiration to the reformation of manners and cultural transformation. Whatever the final achievements of that extended historical process which we call the Reformation were, there can be little doubt that there were radical, transformative impulses at work within it nor of their capacity to draw together all three of the target areas I have tried to distinguish. Despite such convergence, there may be, as I hope to show shortly, heuristic and analytical value in making these distinctions, in separating out these three dimensions of transformative thinking and action.

Such an approach necessarily draws us into more or less vexed, but historical, questions. What were the institutions, processes and procedures of rule that mattered? What was the state and what were its external and internal relationships of power? To take a critical case, there is an enormous difference between thinking of the state as predominantly the central, hierarchical apparatus of Crown, Council, Court, Parliament, attendant bureaucracies including the judiciary and the episcopal bench, on the one hand, and the state as networks of governance in urban, parish and county communities throughout the land. The first is an evocation of a monarchical state, limited perhaps but irresistible; the second, a highly participatory, mediatory, discretionary and quasi-republican state. How we describe the state will to some extent determine what we think of as radical. Equally, how we understand the government or the state in past societies will circumscribe our view of the relationship between state and society, as will our understanding of the nature of historical societies.

In the mid 1980s the debate on the nature of early modern English society was reopened. Keith Wrightson suggested that it was difficult to describe early modern England as either a vertically aligned or a class society. Was it a hierarchical society experiencing the first stirrings of a class society or was it an immature class society with residues of early social formation or was it an altogether distinctive kind of society? His answer was to emphasize ambiguity and regional variation.[6] Almost simultaneously, David Underdown was arguing for the shaping of civil war allegiances around variations in regional ecology and land management and use patterns, although regional cultural differences were seen as 'at most marginal'.[7] The old sociology of knowledge was collapsing in the face of uncertainties about the balance between horizontal and vertical social articulations and between local distinctiveness and social uniformities. One response was to emphasize cultural factors. Kevin Sharpe attempted to spell this out in terms of a shared contemporary 'ideology' which stressed ideals of organic unity, a state at once natural and divine, the elevation of the commonweal above the sectional discriminators of public/private, community/individual. and the ruler as moderator in pursuit of social harmony.[8] Sharpe widened our perception of the 'political' in early modern society and reasserted its character as a community with shared assumptions. But those assumptions tended to lead away from conflict and towards consensus in a society whose history, we knew, was wracked by the worst civil strife in English history. If we are to relate government and society in an age of crisis, as well as of radical challenges to those relationships, something more is required; a new basis for a sociology of knowledge capable of embracing both consensus and conflict.

Any satisfactory history of radicalism must also allow for the possibility of unselfconscious transformations of the state, of society and of the relationships between the two. The technologies of war, communications or financial transfers may change and, in evolving, transform the nature and relationship of rule. Those changes to rule may be without self-conscious intent. So it is sometimes argued that the restored monarchy of 1660 brought back old institutions, procedures, processes and rituals but their adequacy was severely tested by changed social circumstances: an erosion of community by social polarization, a more rapid capitalization of agriculture and cultural bifurcation.[9] None of these social changes was intentional. Social consciousness might catch up with them *post facto* but was unlikely to control the causes, the course or the consequences of such transformation. Put in its simplest form, social transformation, and transformative change of the state and its social relationships, might well result independently of radical thought and action. In turn, this exposes the question of self-consciousness as a necessary precondition of radical identity. It would seem reasonable to argue that the self-consciousness of radical actors must be a prerequisite of characterizing them as radical if we are to retain a capacity to relocate individuals in the past with some discipline. But identifying the self-consciousness of individuals and groups in the past can be a vexed and vexing business. Christopher Hill has argued that the early modern rhetoric of consensus is deceptive, a public and conventional face often masking a private dissent.[10] But, if the argument is that, of the combination of public loyalty and private unease, we must give priority to the latter in face of the conflict we know emerges in the 1640s, we should pause. Such a privileging of the private would be to minimize public convention although we know that this was a society attaching considerable importance to the observance of public conventions. In this context, should self-consciousness be reduced to the private or kept open to include public observance and performance?

Despite the difficulties, self-consciousness remains a prerequisite for the description of ideas or activities as radical. If the transformation of rule (substantive radicalism) is necessarily linked to the language we use and which contemporaries may have used to depict such transformations, this is all the more imperative. Otherwise, as Conal Condren suggests, radical moments look like 'moments of mishap'.[11] The nature of that self-consciousness might involve a grasp of continuities, a sense of membership of a 'radical tradition' and a desire to emulate the high points of the identified tradition. But in what sense might it be awareness of these continuities which drives the pursuit of a radical agenda or should we see radical self-consciousness as a series of moments, driven by the need to respond to particular problems, situations and contingencies – even if accompanied by awareness or 'construction' of a 'radical tradition'? The changing balance between these two – from pragmatic responsiveness to awareness of tradition – is surely a key feature of the history of radicalism. But this is not the same as saying that one is more radical or a more mature radicalism than the other.

II. THE QUESTION OF LANGUAGE

Assuming that there have been moments in the more distant English past, specifically in the early modern period, when individuals and groups have self-consciously aspired to transform the nature of rule over them, the relationship between that rule and society, or the nature of society itself, how might we appropriately describe those moments or the traditions in which they might be linked? The semantic problem revolves in particular around the question as to whether use of the terms 'radical' or 'radicalism', before the 1800s, might be justified and whether adjectival or nominative usage make any difference in answering that question. For J.C.D. Clark, as for Conal Condren, tracing a radical tradition from the 1640s onwards involved 'a deliberate act of anachronism' since the secularized concept and language of 'the radical' only emerged in the 1820s and 1830s.[12] Others have argued that the restriction of language to contemporary usage is damaged by its partisan exploitation.[13] Ian Hampsher-Monk appears to see, in the plurality of political languages available to political writers and activists in the 1790s, a platform for claims as to their agency and some liberation of them and of later commentators from the restrictions of contemporary usage.[14] Finally, John Pocock has suggested that it might be legitimate to use the word 'radical' adjectivally but not as a noun in application to the prenineteenth-century past. There were radical ideas, individuals, moments, actions and groups but not radicals or radicalisms.[15] The validity of applying the categories of 'radical' and 'radicalism' to the periods before 1800 has been called into question but that questioning itself has proved to be problematic.

III. TRANSFORMATION OF RULE SUBSTANTIALLY APPLIED

So questions multiply. Let us begin by assuming that there may be a history of the intention to bring about the transformation of rule in England which stretches well back before 1800. (For the moment I will also assume that we may use the language of 'radicalism' to describe it; in the same way that one might talk about the 'nuclear' family of the early modern period, or about the 'linguistic contexts' within which they articulated their ideas, although this terminology was unknown to contemporaries). When would it begin? Is it inextricably linked to the maturation of the state? Did radicalism emerge, as is so often suggested in both diachronic and synchronic terms, uniquely in seventeenth century England? Was this because, by the seventeenth century, there was some sense of a unitary state in England? And whose sense was it? Was such a sense of the state confined to the gentry and London citizens or was it more socially and geographically widespread? What was the nature of that state? Was it the unitary state of King, Lords and Commons, the Privy Council and the Court (the state of Sir Geoffrey Elton's points of contact)? Was it the state – holy or backsliding – of the godly? Even the last of these questions leaves open the possibility of addressing the history of the state as that of a set of secular institutions and processes. But is this right? Are the issues of ecclesiastical governance, the importance of the parish, the government and informing of consciences so important that we need to think of a complex of secular/religious institutions comprising the church-state?[16] It is in this sense that the massive breach and transformation of rule, setting aside key parts of Magna Carta, which the Reformation represented might be seen as radical events. But, just as we should beware of thinking of the early modern state in too secular terms, so we should also beware of assuming its centralized character. Recent work on the early modern state has emphasized its dispersed, participatory, mediatory and discretionary character – the state of the 'unacknowledged republic'.[17] What differences does thinking of the early modern state in these terms make to our perception of early modern radicalism?

So there are, as always in history, many questions. What hinders progress is the current state of diversity as to where to begin and what is under scrutiny. On the one hand, Luc Borot sees Levellers as the dawn of English radicalism, the end of premodern grievance rites. He associates this with a move from (to use his terminology) heteronomy to autonomy with the implication of a shift to more secular forms of legitimation.[18] On the other hand, Stephen Alford's essay suggests a sixteenth century justification for resistance, even for deposition, in reaction against idolatry with the further implication, made almost explicit in the 1584 Bond of Association, that there is a republic-in-waiting capable of acting independently of the monarch.[19] In turn, this raises the question of collective oaths and engagements running through from at least the Bond of 1584 to the Solemn League and Covenant of 1643, the Engagement of 1649/50 and beyond. In so far as these represent ways of defining and declaring one's membership of civil society, they impinge on the issues, raised earlier, of the relationship between state and society and the nature of the society to which the state must relate.[20]

The history of radicalism as the transformation, or envisaging of the transformation, of rule is then intimately connected with both the history of the state as a set of processes, institutions and procedures through which rule may be exercised and the history of society as a self-consciously identified association and as an unself-consciously evolving community or set of communities. We should avoid seeing the exercise of rule only in secular or only in centralized terms. Equally, we should seek to balance contemporary awareness and articulation of social relationships with the changing social problems of which contemporaries may have been only dimly aware but which the work of social historians may reveal to us. Radicalism will always be specific to, functionally related to, the nature and forms of rule in any particular period. What are the things that we should be focusing on when we think of the nature of rule, of government, or of the state, in the mid seventeenth century, in 'revolutionary' England?

III. i The state/government

What might the approach I am moving towards involve if we related it to the nature of the state/government, the relationship between government and society and the nature of society in the critical decades for early modern radicalism, the 1630s to the 1650s?

One way of representing the history of the period from 1629 to 1647 would be to focus on the struggle as not so much one between state and society as one within the state and over different perceptions as to how the state should operate. The Stuarts found themselves presiding over a dispersed state, with high levels of participation in office holding, one in which the unpaid justices, juries, constables, churchwardens, overseers and other office holders show themselves as possessed of discretionary authority, mediating the orders of the Crown and the provisions of statutory legislation to meet local circumstances and perceived local needs.[21] The 1620s had been a humiliating reminder to the Stuarts that their capacity for warfare and for the creation of a 'modern' military establishment could all too easily founder on the lack of co-operation from this 'unacknowledged republic' and their representatives in Parliament. In both Church and State, or the church-state, the 1630s saw attempts to override, circumvent and sidestep the resistance of the unacknowledged republic to the requirement of a standardized response to the ecclesiastical and civil policies of the Crown. This was a struggle within the 'State' involving a redefinition of its character. From the successful raising of a standard national tax – shipmoney – to make possible the first steps towards a modern navy,[22] to the Declaration of Sports,[23] to Laud's insistence on standard observance of the liturgy, discretion was being taken out of the hands of local officeholders. For Charles I's policies to succeed, the balance of the state would have to be shifted so that the Crown might assume a less mediated and more deferential responsiveness from the officeholders of the dispersed state. Here there is a real sense in which he and his ministers were – as contemporaries recognized – the radical innovators.[24] The parliamentary reaction of 1640/1641 was intended to restore the authority of local officeholders, characteristic of the unacknowledged republic, and to provide insurance for that disposition of power by further weakening the Crown. The institutional and financial props of personal rule were taken away. The King's principal ministers were arrested, impeached and, in the case of Strafford, executed. Parliament was made an effectively, regular part of the operation of government. What looks like a constitutional revolution was essentially a restoration which, in order to guarantee that it would be a permanent restoration, introduced a number of constitutional innovations. From the Grand Remonstrance to the Nineteen Propositions the defence of these changes was essentially conservative: a restoration of discretionary judgement by unpaid local officeholders. The more complex problem remained the Church. If a loosely 'uniform' Church has been unacceptable to Archbishop Laud, so it was also to some of the godly opposed to him. They also wanted to override the autonomy of local parishes and patrons. For these 'Puritan' zealots the Reformation had been too loosely, laxly and ineffectively policed. It was time to reform the Reformation. Over the question of the Church – whether to restore the loosely coordinated, comprehensive church of pre-1633, or whether to reform the Reformation – the angry officeholders of 1640–1641 were to split and this, in large part, made possible the English Civil War, even if the description 'England's War of Religion' is to privilege this aspect of the struggle.[25]

With war came a new and double threat to the discretionary autonomies of the unacknowledged republic, this time from within the parliamentary cause. The irony of this development was manifest not only in the Presbyterians' drive to national religious uniformity but also in the fiscal, legal and administrative demands of the developing parliamentary war machine. Taxes were levied on an unprecedented scale and in the case of the excise by a new, centrally controlled bureaucracy. Juries were set aside, the provisions of the Petition of Right broken and local processes usurped by county committees. The counties' control of their own militias was first mitigated by the Associations and them nullified by the creation of a national standing force, the New Model Army. Weakening the Crown had seemed to be the way to protect the unacknowledged republic. Between 1642 and 1646 Parliament reformed the State without the King. It is estimated that, in those four years, 550 parliamentary ordinances were passed cumulatively reshaping the relationship between central and local government.[26] By the mid-1640s Henry Parker was defending not merely Parliament, but parliamentary absolutism.[27] As peace returned in 1646, the questions were whether reform without the King had been a purely temporary phase and whether a negotiated settlement could restore the status quo, immediately *ante bellum* (that is incorporating the reforms of 1641). As we know, the subsequent crisis of 1648–9 seemed to suggest that reform without the King might be a permanent condition. In religion too, the issue of the 1640s was not that of a radical move from discipline to liberty but a radical (and non-discretionary) transformation of discipline.[28]

By 1647, the oft cited *annus mirabilis* of the emergence of political radicalism, three issues predominated. The first was how to restore both the religious and civil dimensions of rule by the unacknowledged republic in face of the demands of military security and of both Scots and English Presbyterians for greater centralized control over religious heterodoxy. Second, the problem of the legal status of many acts committed by combatants during the wars was one of balancing the rights of civilians and those of soldiers acting under orders. But the pressing problem of military indemnity[29] was also both a political and a constitutional issue. How was military unrest to be quelled without such an indemnity and how was an authority capable of providing adequate protection for both soldiers and citizens to be re-established? The soldiers were well aware that an ordinance offering them indemnity and passed by one parliament could be rescinded by another. The same was true of parliamentary statute, were the parliamentary trinity to be set functioning again. Everything therefore hung on the nature of a settlement with the King and the possibility of a 'law paramount'. Hence the anxieties of later 1647 occasioned by the Grandees' negotiations over the Heads of Proposals and growing unease at the King's duplicitousness and lack of realism. Settlement, thirdly, could be seen as anchored by the conservative engagements of the Solemn League and Covenant, with its promise of protection for the person, authority and dignity of the King. But what if the 'insanity' of royal policies made this unsustainable?

Here then, is one way of looking at the dynamic of the state's development in the 1640s. It is against such a dynamic that the question of the transformation of rule, of radicalism, should be read but also against the shifting relationship between this state dynamic and society, taking account too of the transforming impact of war upon society.

III. ii Government and society

There are a number of dimensions which it is useful to consider in connection with the relationship between government and society in the 1640s and 1650s. Most of these have emerged in relatively recent research and thinking about early modern civil society, governance and the state. Cumulatively, they amount to a substantial setting aside of the two models of state/society relations which dominated historical thinking for over a century and a half but which could be traced as far back as James Harrington's writings of the 1650s. Both models rested on the assumption of a horizontally integrated 'class' society in which structural antagonisms showed themselves in terms of vertical conflict. They depicted the early modern period as one of transition *via* class, from an aristocratically dominated polity with its roots in a medieval order of government/society relationships to a society substantially shaped by, and in the interests of the middle class, merchants, professionals and gentlemen and looking forward to the commercial/industrial, scientific, secular and democratic society/state relationships of the future. Both Whig and Marxist accounts of this transition, the great arch, shared assumptions in common. But behind both schema was also the view that the state was an instrument of power, centralized in such a way that its seizure could be made to serve the interests of the dominant class on a national basis. Both models have suffered not only from growing doubts about the class basis of early modern society but also from the development of new themes explanatory of the relationship between government and society. I want to look briefly at five of those themes here. Together they amount to a call for a new sociology of knowledge underpinning our treatment of seventeenth century radicalism.

First, and we have already seen something of this, come the ideas behind regarding early modern England as an 'unacknowledged republic'. The notion that 'common consent' informed the rule of civil law within a framework of divine and natural law, that without law 'neither household, nor city, nor commonwealth, nor the world itself can stand', implied many points of consent and diverse structures of governance. What was apparent, to writers like Althusius and Grotius, in relation to the Empire and the United Provinces, also described a reality basically familiar to Englishmen.[30] The state of early modern England might be seen as a network of activities with widely dispersed discretion, high levels of participation reaching deep into the status ranges of society, and a culture of mediation between complementary authorities. Royal policy, writ and indeed parliamentary statute had to do business with these patterns of civic duty and autonomy.[31] The unpaid workhorses of the system, as Cynthia Herrup stressed in anticipation of much of the shift of historiographical emphasis in the last decade, were recruited from the sub-gentry: constables, churchwardens, jurymen and overseers of many kinds. They and their discretion were central to the operation of the parish, hundred, county and, in a very real sense, the government of the country. There was no single ruling class in England.[32] But, if there was no single ruling class, how could revolution be a struggle against *the* ruling class? In this context, the notion of limited or mixed government became bound up with the *potestas irritans* of this dispersed, participatory state; the revolutionary or radical threat with those forces which would overthrow its restraining and protective capacities. This is not to suggest that all was sweetness and light in the realms of parish and shire officeholding but the dispersed and rotational nature of officeholding did something to ensure a large measure of communal self-governance by male heads of households, oppressive or not as its governance of non-male, non-heads of households may potentially have been.

A second theme in state/society relations in this period is that of religion, in particular of ideas of the confessional society and of casuistry as a means of government and self-government. A well-ordered society was assumed to be a godly society and one of shared orthodoxy rather than of competing heterodoxies. The vicious religious wars of the period bore ample witness to these truths. By 1640 the key questions were to what extent and in what respects was godly uniformity to be insisted upon; what was the range of things indifferent over which some latitude of observance might be allowed?[33] Laud had insisted on a strictly literal – and legal – uniformity overriding local discretion and tender consciences. The reaction was an inextricable amalgam of civil outrage and religious fury. But within the ranks of the parliamentary godly there was also an impulse to discipline, purify and reform the nation which would equally not brook local discretion and variation.

Where did reforming authority and discretion lie: in the majority votes of the Westminster Assembly and the committees of Parliament or in the parishes and congregations? In either case, it was a common view that the governing of consciences, structuring internal self-discipline, was inevitably a greater priority than coercion. Casuistry, the schooling of conscience, was thus a social and governmental necessity as well as a spiritual one.[34] To question who was to control casuist discourse was immediately to question the role of the church-state. But there was a tension between the aspiration for, on the one hand, a national community of individuals operating according to shared, conscientious norms and, on the other, for one which implied some claim for individuals and groups to enjoy such liberty of conscience as would enable them to follow God's promptings whether mediated through Scripture, the teaching of the church, or other casuists' advice or more immediately communicated through providential experience. In a period of contested confessional authority and civil dispute those tensions were bound to become more acute. Where authority had become fragmented the scope for variations in the casuists' attempts to accommodate circumstantial and prudential considerations in the guidance of conscience was drastically enlarged.

Contemporaries had repeatedly attempted to overcome this fragmentation of the confessional and conscientious society by reasserting a community of values and moral intentions through subscriptional mechanisms: the oath or engagement. This third theme, the vision of a covenanted society, also has its quasi-republican overtones. Men acting as self-ruling citizens joined together conscientiously declaring themselves members of a civic, subscriptional community with common values and objectives. It was inevitable that early modern government would seek to relate to, and indeed engender, such a covenanted society. From the Oath of Succession in 1534, through the Bond of Association of 1584, the Protestation of May 1641, the Sacred Vow and Covenant of June 1643, the Solemn League and Covenant of 1643 to the Engagement of 1649, the state was involved in administering oaths of engagement with simultaneous republican and authoritarian implications.[35] Clearly in a dramatically shifting political environment there were strong links between a covenanted society and a casuistically managed one. How could consciences be released, for example, from the Solemn League and Covenant to undertake the obligations of the Engagement? Could the acts of men – even of those in authority – release subscribers covenanted with God? A substantial and contested literature was generated on these issues and the consideration of the impact of prudential and circumstantial factors on conscientious obligation.[36] But, if casuistry became a battlefield in the war of words, the question became who should control this process and how? Thomas Hobbes, in one sense himself a doctor of conscience, was against the unfettered invocation of conscience and was clear that it was the sovereign's right to impose appropriate fetters. Alternatively, not swearing could come to seem an important feat of disengagement, not so much from society as from the moral complexities to which the diversity of engagements gave rise. But the resistance to oaths, of the Quakers, for example, could also be seen by contemporaries as menacing to social and governmental order. As in the case of the Solemn League and Covenant, God was often cast as actively involved in creating a framework of civic authority, in the act of state building which these engagements involved. But what kind of God was He?

This brings us to a fourth theme: that of the 'chosen people' or a God-driven society and the question of what the relationship between civil authority and such a society might be. Looking at the balance between the potential for revolution of the 1640s and the limitations of those possibilities, John Walter has observed that in the crisis years of 1640–1642 there may have been more iconoclasm than anti-enclosure activity.[37] Idolatry could be a more explosive issue than economic oppression. The majority of us are secular historians, unbelievers, and the ethos of our profession is secular. It has taken us a long time to find a place for religion alongside social, economic and constitutional/political factors. The problem now is exactly what that place might be. Glen Burgess' essay in this collection pinpoints one critical aspect of the problem. He does so by offering us a new separation of religion and politics, or of the spheres of grace and nature. Those – and they were legion – whose primary allegiance was to a living God, disposed to intervene directly in the affairs of his chosen people, were left with a political realm which had only a very precarious existence. 'God not man was the radical activist'. Believers in such a God imagined the transformation of the world as something engineered outside of politics, by a literal *deus ex machina*.[38] The assumption that appears questionable, in the line pursued here by Burgess, is that writers in the early modern period saw the living God as Deus *ex* rather than *in* machina. But the extent to which they were willing to separate grace and nature may be exaggerated by this approach. For Cromwell, to take one instance, politics was a partnership with the Almighty.[39] For many more, politics was about submission to an absolute God and a defence of that obligation against all worldly interference with it.[40] Such a defence, the service of God, almost necessarily meant worldly engagement. As one of the most admired expressions of godly sentiment and aspiration in its day, the Musselburgh Declaration of 1 August 1650 demonstrates that covenants were seen as binding, subject to God's providential guidance. Nevertheless, 'we do not think providences alone a sufficient rule for God's people to walk by'. Scripture too, read in part prudentially and in the light of prevailing circumstances, provided a supplementary guide. Without doubt, the primary objective remained to submit to Jesus Christ 'upon this own terms' and 'to follow him withersoever he goeth'.[41] The means of charting that course were those that we might describe as both secular and religious but contemporaries made no such category discrimination. Necessity, justice, prudence and divine direction were inextricably mixed, fusing politics and religion into an amalgam foreign to most of us but central to the thought and deed of seventeenth-century actors. Burgess is right to point to the primacy of divine will for so many of them but following the divine will meant human agents exercising their instrumentality by engagement with the world, bloodying their hands when it was required of them. Indeed, ignorance of 'the deep policies of worldly statesmen' could lead the saints into false commitments. It was this which had obliged God to give 'a second testimony ... from heaven', the King's defeat in the second civil war, 'he being a man of so much blood that the Lord would have no peace with him'. God's instruments on earth accordingly decapitated the 'man of blood'.[42] Instrumentality and submission went together in knowing engagement with the world by God's saints on his behalf. Politics and religion then merged where God and his instruments acted or performed speech acts in the world.

The final theme to inform discussion of the government/state and society relationship in this period is the development of a print culture, particularly in relation to the expansion of unlicensed printing from the 1640s onwards. Jürgen Habermas located the emergence of a public sphere, associated with the development of print culture, in the later seventeenth century. David Zaret has argued that this is a chronological error. For him the breaking open of an encapsulated political culture, intact through the sixteenth century, occurs in mid seventeenth-century England in association with the democratization of 'patterns of debate and dissent in the English Revolution'. Popular participation in religious debates, new standards of public reason and printing's capacity to create a public space (in these circumstances accessible to a much wider range of actors) fundamentally transformed the relationships of rule between government and society.[43] One may question some of the premises on which

Zaret's arguments are based, but the importance of the radical expansion of unlicensed printing and the emergence of a 'news' media can hardly be denied. We are only beginning to assimilate the significance of print culture, and the extension of those able and free to participate in the war of words, for the relationship between government and a more autonomously evolving political society.

The links between government and society were then mediated by ideas, practice and expectations associated with the 'unacknowledged republic', the confessional society and the demands of casuistry (particularly as confessional unity fractured), a society covenanted in a series of sometimes mutually incompatible engagements, and one driven by, on the one hand, the demands of a wilful and sometimes barely scrutable living God, and, on the other, by a widely divergent, accessible and relatively autonomous print culture.

Beyond the nexus of these interfaces between government and society, how can we depict the society with which we wish to connect contemporary radicalism? The old sociology of knowledge associated radical thought with class, either on the model of class transition driven by broadly envisaged economic and social changes, or of the fracturing of the old or nascent ruling classes by pressures from below. This will no longer do. As Glenn Burgess has suggested here, these approaches have tended to treat radicalism too monolithically, to characterize and privilege the radical as an anticipation of the modern and to rely on class analysis as a means of 'understanding' radicalism. As we have seen, some social historians have come to see early modern society as only ambiguously a class society. But, even were this not so, it has become obvious that 'the radical option was a minority choice for every social group'.[44] The association of radical words and actions with class and class conflict has worn so thin as to become unhelpful.

What then shall we put in its place? If we wish to end the monolithic treatment of radicalism, would it be best to assume communities of discourse, a number of linguistic contexts, some of which might be amenable to ideas of the transformation of rule while others might be inimical to it? The problem with the linguistic turn, in this respect, is that it does not of itself provide answers as to how choices between competing languages were made or why new languages became necessary. An alternative would be to adopt an approach similar to that of many contemporaries in their thinking about pre-civil society and to envisage seventeenth-century England as primarily a society of households. The patriarchal basis of authority and the strains upon it would not be the only subjects made more accessible to us by adopting this framework.[45] The functioning of government in relation to the nurture or destruction of households and their godliness, the pressures upon them of economic crisis and war, would all offer a basis for assessing political ideas and their transformative or other significance.[46] Ann Hughes has provided a perceptive analysis of Leveller agitation in terms of 'honest households'.[47] But beyond individual households were largely self-governing communities of households with officeholding widely dispersed amongst them and with sufficient autonomy to regard most legislation as permissive and themselves as having wide powers of discretion in relation to it. We come back then to the realities of the unacknowledged republic.

In practice, many of the legislative programmes which have come to be associated with the central government (for example, the Elizabethan Poor Law) were the result of cumulative local initiatives. In this respect, society begins to be almost impossible to dissociate from complex networks of governance and mediation running across the spectrum from household, parish, borough and county officeholders through to the personnel of crown and court. Many individuals were simultaneously operating at several points on the spectrum. Much political discourse, claim and counterclaim, petition and response represented a dialogue within the layers, branches and regions of this unacknowledged republic. The 'framework that can bring together society and economy, politics and culture'[48] may indeed be not so much a revival of the classical sociology of knowledge, but a new political sociology of knowledge rooted in an understanding of this matrix of rule and social organization. In this way, fresh approaches to *De Republica Anglorum* may not only shape our understanding of state/society relationships but our understanding of civil society itself.

IV. REASSESSING SOME MID-SEVENTEENTH-CENTURY RADICALS: THE LEVELLERS, WINSTANLEY AND HARRINGTON

To give some indication of the potential here, I offer an all-too-brief sketch of what might be involved in rereading the 'radicalism' of some individuals or groups commonly held to represent mid-seventeenth-century radicalism. All three have raised issues of tradition, of self-consciousness, of continuity and discontinuity (particularly perhaps in relation to the balance of secular and religious) and all three have things to say about the institutions of rule, the relationship between state and society and about social transformation.

IV. i The Levellers

The late nineteenth to mid-twentieth century rediscovery of the Levellers as liberal democrats, far removed from the social and state/society contexts we have just been discussing, is all too easy to depict as a chronological and contextual displacement which ends in the confusion of backward-looking progressives. The problem is, as Glenn Burgess indicates, how to put a comprehensive, post-revisionist assessment of them (and other 'radicals') in place and what its meaning for their status as radicals would be.[49]

That coalition, which came to be branded as the 'Levellers' in the immediate aftermath of the Putney debates,[50] began to coalesce in 1645/6 in a series of protests against the developing tyranny of Parliament. The creation of a military/fiscal machine, by a parliamentary leadership now desperate to avoid defeat in the Civil War, inevitably involved the paradox of the overriding of the discretionary autonomies of the unacknowledged republic by those who had been elected to defend those autonomies against the tyrannies of the eleven years' personal rule. New, and unprecedentedly heavy, taxation; administration through county communities side stepping local office holders; military pressures to override the mediatory processes of local regional authorities, and the creation of a national standing army with little, if any, accountability at the local level: all of these looked far more oppressive than the policies of the Stuart monarchy in the 1630s. Equally objectionable to members of the Leveller coalition were the growing threat of an unmediated religious uniformity and the setting aside of due process of law by arbitrary arrests, imprisonment without trial, and the forgoing of jury participation in the trials of commoners. By the mid 1640s it was clear that even an elected assembly could not, in all circumstances, be trusted to sustain the principles of the Petition of Right. The threat to liberty and property represented by the parliamentary policies of 1643 and 1645 was then a cry not only of royalists but also of many on the parliamentary side, in particular of the Leveller coalition.[51] Even in relation to the achievement of a godly society, one can see the Levellers as defenders of the discretionary 'tolerances' of the unacknowledged republic's operation pre-1633. The threat to such liberty of conscience no longer came from the idolatrous leanings of Laudianism but from the godly formality and rigidity of the Presbyterians. So, in this sense, it would be possible to present the Levellers as defenders of traditional 'freedoms', for whom the myth of the freeborn Englishman, sustained in his liberties by Magna Carta and the Petition of Right, was entirely appropriate; not so much radicals as conservative defenders of customary rights.[52] The languages they operated with could be seen as entirely consistent with this: the language of the 'common law mind', heavily reliant on Sir Edward Coke, and the language of practical Christianity with its devaluing of forms and privileging of mutual support and tolerance. Neither threatened the loosening of ties with customary ways that were inherent, for instance, in the languages of apocalyptic millennialism or more hardline classical republicanism. Rather than transforming the nature of government and its accommodation with contemporary society, the Levellers might be seen as wishing for the substantial restoration of what had been in place before the troubles.

But that, of course, is not the whole story and it will be instructive to ask 'Why not?' Two very practical sets of considerations seem to have driven Leveller thinking beyond the restoration of the customary and into envisaging a transformation or rule and the relationship between government and society. The first of these was the recognition that a representative assembly could tyrannize over the bodies, property and consciences of those it represented. What was to be done about this? In seeking to prevent a return to the 'old' tyrannical potential of prerogative monarchy and to curb the potential of the Commons for corruption and absolution, the Levellers had to consider the transformation of the relationship between government and governed. The second set of practical considerations were precipitated by their alliance with the soldiers and the anxious concern of the latter with the problem of indemnity.[53] Indemnity from prosecution for acts committed as soldiers under orders (rather than acts without discipline *while* soldiers) was vital to the army. But where was the civil authority capable of providing secure indemnity for the military? The indemnity ordinances of 27 May and 7 June 1647 were unsatisfactory because, on the one hand, they set the problematic challenge of establishing the direct authority of Parliament for individual acts in wartime and, on the other, there was the danger of citizens being deprived of reasonable legal redress. The dubious nature of parliamentary ordinances was a further worry for the military but of even greater concern was the reversibility of any parliamentary enactment by a future Parliament. The best hope of legal security for the soldiers rested in a comprehensive settlement into which their protections would be written. It is to this quest that the Levellers responded with the idea of an Agreement of the People, capable of binding future Parliaments and protecting the interests of both citizens and soldiers. Such a settlement would provide for frequently elected assemblies with limits on eligibility for election and re-election designed to safeguard against corruption. Power over the consciences of the godly with respect to religious practice and military conscription was also taken away. The provisions of the Petition of Right were written into the settlement. No 'publike officer' was to be imposed on counties, hundreds, cities, town or boroughs. They were to be chosen by the people on an annual basis. Similar provision was made for the appointment of future military commanders. The balance of accountability in the operation of the dispersed state was firmly shifted to local communities, but, in restoring the unacknowledged republic, the Levellers made a number of highly significant moves which we might reasonably wish to describe as 'radical'. First, they gave acknowledgement to the 'unacknowledged' in the form of a written, binding constitution. Second, they transformed the old parliamentary trinity into a unicameral assembly with limited powers. Third, the relationship between state and society was further transformed into one between this state and not so much a covenanted or god-driven society as a subscriptional community since full citizenship for adult male heads of household was dependent on their endorsement of the Agreement. At the same time, the security of parliamentary soldiers from future prosecution was written into a constitution unalterable by future parliaments.[54] The Leveller's defence of the freedom of press and pulpit can also be seen as the maintenance of an open public sphere as a further check on the corruptibility of even representative governors.

By placing the Levellers in the contexts of rule, state/society relations and the changing nature of society, we can see them as attempting both to restore the political culture of the unacknowledged republic, and seeking to achieve this by transformative means. This formulation may not be new but the means of getting to it are. The virtue of this is that it enables us to escape the anachronistic monolith of freedom loving liberals and democrats sprung out of nowhere or out of submerged traditions barely recoverable by the historian. In their place we have a coalition with a flexible programme, capable of making broad, pragmatic adjustments, both in language and objectives, around a core of fixed principle (liberty of conscience, the rule of law, consent, dispersed or limited authority) and driven by immediate, practical concerns.

IV. ii Winstanley

Like many of the Levellers, Winstanley came from and returned to a background of local office holding and it is to this context and that of the confessional, covenanted society that he and his radicalism are best related. The allegation of his 'modernity', associated with the notions that human nature could be changed and that equality of freedom could result from the abolition of property and wage labour, now seems to miss more than it explains.[55] Equally misleading are characterizations of Winstanley as leading a movement of the landless poor, alienated from the mainstream of the English Revolution. This was not how Winstanley saw it.[56] His participation in parish politics as a vestryman and local office holder, both before and after the famous digging experiments, suggests much greater integration with the parochial communities of London and Surrey than has commonly been allowed. Closer reading of his first published works of 1648, hitherto generally available only in severely truncated extracts, reveals a casuist concern with the problems of allegiance and obligation in the military and political crisis of that year. It became clear to him that the driving force of material necessity prevented the poor from adequately weighing the issues of conscience confronting them. Alternative social and economic infrastructures capable of ameliorating economic desperation and liberating conscience for the service of God became essential. Winstanley was not rejecting the conscientious society but endorsing it. Freedom was a moment enabling one to submit to the divine will. The fall of 'Kingly Government' was part of the unfolding of divine history, and the restoration of 'Creation Right' through communist community accordingly had an apocalyptic dimension. This was combined, in Winstanley's thought, not with alienation from the parliamentary revolution, but with the attempt to draw out what he regarded as its full potential. From the Solemn League and Covenant to the ordinances establishing a republic and the Engagement of 1649, Parliament's own words seemed to him to justify the wholesale social restructuring for which he campaigned, the displacement of Kingly Government by Commonwealth's Government. In this respect, Winstanley claimed to be at the heart of the true mainstream of the English Revolution.

One of his points of contact with contemporary political culture was then a casuistry, densely informed by scriptural readings and underpinned by a sense of the purpose and dynamic of the parliamentary cause. The other was his faith in a network of local officeholders closely governing the affairs of householders, parishes, boroughs and counties. *The Law of Freedom* (1652), his best known work, was, in this respect, an attempt to re-establish the self-governing communities (in which he had held office and would again) which had been put under intense pressure by socio-economic polarization and the ravages of war. So that, for Winstanley, the conscientious community and the republic of office-holders were to be restored but this could only be achieved by the transformative reconstituting of society. Lotte Mulligan and Judith Richards were right to insist that Winstanley and his contemporaries shared much of a mental map in common. But, to retain much of that commonality, he also embraced a radical set of discontinuities, in the form of 'dramatic social change', the end of property and wage labour.[57]

IV. iii Harrington

Winstanley did not have, but appealed to, the force which Cromwell possessed to transform rule. As the events of 1648/9 and 1653 demonstrated, the temptation to military intervention could prove overwhelming but there remained a reluctance to convert such intervention into permanent military control or to transform rather than restore the forms of civilian rule. An unstable stalemate ensued. Responsible government was still the goal of those who had begun the struggle in defence of civil and religious liberties. This meant accountability, not to the soldiers, but to what Cromwell himself called the 'witnesses' of the dispersed state, those whose active participation in largely unpaid office mediated and shaped the state across the parishes, hundreds, counties and boroughs of the nation.[58] A crucial question facing the Protectorate was whether these people, or their representatives in Parliament, would be prepared to work with the constitutional arrangements devised by the army *and* bear the heavy costs of military establishments in England, Wales, Scotland and Ireland.

The most systematic attempt to address these issues was James Harrington's *Oceana* (1656) and its associated publications. Over the last four decades, scholars have moved from a preoccupation with Harrington's Agrarian Laws and his imputed role as the class spokesman for a bourgeois imperialism to an engagement with his use, or abuse, of the languages of classical and Machiavellian republicanism. The relationship between society and the state was certainly one of Harrington's preoccupations and his argument rested on an historical analysis of the collapse of the baronage and of the military and governmental consequences of that collapse. In this sense, Harrington's advocated republic was post-baronial and John Pocock was right to describe *Oceana* as a Machiavellian meditation on the end of feudalism.[59] But there is also force in Blair Worden's description of it as a meditation on the expulsion of the Rump and, in that sense, much more closely engaged with the immediate problems of the 1650s.[60] It is a suggestion reinforced by the recent demonstration of Harrington's close reading of contemporary debates about the military and, in particular, the Militia Bill of October 1656.[61] His advocacy of a citizen militia and failure to recognize the irreversible implications of the military revolution embodied in the Protectorate's army and navy have been taken as evidence that he was in the grip of a classically derived, republican language. What he was doing with that language, however, has become the subject of substantial debate. Pocock's thesis in *The Machiavellian Moment* (1975) was that Harrington's work was the means by which such a language was adjusted from the needs of compact city-states to the requirements of extensive agrarian societies and made available for American resistance to imperial and monarchical presentations in the eighteenth century. Others have argued that a preoccupation with settlement, perhaps in competition with Hobbes, pushed Harrington in the direction of institutional constraints and a subversion of the values, while using the language, of classical republicanism.[62] It is now clear that future readings of Harrington's work must engage with his agenda of elaborate rituals designed to restore and maintain the civil and military machinery of government through the dispersed state of parish, hundred and county as well as the bicameral balances of his legislature. The people were once more to be 'equally possest of the government' and the militia. Provision for participatory office-holding was on an impressive scale. Over two years, half of adult citizens would be required to discharge some public office. This was the rule of 'King PEOPLE'. Oceanic government was co-ordinated not only in the relationships between the central institutions of council and bicameral legislature, but also between them and the state in its local and regional forms of expression. Harrington's civil religion falls into a similar pattern: national provision with a good deal of local mediation and discretion plus provision for the liberty of godly, Protestant consciences.

Harrington, like Winstanley and the Levellers, saw some form of restoration of the unacknowledged republic as essential. How else was England to be governed? How else was there to be an English state with any effective meaning? But, to make that work, there had to be a transformation of other aspects of rule in order to achieve the following: a halt to the unselfconscious process of social transformation (an Agrarian Law); a series of checks on the tendency of the mixed polity to self-destruct (the Equal Commonwealth); and an elimination of the military/fiscal state which threatened to overwhelm the unacknowledged republic (the citizen militia).

IV. iv Three Radicalisms Reconsidered

In the Levellers we witness an attempt to put the unacknowledged republic back on its feet but with transforming constitutional constraints on even a body representative of this 'state'. Theirs would have been a settlement providing for plurality of voices, both in print and oral culture, a public sphere designed to protect liberty for godly consciences within the framework of a subscriptional community of those who endorsed the Agreement of the People. Winstanley too sought the restoration of many features of the unacknowledged republic but to preserve the possibility of a conscientious society, open and responsive to casuist reasoning, he advocated the transformation of society. The introduction of Commonwealth's Government was a means of removing the constricting social and economic pressures, as he saw it, on conscience. The unacknowledged republic was also be set working again in Harrington's *Oceana* but this was only possible, he thought, if, by eliminating the military/fiscal state, the immediate threats to it were removed and both socio-economic change and inter-institutional conflict were brought under control by 'political architecture'.

Twenty years ago I tried to explore an alternative to the teleological identification of radicalism in our early modern past. My functionalist approach of identification *via* the processes of delegitimation of the status quo, legitimation of a preferred alternative and the envisaging of the means of transfer from one to the other now appears, at best, a flawed starting point. I would want to qualify or modify it in four respects. More scope needs to be left for the antiformalism of much of the thinking of the 1640s and 1650s[63] and its predilection for demolition and aversion to construction save under the guiding hand of King Jesus. Second, I would concede much more influence not only to the linguistic turn but also to the linguistic choices and linguistically subversive plays that contemporaries were capable of making, to their linguistic agency. Third, as an extension of this, I would advocate the necessity of caution in the face of linguistic projection, labelling, the imposition of identities by contemporaries, such as we see in respect of, not only the Ranters,[64] but of Levellers, Diggers and many others. Finally, readers will be aware by now that I consider the work of Collinson, Braddick, Hindle and others to be seminal for the reading of the political thought of the period in its socio-political context. This applies not only to those who have advocated some sort of transformation of rule but to more cautious thinkers such as George Lawson or to practical politicians like the Lord Protector himself.

V CONCLUSION

Before drawing some general conclusions, I want to suggest four preliminary considerations. A historiography of radicalism, or of political thought more generally, which is based on political approval or disapproval carries an interpretative deadweight – the metaphoric bestowal of medals, awards and certificates which is entirely inappropriate, condescending and invariably anachronistic.[65] The trajectories or premodern to modern, authoritarian to liberal/pluralist, elite to popular/democratic, religious to secular, exploitation to socially just may all contain the bacillus of progressive ideology and its attendant condescension to the past. It is this which makes so many commentators see, as Conal Condren notes, any form of republicanism as radical by default.[66] Does some sort of functionalist approach offer the only prospect of liberation from this dubious teleology and its historical consequences?

Second, nearly always – as in the three examples discussed above – we will find a mixture of the restorative and the transformative.[67] This should not surprise us. In a period of elemental upheaval those things which were valued in present rule might only be sustained if transformed circumstances were adjusted to by transformed institutions, relationships of rule and social dispositions. Third, degrees of self-consciousness and unselfconsciousness are in evidence and need to be worked on further. We should not, however, automatically assume that this separates into a self-conscious awareness of tradition, the customary, and an unselfconsciousness of transformation and its consequences. An instructive test case here is consciousness of God as a *living God*, a wilful, arbitrary, unpredictable and transformative God to whom the self must consciously be submitted.[68] Finally, I would argue that the issues of print culture, the confessional or conscientious society, and of the unacknowledged republic or dispersed state provide a more productive and historically appropriate base for a political sociology of knowledge, for this period, than does a chronologically displaced class analysis.

Many of the essays in this volume raise the question of a long-term history of radicalism, a meta-narrative of radical ideas and movements, the possibility of a tradition of English radicalism. Like the history of the state, to which it would almost necessarily be functionally related, the long-term history of radicalism appears problematic because the discontinuities can appear so great as to forbid a continuous narrative. The radicalism of the twenty-first century may appear so different to that of the seventeenth as not to be part of the same story.

Beyond showing that the ideas of the past are relevant to the present, there has been an urge to demonstrate a substantive continuity, an urge represented at its best perhaps in the work of Christopher Hill and E. P. Thompson. The greater the emphasis on radical continuity, the more we are obliged to assume that we are in some sense constructed in ways similar to our predecessors if only in our willingness to pick up and pass on the same baton of the radical cause. Differences in the sources of ideas, objectives, language and context are downplayed in the search for a socially innate, if not genetic, radical germ. But this itself involved a process of reading, memory and construction which has little affinity with history as an exercise in scrupulous and self-critical recovery of the past. Its links to social history are typically either to the history of the processes and rituals of protest[69] or to the history of oppression, marginalization and alienation. The latter leaves us with the problem of how radicals were able to access the linguistic resources of, and exercise leverage over, their society; the former with how to distinguish radical forms of protest from others. If we move away from a class basis for the analysis of social change over long periods and recognize that radical movements can be coalitions of individuals from different social backgrounds, alliances of a spectrum of minorities, the problem is how to tell the history of those shifting coalitions.

By contrast, Mark Philp has argued here for the denial of any consistent ideological (or sociological) tradition emphasizing instead the specificity of each struggle and its context, of tactical dynamics and the contingencies of pragmatic responses.[70] For J. C. D. Clark the question, as to whether English radicalism can be traced to the 1640s or the 1760s, asks a meaningless question because the vocabulary of radicalism was itself only established in the 1820s.[71] The 'no thing before the word' view of the history of radicalism is one shared by Conal Condren.[72] Richard Greaves likewise, argues that no assumptions of radical continuity can be made over long periods of time, that – even allowing for the use of the word – we damage the historical specificity of radical episodes or moments if we invoke the continuity of a never-ending tradition. In the wake of these critiques, we are left wondering whether there is anything to be gained by diachronic comparisons or narrative linkage of these historically specific moments and whether there can be any justification for describing those moments pre-1820 as 'radical'.

Yet, in this reaction to the teleological, linguistic and generalizing excesses of an earlier pursuit of the great radical tradition, is there a danger of throwing out the baby with the bathwater, of losing something of value to historical discourse? A middle-way in dealing with the history of moments of politically or socially transformative aspirations which might be called 'radical' can be argued. John Pocock has interestingly suggested that the concept of, if not the word for, the radical was evident in the 1640s in notions of 'Root and Branch' reform. In this view the danger lies in moving from 'radical' as adjective to 'radical' as noun in our discourse on the period.[73] But beyond linguistic considerations, to which, since we deal with words, we shall always have to return, I would like to suggest five considerations why, even allowing for the imperatives of historical specificity, we might want to raise our enquiry on to a longer-term basis. First, at the most precise level of specificity there are questions of comparison and contrast. The pragmatics of practical considerations which prompted a transformative response either in Stephen Alford's dynastic crisis of the 1560s or 1580s, or in the indemnity/settlement issues of the later 1640s pose exactly these questions and it is not our business to evade them. Philp identifies ways of looking at the politics of exclusion/inclusion and at the transactional costs involved in pursuing one option or the other. Are there analyses of this type which might link the study of radical response in discrete situations? Second, we must think less monolithically: of radical moments rather than of radical individuals[74] or radical movements. What, if anything, links these moments? A substantial reality (the 'radical' as noun); functional requirements; linguistic or rhetorical continuities; self-conscious historical references? Third, the meta-narrative of rule, if it is feasible, must have significance for the possibility of a story linking those attempts to transform it. Fourth, since rule requires resources, the socio-political history of power and property will involve the story of how their disposition was legitimated or challenged. This too must presage some elements of the history of radicalism. Finally, the metahistory of the confessional society, even at the crude level of the transition from a conscientious society to one of 'interests' should have implications for a longer-term history of radicalism. As long as we see religion as an antithesis to politics we will end up with a terminal problem for that history. Either, following Christopher Hill, radicalism in a traditional society must tend to the heterodox or the irreligious (but this flies in the face of the evidence), or, as Glenn Burgess argues, early modern radicalism is God-centred and therefore not political. The claim I have made above is that we need to readdress the basic assumption behind both positions.

Linguistically one of the longer-term historical questions is how we moved from a prevailing and sustaining language of tradition and custom to one of innovation, reconceptualism and transformation. Here is a complex of issues which needs disentangling. Language itself is a set of conventions, From this perspective, for radicalism to emerge it has to be either a dissonant or an innovative language. In both cases, it has to breach convention and the process involved here requires explanation. Is it a product of the subversion of a conventional language? Harrington, for example, finding the ancient constitution and the language which sustained it subverted by social change, substituted (but also subverted) the language of classical republicanism. Where does the linguistic challenge inherent in these transformative dispositions come from?

We cannot understand the processes of linguistic transformation, any more than we can understand movements and moments of political and social transformation and action, without invoking something more substantial than linguistic conventions. The preconditions of the further prosecution of this line are clarity about the meaning of the categories we use and, secondly, close linkage of the discussion to the recovery of the historical meaning of rule, the relationship between state and society and the nature of society. Ideas reflect changing social circumstances but how are we to recover these links? The sociology of knowledge of the old marxist type is discredited. But a political sociology of knowledge, based on patterns of governance and office-holding from the unacknowledged republic onwards may have important things to teach us as has been suggested above. Such an approach may lead to a history of radical ideas, episodes and moments which is less monolithic but more integrationist. The classic sociology of knowledge and the history of radicalism based on it pitted oppressed against oppressors, excluded versus included, exploited against exploiters and made little allowance for conflict within that state or amongst the powerful which could generate transformative aspirations and coalitions. When we concede the reality of the dispersed, highly participatory state of the self-governing communities of the unacknowledged republic, it becomes possible to conceive of a radicalism emerging from within the structures of that state and, to a highly integrated extent, sharing a political culture with it. In turn, this opens up the possibility of a history of a radicalism which, while standing in a critical relationship to the status quo and seeking transformation, is not coming to that task from a position of *radical* alienation. Such a history would have to acknowledge local distinctiveness and contextual specificity. It would also acknowledge the radical moments of actors devoid of a programmatic radicalism, that is the development of radically pragmatic responses under the sheer pressure of events and circumstances.[75] These sensitivities, valuable and essential as they are, should not preclude the history of radicalism. The risk inherent in over-scrupulosity about language or in an over-emphasis on historical specificity is that we lose what might be learned from a comparative, diachronic perspective on these moments. The reward for pursuing such learning, despite the difficulties, would be a richer and more human appreciation of the fitful impulse towards transformative change in our history.

NOTES

1 Richard L. Greaves, 'That Kind of People': Late Stuart Radicals and Their Manifestoes: A Functional Approach', p. 89, this volume.
2 Luc Borot, 'Richard Overton and Radicalism: the New Intertext of the Civic Ethos in Mid-Seventeenth-Century England', p. 38, this volume.
3 Glenn Burgess, 'Introduction', p. 1, this volume; Glenn Burgess, 'Radicalism and the English Revolution', Ian Hampsher-Monk, 'The Languages of Radicalism: the 'Failed' English Revolution of the 1790s as Linguistic Non-Performance?', p. 143, this volume.
4 J. C. Davis, 'Radicalism in a Traditional Society: The Evaluation of Radical Thought in the English Commonwealth', *History of Political Thought*, 3:2 (1982) pp. 193–213. See also the comments of Burgess, 'Introduction', p. 8, this volume.
5 J. C. Davis, 'Radical Lives', *Political Science*, 37, (1985) pp. 167–172.
6 Keith Wrightson, 'The Social Order of Early Modern England: Three Approaches', in Lloyd Bonfield, Richard M. Smith and Keith Wrightson (eds.), *The World We Have Gained: Histories of Population and Social Structure: Essays presented to Peter Laslett on his Seventieth Birthday* (Oxford, 1986) pp. 198–199.
7 David Underdown, *Revel, Riot and Rebellion: Popular Politics and Culture in England 1603–1660* (Oxford, 1985) p. 45 and passim.
8 Kevin Sharpe, *Politics and Ideas in Early Stuart England* (London and New York, 1989) pp. 10, 14.
9 Underdown, *Revel, Riot and Rebellion*, Conclusion.
10 Christopher Hill, *A Nation of Change and Novelty: Radical politics, religion and literature in seventeenth-century England* (London and New York, 1990) Chapter 3 especially p. 52.
11 Conal Condren, 'Radicalism Revisited', p. 311, this volume.

12 J. C. D. Clark, *Revolution and Rebellion: State and Society in England in the seventeenth and eighteenth centuries* (Cambridge, 1986) pp. 98, 108. See also *idem.*, 'Religion and the Origins of Radicalism in Nineteenth Century Britain', above. Cf. Conal Condren, 'Radicals, Moderates and Conservatives in Early-Modern Political Thought: A case of the Sandwich Islands Syndrome', *History of Political Thought*, 10 (1989).

13 Richard L. Greaves, '"That Kind of People": Late Stuart Radicals and their Manifestoes: A Functional Approach', pp. 87-114, this volume.

14 Ian Hampsher-Monk, 'The Languages of Radicalism: the "Failed" English Revolution of the 1790s as Linguistic Non-Performance?', p. 135–155, this volume.

15 J. G. Pocock, 'The true Leveller's standard revisited: an afterword', in Michael Mendle (ed.) *The Putney Debates of 1647: The Army, the Levellers and the English State* (Cambridge, 2001) pp. 283–291.

16 J. C. Davis, 'A Short Course of Discourse: Studies in Early Modern Conscience, Duty and the 'English Protestant Interest'', *The Journal of Ecclesiastical History*, 46:2 (1995) pp. 302–309.

17 Michael J. Braddick, *State Formation in Early Modern England c.1550–1700* (Cambridge, 2000); Steve Hindle, *The State and Social Change in early Modern England c.1550–1640* (London, 2000); Mark Goldie, 'The Unacknowledged Republic: Officeholding in Early Modern England', in Tim Harris (ed.), *The Politics of the Excluded c.1500–1850* (Basingstoke, 2001) pp. 153–194.

18 Luc Borot, 'Richard Overton and Radicalism: the New Intertext of the Civic Ethos in Mid-Seventeenth-Century England', pp. 56–57, this volume.

19 Stephen Alford, 'A Politics of Emergency in the Reign of Elizabeth I', above. See also Patrick Collinson, *De Republica Anglorum: Or, History with the Politics Put Back* (Cambridge, 1990).

20 David Martin Jones, *Conscience and Allegiance in Seventeenth Century England: The Political Significance of Oaths and Engagements* (New York, 1999); Edward Vallance, 'Oaths, Casuistry and Equivocation: Anglican Responses to the Engagement Controversy', *The Historical Journal*, 44:1 (2001) pp. 59–77. I am also grateful to Dr Vallance for a prepublication copy of his paper, 'Puritanism and Liberty: The Radicals and the Idea of a National Covenant'.

21 Michael J. Braddick, *State Formation in Early Modern England c.1550-1700* (Cambridge, 2000), Part I.

22 James Scott Wheeler, *The Making of a World Power: War and the Military Revolution in Seventeenth-Century England* (Stroud, Gloucestershire, 1999).

23 For example, the 1633 Declaration of Sports was seen as overthrowing western Assize orders forbidding ales and revels. Defence of local authority and discretion against such incursions remains a feature of officeholders' behaviour down to the Clubmen assemblies of the 1640s. Underdown, *Revel, Riot and Rebellion*, pp. 65–66, 150–158.

24 Hugh Kearney, *The Eleven Years Tyranny of Charles I* (London, 1962): Kevin Sharpe, *The Personal Rule of Charles I* (New Haven, 1992).

25 John Morrill, *The Nature of the English Revolution* (London, 1993) Part One.

26 David L. Smith, 'The Impact on Government', in John Morrill (ed.), *The Impact of the English Civil War* (London, 1991) pp. 38–9.

27 Michael Mendle, *Henry Parker and the English Civil War: the political thought of the public's privado* (Cambridge, 1995).

28 William Lamont, 'Pamphleteering, the Protestant Consensus and the English Revolution', in R. C. Richardson and G. M. Ridden (eds.) *Freedom and the English Revolution: Essays in History and Literature* (Manchester, 1986) pp. 72–92.

29 Barbara Donagan, 'The army, the state and the soldier in the English civil war', in Mendle (ed.) *The Putney Debates*, pp.79–102; Michael Mendle, 'Putney's pronouns: identity and indemnity in the great debate', in *ibid.*, pp. 125–127.

30 See Howell A. Lloyd, 'Constitutionalism', in J. H. Burns with Mark Goldie (eds.) *The Cambridge History of Political Thought 1450–1700* (Cambridge, 1991) p. 289.

31 Collinson, *De Republica Anglorum*. Of particular interest here in this seminal discussion is Professor Collinson's reading of Sir Thomas Smith's *De Republica Anglorum* (1583).

32 Cynthia Herrup, 'The Counties and the Country: Some Thoughts on Seventeenth century Historiography', in Geoff Eley and William Hunt (eds.), *Reviving the English Revolution: Reflections and Elaborations on the work of Christopher Hill* (London, 1988) pp. 289–304 especially pp. 292–293.

33 For a useful discussion see John Morrill, 'The Impact of Puritanism', in Morrill (ed.) *Impact*, pp.51–56. J. C. Davis, 'Against Formality: One Aspect of the English Revolution', *Transactions of the Royal Historical Society*, 6th series, 3 (1993) pp. 265–288.

34 Keith Thomas, 'Cases of Conscience in Seventeenth Century England', in John Morrill, Paul Slack and Daniel Woolf (eds.), *Public Duty and Private Conscience in Seventeenth Century England* (Oxford, 1993) pp. 29–56.

35 Jones, *Conscience and Allegiance*. On the Bond of Association of 1584 see Stephen Alford, 'A Politics of Emergency in the Reign of Elizabeth I', pp. 17–36, this volume.

36 Vallance, 'Oaths, Casuistry and Equivocation', *idem.*, '"An Holy and Sacramental Paction": Federal Theology and the Solemn League and Covenant in England', *The English Historical Review*, 116:465 (2001) pp. 50–75.

37 John Walter, 'The Impact on Society: A World Turned Upside Down', in Morrill (ed.), *Impact*, pp. 105–107.

38 Glenn Burgess, 'Radicalism and the English Revolution' pp. 78–9, this volume. Cf. Clark, 'Religion and the Origins of Radicalism', p. 266, this volume.

39 J. C. Davis, *Oliver Cromwell* (London, 2000) Chapter 6.

40 J. C. Davis, 'Religion and the Struggle for Freedom in the English Revolution', *The Historical Journal*, 35:3 (1992) pp. 507–530.

41 *A Declaration of the English Army now in Scotland, Touching the Justnes & Necessity of the Present Proceeding in that Nation*, (1650) in A. S. P. Woodhouse (ed.) *Puritanism and Liberty* (London, 1938) pp. 476–478.

42 *Ibid.*, pp. 476–477.

43 David Zaret, 'Religion, Science and Printing in the Public Spheres in Seventeenth-Century England', in Craig Calhoun (ed.), *Habermas and the Public Sphere* (Cambridge, Massachusetts, 1992) pp. 212–235. See also *idem.*, *Origins of a Democratic Culture: Printing, Petitions and the Public Sphere in Early Modern England* (Princeton, 2000).

44 Burgess, 'Radicalism and the English Revolution', pp. 64–65, this volume.

45 Gordon Schochet, *Patriarchalism in Political Thought* (Oxford, 1975).

46 For useful perspective on these issues see Braddick, *State Formation.*

47 Ann Hughes, 'Gender and politics in Leveller literature', in Susan D. Amussen and Mark A. Kishlansky (eds.), *Political culture and cultural politics in early modern England: Essays presented to David Underdown* (Manchester, 1995) pp. 162–188.

48 Burgess, 'Radicalism and the English Revolution', p. 65, this volume.

49 Burgess, 'Radicalism and the English Revolution', p. 64, this volume.

50 Blair Worden, 'The Levellers in history and memory c.1660–1960', in Mendle (ed.), *The Putney Debates*, pp. 280–282. See also *idem.*, *Roundhead Reputations: The English Civil Wars and the Passions of Posterity* (London, 2001).

51 Glenn Burgess, 'The Impact on Political Thought: Rhetorics for Troubled Times', in Morrill (ed.), *The Impact*, pp. 77–78.

52 R. B. Seaberg, 'The Norman Conquest and the common law: the Levellers and the argument from continuity', *Historical Journal*, 24 (1981) pp. 791–806.

53 Donagan, 'The army, the state and the soldier'; Mendle, 'Putney's pronouns'.

54 For these provisions see the Third Agreement of 1 May 1649 in Andrew Sharp (ed.), *The English Levellers* (Cambridge, 1998) pp. 168–178. See also Ian Gentles, 'The *Agreements of the people* and their political contexts, 1647–1649', in Mendle (ed.), *The Putney Debates*, pp. 148–174.

55 Christopher Hill, 'Winstanley and Freedom', in R. C. Richardson and G. M. Ridden (eds.), *Freedom and the English Revolution: Essays in history and literature* (Manchester, 1986) pp. 151–168.

56 J. C. Davis with J. D. Alsop, entry on Gerrard Winstanley in *The Oxford Dictionary of National Biography* (Oxford, 2004).

57 Lotte Mulligan and Judith Richards, 'A 'Radical' Problem: The Poor and English Reformers in the mid-seventeenth century', *The Journal of British Studies*, 29:2 (1990) pp. 118–146.

58 For Cromwell's invocation of these "witnesses" see his speech of 12 September 1654 to the first protectoral Parliament in W. C. Abbott (ed.), *The Writings and Speeches of Oliver Cromwell*, 4 volumes (Cambridge, Massachusetts, 1937–1947; Oxford reprint, 1998) Vol. III, pp. 451–462.

59 J. G. A. Pocock (ed.) *James Harrington: The Commonwealth of Oceana and A System of Politics* (Cambridge, 1992) Introduction.

60 Blair Worden, 'English Republicanism', in Burns with Goldie (eds.), *Cambridge History of Political Thought*, pp. 450–455.

61 T. R. W. Kubik, 'How far the sword? Militia tactics and politics in the *Commonwealth of Oceana*, *History of Political Thought*, 19:2 (1998) pp. 186–212.

62 J. C. Davis, *Utopia and the Ideal Society* (Cambridge, 1981) Chapter 8; *idem.*, 'Equality in an unequal commonwealth: James Harrington's republicanism and the meaning of equality', in Ian Gentles, John Morrill and Blair Worden (eds.), *Soldiers, writers and statesmen of the English Revolution* (Cambridge, 1998) pp. 229–242; Jonathan Scott, 'The rapture of motion: James Harrington's republicanism', in Nicholas Phillipson and Quentin Skinner (eds.), *Political Discourse in Early Modern Britain* (Cambridge, 1993) Chapter 8.

63 J. C. Davis, 'Against Formality: One Aspect of the English Revolution', Transactions of the Royal Historical Society, 6th series, 3 (1993) pp. 265–288.

64 J. C. Davis, *Fear, Myth and History: The Ranters and the historians* (Cambridge, 1986).

65 On anxieties about this from a sympathetic commentator see Barry Reay, 'The World Turned Upside Down: A Retrospect', in Eley and Hunt (eds.), *Reviving the English Revolution*, pp. 64–5. See also Phyllis Mack's comment on the '*utterly* conservative scenario' of Winstanley's patriarchalism: 'The Prophet and Her Audience: Gender and Knowledge in The World Turned Upside Down', in *ibid.*, p.143. My emphasis.

66 Conal Condren, 'Radicalism Revisited', pp. 318–320, this volume.

67 Glenn Burgess's remarks on pointillism are suggestive here: Burgess, 'Radicalism and the English Revolution', p. 65, this volume.

68 J. C. Davis, 'Living with the Living God; Radical religion in the English revolution', in Chris Durston and Judith Maltby (eds.), *Religion in the English Revolution* (Manchester, forthcoming)

69 For an example of this see Tim Harris, 'The Leveller legacy: from the Restoration to the Exclusion Crisis', in Mendle (ed.), *The Putney Debates*, pp.219–240. Acknowledging that there was little if any continuity of ideas or programmes as part of a Leveller tradition transcending the Restoration, Harris argues that there were continuities in the technique of mass politics, agitation and the use of cheap print and petitions, appeals to natural justice, popular sovereignty, the laws of God and nature and to fundamental law. But this is to make standard discursive practice and mobilization techniques too much the exclusive legacy of the Levellers and radicalism.

70 Mark Philp, 'Disconcerting ideas: explaining popular radicalism and popular loyalism in the 1790s', pp. 156–188, this volume.

71 J. C. D. Clark, 'Religion and the origins of radicalism in nineteenth-century Britain', p. 241, this volume.

72 Conal Condren, 'Radicalism Revisited', pp. 311–329, this volume.

73 J. G. Pocock, 'The true Leveller's standard revisited: an afterword', in Michael Mendle (ed.), *The Putney Debates of 1647: The Army, the Levellers and the English State* (Cambridge, 2001), pp. 287–288.

74 J. C. Davis, 'Radical Lives', *Political Science*, 37 (1985) pp. 167–172.

75 An illuminating illustration of this approach seems to me to be implicit in F. Rosen, 'Jeremy Bentham's Radicalism', pp. 216–239, this volume.

Index

absolute monarchy/absolutism 20, 57, 105, 198, 348
Adam, John 293–4, 297–9
Addington, Henry, 1st Viscount Sidmouth 261
Addison, Joseph 117
Agreements of the People (1647–9) 42, 49, 52, 54–7, 70–3, 76, 357, 362
Alford, Stephen 321, 327, 328, 345, 365
Alsop, James D. 65
Althusius, Johannes 345, 350
Ambrose, Saint 263
American foundation *see* American Revolution
American Revolution and War of Independence (1775–83) 142, 146, 179, 242, 263, 299
Amherst, William, 1st earl Amherst 293–4, 296–9
anachronism 12–14, 66, 90, 91, 242, 311, 312, 315, 328, 339, 340, 344
ancient constitution 68, 71, 73–4, 135, 137, 146, 160, 326 (*see also* common law)
Anderson, Perry 3
Annesley, Arthur, earl of Anglesey 89
antiformalism 362
anti-popery *see* Catholicism
Apologetical Narration (1644) 73
Argyll rebellion (1685) 94, 96–108
Arnot, Sandford 293
Asa 24
Associations, loyalist (1790s) *see* Reeves, John
asymmetry, explanatory 157–9, 162, 170, 180, 183, 184
Athalia 23
atheism 97, 257, 258, 265, 327
Attwood, Thomas 299
Augustine, Saint 57, 263
Aylmer, Gerald 64
Aylmer, John 21, 22

Bacon, Sir Francis 41
Bacon, Nicholas 20, 27
Bahadur, Shamshir 288
Baker, Keith 141, 144
Bamford, Samuel 197, 200, 207, 253
Baptists 87, 90, 91, 95, 98, 107
Barker, Christopher 25
Barrackpore mutiny (1825) 296
Bastwick, John 43
Beccaria 233
begriffsgeschichte: 323
Belchem, John 190–2, 197, 207
Bellers, John 4
Bentham, Jeremy 151, 217–36, 254–63, 286, 292, 296, 313, 323, 328
Bentinck, Lord William 298, 302
Bernstein, Eduard 63
Bethel, Sidney 87
Biagini, Eugenio 190
bible *see* Matthew bible, Geneva bible
biblical word-association 50–1
Birmingham Political Union 299
birth control 232, 233
Blackstone, Sir William 233, 255, 262, 263
Blake, William 4, 6, 7, 137
Blaquiere, Edward 235
Blood, Thomas 92, 94–108
Bond of Association (1584) 17–18, 25–7, 33, 55, 321, 345, 351
  later impact 29–30
bonds, Scottish 29
Bonner, Edmund 40, 44, 47
Borot, Luc 317–19, 327, 328, 330, 331, 339, 345
Bothwell Bridge uprising (1679) 94
Bourbon, Louis de, prince de Condé 29
Bourne, Zachary 96
Bower, Samuel 270–1
Bowles, John 161
Bowring, John 235, 255, 262, 291, 292
Bracton, Henry 20
Braddick, Michael 362
Bradshaw, John 46, 47
Bridle, William, and Mrs Bridle 198–203, 205
Bright, John 190–1, 207
'Britannicus' (pseud.) 247

Brown, John 118
Browne, Sir Thomas 38
Brownists 41
Brroke, Sir James 302
Buckingham, James Silk 293–6, 299, 301, 302
Bullinger, Heinrich 19
Bunyan, John 7, 38, 54
Burdett, Sir Francis 257
Burford mutiny 39, 42, 55
Burgess, Glenn 312, 316, 317, 321–3, 340, 352–4, 356, 366
Burgh, James 17–18, 30, 118, 146
Burghley, Lord *see* Cecil, William
Burke, Edmund 115, 117, 120, 122, 124, 129, 137, 143, 145, 149, 161, 183, 294, 340
Burnley, Mary 289
Burns, J.H. 218
Burton, Henry 43
Butler, James, duke of Ormond 94–108
Byron, Lord 292

Calvin. Jean 104
Cameronians 91, 96–108 (*see also* Covenanters)
Canning, George 293–4
Capel, Arthur, earl of Essex 92, 108
capital punishment 103
Capp, Bernard 68
Carew, Sir Peter 19
Carlile, Robert 200, 206–7, 233, 247, 249, 261, 266
Carlyle, Thomas 3
Caroline, Queen 205
Cartwright, John, Major 21–2, 137, 141, 145, 243
Caspah, battle of (1804) 288
casuistry 55, 350–2, 359
Catholicism 18, 23, 28, 30, 31, 88, 90, 97–8, 101
Cecil, William, lord Burghley 18, 20, 25–9
Chandos, Marquis of *see* Grenville, Richard
Charles I 43, 46–7, 331
Charles II 89, 321
Chartists/Chartism 4, 6, 39, 190, 191, 207, 271
Cheke, John 19
Child, Henry 204
Christianson, Paul 68
Christie, Ian 163
Christie, Thomas 129
Chudleigh, Thomas 88
Church and King riots (1791) 159, 164
Church of England, attacks on 241–72 (*see* further atheism; religion)
Cicero 328, 331
citizenship 27–8, 30, 40, 41, 54, 56, 122, 128, 330, 348
civic ethos *see* citizenship
civic language 137–8 (*see also* citizenship)
civil society 295
civility *see* politeness
Claeys, Gregory 330
Clarendon *see* Hyde, Edward
Clark, Anna 207
Clark, J.C.D. 9, 64, 99, 313, 314, 316, 326–7, 333, 344, 364
Clarridge, Samuel 92
class, social/class struggle 5, 8, 10–12, 64–6, 102, 157, 169–70, 172–5, 177, 181, 184, 190, 191, 208, 230, 232, 242, 349, 363
classical republicanism *see* republicanism
Cobbett, William 141, 145, 150, 161, 207, 258, 267
Cockaygne, land of 5–6
Cohn-Bendit, Daniel 37
Coke, Sir Edward 41, 56, 194, 357
Colchester plunderers 65
Collard, Nicholas 204
College, Stephen 88
Colley, Linda 159
Collinson, Patrick 21, 23, 27, 39, 328, 362
colonies, British 285–6 (*see also* American Revolution; India)
commercial society 117, 136
common law 41, 56, 194, 195, 199, 357 (*see also* ancient constitution; constitutionalism; liberties)
commonwealth tradition 242, 332, 359
  commonwealthsman 332
Communist Party Historians' Group 3, 4, 14, 64
Condren, Conal 8–9, 11, 63, 64, 66, 69, 90, 343, 344, 363, 364
Connolly, William S. 320
conservatism 243, 315
constitutionalism, of radicals 183, 191, 192, 208, 222, 266
continuity (of radicalism) *see* radical tradition
convention, national 146–7, 248 (*see also* parliament)
  England (1794) 146
  Scotland (1793) 146
conventions 224–5
Cooke, Anthony 20
Cookson, J. E. 163, 178
Cooper, Anthony Ashley, 1st earl of Shaftesbury (d. 1683) 100
Cooper, Anthony Ashley, 3rd earl of Shaftesbury (d. 1713) 117
Coppe, Abiezer 79
copyhold 102
Corah 24
Cornwallis, Charles, 1st Marquis Cornwallis 290, 294
corruption 126, 137, 326, 333
  'Old Corruption' 301

counsel 23
County Movement 142
country party 160, 184
covenanted society 351
Covenanters 87, 90, 91, 93–108
Cranmer, Thomas 19, 32
Crawfurd, John 292, 299, 301
Crimmins, James 220, 221
Cromwell, Oliver 10, 39, 42, 43, 48, 55, 69, 76, 352, 360, 363
crowds 41, 162–3
Culpeper, John 46
Curzon, George 285
customary tenure 102

Dalhousie, earl and marquis of *see* Ramsay, James
Darnley, Henry, Lord 29
Dathan 24
David (King) 24, 32
Davis, J.C. 7, 8, 62, 64, 69, 92, 313, 314, 319, 320, 322, 340–1, 362
Declaration of Sports 347
deism 179, 182, 249, 265
Dennis, Jonas 244
Derbyshire miners 65
despotism, in government of India 295, 297
Diggers 4, 78, 79, 193, 264 (*see also* Winstanley, Gerrard)
dissent *see* nonconformity
domestic sphere *see* public/private spheres
domesticity 123–4, 128 (*see also* public/private spheres)
Dozier, Robert R. 163, 164, 167
Dumont, Etienne 219, 256
Dundas, Charles, Baron Amesbury 167
Durston, Christopher 53
Dyer, George 263

East India Company 285–303
Eaton, Daniel Isaac 148, 181
education 119, 122, 124, 128, 150, 287, 290
Edward VI 19, 22, 32
effeminacy 120, 121
elect nation 43
Elizabeth I 23, 24
Ellenborough, Baron *see* Law, Edward
Elton, Sir Geoffrey 345
Elyot, Sir Thomas 40
Emsley, Clive 176
Engagement, the (1649–50) and the Engagement controversy 55, 345, 351, 359
Enlightenment 218, 223–6, 234, 295
Epstein, James 190–2, 207
Erskine, Thomas, Baron Erskine 148
Evangelicals and Evangelical movement 119, 247, 248
Ewart, William 299
Exclusion Crisis 87, 94, 100

family 122–3, 128
family of love 65
fanatics/fanaticism 87–8, 90, 91
Fast sermons 69
Fawlty, Basil 331 (*see also* Charles I)
Ferguson, Robert 87, 96
festive culture *see* popular culture
Fifth Monarchists 77, 80, 90, 94, 95
Filmer, Sir Robert 57, 160
Fink, Z.S. 41
Fitzroy, Augustus, 3rd duke of Grafton 255
Fleet, the (prison) *see* prisons
Forbes, Sir Charles 286, 294, 296, 300
Fortescue, Sir John 20, 21
Fox, Charles James 257
Foxe, John 40, 41, 43–7, 50, 331
franchise, parliamentary 9, 41, 42, 70, 218–21, 234, 243–9, 253, 258, 268, 285, 301, 333 (*see also* parliamentary reform)
Frank, Joseph 39
Franklin, Benjamin 299
freedom of information 227 (*see also* newsbooks and newspapers)
freeborn Englishman, liberties of 46–8, 182, 199, 356
free press *see* newsbooks and newspapers; freedom of information
free-thinkers 160, 179
free trade 235, 287, 289, 292, 300
French Revolution (and debate about) 37, 115, 117, 121, 129, 141–7, 160, 171, 176–8, 180–2, 190, 217–22, 230, 245–50, 265, 318, 321, 325, 328
Friedeburg, Robert von 320
functional definition or approach (of/to radicalism) 8, 67, 90, 92, 338, 340, 362, 363
Furet, François 141
Furneaux, Philip 255

gallantry 118–20, 129
Galloway insurrection (1666) 94, 95
Galt, John 245, 250–3
Gauchet, Marcel 54
gender 44, 116, 192 (*see also* effeminacy)
Geneva 23
Geneva bible 24–5, 28
genre 37–57, 148
George, Henry 147
Gerrald, Joseph 146
Gest, Edmund 25

Gibbs, Sir Vicary 256
Gilby, Anthony 23
Gilchrist, John 293
Gimmelfarb-Brack, Marie 48
Gladstone, John 299
Gladstone, William 190–1, 207
Glassites 264
Glorious Revolution 30, 94, 96, 122, 141, 143–7, 266
Godly rule 53
Godwin, William 115, 117, 119, 147, 161, 232, 249
Good Old Cause 93, 94, 96, 104, 266
Goodman, Christopher 22–5, 28, 31, 321
Goodwin, John 74
Gordon Riots 165
Gordon-Lennox, Charles, 5th duke of Richmond 285
Grafton, duke of *see* Fitzroy, Augustus
Grand Remonstrance (1641) 347
Granovetter, Mark 163
Grant, John 300
Gray, Miss *see* Hunt, Henry
Gray, Alexander 241–7
Greaves, Richard 312, 314, 318, 319, 321, 323, 327, 332, 339, 364
Greek independence 235, 292
Grenville, Richard, Marquis of Chandos, duke of Buckingham and Chandos 285, 286
Greville, George 285
Grote, George 261
Grotius, Hugo 350
Guy, John 22, 28

Haigh, Christopher 45
Halévy, Elie 222, 254, 257
Hall, Charles 264
Hampden, John (1595–1643) 10, 198
Hampden, John (c.1653–1696) 108
Hampden clubs 196, 253
Hampsher-Monk, Iain 312, 313, 318, 319, 322, 324–8, 340, 344
Hancocke, Giles 88
Hardy, Thomas 161, 172, 179
Harford, John 247–9
Harrington, 5th earl of *see* Stanhope, Leicester
Harrington, James 41, 44, 55, 136, 331, 349, 360–2
Harrison, Thomas 76
Hastings, Marquis of *see* Rawdon-Hastings, Francis
Heads of the Proposals (1647) 70, 348
Heinemann, Margot 39, 48, 51
Helvétius, Claude Adrien 224–6, 232–4, 323
Herrup, Cynthia 350
Hezekiah 25
Hill, Christopher 5–7, 11, 62, 63, 65, 66, 343, 364, 365
Hindle, Steve 362
history, Roman 44, 121
history of political thought, methods of 135–7
Hobbes, Thomas 26, 50, 52, 55, 57, 97, 160, 313, 352, 361
Hobhouse, John Cam 292, 302
Hodgskin, Thomas 232
Hodgson, William 129
Holcroft, Thomas 173
Holinshed, Raphael 19
Hollis, Thomas 48
Holloway, James 89
Hone, William 261
Hooker, Richard 22
Höpfl, Harro 327
Huddesford, George 245
Hughes, Anne 44, 355
Hulme, Obadiah 146
Hume, David 17, 117–19, 138–40, 170, 221, 223–6, 233, 234, 323, 329
Hume, Joseph 285–303
Humphrey, John 321
Hunt, Henry 190–208, 246, 266, 267
Hunt, Lynn 141
Hunter, William 45
Hutton, Ronard 53
Hyde, Edward, earl of Clarendon 46

idolatry 18, 23–5, 28, 31
imprisonment for debt 190–208
Independents 10, 49, 51, 52, 55, 71–7, 80, 95, 96, 107
India 285–303
Innes, Joanna 195
Instrument of Association *see* Bond of Association
insurrections *see under* rebellion
interests/public interest 226, 228
intertextuality 37, 38, 40, 48
Ireton, Henry 48, 55, 69–73, 75, 76

Jacobins and anti-Jacobins *see* French Revolution
Jacobites 29
James VI & I 57
James VII & II, earlier duke of York 88, 100
Jebb, John 146, 243
Jehosophat 25
Jenkins, Leoline 88
Jenkinson, Robert, 2nd earl of Liverpool 294
Jessey, Henry 87
Jewel, John 19
Jezebel 23, 24
Joab 32

Johnson, Joseph 119
Johnson, Samuel 243–72
Jones, William 161, 290
Jonsonian comedy 56
Josiah 22, 24, 25, 32
Joyce, Patrick 190

Kaye, Harvey 3
Kedourie, Eli 321
Kenyon, J.P. 64
Killigrew, Henry 20
King's Bench prison *see* prisons
Kinnaird, Douglas 292, 294, 296
Kishlansky, Mark 64
Knox, John 22, 23, 321
Kuhn, Thomas 136

labour movement 190
Lafayette, Marquis de *see* Motier, Gilbert du
Lake, Daniel 202
Lamont, William 68, 322
Lancaster, Joseph 290
Langford, Paul 171
language reform 151
languages, political *see* linguistic approaches
Lansdowne, Marquis of *see* Petty, William
Laud, William, archbishop of Canterbury 347, 350
Law, Edward, Baron Ellenborough 300, 301
law reform 217–36
Lawson, George 363
LeBon, Gustave 163
Lecky, William 95
Lee, 'Citizen Richard' 148
Lefebvre, Georges 162
L'Estrange, Roger 88
Levellers 3–6, 10, 37–57, 62, 65, 69–77, 80, 193–4, 266, 317, 322, 331, 345, 355–8
Liberalism 191, 235, 271, 287
liberties (legal, traditional, civil) 103, 178, 180, 194, 199, 265, 302, 303, 356 (*see also* constitutionalism; freeborn Englishman)
libertinism 118
liberty 121 (*see also* liberties; liberty of conscience)
liberty of conscience 73–5, 77, 92, 93, 98, 100, 356
Lilburne, John 5, 10, 38, 40, 43, 46, 57, 71, 193–4, 199 (*see also* Levellers)
linguistic approaches (to the study of radicalism and political ideas) 8–9, 12–14, 31, 63, 68–9, 90, 135–51, 160, 181–3, 311–33, 339, 340, 344, 354, 361, 362, 366
literary form *see* genre.
Liverpool, 2nd earl of *see* Jenkinson, Robert
localism *see* provincialism
Locke, John 95, 100, 101, 147, 148, 160, 263–4
Lofft, Capel 129
Lollardy 65
London Corresponding Society (LCS) 129, 147, 159, 167, 170, 172, 179, 196
London Greek Committee 235
London Mechanics' Institution 232
Long Parliament 41, 100, 347
lordship 102
Lottes, Gunther 177

Macaulay, Catherine 130
Macaulay, Thomas Babbington, 145, 302
Machiavelli, Niccolò 44, 331
Mackintosh, James 115, 120, 143–5, 300
MacLachlan, Alistair 316
Malcolm, Sir John 285, 286, 294, 298, 300, 301
Malthusianism 232, 247
manners 116, 117, 121–30
Maratha war, second (1802–4) 288, 292
Marprelate, Martin/Marprelate tracts 39, 40, 47, 56
Marsh, Christopher 65
Marshall, Stephen 93, 94
Marshalsea prison *see* prisons
martyrs, Marian/martyrdom 40, 41, 43–7, 54 (*see also* Foxe, John)
Marvell, Andrew 331
Marx, Karl 1, 37, 233
Marxist historiography 2–8, 10, 63, 65, 157, 229, 234, 235, 349
Mary, Queen of Scots 18, 24, 25
Mary I 23
Maryland 30
mass politics, emergence of 160
Matthew bible 44–5
May, Daphne 4–5
memory 10, 54
militia *see* volunteer movement
Mill, Harriet Taylor 115
Mill, James 230, 231, 254, 256–8, 261, 289–92, 294
Mill, John Stuart 115, 218, 252, 254, 257
Millar, John 139–40
millenarianism 68–9, 74, 98, 137–8, 179, 264, 322
Milton, John 38, 331
Mirabeau, Comte de *see* Riqueti, Honoré Gabriel
mixed government 21–2, 160
The Moderate: 42
Monmouth rebellion (1685) 94, 96–108
Montesquieu *see* Secondat, Charles de
morality, 'moral meritorcracy' 121–2, 125, 126, 129

More, Hannah 119, 149, 161
More, Thomas 1, 6
Morice, James 20
Morrill, J.S. 53, 64
Morris, William 6, 233
Morton, A.L. 2, 4–6
Motier, Gilbert du, Marquis de Lafayette 171
Mudge, John 243
Muggletonians 3, 79, 179
Mulligan, Lotte 360
Munz, Peter 13
Munzer, Thomas 6
Murray, James 264
Musselburgh Declaration (1650) 353

Napoleon 250
natural law and natural rights 70, 72, 93, 116–17, 121, 122, 125, 128–9, 135, 137–8, 143, 145, 147, 160, 199, 205, 221, 248, 250, 263, 265, 266, 326
Nedham, Marchamont 318, 332
Netherlands 87, 88
Neville, Henry 331
New Model Army 42, 53, 69–75, 348, 357
Newman, Francis 271
Newman, John Henry 257
newsbooks and newspapers 41, 42, 46, 88, 227, 287, 293–6, 358
Nietzsche, Friedrich 323
Nineteen Propositions (1642) 347
nonconformity and dissent 66, 87–9, 92, 93, 117, 121, 171, 179, 242, 255, 257, 272
Norbrook, David 331
Norman Yoke 5
North, Francis, Baron Guilford 97
northern rebellion (1663) 87, 94, 95

O'Connell, Daniel:L 235
O'Connor, Feargus 191, 193, 207
Ogilvie, William 147–8, 263
Oglethorpe, James 194–5
O'Gorman, Frank 163, 165, 171
order, theories of 19
Ormond, duke of *see* Butler, James
Orwell, George 11
Overton, Richard 37–57, 317, 332 (*see also* Levellers)
Owen, John 96
Owen, Robert 4, 269

Paget, Edward 296, 297
Paine, Thomas 115, 129, 137–8, 144, 145, 147, 149, 159, 161, 170, 172, 181–2, 242, 243, 247, 249, 263, 265
Paine riots and burnings (1791–3) 159, 164–6, 176
Paley, William 119, 262
panopticon *see* prison, prison reform
Paris commune (1871) 37
Parker, Henry 348
parliament, sessions and debates (*see also* Long Parliament)
  1572 24, 25, 32
  1576 41
  Barebones (1653) 193
  Oxford (1681) 88
  Convention (1689) 143, 340
Parliamentary Candidate Society 290
parliamentary reform 100–1, 106, 121, 169–80, 218–21, 226, 234, 235, 243–9, 251, 253, 257–61, 268, 357 (*see also* Chartists/Chartism; franchise; Reform Bill)
Parr, Samuel 217
passions 120, 123, 125
patriarchy, patriarchalism 122, 128
patriotism 123, 130, 159, 167–8, 181, 196, 198, 248, 251, 266
peasants' rising (1381) 3
Peel, Sir Robert 243, 298
Peltonen, Markku 27
Peterloo massacre (1819) 192
petitions and petitioning 41, 42, 44, 48, 159, 164
Petty, William, earl of Shelburne and Marquis of Lansdowne 219
philohellenism 292
Philosophic Radicalism 218, 229, 254, 286 (*see also* Bentham, Jeremy)
Philp, Mark 144, 314, 319, 321, 331, 364, 365
Pitt, William, the Younger 147
Place, Francis 218, 230–5, 262, 290
plain style, plain speaking 149–50
Pocock, J.G.A. 41, 135, 325, 326, 328, 331, 344, 360, 361, 365
politeness 117–18, 120, 149
political economy 139, 160, 232, 249
Ponet, John 19–22, 31, 321
Popper, Karl 13
popular culture and politics 38–40, 48–9, 51–4, 65, 95, 148, 157–84, 190, 205
  popular loyalism 157–84
  popular radicalism 157–84
Porsenna, king 44
Porter, Roy 218
postmasters, in India 288
postmodernism 136
Powell, Lt. Colonel Peregrine 288
prerogative, royal 20
presbyterians 41, 43, 49, 52, 73, 90, 95, 96, 98, 348

press, the *see* newsbooks and newspapers
Price, Richard 122, 141, 143–5, 340
Priestly, Joseph 137, 182, 255
primogeniture 102, 140
Prince, Thomas 46
print culture 353–4, 362, 363
prisons, prison reform 190–208, 219, 221
property/property rights 70, 73, 78, 117, 120, 125, 138–40, 147–8, 219, 251, 252, 260, 262–72
Protestation, the (1641) 351
Proudhon, Pierre-Joseph 147
provincialism, provincial radicalism 172
proverbs 49, 51
providence *see* religion (and radicalism)/religious radicalism
Prynne, William 43, 46, 48, 198
'public, the', in India 294–9, 301
public behaviour *see* theatricality
public interest *see* interests
public opinion 42, 222, 224, 227–9, 235
public/private spheres 116, 122–3, 127, 128, 202, 330 (*see also* domesticity; sexual rights)
  Habermasian public sphere 329, 353, 358
puritans/puritanism 39, 41, 43, 44, 52–4, 347
Putney debates (1647) 42, 69–70, 356
Pym, John 10

Quakers 66, 79, 90, 92, 93, 95, 107
Quine, W.V. 315

Radical, The: 267, 268
radical/radicalism, definition and usage 1, 7–9, 31, 37–8, 40, 45, 55, 62–4, 66–7, 69, 79–81, 89–94, 106, 135, 145, 148, 157, 183–4, 217–18, 235, 241–5, 249, 252, 254, 257, 264, 267–72, 302, 312–33, 338–67
  evidence and propaganda 181–3
  ideology 181–3, 206, 252, 259, 313, 326
  historiography 2–9, 62–9, 135–7, 157–9, 162–4, 190–2, 234, 235, 312–33
  'gentlemanly radicalism' 190–2, 206, 208
  as 'transformation of rule' 338–67 (*see also* functional definition; linguistic approaches; radical tradition; social history)
radical Enlightenment *see* Enlightenment
'radical reform' *see* parliamentary reform
Radical Reformer, The: 266
radical tradition 1, 3–10, 38–40, 64, 66, 67, 91, 104–5, 116, 128, 160, 168–9, 183–4, 190–2, 195, 196, 198, 241–5, 266, 321, 339, 340, 344, 345, 364–7 (*see also* intertextuality)
radicalism *see* radical
Rainsborough, Thomas 39
Raleigh, Sir Walter 198
Ramsay, James, earl and marquis of Dalhousie 302
Ranters 4, 6, 7, 79
Rathbone, William 299
Rawdon-Hastings, Francis, 1st Marquis of Hastings 290, 293, 294
reading 10
rebellions
  1549 19, 24
  Restoration insurrections and plots 93–108
Reeve, John 79
Reeves, John 161, 163–7, 181
Reform Bill (1831–2) 252, 268, 269, 285–303
Reformation, English 341
Reformation, radical 241
reformation of manners 118, 128
Reid, William Hamilton 160, 161
religion (and radicalism)/religious radicalism 11–12, 46, 54, 68–9, 71, 73–81, 92, 93, 97–9, 104–5, 116, 121, 123, 125, 128–9, 160, 179, 241–72, 321–3, 326, 350–3, 365
religious festivals 53
Remonstrance (1648) *see* Ireton, Henry
republicans, republicanism 21, 27–8, 41, 44, 45, 81, 90, 92, 97, 99–100, 103, 108, 118, 120, 123, 128, 136, 160, 221, 226, 262, 327–33, 342, 345, 360–3 (*see also* 'unacknowledged republic')
resistance theory 23, 223, 228
revolution 37, 79, 141–7, 227, 228, 252, 316
Ricardo, David 249, 265, 267
Richards, Judith 360
Richardson, Edward 95
Richmond, duke of *see* Gordon-Lennox, Charles
rights *see* liberties; natural law and natural rights; women, women's rights
Riqueti, Honoré Gabriel, Comte de Mirabeau 219
Ritson, Joseph 161
Rizzio, David 29
Robertson, Joseph Clinton 232, 234
Rogers, John 44
Roman history *see under* history
Romilly, Sir Samuel 219, 256, 261
Rosen, Fred 313, 316
Rousseau, Jean-Jacques 122
Roy, Ram Mohan 286, 295
Russell, William, Lord Russell 90, 91
Russian Revolution 37
Rye House Plot (1683) 88, 91, 96–108

Sacheverall, Dr Henry 143
Sacred Vow and Covenant (1643) 351
Sainsbury, John 196
satire 56, 252

Saul 24
Scaevola, Mucius 43
Schofield, Philip 219–21
Scholey, Joseph 206
Scott, Jonathan 89, 328
Scott, Thomas 95–108
Scott, Sir Walter 3, 244
Secondat, Charles de, baron de Montesquieu 218, 221, 233
sects/sectarianism 74, 88
Seres, William 29
Sexby, Edward 44
sexual rights 199, 200, 203–5
Shaftesbury, earl of *see* Cooper, Anthony Ashley
Shakespeare, William 51
Sharp, Anthony 92
Sharp, James, archbishop of St Andrews 94
Sharpe, Kevin 342
Sidmouth Viscount *see* Addington, Henry
'Sidney' (pseud.) *see* Millar, John
Sidney, Algernon 41, 44, 91, 95, 108, 198, 266, 318, 319, 331, 332
Sieyes, Emmanuel Joseph, Abbé, 145
Simon, Louis 254
Skinner, Quentin 26, 137, 148
slave emancipation 285
Smith, Adam 126, 233
Smith, Nigel 39, 47, 49, 51
Smith, S.C. 167
Smith, Sir Thomas 21, 22
social history, of radicalism 10–11, 64–6, 169–70, 172–4, 338–9, 346–55, 366–7 (*see also* class, social)
social rank 125, 174
socialism/socialist movement 190, 231, 264, 265, 269–72, 326, 327
Society for Constitutional Information (SCI) 159, 170, 171
Solemn League and Covenant (1643) 96, 98, 104, 345, 348, 351, 359
Sorel, Georges 162
Spanish Armada (1588) 322
speech-act theory 135–7, 141, 149
Speke, Hugh 96–108
Spelman, Sir Henry 322
Spence, Thomas 148, 151, 172, 264, 266
Spencians 177
Sprigge, Joshua 76
Spufford, Margaret 64
Stamp Act (1827) 298
standing armies 126
Stanhope, Leicester, 5th earl of Harrington 292, 294, 296
Stapleton, Thomas 23
state, terminology and nature of 26, 341–2, 344–9
Steele, Richard 117
Stephen, James 195
Stewart, James 87
Stormont, lord 243
Stuart, Sir James 258
style, literary 149–51
suffrage *see* franchise
Swallowfield 27–9
Swedenborgians 179

taxes, taxation 101–2, 182, 249, 267, 268
Tell, William 198
theatricality 48
Thelwall, John 137–8, 147, 150, 173, 181
Thomas, William 254
Thompson, E.P. 2–4, 7, 157–9, 162, 163, 174, 182, 196, 218, 229–31, 235, 364
Thompson, William 115
Thoms, William 323
Thornley, Thomas 299
Tillinghast, John 80
tithes 249, 268, 285
Tomkins, Thomas 43–4
Tong, Thomas 95–108
Tooke, Rev. John Horne 151, 161, 171, 182, 257
Tories 88, 89, 161, 285, 333
Torr, Donna 4
town government 103
Toynbee, Arnold 271
tradition *see* radical tradition
traditionalism 104–5, 116 (*see also* ancient constitution; Norman Yoke)
transmission (of radical ideas) 9–10, 91, 137, 142–7
Trimmer, Sarah 161, 166
Truth, The: 268
Turton, Thomas 206

'unacknowledged republic' 345, 349–50, 356, 358, 361–3
Underdown, David 65, 342
United Britons 177
United Englishmen 177
United Irishmen 177
utility, utilitarianism 135, 139–40, 217–36, 252, 254, 262, 265, 266, 272, 290, 302
utopianism 56, 151

Vane, Sir Henry 44, 322
Venner, Thomas 94–108
Venner's rising 93–108
Vernon, James 190
Vince, Mrs *see* Hunt, Henry
virtue 116, 121, 124, 127

Voltaire (pen-name of Arouet, François-Marie) 218, 255
volunteer movement 159, 164, 167–8
  Scottish 167

Wade, John 231–2, 234
Walcheren expedition (1809) 256
Walcott, Thomas 97, 100
Wallace, William 198
Wallington, Nehemiah 53–4
Wallis, Alexander 89
Walsingham, Sir Francis 18, 25
Walter, John 65, 352
Walwyn, William 46, 50
Warne family 45
Warren, Edward 94
Watson, Richard, bishop of Llandaff 264
Weber, Max 13
Wellesley, Arthur, 1st duke of Wellington 298, 300
Wellington, duke of *see* Wellesley, Arthur
Wells, Roger 163
Wentworth, Sir Peter 41
West, Edward 297
West, Robert 91, 97, 100
Westminster Assembly 351
Wheeler, Anna 115
Whetherell, Sir Charles 285
Whigs and Whiggism 87–9, 100, 265–72, 285–303
  'radical Whigs' 95, 120
Whitehall debates (1648–9) 70, 73, 75–6
Whitgift, John 21–2
Whitmore, William 300
Whittingham, William 23
Will Waver: 267
Wilberforce, William 119, 243
Wildman, John 75, 96
Wilkes, John 4, 39, 142, 190, 195–7, 242
William III, previously William of Orange 96
  association to defend (1696) 29–30
Williams, George 241
Windham, William 173
Winstanley, Gerrard 1, 4, 5, 10, 55, 65, 78–9, 193, 264, 358–60 (*see also* Diggers)
Wolfe, D.M. 48
Wooler, Thomas 198, 199, 207
Wollestonecraft, Mary 115–30, 149, 330
women, women's rights, women's movement 116, 122–30, 260 (*see also* effeminacy; gallantry; gender)
Wood, Andy 65
Worden, Blair 360
Wortham, Christopher 331
Wrightson, Keith 65, 342
Wynn, Charles Williams 297
Wyville, Christopher 137, 145, 243–4

Yorke, Henry Redhead 148, 161

Zaret, David 353–4

Lightning Source UK Ltd.
Milton Keynes UK
173690UK00007B/33/P